TANZANIA
Party Transformation and Economic Development

PUBLISHED FOR THE CENTER OF
INTERNATIONAL STUDIES
PRINCETON UNIVERSITY

*A list of other Center publications appears
at the back of the book*

TANZANIA

Party Transformation and Economic Development

HENRY BIENEN

PRINCETON UNIVERSITY PRESS
PRINCETON, NEW JERSEY
1967

TO LEIGH

Preface

KNOWLEDGE OF African political systems is difficult to gain and even more difficult to correlate. Analysts have devised typologies in an effort to organize information about African politics and to make it more meaningful for the comparative study of developing areas. However, the scarcity of empirical studies of whole political systems has resulted in profound disagreements among observers as to the suitability of the various typologies, the nature of African polities, and their prospects for democracy or totalitarianism.

I have attempted to present a case study of the Tanganyika African National Union as it tries to govern Tanzania. My aim is to relate economic and political development by showing how a ruling party interacts with the economy it undertakes to transform.

When the union of Zanzibar and Tanganyika occurred in April 1964, one sovereign state was created.[1] It was originally called the United Republic of Tanganyika and Zanzibar; but the name was subsequently changed to the United Republic of Tanzania. Although the area is now commonly known as Tanzania, I have not always referred to it as such in this book, since my primary concern is with the country prior to its union. It would make no more sense to refer to the country as Tanzania before April 1964, than it would to call Russia the Soviet Union before 1917. Even when discussing events after the Union, I often use the name Tanganyika because my analysis deals with the Tanganyika Afri-

[1] On April 22, 1964, the President of the Republic of Tanganyika, Julius Nyerere, and the President of the People's Republic of Zanzibar and Pemba, Sheikh Abeid Karume, signed the Articles of Union between their two countries at Zanzibar. The Articles were ratified on April 25 by the Parliament of Tanganyika and the Revolutionary Council of Zanzibar. On April 27, the Instruments of Ratification of the Agreement were exchanged and the new Republic of Tanganyika and Zanzibar came into being.

can National Union (TANU), which is the ruling party only on the mainland of the United Republic. I have used the name Tanzania when I wish to stress the United Republic as a whole or to emphasize aspects of the Union which affect politics in mainland Tanganyika (for example, the entrance of Zanzibaris into the Cabinet or new streams of political thought into the mainland from Zanzibar).

I have abandoned correct Swahili reference to tribes and have simply used root names; thus, the people who live on the slopes of Kilimanjaro are referred to as Chagga instead of Wachagga, a man is a Chagga instead of a Mchagga. The only usage I have kept is to denote places with the Swahili prefix "U"; for example, parts of Tanganyika are referred to as Ugogo or Uhehe.

The present demarcations in Tanganyika are called districts and regions; during the colonial period they were known as provinces and districts. TANU uses the term region to refer to its administrative units, but it uses "area" instead of "district" for demarcations. I have used area and district interchangeably.

Without help from a variety of sources this study would not have been possible. I was able to go to East Africa for twenty-two months in 1963-65 on an exchange program between the Department of Political Science, University of Chicago, and the Department of Political Science, Makerere College, University of East Africa. As a one-year Visiting Research Fellow and then as a Visiting Professor to Makerere, I greatly benefited from the advantages which accrue to a scholar connected with Makerere. I also received financial assistance for typing and traveling from a Public Administration vote in the Department of Political Science at Makerere. Further typing assistance was provided by the Center for the Comparative Study of Political Development at the University of Chicago and the Center of International

Studies at Princeton University. The University Research Fund of Princeton University did the photoduplication.

Special thanks are due to several of my colleagues for their thoughtful comments: among them, Professor Carl Rosberg of the University of California at Berkeley; Professors Theodore Lowi and J. David Greenstone of the University of Chicago; Dr. T. V. Sathyamurthy of Strathclyde University; Professors Raymond Apthorpe and Ali Mazuri of Makerere College, and Professor William Tordoff of the University of Zambia. Professor Harvey Glickman of Haverford College made many documents available to me and was most generous with his insights into Tanganyikan politics. Professors Jeremy Azrael and Leonard Binder of the University of Chicago offered helpful criticism and invaluable assistance throughout.

My work could not have gone forward without the full cooperation of many Tanzanians. Although it would be impossible to mention each individually, I would like to single out for special thanks the Honorable Rashidi Kawawa, Second Vice President of the United Republic of Tanzania, who met with me and recommended me to TANU officials. Many of these officials were not only generous with their time but were personally hospitable as well. S. K. Luangisa, O. M. Marwa, A. W. Chambiri, A. N. Laicer, A. Suleiman, I.S.A. Kajembo, and S. S. Chamshama were among the regional and area commissioners who facilitated my work. I am also grateful to the many ministers and junior ministers who gave of their time and knowledge: the Honorable A. K. Hanga, the Honorable A.Z.N. Swai, the Honorable A. S. Mtaki, N. Buhatwa, E. Kisenege, and E. Barongo. Among the civil servants in the central government, M. C. Othman, A. J. Nsekela, F. K. Burengelo, and Jacob Namfua also provided assistance. Special thanks are owed to M. Milando, formerly President Nyerere's personal secretary and E. Kahatano, agricultural officer. Both local and central government officers from Community Development and Agriculture were invaluable informants. Elected and appointed members of TANU's branch, area, and regional organizations were courteous and most helpful. I hope that this work, in turn, may be of some use to them.

The friendliness and spirit of inquiry for which the President of the United Republic of Tanzania, Mwalimu Julius K. Nyerere, is noted can be found widely throughout Tanzania. I would like to thank the many people with whom I spoke for the honesty they manifested; although some may disagree with my conclusions, I trust they will recognize the sincerity of my efforts. I am particularly grateful to P. O. Yamo and to the Tanzanian students at Makerere College, especially Paul Mushi and Bismark Mwansasu. Mr. Griffith Cunningham, principal of Kivukoni College at Dar es Salaam, welcomed me to Kivukoni and gave me an invaluable base for making contact with other Tanzanians. Mr. Lionel Cliffe shared his insights and his friendships in Tanzania with me.

Professor Colin Leys at the University of Sussex encouraged and aided my work at every step, as he has done for so many people who came to Makerere. Professor Aristide Zolberg of the University of Chicago taught me a great deal about African politics; he has been teacher, colleague, critic, and friend. Thanks are also due to Miss Lalor Cadley of Princeton University Press for her editorial assistance.

To my wife, Leigh Buchanan Bienen, I owe thanks both personal and professional. She has invariably been an understanding wife and a helpful critic.

Princeton
January 1967

HENRY BIENEN

Contents

xi

CONTENTS

xii

CONTENTS

CONTENTS

List of Tables and Figures

TABLES

FIGURES

xv

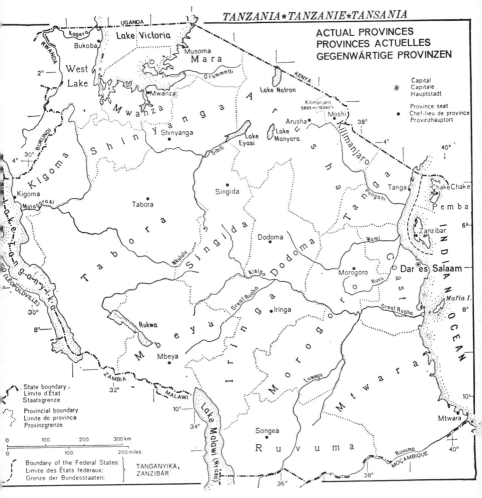

Map reproduced with permission of Cartactual, Topical Map Service,
Budapest, Hungary

ABBREVIATIONS

ASP	Afro-Shirazi Party
DDCS	District Development Committees
EACSO	East African Common Service Organization
EAISR	East African Institute of Social Research
EDC	Economic Development Commission
EDRP	East African Development Research Project
MNE	Members of the National Executive Committee of the Tanganyika African National Union
NEC	National Executive Committee of the Tanganyika African National Union
NUC	National Union of Cooperatives
NUTA	National Union of Tanganyika Workers
RDCS	Regional Development Committees
TAA	Tanganyika African Association
TAC	Tanganyika Agricultural Corporation
TANU	Tanganyika African National Union
TPP	Tanganyika Parliamentary Party
VDCS	Village Development Committees

Introduction

ON THE EVE of independence, Kasela Bantu, the Publicity Secretary of the Tanganyika African National Union (TANU), wrote a pamphlet called *What TANU Is and How It Works* in an effort to describe Tanganyika's national movement to an overseas audience and to non-Africans in Tanganyika. He was also trying to explain the organization and aims of TANU to its own members. Bantu's attempt reflects a perpetual concern of TANU leaders with establishing the identity of the party, elucidating its structure and functions, and defining new roles for TANU. It may seem paradoxical that a national movement, having become a ruling party, should worry so much about its purpose and place within the nation. Yet, any understanding of the way Tanganyika is ruled, any explanation of what TANU actually does, depends on recognizing that leaders and followers alike are still asking: What is TANU and How Does It Work?

I have tried to provide answers to these questions by looking at what TANU does in Tanganyika. I found the models which have so far been constructed for the study of African political parties inadequate to explain politics in Tanganyika. TANU has been described as a monolithic party.[1] And according to the criteria given for various political typologies, Tanganyika should fit within the categories of "revolutionary-centralizing system,"[2] "revolutionary mass-movement regime,"[3] or "mobilization system."[4]

For example, David Apter describes the mobilization model in Africa as follows: power resides at the top of the

[1] James S. Coleman and Carl Rosberg, Jr. (eds.), *Political Parties and National Integration in Tropical Africa* (Berkeley and Los Angeles: University of California Press, 1964), p. 677.

[2] *Ibid.*, "Introduction" and "Conclusion."

[3] Robert Tucker, *The Soviet Political Mind* (New York: Frederick Praeger, 1963), pp. 3-19.

[4] David Apter, *The Political Kingdom in Uganda* (Princeton: Princeton University Press, 1961), pp. 22-24.

3

organization, generally in a single leader who monopolizes legitimacy; the party demands a fundamental commitment on the part of the individual; it can make quick changes in its alliances and alter its goals and targets; the organization is devoted to the establishment of political units which are essentially new, subordinate solidarity groupings; the party or state will most often act on grounds of expediency and necessity, using ideology to give perspective and justification for what appears necessary.[5] The mobilization system is essentially defined by the characteristics of the party system; some other political typologies are similarly defined. Superficially, TANU does comply with these characteristics: it seems to have hierarchical authority, claims total allegiance, and appears to be tactically flexible; the party has linked functional organizations, and it voices its political programs in terms of moral claims and slogans.

TANU's history makes it eligible for a place in the "revolutionary mass-movement regime" classification as well. It is indeed a mass movement, organized during a struggle for power as a means for waging this struggle, which became an ostensibly revolutionary, centralized, militant party, gained control, and was transformed into the ruling single party. In terms of the differentiating factors of ideology, modes of popular participation, and organizational aspects, TANU would also fit Coleman and Rosberg's "revolutionary-centralizing" rather than "pragmatic-pluralistic" pattern of uni-party and one-party dominant African states.[6]

But the images which these typologies convey are essentially misleading when one considers that TANU is unable to manage political affairs at the local level, that central TANU organs cannot exact the desired responses from regional and district party bodies; and that there is a great deal of deflec-

[5] *Ibid.*, p. 23. I have not included all the points Apter makes under each characteristic.
[6] Coleman and Rosberg, p. 5.

tion from orders and plans made at the center. These problems cannot be explained simply by stating that this particular party does not "really" fit the models which are postulated for dynamic, highly centralized, hierarchically organized and monolithic parties which dominate, if not monopolize, political processes.

Too often the politics of new states have been described as if intentions were facts, as if the word had become flesh; the characterizations of political systems in Africa are based on images conveyed to the world by party leaders. But these images cannot be used as the crucial differentiate systems images, for such images are variables. It is false to assume that explicit ideologies in African states have any general relevance; they may be espoused by only a select few who themselves may be removed from the center of power within the party. The aspirations of certain elites to transform their societies through a single party which penetrates all communities and social structures and mobilizes society's resources may or may not be significant.

One problem with typologies is that they are not derived from the study of processes, but are based instead on roles and statuses which supply us with no more than a map of the socio-political terrain, or an idea of the elites' normative expectations. Neither the characterizations nor the maps from which they are derived specify the ways in which central institutions work. They provide no information as to the nature of relationships within the party, nor do they show how the party relates to society as a whole—not merely to the modern, urban, or town sectors.[7] We cannot tell from them

[7] The aforementioned authors are themselves conscious of these questions. In fact, their typologies are designed to seek out the data that will reveal how much tactical flexibility parties have, or how hierarchical their authority is. (See Apter, *op.cit.*) Nonetheless, the typologies are dependent on formal structures and political rhetoric rather than on hypotheses about party function insofar as they purport to describe concrete African systems.

whether normative expectations, which may be stated in explicit ideologies at the center, are shared throughout society.

The difficulty lies in focusing on political structures—parties in particular—as organizations which operate in an environment coterminous with society or the territorial entity called the nation. The primacy of party has been asserted by political leaders of African states and commentators alike,[8] an assertion which entails neglecting the traditional sector or assuming that the party allocates values for that sector.[9] There is little evidence to support such views. Quite the contrary, the data available seems to indicate that the structures of the party and the state do not operate everywhere in society; nor do they operate in the same way in town and countryside. Local communities exist in which there is no effective party presence. Choices are being made there, and authoritative values are being allocated, often without reference to the agencies of central rule.[10]

Even within the "modern" sectors—in the towns and in

[8] See Rosberg and Coleman, op.cit., p. 1; Martin Kilson, "Authoritarian and Single-Party Tendencies in African Politics," World Politics, xv (January 1963), pp. 262-94; Gwendolen Carter (ed.), African One-Party States (Ithaca: Cornell University Press, 1962); Thomas Hodgkin, African Political Parties (Baltimore: Penguin Books, 1961); Ruth Schachter, "Single-Party Systems in West Africa," American Political Science Review, LV (June 1961), 294-307.

[9] By traditional sector I mean more than the society which is defined by patterns of subsistence agriculture. The duality of society in many underdeveloped countries is not only a matter of "dual economies"—subsistence and monetary. Within the same territorial boundaries of a new state, we may speak of "mobilized and non-mobilized" sets of the population. Cf. Karl Deutsch, "Social Mobilization and Political Development," American Political Science Review, LV (September 1961), 497-514. This concept calls attention to participation in supra-local communication networks.

[10] In Aristide Zolberg's Creating Political Order: The Party-States of West Africa (Chicago: Rand McNally, 1966), p. 131, the distinction is made between a "modern" and a "residual" sector. Authoritative values do get allocated within one political system; but there are two sets of values, and the structures which operate in the modern sector do not deal with values in the residual sector by definition.

the market economies—ruling single parties cannot mobilize all the resources; nor have they become totalitarian parties (although they may be authoritarian).

Some have implied that certain African parties might become totalitarian if they themselves were stronger or the commitment of leaders and people to democracy weaker.[11] On the former point, one writer, commenting that Ghana may pass through a pronounced non-democratic, "in all probability authoritarian-totalitarian movement," notes that this form might be not only Marxist but Fascist, although perhaps in a modified form "making allowances for organizational deficiencies."[12] But are not organizational deficiencies the very crux of the matter, since they stem from the nature of the resources available to elites? (By resources I mean not only the economic base but also the abilities of national elites and the availability of elites that operate at a subnational level.)

This concern with relating resources to political organizations is posed in the comparative study of politics as a concern with the relationship between economic and political development. The two have been tied together in various formulas:[13] performance in the political sphere has been seen as a precondition for economic development;[14] the relationship between various economic and political stages have been outlined so that correlations between political types and eco-

[11] David Mlay, "Our Child Is Growing Up," *Nationalist* (Dar es Salaam) July 15, 1965, p. 10. Mr. Mlay was referring to TANU in Tanganyika.

[12] Henry Bretton, "Current Political Thought and Practice in Ghana," *American Political Science Review*, LII (March 1958), 49-50, 57.

[13] For a review of the formulas see Lucien Pye, *Aspects of Political Development* (Boston: Little, Brown and Co., 1966), pp. 31-48.

[14] Many economists have stressed the political forms and conditions which may impede economic development. Cf. Norman S. Buchanan and Howard S. Ellis, *Approaches to Economic Development* (New York: The Twentieth Century Fund, 1955).

nomic indices appear.[15] Often the concern is to specify the possibilities for democratic systems. Attempts have also been made to discover the capacity of regimes to mobilize resources. Many discussions of totalitarian systems have been couched in terms of the power potential of governments which exists in industrial society. Thus the industrialization of the Soviet Union and the increasing centralization of the Communist Party have been seen as interacting processes.

Political analysts of new states are aware of the underdeveloped economies of their subjects and the impotency of those who command the party and government structures to implement policy objectives. And yet the aforementioned typologies which convey the picture of dynamic and mobilizing parties have been applied to countries where the economies are among some of the least developed of new states (e.g., Guinea and Mali). We cannot describe African states as possibly becoming totalitarian when subsistence sectors account for more than one-third of the total Gross Domestic Product, when many people still spend most of their time working for their subsistence, when the government collects about one-half of its assigned taxes at district levels.

With these pertinent facts in mind, I have studied the relationship between economic and political development in Tanganyika by focusing on the connection between economic factors and TANU's organization and operation. I have tried not merely to describe the physical and economic environment in which TANU lives, but also to show what the party is doing to change the economy of Tanganyika and what

[15] E.g., James S. Coleman, "The Political Systems of the Developing Areas," in Gabriel Almond and James S. Coleman (eds.), *Politics of Developing Areas* (Princeton: Princeton University Press, 1960); Seymour Martin Lipset, "Some Social Requisites of Democracy: Economic Development and Political Legitimacy," *American Political Science Review*, LIII, No. 1 (March 1959), pp. 69-105. Walt W. Rostow, *The Stages of Economic Growth* (Cambridge: Cambridge University Press, 1960), looks at stages of growth and forms of political organization, as Pye, *op.cit.*, p. 35 points out.

changes, if any, are taking place in TANU as it organizes to achieve economic development.

Another general area of concern in the comparative politics of new states has been variously subsumed under the headings "nation-building" or "national integration." The implication here is that a territorial unit, a country with an international identity, has not yet become a nation. This absence of nationhood has been described in terms of ethnic heterogeneity,[16] the lack of a shared political culture,[17] social cleavages (rural/urban gaps, disparate levels of development within a territory,[18] the gaps between elite and non-elite), and the difficulty in creating legitimizing doctrines.[19]

Many analyses of new states assume a linkage between development and integration; national integration is seen to be positively correlated with economic development.[20] And more generally, increasing national integration is equated with modernity; for a state to be modern, it must have a politics of nationalism within the context of state institutions.[21] Such a politics can be brought about only after the gaps between elites and non-elites have been closed—gaps which are expressed as social, political, and cultural discontinuities in the "modern" and "traditional" sectors of society. The performance of the so-called middle-level elites is crucial for the way in which these gaps are closed,[22] for they are the ones

[16] Cf. Clifford Geertz (ed.), "The Integrative Revolution," *Old Societies and New States* (Glencoe: The Free Press, 1963), pp. 105-57.

[17] Lucien Pye, *Politics, Personality and Nation-Building in Burma* (New Haven: Yale University Press, 1962).

[18] Edward Shils, *Political Development in the New States* (The Hague: Mouton and Company, 1962); Aristide Zolberg, *One-Party Government in the Ivory Coast* (Princeton: Princeton University Press, 1964).

[19] Leonard Binder, "National Integration and Political Development," *American Political Science Review*, LVII (September 1964), 622-31.

[20] Cf. Almond and Coleman, *loc.cit.*; Lipset, *loc.cit.*; Deutsch, *loc.cit.*

[21] Pye, *Aspects of Political Development*, p. 37.

[22] Binder, *op.cit.*, p. 630.

involved in mobilizing resources; they must straddle the traditional and the modern sectors in order to "reinterpret traditional beliefs, adapt them to modern needs, and translate them into a modern idiom."[23]

I have approached the subject of national integration in Tanganyika through an analysis of intra-party relationships. My understanding of TANU is as a complex of interacting organizations, not as a monolithic structure which exists in imaginations only. The cleavages and discontinuities in Tanganyika are analyzed by looking at recruitment to party posts, and by describing the way in which TANU hierarchies communicate, both vertically (from district to region to national level) and horizontally (from one district to another). I have also investigated the components of political ideology in Tanganyika in order to see what kinds of formulas are put forward as legitimizing doctrines and guides to action. I have explored the way ideology is disseminated, transformed as it is articulated by national leaders, and channeled through middle-level elites, in an effort to understand how and what TANU communicates.

In order to pursue these objectives, I went to those in political positions at the regional and district headquarters as well as in Dar es Salaam, the capital.[24] I did not go to the grass roots, which would have entailed doing research at the village level, but concentrated on party and state officeholders because they constitute the political elite at these levels,[25]

---

[23] Shils, *op.cit.*, p. 89.

[24] A district is often around 6,000 square miles although it may be as small as 1,000 square miles. Regional headquarters are set up in towns varying in size from 5,000 to 10,000 people. A few regional centers are much larger (e.g., Tanga with more than 50,000 and Mwanza with more than 20,000). The district towns sometimes had less than 1,000 people living in the town itself. I carried out interviews and traveled with TANU officials and civil servants in 6 of the 17 regions and 8 of the 60 districts. I also visited many other districts in which I did not do research.

[25] In the regional and district headquarters the elite of power (the

10

and my aim was to approach politics in Tanganyika by trying to analyze the political functioning of these elites.[26]

What are sometimes loosely referred to as central/local relationships can perhaps better be described in terms of elite/non-elite and intra-elite ties. Within the elite group, I have made a distinction between central and non-central. A central elite member is any party or state officeholder operating in Dar es Salaam; a non-central elite is one who is appointed from the center and remains responsible to it, but is assigned to work in the regions and districts in Tanganyika. Individuals may be members of both central and non-central elites simultaneously (for example, when a minister returns to his district and plays local roles). I have also distinguished between high- and middle-level elites, depending upon their position within the political or administrative hierarchy. Not all members of the central or national elite are high-level elite members.

This framework has enabled me to translate problems of national integration—often discussed in terms of persistence and/or paramountcy of primordial ties, rural/urban gaps, subsistence and monetary sectors—into questions about the political functioning of rulers; by looking at interacting hierarchies, one can see the system in motion. This approach offers the added possibility of generalizing about Tanganyika

political elite) is almost synonymous with the elite of wealth and status. Where there has been little indigenous private ownership of the means of production, wealth and status are derived from holding political or civil service offices. "The dearth of trained manpower ensures that there are very few free-lancers in any elite field" (Aidan Southall, "Traditional Role Structure and the Formation of Elites in East Africa." Paper presented to the African Studies Association, Philadelphia, October 27-29, 1965), p. 14.

26 This study, however, is not a systematic study of elites. I did not accumulate data on the social demographic basis of entire elites, nor did I trace genealogies; this would require a research team. My judgments were not based on questionnaires but on personal interviews and observations of men working in their offices and in the field. I was also able to use reports made by TANU officials of their own activities.

as a whole, while at the same time focusing on politics outside the capital. It is my hope that this work will be both useful to scholars who wish to do micro-political studies within Tanganyika and relevant to the growing literature on comparative development of new states.

The major advantage of combining research at district and regional levels with research in Dar es Salaam was that it became possible to get beyond the TANU which appears on organization charts and in the descriptions given by central leaders. When we begin to examine how TANU institutions work and interrelate, we find that TANU remains a party which itself suffers from integrative problems. TANU is a party without a powerful center: its central staff at National Headquarters consists of less than 25 permanent and full-time officials; there is no central filing system which enables officials to know where TANU members are located or even who they are. Thus TANU, the instrument designed to bring about national integration and economic development, reflects the very same lack of integration found in society. There is a dire need for concrete institutions to link developmental and integrative processes; but TANU cannot yet provide this institutional link.

TANU is the only political party in Tanganyika, *de jure* and *de facto*. It faces no organized interest groups; functional organizations are linked to it (for example, the National Union of Tanganyika Workers [NUTA]); the position of high-level leaders within the party is not being challenged. TANU is, indeed, hierarchically organized and led by a charismatic leader. Yet Tanganyika is only partially and intermittently ruled by the national TANU elite. TANU is still a party where the relationships between the center and the organizations outside Dar es Salaam pose problems for the leaders. A number of interrelationships exist: between the center and the local units directly; between the center and regional, district, and local organizations; between various regional and district organizations; and between TANU and associated organizations. As we shall see, the loose, decentralized forms of party organization inherited from the period of the anti-colonial struggle have not been overcome.

These organizational inheritances of the pre-independence period have proved durable for a number of reasons. Periods of development which have unfolded gradually in other ex-colonial countries have been telescoped in Tanganyika. The political movement was formed, became the ruling party, and embarked on a major five year plan all within ten years. Thus there has been little time to confront the organizational deficiencies of the past. Furthermore, the low levels of economic development and the large share of the subsistence sector as a percentage of total GDP (more than 25 per cent) have persisted.

It is this very lack of economic development which has discouraged the formation of economic interest groups potentially hostile to the regime. Economic development often creates new tensions and gives rise to organized interest groups which make explicit demands on government and party; it may also encourage new definitions of tribal identity and thus increase social cleavage.[27] Urbanization or change in demographic and other social patterns which is not necessarily accompanied by economic growth may also confront a regime with opposition groups. Because TANU has not been threatened by indigenous opposition groups, it did not have to centralize in order to gain power. But, by the same token, no interest and associational groups exist which could be used by TANU to effectuate its rule. Thus TANU must itself organize such associational and interest groups (for example, TANU farmers or cooperative organizations, TANU literacy groups). The material conditions needed to centralize TANU and enable it to control from the center do not exist either.

Tanganyika's leaders are politically ineffective when try-

[27] Cf. Zolberg, op.cit., for a discussion of these in the Ivory Coast.

ing to impose commands over a wide area. There is too little centralized authority at every level and throughout the system as a whole. In question is whether the central TANU government does in fact "rule" Tanganyika and what it means by central government rule. Of course "central rule," "political effectiveness," and "control" are political variables not static states; they can only be measured over a period of time and in relation to other changes. Thus any judgment about central rule or political effectiveness depends on implicit or explicit comparisons with other systems and/or on changes within Tanganyika.

When I say that TANU is a party without a powerful center and that it rules Tanganyika only partially, I am not maintaining that party functions are atrophying. Nor am I arguing that power and prestige are gravitating to state agencies or to interest groups. Tanganyika is not a no-party state; TANU performs crucial functions and we must examine them. But it is not a polity within which power and effectiveness reside and can be parceled out to the various structures. Power must be created by structures out of potentialities. This is a dynamic process. In Tanganyika, it is the relative weakness of structures, even within the modern sector, which is striking, not their relative strengths.

One of the major questions which must be considered is how such seemingly fragile institutions survive. We shall see that the very looseness of TANU works to maintain party rule in Tanganyika. And while the material conditions of Tanganyika do not facilitate the building of a centralized, disciplined party, they have impeded the formation of social classes or emergent political elites who might threaten the present regime. This is not to say there are no threats to the presently constituted TANU rule; the "grave-diggers" of a regime are not simply a function of material conditions any more than is the nature of a party's organization. Ideology and organization must be considered in their own right.

14

A great deal of descriptive material is included, not only because Tanzania is interesting in its own right, but also because I am concerned with structural models.

A functional model is like the electrical engineers proverbial "black box" where something goes in and something comes out, and what is inside is unknown or relevant only to the extent of somehow relating outputs to inputs. A structural model emphasizes the contents of the box.[28]

We learn about the politics of a particular system and make what we learn relevant to other systems by constructing structural and functional models. My quarrel with certain typologies is not that they have chosen differentiating factors poorly, but that when it comes time to see what systems fit the typologies, function is not linked to structure and thus truly structural models are not created.

I have tried to describe TANU in detail in order to build towards such a model and thus make the study of a particular system meaningful for the comparative study of politics. Toward this end, I have constructed an analytical framework which focuses on the political party and its interaction with the economy.[29] The key variables I have singled out—intraparty relationships, levels of and structure of economy—are themselves found within the overarching frameworks of mobilization system or revolutionary-centralizing system.[30] But these typologies have paid more attention to the nature of party than to economic factors. The explicit variables contained therein are political rather than economic ones; the attempt to relate economic factors to political ones has been

[28] Anthony G. Oettinger, "The Uses of Computers in Science," *Scientific American*, Vol. 215, No. 3 (September 1966), p. 163.

[29] No formal model is proposed because at this point I do not want to generalize the relationships between political institutions and economic variables; this, I believe, will constitute the core of a future model.

[30] See Apter, *loc.cit.*; Rosberg and Coleman, *loc.cit.*

15

more evident in "stage theories" of development. Very little analysis has been done on the evolution of specific political structures as this evolution relates to economic change.[31] My book represents an attempt to do precisely this.

I have also tried to demonstrate the importance of variables which pertain to a political party and which are omitted or treated indirectly in more general formulations of political types and in the current typologies being used for African political systems. These variables appear in the following outline as patterns of recruitment to party offices; elite interactions; ideology; structure of the economy and economic goals; and the attempt of the party to handle economic tasks.

This study is organized into four parts. Part I, "TANU Before Independence: A Political History," examines the historical factors which have molded TANU's present structure —the legacies of colonial rule, social heterogeneity, and the position of traditional rulers. We see here how TANU grew rapidly by capitalizing on the general opposition to British policy and presence, but was unable, before Tanganyika gained its independence, to establish central institutions capable of imposing a central will on regional, district, and local TANU organizations.

Part II, "Organization, Recruitment, and Ideology," describes the patterns of recruiting party officials and analyzes TANU in terms of elite interactions. The chapter on ideology serves as a bridge to the rest of the study, by revealing the leaders' own perceptions of the task of nation-building in Tanganyika.

[31] This kind of analysis has been done for bureaucracy and economic development in Joseph LaPalombara (ed.), *Bureaucracy and Political Development* (Princeton: Princeton University Press, 1963), particularly Bert F. Hoselitz, "Levels of Economic Performance and Bureaucratic Structures," pp. 169-198. See also Deutsch, *loc.cit.*; Alexander Gerschenkron, *Economic Backwardness in Historical Perspective* (Cambridge: Harvard University Press, 1962).

Part III, "TANU and the Economy of Tanganyika: Conditions, Apparatus, and Goals," is an attempt to establish the meaning of economic configuration for those who govern Tanganyika. This section moves from a description of the structure of the economy to an examination of the way in which TANU structures operate as new goals are formulated and established ones implemented.

The final section, "Crises and Conclusions," deals with the nature of TANU in terms of two major events in the history of independent Tanganyika: the army revolt of January 1964, and the presidential and parliamentary elections of September 1965, both of which provide a dramatic illumination of TANU and the politics of Tanganyika.

TANU Before Independence · A Political History

CHAPTER I

Origin and Inheritance of the Tanganyika African National Union

ON JULY 7, 1954 (the day known as *Saba Saba*—the seventh day of the seventh month), TANU was founded in Dar es Salaam. Within four years, it had become overwhelmingly the dominant non-governmental political organization in the country. In 1960, TANU formed a "responsible government" with Julius Nyerere as chief minister; on December 9 of the following year, Tanganyika gained its independence, and Nyerere led the new TANU government as the first Prime Minister of Tanganyika. A new Constitution was framed at the end of 1962, and Julius Nyerere was elected the first President of Tanganyika. Thus in eight years, the President of TANU had become the President of an independent Tanganyika.

Tanganyika's progress to independence under the leadership both of TANU and of Julius Nyerere is one of the most dramatic stories of African postwar history. Tanganyika's evolution in the 1950's has generally been described against a background of earlier political quiescence.[1] However, as more information is gathered on the history of political organizations which predate TANU, it appears that before World War II there was greater political activity among Tanganyika Africans than had been assumed.[2]

Pre-TANU Political Organizations

Dar es Salaam, the capital of Tanganyika, did not become the major administrative, political, and economic center of Tanganyika until well into the period of British rule. Under

[1] George Bennett, "An Outline History of TANU," *Makerere Journal*, No. 7 (1963), p. 1.
[2] Ralph A. Austen, "Notes on the Pre-History of TANU," *Makerere Journal*, No. 9 (March 1964), p. 1.

21

German rule, which lasted from the late 1880's until the defeat of Germany in World War I and the subsequent loss of her colonial territories in East Africa, it was merely one among several centers. The Germans in East Africa looked West towards the Congo and Ruanda-Urundi and set up a large administrative center in Kigoma on the eastern shores of Lake Tanganyika which was intended as the great railhead for German East Africa. (The outbreak of the First World War disrupted German plans for this.[3]) Tabora in central Tanganyika was also a major center and railhead under both the Germans and the British. Tanga, in the extreme northeastern part of Tanganyika, was another city equally as important as Dar es Salaam in German times; an advanced government school was located there, in which the German East African administration trained its African civil servants.[4] Tanga was more exposed than the capital to the influences of missionaries and white settlers; and it was nearer to the more economically developed areas of Kenya and the cluster of sisal plantations and coffee estates in northern Tanganyika.

Because the capital city did not overshadow all other towns, political activity was not concentrated within it. In fact, the first voluntary association founded by Africans—the Tanganyika African Civil Servants Association—was formed by government employees in Tanga in 1924. This Association pursued the interests of African government employees and introduced into public life some of Tanganyika's educated Africans.[5] Although a few of these people reappeared later in the Tanganyika African Association (TAA) from which TANU itself was formed,[6] none of them fig-

---

[3] The railroad station and the houses of the regional and area commissioners are perhaps the most imposing buildings from the German period. The commissioners inhabit the dwellings built for the Kaiser's son whose inhabitance of them was prevented by the advent of World War I.

[4] Austen, *loc.cit.*   [5] *Ibid.*, pp. 2-3.

[6] Perhaps most important among them was Joseph Kayamba, a

ures prominently in the current Tanganyikan political scene. Two other significant voluntary associations were formed in the interwar period; both were based in Dar es Salaam. The Tanganyika African Welfare and Commercial Association (TAWCA) was formed in the mid-1930's. Despite its title, which suggested non-political aims, it was considered by the British administration to be more political than the TAA, which began sometime between 1927 and 1929 and at first seemed to have no political ambitions. Sir Harold Mac-Michael, British governor from 1934 to 1938, referred to TAWCA members as "semi-literate, politically minded, mission trained youth"; but he allowed the organization to operate because he realized that it would be a mistake to stamp on all such activities.[7] Attempts were made to merge it with the TAA before World War II, but they were largely unsuccessful; and TAWCA never did emerge as the parent of a major political organization.

The TAA's history was quite different. For some time it functioned chiefly as a mutual benefit organization for urban Africans.[8] Sir Donald Cameron, Governor from 1925 to 1931, described the TAA to the Colonial Office as happily "a social rather than a political organization" whose members constituted "some of the better-educated natives who are employed in Government service or engaged in business and trade in Dar-es-Salaam." There were about 120 members "many not Tanganyika nationals . . . and though a reasonable and respectable society it did not profess to be representative."[9] But no organization could hope to have a national impact in Tanganyika if it remained solely an urban

Tanga civil servant. See "The Story of Joseph Kayamba," *Ten Africans*, Margey Perhan (ed.) (London: Faber and Faber, 1935).

[7] Austen, *op.cit.*, p. 4, citing the Archives of the former Tanganyika Territorial Secretary as S.M.P. 22444, pp. 69-70.

[8] Bennett, *op.cit.*, p. 15.

[9] Austen, *op.cit.*, p. 2, citing Cameron to Colonial Office, August 22, 1930, S.M.P. 19325, p. 15.

phenomenon; in order to succeed, it was essential to make contact not only with the small towns, but with the villages as well. After World War II, the TAA became increasingly political, as it extended its sphere of influence into the rural areas. From an urban-based interest group, the TAA was developing into a national movement. Its new connection with the countryside had apparently been effected through tribal unions.

Tribal unions developed among the Chagga of Kilimanjaro, the Haya of West Lake around Bukoba, the Zaramo of the Coast and Dar es Salaam, the Sukuma of East Lake Region, and the Sambaa in northeastern Tanganyika, close to Tanga. These tribal unions usually had little connection with one another, but some were acquainted through membership in the TAA.[10] In some instances, the tribal unions even competed with the TAA. In 1951, for example, the colonial government accepted the demand of the Kilimanjaro Chagga Citizens' Union (KCCU), a tribal union of the Chagga, for the election of a paramount Chagga chief. At that time, a branch of the TAA in Moshi, the capital of the region inhabited by the Chagga, took the name of the Chagga Congress, both to indicate its local affiliation and in order to compete with the KCCU. The tribal union dominated the election nonetheless; and after the KCCU's winning candidate, Thomas Marealle, became paramount chief, the TAA branch was absorbed into the KCCU.

It would be a mistake to see this election, and the growth of the tribal unions, as a victory for tribal traditionalism over a modern political movement. The tribal unions grew in opposition to both the British administration and its chiefly agents. Within their ranks were leaders opposed—in varying degrees—to traditional tribal leaders, who were thought to have a previously established right to rule based on clan and lineage. In the Chagga election, the TAA supported a chief

[10] Bennett, *op.cit.*, p. 15.

24

who was a representative of the native administration and associated with the Chagga Council of Chiefs formed by the British administration.[11]

It is important to note these facts because the history of the tribal unions has a tendency to be distorted now that TANU needs operative myths. TANU spokesmen now trace TANU's roots to the TAA and to cooperative societies, denying a share in its parentage to the tribal unions, which are described as tribalistic and disruptive of national unity. For example, Edward Barongo, one of the founders of TANU in Buhaya, West Lake Region, said in 1965 that the Bukoba Buhaya Union was tribalistic and that the TAA, not the Bahaya Union, was the forerunner of TANU in Bukoba, the capital of West Lake.[12] He asserted that most of the leaders of the Bahaya Union did not even reside in Bukoba or its environs, but were in the capitals of Kenya or Uganda. This last point calls attention to the fact that the men who were active in the Union were certainly not traditional elders since they lived outside their home areas. But Mr. Barongo's version ignores the fact that the Bukoba Bahaya Union changed its name to the African Association after contact with the TAA. One historian of West Lake Region says that the Bukoba Buhaya Union was formed in 1924 and developed like the TAA through official patronage and successful petition on minor issues.[13] Furthermore, the tribal unions in general and the Bahaya Union in particular fed on reactions against British efforts to enforce unpopular agricultural policies, just as the TAA did.

The British administration, like other colonial regimes in Africa, imposed regulations as it tried to promote rural

[11] For this election see *ibid.*, p. 16.

[12] Interview with Mr. Barongo, who has held the positions of junior minister, Deputy Secretary General of TANU, district and provincial chairman of TANU in West Lake.

[13] Austen, *op.cit.*, p. 5. Governor Cameron presented the TAA with its first headquarters building as a gift (*ibid.*, p. 3).

change. These regulations were first introduced in the late 1920's and became widespread by the late 1930's. From about 1946 to 1957, laws enforcing agricultural change—which were concerned with anti-erosion measures, cattle-culling, disease prevention, and the inspection of crops—constituted the main plank in the government's efforts for agricultural improvement.[14] Reaction against these regulations was sometimes led by the tribal unions. The most celebrated single case of opposition, the Meru Land Case, which was debated in the General Assembly of the United Nations, was crucial in stimulating the creation of TANU. Meru opposition to forcible alienation from their land in 1951 (to make way for the expansion of a settler area) gave rise to explicit links between a tribal union and the TAA—which later became TANU. The Meru Citizen's Union, a tribal union led by Kirilo Japhet, was formed in protest against land alienation.[15] In 1953, Japhet toured Tanganyika under the auspices of the TAA. (He later became the first TANU chairman of Northern Province.[16]) TANU representatives in 1954 always raised the Meru Case to the UN Visiting Missions.[17] The widespread discontent arising from the Meru Land Case and the publicity attendant on Kirilo Japhet's appearance in 1952 as the first Tanganyika African to address the UN broke the ground for the formation of a national movement.[18]

Yet in 1961, the TANU Deputy Secretary General, Edward Barongo, announced that the Meru Citizen's Union had been closed down, and TANU leaders launched attacks against organizations based upon tribal or religious affiliations.[19] In

[14] Lionel Cliffe, "Nationalism and the Reaction to Enforced Agricultural Change in Tanganyika During the Colonial Period," Paper presented to the EAISR Conference, Makerere College, Kampala, December 1964, p. 1.

[15] Japhet is also known as Kirilo Japhet Ayo.

[16] And was narrowly defeated in Parliament in September 1965.

[17] Cliffe, *op.cit.*, p. 5.   [18] *Ibid.*, Bennett, *op.cit.*, pp. 16-17.

[19] *Ibid.*, p. 28. The *Tanganyika Standard*, August 23, 1961, published Barongo's statement.

order to understand this policy shift, it is necessary to examine further the growth of political organizations predating TANU.

The TAA was able to make contact with rural people partly because political consciousness developed among farmers as the issues of land alienation and enforcement became aggravated. Cliffe writes:

In most areas, even if the rural peasantry was not part of the formal membership, the [Tanganyika African] Association's officials represented them in the sense that they received and took up complaints and were thus, among other things, concerned with the very regulations [on agricultural enforcement] with which we are concerned.[20]

But there had to be people to follow up these complaints; and in 1940 Lord Hailey reported that the TAA had less than 100 members and only one branch outside Dar es Salaam (in Dodoma, central Tanganyika).[21] By 1947, however, membership had increased substantially in the towns, due no doubt to growing unrest in the countryside; Lord Hailey now reported TAA branches "in a considerable number of places in the Lake, Northern, Eastern and Tanga Provinces." Furthermore, membership was extending to new categories of people: the early TAA had been made up almost entirely of junior government officials and teachers; by 1948, traders and African farmers were joining as well as government and Native Authority employees.[22] In 1948, the TAA told the UN Visiting Mission that it had 39 branches, 1,780 members,

[20] Cliffe, *op.cit.*, p. 6.

[21] Bennett, *op.cit.*, p. 15, citing Lord Hailey, *Native Administration and Political Development in British Tropical Africa* (London: H. M. Stationery Office, 1940), p. 23.

[22] *Ibid.*, citing Lord Hailey, *Native Administration in British African Territories*, Part I (London: H. M. Stationery Office, 1950), p. 357.

and a central committee of 30.[23] The next Visiting Mission in 1951 found TAA branches in practically every town of importance they visited. By then, the TAA claimed to have 5,000 members, and a member paid a subscription fee of six shillings a year.

The growth of the TAA received impetus from two other sources in addition to the reaction to enforced rural change. In 1947, the TAA had its first large public meeting to protest the revised proposals for a Central Legislative Assembly in East Africa. Tentative proposals had first been put forward in 1945 by the British Colonial Office members to the Central Legislative Assembly, but had been rejected by European spokesmen. The Colonial Office consequently revised its proposals so that European representation was increased in Colonial Paper 210, which was brought into effect at an Extraordinary Meeting of the Tanganyika Legislative Council on April 17, 1947. Africans, rural and urban alike, feared that this was the first step in tying Tanganyika to an East African Federation which would be dominated by Kenya white settlers; it was to protest this attempt that the TAA called its first meeting. Thus once again, as in the Meru Land Case, racial questions came to the fore, and the TAA was able to exploit them.

The other stimulus to activity came from the colonial administration itself, which appointed a committee on constitutional development in 1949. Educated people and town-dwellers followed these constitutional issues and transmitted them to the rural populace in terms of racial dominance and greater independence for Africans.

Thus by the 1950's, the TAA was firmly involved in the political life of Tanganyika. And it was connected not only with tribal unions, but with other organizations which were not expressly formed to protest against colonial regulations and

[23] *Ibid.*, p. 16, citing United Nations: Report of the Visiting Mission to the Trust Territory of Tanganyika: Petitions T/218/Add. 1, November 1948, p. 17.

rule, but became politicized in the course of events. The most significant of these organizations were the cooperative societies, which became especially important in Sukumaland where the cotton cooperatives of the Victoria Federation of Cooperatives Union became the vehicle for the national movement after a TANU branch was banned from Lake Province. But even before TANU came into existence, the cooperatives played a political role.

Although by 1953 the TAA had grown in size and had officers and an executive committee chosen by its branches at an annual conference, coordination between the center and the branches was weak.[24] It was in order to overcome this weakness that Julius Nyerere determined to transform the TAA and reconstituted it as the Tanganyika African National Union in 1954.

Julius Nyerere is the son of a chief of the Zanaki, a small tribe that inhabits the shores of Lake Victoria in what is now Mara Region. Nyerere attended Roman Catholic mission schools (including St. Francis Pugu, one of Tanganyika's most prominent secondary schools), Makerere College in Kampala, Uganda, and the University of Edinburgh where he received an M.A. degree. When he returned to Tanganyika in 1952, at the age of 30, he became a teacher at St. Francis Pugu school located twelve miles outside of Dar es Salaam. Nyerere had been a member of the TAA before going abroad; in April 1953, he was made the organization's president. In 1954, Nyerere invited a group of TAA members to Dodoma to discuss his proposals for a new constitution. In July 1954, a four-day conference of the TAA was held at Dar es Salaam to discuss these proposals and their modifications made at Dodoma. On July 7, a new constitution was adopted and the Tanganyika African National Union came into existence.[25]

[24] *Ibid.* [25] *Ibid.*, p. 17.

Cooperation from local TAA branches, which usually turned themselves into TANU branches, and from other organizations facilitated TANU's development. (For example, a football club was instrumental in popularizing TANU in Dar es Salaam.[26]) While the TAA provided TANU with a nucleus of branch organization, it also left behind a tradition of little central control, lack of communication between branches, domination of the movement by town-based people, and a lack of clearly defined aims. The TAA had absorbed local tribal-based groups, and its local branches often expressed parochial sentiments—a condition which was to prove embarrassing to central TANU leadership on a number of occasions. Individuals who led branches and sub-branches took positions that TANU leadership was not willing to endorse. For example, at Korogwe in Tanga Province the chairman of a TANU sub-branch was convicted of sedition in January 1957, when he maintained that TANU was now the government and the people need no longer obey agricultural rules. Nyerere repudiated and dismissed this man,[27] but the government nonetheless banned the Korogwe TANU branch. As TANU grew rapidly in size and spread across Tanganyika, the problem of controlling the local TANU organizations became acute.

Thus the inherent inadequacies of the TAA were transmitted to TANU, where they took on far greater magnitude. The same problems now became more serious because of TANU's larger membership and its aspiration to lead an all-out assault against the colonial government to win national independence. Although TANU did achieve its major aim in 1961 by forming an independent government, it did not solve the problem of forging a centrally directed political movement in the pre-independence period. How then did TANU win independence? To answer this complex, multi-faceted

[26] Cliffe, *op.cit.*, p. 6.
[27] M.F.K. Chagga who was elected to Parliament in September 1965.

question, we must begin with an examination of the nature of heterogeneity in Tanganyika.

Any political movement which aspired to lead Tanganyika's Africans from colonial rule to national independence in the 1950's faced the difficult task of unifying the disparate African populace. Insistence upon the need for African unity was essential, since important groups of people existed, who were indifferent or absolutely opposed to Tanganyika's independence—especially if the country was to be governed under the principle of unqualified majority rule. Tanganyika is a society that has significant, if numerically small, European and Asian groups, and segments of these groups saw British colonial rule as the best guarantee of their security and prosperity. Among the Tanganyikan Africans themselves, ethnic and cultural divisions are evident. Over 120 distinct tribal groups are said to inhabit Tanganyika; and there are people of Nilotio, Nilo-Hamitic, Hamitic, and Bantu origins.[28] Coastal inhabitants with the physical characteristics of Africans sometimes referred to themselves as Arabs (before independence), often as a reflection of their commitment to Islam. Other religious groups are found here as well: Protestants, Catholics, and indigenous religious groups. (The 1957 census indicated that 7.8 per cent of the African population were Protestant, 17.1 per cent Roman

[28] I am aware that classification of peoples into these five groups has been called into question by many ethnographers and anthropologists. I am certainly avoiding associating any group with particular qualities (e.g., "Hamites have talent for rule"); I am merely calling attention to possible classifications of peoples in different ethnic categories. While these groups have often interbred there still are some physical and linguistic distinctions to be made among them. Similarly, I am aware of the difficulties in employing descriptions of peoples on the basis of "tribal" categories (e.g., not all people that outside observers call Haya would necessarily describe themselves this way). A further problem is that many so-called "tribes" in Tanganyika are creations of very recent origin. Nonetheless, I have decided to use the word "tribe" since most of the ethnographic literature on Tanganyika refers to tribes or tribal groups.

Catholics, and 30.9 per cent Muslim.[29]) There are important cultural differences as well; some people speak Swahili as a first language while others speak a tribal tongue. Further evidences of disparity may be found in the "mass/elite gap," the "rural/urban dualism," which is a reality in Tanganyika: political leaders are very conscious of themselves as an educated minority.

It was essential that none of these facts of social existence be allowed to inhibit the formation of a national movement.

Tribalism

What is commonly called tribalism would seem, on the face of it, to be the most threatening of all Tanganyika's primordial attachments to the formation of a national movement.[30] In 1955, a special representative of the Tanganyika government at the Trusteeship Council meeting said:

> . . . many of the tribes differed from each other to a greater degree than the educated sections of Africans differed from Europeans. . . . Because of the fear and distrust between neighbouring tribes it was doubtful whether any one tribe would be prepared at that time to accept a member of another tribe as its representative.[31]

This was a mistaken view. The fact that Tanganyika has over 120 tribes did not prevent TANU's coming to power. As one observer has said: "Although forms of tribal patriotism

[29] *Statistical Abstract, 1962* (Dar es Salaam: Government Printer, 1963), p. 24, Table C 14.

[30] "By a primordial attachment is meant one that stems from the 'givens'—or, more precisely, as culture is inevitably involved in such matters, the assumed 'givens'—of social existence: immediate contiguity and kin connection mainly, but beyond them the givenness that stems from being born into a particular religious community, speaking a particular language, or even a dialect of a language, and following particular social customs" (Geertz, *op.cit.*, p. 109).

[31] UN Trusteeship Council, *Verbatim Records* (T/PV. 584), p. 86. Cited by J. Clagett Taylor, *Political Development of Tanganyika* (Stanford: Stanford University Press, 1963), p. 132.

emerged, the spirit of sub-national separatism never seriously took hold."[32] The types of traditional political systems among Tanganyika's major tribes were important factors in this outcome.

Tanganyika does not have large, centralized chiefdoms which might have become the focus for ethnic nationalism;[33] most of the large tribes are recent, loosely knit federations, not historic kingdoms with strong central rulers. The Sukuma, for example, the largest tribe in Tanganyika, comprised about 12 per cent of the 8,665,000 people counted in the 1957 census,[34] a figure quite close to that of the Baganda tribe in Uganda with 16 per cent.[35] And in both countries, there are quite a few other tribes with one-quarter to one-third the numbers of the Sukuma and the Baganda.[36] But

[32] Harvey Glickman, "Traditionalism, Pluralism and Democratic Processes in Tanganyika," Paper presented at the 1964 annual meeting of the American Political Science Association, Chicago, Illinois, September 9-12, 1964, p. 3.

[33] James Coleman, "The Politics of Sub-Sahara Africa," in Almond and Coleman, *op.cit.*, pp. 254, 258-60; Margaret Bates, "Tanganyika," in Carter, *op.cit.*, p. 398, characterizes the "typical" authority pattern in Tanganyika as one where a number of chiefs might exist within one tribe without being under a central authority.

[34] For materials on the Sukuma see Hans Cory, *The Ntemi: The Traditional Role of a Sukuma Chief in Tanganyika* (London: Macmillan, Oxford University Press, 1951); Hans Cory, *The Political Indigenous System of the Sukuma* (London: Oxford University Press, 1953); Hans Cory and W. Malcolm, *Sukumaland* (London: Oxford University Press, 1943). A most valuable contribution has recently been made by Gene Andrew Maguire, *Toward "Uhuru" in Sukumaland: A Study of Micropolitics in Tanzania, 1945-1954* (Unpublished Ph.D. dissertation, Harvard University, 1966).

[35] If we consider that the Nyamwezis, the second largest tribe in Tanganyika, are both ethnically akin to the Sukuma and geographically contiguous, we would get a possible tribal grouping of more than one-fifth of the total population.

[36] The Nyamwezi, Makonde, Haya, Chagga, Gogo, Ha, Hehe, Nyakusa, and Luguru are all between 200,000 and 360,000 people. For a population breakdown by tribes in Tanganyika see *Statistical Abstract, 1962*. For Uganda, see *The Economic Development of Uganda* (Baltimore: Johns Hopkins Press, 1963), p. 439.

while the centralized kingdom of Buganda did become the focus for an ethnic nationalism,[37] the Sukuma have not expressed any such sub-nationalism.

The Sukuma are an example of a tribal group which became a political unit only recently; traditionally, they were grouped in independent tribes. In 1942, the question of a formal union of the Sukuma chiefdoms was broached by the British, and four years later 51 Sukuma chiefs came together to form a Sukuma federation. The federation was sponsored by the British as part of the colonial administration policy of creating chiefly councils and provincial councils; but the indigenous political system of the Sukuma with its elements of tribal checks and balances was never fully transcended by federal or provincial institutions. Moreover, by the time the Sukuma Union became active, TANU had been formed, and there was some overlapping of membership. The establishment of a vigorous cooperative federation, the Victoria Federation of Cooperatives, in 1954 increased the cross-cutting of political allegiance; and a separate Sukuma sub-nationalism based solely on tribal loyalties did not emerge.[38] The grievances of both the Sukuma Union and the Victorian Federation were channeled into TANU, where local discontents grew into the basis for a national movement. Educated young men—often from chiefly families but opposed to the chiefs— who were active in the Sukuma Union and the cooperatives, gave TANU their sympathetic response.

Other large tribes were not formed into single political units until after World War II. The Chaggas in fact did not establish a council of chiefs until 1946. Chagga families and clans had often developed with few ties despite their geographic proximity around Mt. Kilimanjaro.[39] Their internal

---

[37] See Apter, *The Political Kingdom in Uganda.*

[38] Glickman, *op.cit.,* pp. 4-5.

[39] For a history of the Chagga see Catherine Stahl, *History of the Chagga People of Kilimanjaro* (The Hague: Mouton and Company, 1964).

politics have been intense, and have been manifested through local TANU branches. Though the Chagga, along with the Haya, are the best-educated tribal group, they have not dominated either the TANU government or the TANU party organs. Nor have the Chagga acted as a group vis-à-vis the rest of Tanganyika.

Some of the tribes of West Lake and western Tanganyika had a traditional system of hierarchical and authoritarian rulers. But there was no single *Mwami* of all the Haya as there was for the Tutsi (in Ruanda), nor was there a *Mukama* as in Bunyoro (in Uganda), despite the fact that Haya clans claim origin in Bunyoro.[40] Sub-units within the Haya tribe have very strong claims on individual attachments; in certain parts of Buhaya, people are more likely to refer to themselves by clan than by tribe.[41] Although some chiefs in West Lake Region have overtly challenged TANU over local issues, most Tanganyika tribes were not centralized tribal systems with strong chiefs who could challenge TANU.

The impact of the European powers in Tanganyika, variable though it was, did weaken traditional systems. And even before the Germans penetrated Tanganyika, the slave trade had affected tribal systems. It has often been said that the slave trade destroyed the fabric of traditional tribal society in the nineteenth century. Actually it had different impacts upon various tribes: undoubtedly some were weakened; but others —the Yao, for example—grew stronger from the slave trade.[42] Another result of the slave trade was the spread of

[40] Glickman, *op.cit.*, p. 4. The Bahaya were divided into a series of autonomous kingdoms which were not under a central *Kabaka* as in Buganda or *Mukama* as in Bunyoro. See P. Reining, "Village Organization in Buhaya," Paper presented at the EAISR, 1952, p. 1.

[41] For the Haya, see Hans Cory and M. Hartnall, *Customary Law of the Haya* (London: Laird Humphries, 1945), and Audrey Richards (ed.), *East African Chiefs* (New York: Frederick Praeger, 1959).

[42] Joan Vincent, "Prolegmena to the Study of Tanganyikan Unity." Unpublished paper. Cited with permission of the author.

the Swahili language inland, which greatly facilitated the formation of a national movement in the future. The Germans strengthened Swahili as a *lingua franca* by their use of Swahili speaking *akidas* (African or Arab agents) as their administrators; and the British used Swahili as a language of administration. But the initial carriers of Swahili were the slave-trading caravans. Furthermore, the slave trade may have paved the way for the acceptance of shared authoritarian rule because the slave caravans required a chieftain structure.[43] And the amalgamation of peoples arising out of organized raiding may have facilitated the acceptance of extra-tribal leadership, since disparate peoples came under "foreign" tribal rulers.

The German period of rule, which has usually been characterized as having wrought havoc in Tanganyika, may also have had some positive effects on later unity. President Nyerere has said that the Maji-Maji revolt of 1905 (when the tribes of the south, particularly the Hehe led by Mkwawa, rose against the Germans) was part of the foundation of Tanganyikan unity. Nyerere claimed that the revolt brought different tribes together, and that TANU's calls for unity could be understood by the masses because the uprisings against the Germans had fostered a Tanganyikan nationalism.[44] It is difficult to be as certain of the real impact of the anti-German

[43] Roland Oliver and G. Mathew, *History of East Africa*, I (Oxford: Clarendon Press, 1963), 205.

[44] Julius Nyerere's "Foreword" to Catherine Stahl, *Tanganyika: Sail in the Wilderness* (The Hague: Mouton and Company, 1961), pp. 6-7. Also see R. F. Eberlies, "The German Achievement in East Africa," *Tanganyika Notes and Records*, No. 55 (September 1960), pp. 181-212. Vincent suggests that the impact of German rule on Africans in Tanganyika may have been less far-reaching than ethnocentric European studies lead us to believe. A Tanzanian author suggests that "the Nyamewezi under the courageous Mirambo were the first nationalists to take up arms against external aggression," when they fought the Arabs in the 1880's. Cf. Daudi Mwakawago, "Growth of Nationalism in Tanganyika," *Mbioni*, II (November 1965), 5.

revolts. Since they were one of the few examples of fairly large-scale African military opposition to European rule, a mythology has been constructed around them. There is not much evidence that inter-tribal unity was furthered in the immediate aftermath of the revolts. However, the revolts did affect the way in which national leaders later formulated their demands. The wholesale slaughter wrought by German reprisals influenced Nyerere to opt for a peaceful path to independence. And perhaps the slaughter prepared the ground for a national movement in which all partial claims were diminished through the realization that unity was necessary for an anti-colonial struggle.

We are on firmer ground when we consider the alterations wrought in the traditional tribal systems by British colonial rule.

Native Authorities

The Native Authority Ordinance came into effect in Tanganyika in 1923. This ordinance and the Native Courts Ordinance of 1929 provided for the functions of Native Authorities and established the system now known as "indirect rule," which is associated with the name of Sir Donald Cameron.[45] Since the traditional patterns of rule varied, legislative measures were deliberately made elastic, and various ordinances formulated different patterns. Four broad categories of native administration could be distinguished: (1) the chief as Native Authority with subordinate chiefs under him; (2) a federation of chiefs recognized as a Native Authority;[46] (3) a tribal council composed of several petty chiefs, or headmen,

[45] Cameron outlined his views on indirect rule in *My Tanganyika Service and Some Nigeria* (London: Allen and Unwin, 1939); "Native Administration in Nigeria and Tanganyika," supplement to the *Journal of the Royal Africa Society*, xxxvi (November 30, 1937), pp. 1-20.

[46] Hereditary chiefs retained their separate entities and executive powers as Native Authorities of their separate units, but they combined for certain purposes.

of the same tribe recognized as a Native Authority; and (4) a small chief or village headman of a more or less isolated portion of a tribe who was designated as a Native Authority. The system of indirect rule worked to undermine the very institutions it sought to uphold.[47] For one thing, the Native Authorities had to enforce rules made by the colonial administrators. After World War II this became a serious problem for them when the British tried to enforce agricultural changes. Complaints about enforced agricultural change went to the heart of the Native Authority system. The Native Authorities' role in imposing unpopular measures worked to discredit the local rulers;[48] complaints against regulations went hand-in-hand with criticisms of chiefs and the chiefly system.[49] The feeling was expressed by a TANU representative from Musoma who told a UN Visiting Mission in 1954 that cattle-culling "was introduced without consultation with Africans except chiefs, whom we consider to be government employees unable to object before the District Commissioner or the District Officer."[50]

Secondly, a large body of anthropological literature has established that very often the indigenous rulers were not those eventually supported by the British.[51] Sometimes the British were unable to locate the rulers in the system, particularly in societies where the political authority was decentralized. When installing rulers for these clans, men who were

[47] In another context, see, e.g., David Apter, *Ghana in Transition* (New York: Atheneum, 1963), pp. 119-58.

[48] Cliffe, *op.cit.*, p. 2.

[49] J. Gus Liebenow, "Responses to Planned Political Change in a Tanganyika Tribal Group," *American Political Science Review*, L (June 1962), 442-61; Roland Young and H. Fosbrooke, *Land and Politics Among the Luguru of Tanganyika* (London: Routledge and Kegan Paul, 1960), p. 163.

[50] Cliffe, *op.cit.*, p. 4, citing from UN Visiting Mission Report, 1954, p. 12.

[51] Cf. Richards, *op.cit.*

thought to have a previously established right to rule were sometimes ignored; in Tanganyika, many chiefs were appointed who had no traditional right. At times, in the interest of "taking every possible step to hasten the change over from traditional to modern system of administration," unsuitable chiefs were deposed and replaced by better-educated (or more pliable) ones. If a ruler had a legitimate position within the tribe, it was often jeopardized by acceptance of a new authority bestowed by the colonial government.

The position of the chiefs was weakened after World War II when the British modified the Native Authority system. Hitherto unrecognized advisers of the chiefs became an integral part of local government; by 1948, Native Authorities were commonly referred to as the "Chief in Council" rather than simply as the "Chief."[52] Just when political activity began to quicken in Tanganyika in the 1940's, the Native Authorities were further undermined by the decision to introduce elected bodies at local levels. These proposals were under discussion from 1945 on.[53] By 1951, there already existed different types of elected councils: those with mixed chiefly and commoner representation; and those composed of representatives elected by age-grades and kinship units (in Masailand).

In 1952, Oliver Littleton, Secretary of State for the colonies, indicated that under the Trusteeship System of the UN Administering Authority, the United Kingdom had an obligation to provide for the full participation of all sections of the population, irrespective of race or origin, in the progressive development of political institutions and the economic and social advancement of the territory.[54] The policy of multi-

[52] Taylor, *op.cit.*, p. 16.
[53] Lord Hailey, *An African Survey* (London: Oxford University Press, 1957), p. 473.
[54] Taylor, *op.cit.*, p. 76, citing from House of Commons, Parliamentary Debates, DII, Col. 2240.

racialism in Tanganyika was to be implemented by having multi-racial elected councils.[55] Not only did the extension of the elective principle further undermine appointed chiefs, but it forced them to defend the protection of Asian and European minority representation to an increasingly aroused African population. When a local government ordinance was enacted in 1953 to provide for county and local councils, and certain powers of the Native Authorities were delegated to the councils, it became clear that these councils were intended eventually to replace Native Authorities. And when the first local council was established at Newala in 1954, it took over full executive responsibility in the area at the local level.[56] Africans observed that the British did not see Native Authorities as an indispensable feature of local government.

Native Authorities were themselves dispersed and disorganized. It was only in 1957, when TANU had already achieved national prominence, that 57 chiefs gathered at the First Territorial Chiefs' Convention in an effort to create a formal body. But neither this, nor Governor Twining's statement that the office of chief ought not to be eliminated,[57] could strengthen the chiefs' position. They were too weak to be rallying points for traditionalist groupings; they had no strong base from which to challenge new economic organizations, such as cooperatives, or tribal-interest groups, such as the tribal unions. These groups could only be amalgamated within a national movement.

[55] For the institution of multi-racialism in Tanganyika, see Cranford Pratt, "Multiracialism and Local Government in Tanganyika," *Race*, II, No. 1 (November 1960), pp. 33-49.

[56] The system was to be a two-tiered one with county councils embracing several districts, and being large enough to afford their own staff and support extensive local government functions. The second tier was the local councils established at the district level. The county councils were to be multi-racial, the district ones African. These councils were to be made up of nominated and elected members or a combination of both; no specific reference was made to traditional status as a qualification for members, nor was membership limited to Africans even in the African councils (*ibid.*).

[57] Glickman, *op.cit.*, p. 12; Taylor, *op.cit.*, p. 158.

The chiefs might have been able to exploit intense hostility between tribes if this had existed; at the least, such hostility would have been disruptive for an all-embracing national movement. But there have been no rivalries in recent Tanganyika history which correspond to the present competition among large tribes in Kenya or Nigeria. Of the 9 largest tribal groups, 7 are located on the periphery of Tanganyika, but they are separated by arid and relatively uninhabited land.[58] Some migration still goes on of course; the Sukuma, for example, have been moving into West Lake and areas of Haya settlement. But this has not provoked any far-reaching Sukuma-Haya antagonism, perhaps because the Sukuma are themselves so loosely knit that the movement of small Sukuma groups is not viewed as a Sukuma invasion.

The absence of centralized tribal systems with strong chiefs improved TANU's chances for organizing a national movement in a negative way. Was there anything in the tribal configuration of Tanganyika which operated as a positive spur to the formation and victory of TANU?

One commentator has said:

The fact that a territory embraces relatively small, numerous and dispersed tribes need not act as a deterrent to the centralization of government or to the enlistment of loyalties on a national basis. If one tribe strives for domination of a particular region, it is possible for many small unrelated tribes to support a broadly based nationalist party.[59]

Julius Nyerere has been even less equivocal. He has said that his organization was helped by the fact that the African population is divided into many tribes:

[58] For tribal distribution in Tanganyika, see J. E. Goldthorpe and F. B. Wilson, *Tribal Maps of East Africa and Zanzibar*, East African Institute of Social Research, Kampala, 1960, Map 2.
[59] Glickman, *op.cit.*, p. 4.

The more tribes we have the better. . . . If there were only five tribes, there might be serious clashes. . . . My own tribe is 35,000 people; my brother is the chief. If my brother wanted to be a nuisance, he couldn't be much of a nuisance.[60]

But there is no evidence that smaller tribes opposed larger ones by banding together with TANU. TANU recruited from both large and small tribes; and local TANU branches were stronger among small tribes than large ones. What did happen was that TANU attracted ethnic minorities in given areas. For example, in Masailand and Ugogo, where the main occupation is herding, non-Masai and non-Gogo people who had moved into the areas were more receptive to TANU. Similarly, in towns situated in an area dominated by one tribe, it was likely that *wageni* or "strangers" in the town—that is, people not from the dominant tribe—would take part in TANU activities.

This special interest of local minority groups in politics is not unusual; in Tanganyika a distinct pattern has prevailed.

The towns are the loci of what can be called Swahili political culture and the "strangers" in both the towns and throughout the countryside are the carriers of this political culture. They may be from the dominant tribe in the district, but their absorption of certain values and styles sets them apart from their fellows. Before turning to the place of Swahili political culture in the growth of TANU, I would like to summarize my remarks about tribalism.

In short, TANU did not have tribal roots. Its historical ancestor, the TAA, was not a tribal or a cultural organization. Though TANU worked with and used tribal unions, these did not operate at central TANU levels. It was never dominated by large tribes, nor was it prevented from being all-inclusive by

[60] Taylor, *op.cit.*, p. 96, quoting from H. W. Flannery, "Julius Nyerere, Great Leader," *Catholic Association for International Peace,* XXI (February 1960), 9-10.

tribal hostilities. This lack of tribal opposition stemmed from the fact that traditional tribal systems were not centralized and traditional rulers had no base for opposition. In addition, TANU was not thought of as competing with tribal groups.

This is not to say that the nature of Tanganyika society, made up as it is of many small and dispersed tribes, has had no important consequences for TANU. It was one thing for TANU to organize and become the dominant national movement; it was quite another to establish an effective government over many small-scale and dispersed communities after independence. An examination of the Swahili culture in general, and of the way in which TANU came to power in 1960-61 will reveal that overcoming parochialisms for the sake of organizing a national movement is very different from ruling a society.

Swahili Political Culture and National Integration

I have so far described heterogeneity in Tanganyika primarily in terms of tribal distinctions. Other important aspects of heterogeneity have only been mentioned—religious, linguistic, rural/town, and racial differences. The first three are contained in what I have called the Swahili political culture.

Swahili is spoken over a wide area of East Africa: it is known in the eastern Congo and much of southern Uganda, more widely used in Kenya, and the national language in Tanganyika. It provided an ideal, ready-made vehicle through which TANU officials could communicate with the grass roots of society and operate even in unfamiliar localities. A knowledge of Swahili was therefore a prerequisite to the establishment of a permanent, paid TANU staff, whose members could be posted anywhere in the country.[61]

Swahili was an essential component of Tanganyika's national identity; it was equated with "Tanganyikaness." Before

[61] See W.B.K. Mwanjisi, "Tanganyika African National Union," *Africa Today*, VIII (December 1961), 10-11.

43

independence, TANU promoted literacy and adult education by setting up TANU schools and spreading the use of Swahili;[62] after independence, Swahili became the official national language of Tanganyika. In 1965, Swahili became compulsory in all secondary schools and every pupil must now sit a Swahili language examination at school certificate level.[63] In that same year, Swahili was declared the only language TANU candidates could use in their electioneering. "If the people do not know Swahili, therefore every candidate shall have an interpreter."[64] Implicit in this was the desire to keep TANU free from association with any tribal tongue.

But "Swahili," when used as an adjective—as, for example, in the phrase "Swahili political culture"—refers to more than a language. It is associated with Islam, with the Coast, with TANU, and above all with a style of life.

The slave trade brought to Tanganyika not only a language, but a religion as well—Islam. More Tanganyikans are listed as Muslims than any other category except "pagan." The regional breakdown shows over 70 per cent Muslim in the coastal areas—Tanga, eastern and southern regions; central and western regions are nearly 25 per cent Muslims. As Islam penetrated, in varying degrees, throughout Tanganyika (every district has some Muslims), it served as a medium for regional intercommunication. District centers separated from one another by 500 miles of bush sometimes share similar styles and values. The twin towns of Kigoma and Ujijii on the shores of Lake Tanganyika are hundreds of miles from coastal centers; yet they exhibit a heavy coastal influence in the way their houses are built, in their large Islamic popula-

[62] The late Sheikh Amri Abedi, a former Cabinet minister and mayor of Dar es Salaam, was active in promoting Swahili culture. Julius Nyerere has already translated *Julius Caesar* into Swahili and is at work on another of Shakespeare's plays.

[63] Minister of Education, E. Eliufoo, Speech to Parliament reported in the *Nationalist*, June 30, 1965, p. 2.

[64] From Speech of Second Vice President Kawawa, *Nationalist*, June 10, 1965, p. 4.

tion, and in the weight given to elders in the pattern of leadership. It is not surprising then that area commissioners who have been heads of the party and government in coastal districts are effective in places like Kigoma-Ujijii.

To describe someone as a "Swahili" in Tanganyika can imply many different things. It is not necessary for one to be a Muslim to receive this appellation, nor to be from the Coast.[65] Many of the early TANU activists in Mwanza, the capital of Sukumaland and the present capital of Mwanza Region, were referred to as *wageni* (strangers) and as Swahilis. Some of these are archetypes of the TANU elder-leader: they are Muslims with coastal backgrounds or connections, who have been active at one time in TANU politics in Mwanza. Businessmen in Mwanza who were not from the Coast and were not Muslims were also referred to as Swahilis. Because they were not indigenous Sukumas, they were *wageni*; because they lived in the town, they were Swahilis. Even men from the Nyamwezi tribe, which has strong regional links with the Sukuma, were referred to as Swahilis when they were in Mwanza. (If they had been in their own Nyamwezi country they probably would not have been, depending in part on how they fitted into their indigenous culture.[66])

A number of anthropologists working in Tanganyika have argued that the divisions in tribal societies may not be "between kin and non-kin, literate and illiterate, sub-chiefs and headmen and the rest, but between those who adopt a Swahili way of life and the rest."[67] The Swahili way of life in-

[65] Sometimes Europeans in Tanganyika loosely refer to people from the Coast as Swahilis. Often, people from the Zaramo tribe who live in and around Dar es Salaam are called Swahilis by Europeans in Dar es Salaam.

[66] These ideas were developed at a seminar I gave at Kivukoni College in 1965. I am also indebted to the comments of Lionel Cliffe, John Morris, and Daudi Mwakawaga though none of them are responsible for the use I have made of our discussion.

[67] E.g., Alison Redmayne, "Preliminary Report on a Hehe Com-

volves having "a conviction of one's superiority which is shown by preferring to speak Swahili instead of Kihehe, involvement in the affairs of a minor settlement or Iringa [the major town in Uhehe] where possible, and a minimum involvement in the affairs of one's local community."[68] The commitment to a Swahili way of life is also expressed in dress and often in the choice of a name.[69]

> Just recently it has come to involve the possibility of being some sort of petty official in TANU . . . with opportunities for making speeches and telling other members of the community how they must improve themselves and mend their ways.[70]

Swahili culture, as distinguished from tribal culture, represents a confrontation of the traditional and modern political cultures; it stands for the new life in the town. TANU is both the carrier of this Swahili culture and an expression of it.

Many TANU leaders at the national, regional, and district levels have lived in the towns. TANU appealed to clerks and other lower-level officials in the colonial administration, as well as to the semi-town/semi-rural men—lorry drivers and others in transport services, who moved between the towns and the surrounding countryside, and missionary-educated seminarians. The party also recruited secondary school graduates who did not have the best academic records and thus became primary schoolteachers, and would later qualify as TANU activists at the local level. Former teachers may also be found among the high-level officials. President Nyerere was a secondary schoolteacher and is now known as the

---

munity," EAISR paper, 1962, p. 8. The Hehe are one of the largest tribes in Tanganyika and inhabit what is now the Iringa Region.

[68] *Ibid.*

[69] In the parliamentary elections of 1965, men who have been known by Christian first names and Christianized last names ran under African and often Swahili names. For example, Philip Hosea was listed as P. H. Irungu.

[70] *Ibid.*

Mwalimu (Teacher). Oscar Kambona, TANU Secretary General and Minister for Regional Administration; Nsilo Swai, Minister for Industries, Mineral Reserves and Power and TANU National Treasurer; and Job Lusinde, Minister for Communications and Works, are all former secondary schoolteachers. Among middle-level leaders,[71] on the other hand, very few teachers are to be found. What has caused such a curious scarcity at this particular level?

The successful teachers—the secondary schoolteachers—were not willing to give up their jobs and enter TANU; some even felt TANU was beneath them since local leaders were often less educated than they. Thus, local politics was taken over by dissatisfied primary schoolteachers and school leavers, who later became elected TANU officials—branch or district chairmen, district councilors after independence. The primary schoolteachers did not often move beyond the district level. But if a man pursued his education into secondary school, he almost certainly traveled outside his home district. If he went past secondary school, he was likely to go outside Tanganyika; and then if he became active in TANU affairs, he would enter late in the 1950's as an appointed official. Members of the semi-town/semi-rural strata also became TANU branch chairmen or branch secretaries. Although all of these branch officials aspired to be posted in the towns, only those who showed initiative or happened to be in the right place at

[71] The term "middle-level leaders" refers to all TANU and government leaders at regional and district levels. Leaders of groups linked to TANU at those levels are included too. I also refer to people in Dar es Salaam who are just below the highest-level leaders. Any TANU or government official of high rank who is not a Minister in the Cabinet or part of the TANU Cabinet is a middle-level leader. Parliamentary secretaries, members of Parliament, TANU administrative officials are the highest middle-level leaders. The term is very inclusive and there are obviously wide differences in importance between high middle-level leaders and low middle-level leaders. Thus a TANU area commissioner stands well below a parliamentary secretary; a TANU district chairman just makes it into the middle-level leader category.

the right time became district chairmen or secretaries, and sometimes even regional cabinet officials.

TANU also responded to the needs and values of the rural farmer which it tried to represent as it opposed the colonial administration. As TANU fed on rural discontent, it absorbed tribesmen in their tribal unions and was itself drawn into the countryside as an instrument for voicing rural discontent. In Tanganyika, the emphasis was thus different than in the places Thomas Hodgkin describes, where the "discontent excited by the philosophy of life of which the new town is the symbol and expression" was the catalyst for political organization and provided its most characteristic organizational form.[72]

Tanganyika is not made up of compact villages. A "village" may designate no more than an administrative entity, a collection of families spread over an area of up to 25 square miles; scattered lineage homesteads make up most of the settlements in rural areas.[73] And there are no fixed criteria for distinguishing between small towns of 1,000 people or less and minor village settlements. A divisional headquarters will be the focus for a population spread over 200 square miles. More important than the difference in size among these units is the difference in the ways of living. Daily existence can be substantially altered by the size of a store (*duka*), the presence of a market or a generator for electricity. Thus, in its appeal to the various settlements, TANU often encountered antithetical cultures; it was constantly trying to encompass these wide variations and relieve the many real and potential tensions stemming from them.

[72] I have leaned heavily on Lionel Cliffe, *op.cit.*, p. 9. The citation is from Thomas Hodgkin, *Nationalism in Colonial Africa* (New York: New York University Press, 1957), pp. 91-92.

[73] M. R. Jellicoe, "Political Parties in Tanganyika Since Independence," Unpublished paper, Makerere College, 1963. Cited with permission of the author.

Conclusion

I have shown that TANU was not threatened by any special ethnic particularism, that in fact it could exploit tribal heterogeneity and the Swahili political culture for its goal of organizing for independence. Nonetheless, as TANU tried to extend itself into rural areas it had to straddle disparate ways of life. It had to base its appeal on the common denominator of the demand for independence, avoiding issues that might split Africans. In other words, it had to avoid substantive issues of politics and economics which could set townsman off against farmer or one tribe against another.[74] At the same time, TANU had to work within the loose organization and local chapter autonomy which it had inherited from the TAA. Thus it was vulnerable, as are all African nationalist movements, to attack by the colonial administration, which could bring physical force to bear against individual nationalist leaders, or try to split nationalist movements and play leaders off against each other. The policy of divide and rule was a reality in Africa, not a mythical reconstruction of pre-independence history made in the post-independence period.

One of the most important factors in the rise of TANU was the British administration's attitude toward the formation of a political movement in Tanganyika. The colonial government's hostility, neutrality, and finally, favor toward TANU attitudes were important factors in TANU's development. We must undertake to explain the role of the colonial government in order to understand the way TANU came to power in Tanganyika. And TANU's organization at the end of the 1950's must be described before we can examine TANU as the ruling party of independent Tanganyika.

[74] Nyerere has said that he consciously tried to avoid any such issues with these fears in mind (Stahl, *op.cit.*).

49

CHAPTER II

The Drive to Independence and Dominance

British Policy, Electoral Competition,
and Splinter Parties

UNLIKE KENYA, Tanganyika did not house a large, homogeneous white-settler community; the European population was split between significant minorities of Greeks, Italians and South Africans, as well as the dominant British group. Thus TANU was never confronted by an entrenched, unified European group. The Asian community was also diverse, consisting of Indians, Goans, Pakistanis, and Arabs, many of whom were traders who settled in isolated communities and were vulnerable to hostile action in the countryside. Some Asians threw in with TANU to insure their security; but others supported a policy of postponing independence and insisted on a constitution with built-in racial guarantees.

Because Tanganyika was an international trusteeship held under League of Nations and then UN authority, the colonial administration was more concerned with matters of principle here than elsewhere in Africa.[1] Nonetheless, the British administered Tanganyika essentially as a colony, and opposed TANU until the latter demonstrated its dominant national position in 1958. The British introduced and pressed their policy of multi-racialism, guaranteeing European and Asian minorities a political position which their numbers could not assure through the ballot.[2] They also tried—unsuccessfully—to channel tribalism into sustaining the authority of the chiefs.

[1] B.T.G. Chidzero, *Tanganyika and International Trusteeship* (London: Oxford University Press, 1961), pp. 248-56.

[2] Pratt, *loc.cit.*, reproduces the London *Times* comments of May 24, 1957, for evidence of political oppression in Tanganyika. John Hatch, *Africa Today and Tomorrow* (London: Denis Dobson, 1962), argues that the imposition of multi-racialism was related to British reluctance to undermine Sir Roy Welensky's position in Central Africa or white settlers in Kenya.

50

DRIVE TO INDEPENDENCE

In 1956, the United Tanganyika Party (UTP) was formed under the sponsorship of the colonial administration in support of the multi-racial policy and in opposition to TANU. The UTP was a multi-racial party, whereas TANU was open only to Africans until after 1963. It proposed that Tanganyika form a second chamber which would be a consultative body including outstanding people of all races.[3] It also considered, but never pursued, the possibility of having the chiefs serve as an upper house of Parliament. Although in 1957 the chiefs did gather at a government-sponsored Territorial Chiefs' Convention to see if they might group themselves into a formal body, their position was by now too weak to make the effort successful. They met again in 1959 to endorse TANU's political demands,[4] but for the most part, remained aloof from its electoral struggle with the UTP.

Tanganyika conducted a two-part general election in September 1958, and February 1959, under a tripartite system of voting which guaranteed racial representation. TANU had been opposed to the tripartite system, though Africans could vote for the Asian or European of their choice. Nonetheless, it gave its support to certain Asian and European candidates. Of the 12 seats contested in September 1958, TANU and TANU-supported candidates won every seat; TANU obtained 67 per cent of the 22,769 ballots cast.[5] In order to vote, one needed to have either an educational training equivalent to Standard VII or higher, an income of more than $420 per annum, or experience in certain specified categories of office. Though these restrictions limited the number of Africans who could vote, Africans still made up the majority of possible voters in each constituency; of the 5 constituencies where the 1958 election was contested, Africans comprised two-thirds of the 28,500 registered voters. Although the

[3] Glickman, *op.cit.*, p. 12.
[4] Bennett, *op.cit.*, p. 7; *Tanganyika Standard*, March 13, 1959.
[5] Taylor, *op.cit.*, p. 173, citing from *Colonial Office Report*, 1958, p. 35.

51

franchise was restricted, Africans did vote outside of the towns. There were some 400 polling stations in the five provinces where voting was to take place and there was no voting in Dar es Salaam district for this first phase of the election. Thus Africans who supported TANU were not town-dwellers only.

The first part of Tanganyika's national election resulted in an overwhelming victory for TANU within the context of a very limited vote. By the end of 1958, the UTP had "ceased to function as an effective political organization," according to the administration.[6] Only 3 seats were contested out of the 15 seats in 5 constituencies for the February 1959 phase of the first elections; the UTP had disappeared from the scene. All 5 African candidates, TANU nominees, were unopposed; 2 TANU-supported Asians and 1 TANU-supported European were victorious in their contests.

But what did TANU's victory represent? The UTP did not even have the complete support of the Europeans. One correspondent reported that Europeans in Dar es Salaam remained indifferent to the first elections until two months before they began.[7] By June 1958, Sir Edward Twining's term as governor had come to an end and the following month his replacement, Sir Richard Turnbull, announced his commitment to bring Tanganyika rapidly to self-government.[8] Thus it was clear that the colonial government would not try to determine the results of the election in favor of the UTP. Because the colonial government was not fighting the election against TANU, TANU's victory was not an indication of great organizational strength.

The opposition of a colonial regime can be a significant factor in strengthening the fiber and organization of a national movement. When the British barred civil servants from joining political parties in August 1953, it deprived the TAA

[6] Ibid.
[7] Kenya Weekly News (Nairobi) July 8, 1958, p. 2.
[8] Taylor, op.cit., p. 166.

and later TANU of educated Africans who would not commit themselves totally to the movement. In response to the ban on civil servants in political parties, one group in Western Province asked a UN Visiting Mission: "How can we ever become free?"[9] But this ban also stimulated a number of people, like Nyerere and Kambona, to give up their jobs as teachers or civil servants and devote themselves to the national movement. Similarly, when the British promulgated a provision of the Societies Ordinance, modeled on Kenya legislation, which compelled all organizations to be registered with the government, complaints arose that the requirements were aimed at inhibiting TANU's growth. But the need to comply with the registration provisions forced local TANU branches to seek help from the center; only in this way did TANU in Dar es Salaam learn of the existence of some of its local branches.

Thus, while it is true that a "yielding British policy" was an important element in TANU's pervasive influence in Tanganyika,[10] the lack of a firmly committed colonial enemy also contributed to the deceptive appearance of a "strong" TANU. Another factor which contributed to this impression was the nature of the African opposition to TANU.

We have already seen the weak position of traditional leaders which vitiated any challenge they might pose to TANU. No African political opposition really challenged TANU in the pre-independence elections. Aside from the UTP, two African splinter parties existed in 1958. One of these, the

[9] Bennett, op.cit., p. 19.
[10] John B. George, "How Stable Is Tanganyika?" Africa Report, VIII (March 1963), 3-4. Robert Keith, "Self-Rule in Tanganyika," Africa Special Report, IV (December 1959), 8, saw the possibility that Britain never had a primary interest in Tanganyika as a reason for political unification under TANU. President Nyerere also pointed to the importance of the character of the British administration when he said a non-violent policy would work in Tanganyika against the British administration. Cf. Stahl, op.cit., p. 9.

Tanganyika Federal Independence Party, with headquarters in Tanga, never contested any seats, and disappeared after the 1958 election. It had demanded separate independence for the territory's provinces. But there was no support for regionalism in Tanganyika, and federal arrangements between the provinces were never seriously considered by the British.

The other splinter party, the African National Congress (ANC), was formed as the Tanganyika African Congress in 1958 by Zuberi Mtemvu, a former provincial secretary of TANU. When the Tanganyika African National Congress was refused registration in May 1958, it was renamed the African National Congress, and was allowed to register. It contested one seat in the September 1958 election: Mtemvu ran against the TANU candidate (John Keto) and the UTP candidate (P. C. Mntambo) in Tanga Province; he received 53 votes, Keto 3,455, and Mntambo 1,854. Mtemvu lost his deposit; and the ANC did not contest the February 1959 part of the election. It did, however, field candidates for elections in 1960 and 1962. Although it was decisively beaten again, some of the notes Mtemvu struck continued to ring within TANU itself.

In a memorandum written in 1958, Mtemvu stated that TANU and the UTP were too much alike. He held that Tanganyika should be not primarily but completely African, and alleged that Nyerere was trying to protect his Asian and European friends. He said that the ANC would be "extreme" and "radical"; but aside from advocating internal self-government by 1962 and expressing a more racialistic point of view, Mtemvu's "radicalism" was not evident.[11] His "extremism" consisted largely of African nationalism with references to socialism.

Mtemvu opposed the possibility of TANU being opened to

[11] Mtemvu's memorandum is cited by Taylor, *op.cit.*, p. 163.

non-Africans; after breaking with TANU he called for even more rapid Africanization of the civil service, and took a stridently racial stand on citizenship for non-Africans. But TANU had preempted political organizing among Africans by getting there first, and had made successful demands for allegiance. This, plus Nyerere's personal popularity, precluded the possibility of Mtemvu's issues being able to galvanize voters against TANU. But later on, Nyerere was to battle within TANU against the same tendencies that Mtemvu expressed.

The ANC—which ran 2 candidates, both of whom were unsuccessful—was the only organized opposition to TANU in the general election of 1960. Whereas the elections of 1958-59 were designated to make the Legislative Council more representative and responsive, the 1960 election ushered in "responsible government." A new Legislative Council was elected with a majority of elected rather than appointed members.[12] The election took place on August 30, 1960, with an enlarged franchise. Fifty seats were open to members of any race; 11 were reserved for Asians and 10 for Europeans. Registration was based on three alternative qualifications: the voter must be able to read and write in Swahili or English; he (she) must possess an annual income of $210; or he (she) must be the present or past holder of a prescribed office. There were 885,000 voters registered. By the end of July, 58 TANU-supported candidates had been elected without opposition; of these, 39 were Africans. TANU won 12 of the 13 contested seats. The unsuccessful TANU candidate was defeated by an independent, Mr. Sarwatt, who had originally

[12] The Tanganyika Parliament was called the Legislative Council until May 1, 1961, when Tanganyika officially received self-government. Then it became the National Assembly without new elections. In practice, Tanganyika enjoyed internal self-government for eight months before independence was officially granted on December 9, 1961. TANU formed a majority in the Council on October 11, 1960.

been the TANU Mbulu-branch candidate in Northern Province but was rejected by the TANU National Headquarters.[13] National Headquarters also imposed an unpopular candidate in Tukuyu in southwest Tanganyika. The TANU candidate won, but he did not win a majority of all votes cast in a poor turnout. All told, TANU won 100,581 votes or 82.8 per cent of the total votes cast; the ANC won 337 votes or 0.3 per cent; and independent candidates won 20,527 votes or 16.9 per cent.[14] Sarwatt received close to one-third of all independent votes.

While TANU won a heavy majority of the votes cast, the 1960 election did not attest to TANU's organizational strength. The 885,000 registered voters represented only about half of the persons estimated as potentially eligible to register. Since less than one-seventh of the registered voters actually voted,[15] less than one-fourteenth of the possible electorate voted. The small turnout was due in part to the fact that few seats were contested. But it was also a direct reflection of apathy and the inability of TANU to organize a larger registration, since it is reasonable to assume that TANU wanted a large turnout. The same pattern was evident in elections after independence: in 1962, only 15,000 out of 100,000 eligible voters turned out for municipal elections. Even though it was clear that the TANU candidates would carry the day and this perception reduced the turnout, the number of people mobilized to go to the polls was again a reflection of TANU's organizational weakness.

Perhaps the most revealing election of all was the presidential election of 1962. During the first year of Tanganyika's

[13] Sarwatt was allowed to take part in the parliamentary party meetings of TANU, and he rejoined the TANU fold.

[14] Colin Leys, "Elections," *East African Study Materials in Political Science* (Makerere College, Kampala, 1964-65). Sources: *Tanganyika Gazette*; Martin Lowenkopf, "Tanganyika Achieves Responsible Government," *Parliamentary Affairs*, XIV (Spring 1960), 244-57.

[15] No voting took place in uncontested elections.

independence, the TANU government determined to replace the office of prime minister with an elected president. A presidential election was held under universal suffrage; the only qualification was that the candidate be twenty-one or over. Under the Republican Constitution which was introduced in 1962, the president would be chosen by the members of the National Assembly on the basis of a commitment made by each assembly candidate at the time of this election to vote for a particular presidential candidate. But when the Republican Constitution was inaugurated, it was decided to defer the holding of the National Assembly elections as the Assembly was then only two years old. Special legislation was passed providing for a nationwide poll for the first president.

TANU was opposed by the ANC, which had remained in existence, though it had shown almost no electoral support in the 1960 election. At the end of 1960, it had 9 organized branches as against 498 organized branches attributed to TANU.[16] Mtemvu ran for president against Nyerere. Nyerere received 1,127,978 votes, Mtemvu 21,276. The little over 1.1 million votes cast was less than one-fourth of the potential electorate.[17] At the time of the election, TANU claimed 1½ to 2 million members. This would appear to include almost anyone who ever held a TANU card. In 1962, there were 450,000 dues-paying members. The actual vote for Nyerere was less than membership claimed for TANU. If we assume that most of the dues-paying members of TANU voted (as they are a more politically active part of the population), the voter turnout for non-dues-paying TANU members was very small. Of the population who were not TANU dues-payers, only about 15 per cent of those entitled to vote can have done so.

---

[16] I say "attributed" because there has never been an accepted number. The figure 498 is given in the *Colonial Office Report*, Part I, 1960, p. 32, cited by Taylor, *op.cit.*, p. 199.

[17] Over half of Tanganyika's 10 million people are under 18.

The elections revealed that TANU would win any contest but that it had not organized the population to support it overwhelmingly at the polls. Its organizational strength had never been tested by a vigorous opposition party which could seriously threaten it in a contest for votes. Because of the nature of the opposition and the nature of its own growth, TANU's electoral dominance was deceptive: it did not illustrate TANU's great strength; in fact, it reflected an organizational weakness.

In 1962 another party, the People's Democratic Party (PDC), was formed under the leadership of an ex-TANU leader and onetime head of the railway workers union, C. K. Tumbo. As early as 1960, Tumbo had attacked Nyerere's plan for ending the separate school systems for Asians, Europeans, and Africans, as too mild an integration program. Like Mtemvu, Tumbo believed in rapid Africanization and opposed the racial policies of the government. In order to get him out of Tanganyika, Nyerere made him High Commissioner to Great Britain. After a year, he resigned and returned to Tanganyika to form the PDC.[18]

The PDC, like the ANC and the splinter groups which were to follow it, was racialistically "African" and demanded the right to be an opposition. While these splinter parties were "radical" on citizenship, Africanization, and the future role of non-Africans in Tanganyika society, they were often conservative on social issues in an attempt to play to specific grievances. A new party was formed at Mwanza in 1962, the People's Convention Party (PCP), in opposition to this "radical" legislation. It opposed government land bills which set conditions for continued rights of occupancy, and at the same time tried to appeal to African farmers with a stake in land by playing on their fears that their land would be con-

[18] Tumbo was arrested in 1964 in Mombassa and extradited to Tanganyika where he was put in preventive detention.

fiscated. The PDC had disbanded itself within a year and some of its founders were appropriated by the PCP.

In fact, the splinter movements have been a kaleidoscope of interpersonal attachments and alliances of various spokesmen. For example, J. D. Chipaka, one of the founders of the PDC, was an ex-ANC member. Sheikh Yahya Hussein was the head of a very short-lived Nationalist Enterprise Party. He appeared at a press conference in Dar es Salaam in 1963 with Samson Masalla who had been president of the PCP (which was refused registration by the regional commissioner in Mwanza) to announce a new party called the African Independence Movement.[19] Sheikh Hussein called for Tumbo, who was at that time outside Tanganyika, to return and lead the African Independence Party. (Tumbo, for all his "radicalism," had at times bid for support of the chiefs; and Sheikh Hussein himself was both a Muslim leader and a supporter of chiefly institutions.) Sheikh Hussein also put forward the name of one Chief Fundikira as a desirable head of the African Independence Party.

Fundikira has been approached at various times by dissident groups interested in restoring chiefs to positions of influence. He is a chief of the Nyamwezi, the second largest tribe in Tanzania;[20] but he is also, and above all, a Muslim leader, active in Islamic affairs who appeared at Muslim conventions in Mombassa and Tanga. His brother-in-law was President of the All-Muslim National Union of Tanganyika.

Chief Fundikira was elected to the Legislative Council in 1959 with TANU backing, but he did not join TANU until

[19] Sheikh Hussein claimed that 21 members of the TANU National Executive Committee supported the positions he took at the press conference. This was never substantiated.

[20] Tumbo and Samson Masalla were also Nyamwezi; and Tumbo's railroad union agitated in Tabora which is a main railhead. However, the Nyamwezi as a tribe have not been anti-TANU. (In the 1965 presidential elections, abstentions were high in three Tabora constituencies, but registration was relatively high also.)

1960. He became a minister before independence, holding the portfolios of Lands and Surveys and later Justice. In May 1960, he spoke out against Nyerere, repudiating an inference of Nyerere's that justice in the hands of chiefs could be bought. In 1963, Fundikira also opposed the government's land bills which set conditions for maintaining leaseholds and abrogating freehold. He left the Cabinet early in 1963 in protest against the land policy. Fundikira also protested that TANU did not have a mandate for legislating into existence a one-party state; he claimed the foundations for this legislation were laid when area and regional commissioners were constituted in 1962. Shortly thereafter, he was arrested and tried for allegedly accepting bribes as chairman of the National Agricultural Products Board. Many people considered this a political arrest, and when he was acquitted in June 1963, there was a large demonstration for him in Dar es Salaam. The Dar demonstration was based neither on his chiefly status nor on his Nyamwezi ties; it was an outpouring of Muslim support on the Coast. Fundikira rejoined TANU after the army mutiny of January 1964, as a gesture of national solidarity. It has since fallen to him to defend government policy on a number of economic issues.[21]

When Fundikira rejoined TANU, there were no longer any well-known figures in opposition: Tumbo was under arrest; Mtemvu had rejoined TANU in 1963 and is now in the Ministry of Lands as Assistant Secretary to the Village Settlement, Water Development, and Irrigation Divisions.

TANU's Organization in the 1950's

TANU's rapid growth into a mass movement in the 1950's was characterized by an absence of central direction, due largely to the fact that there existed neither a central staff nor

[21] He has been made chairman of the East African Aviation Board by the same government that was instrumental in having him tried for corruption when he held another important economic post.

a firm base for central finances. It has been asserted that Nyerere was well aware of the difficulties of controlling a mass movement, and had intended TANU as a "close-knit" organization.[22] He was concerned that local branches would obstruct a non-violent path to independence by making extreme demands; and he was conscious of the critical lack of qualified leaders.[23] Despite Nyerere's intentions, TANU was at first a party characterized by narrow recruitment and dependent upon private financing.[24] In the absence of a large, trained central staff, TANU relied on well-known individuals to recruit new members and bring in money. Branches with self-selected leaders sprang up as TANU's influence spread into rural areas. Nyerere welcomed all Africans to TANU regardless of social or ideological orientation. Thus ensued an almost uncontrolled transition from a small group in Dar es Salaam with links to tribal and associational groups to a mass national movement.

But even as TANU grew in size, it did not develop into a "mass party" with a hard-core party bureaucracy. It qualified for this name only insofar as it was large; but it had not the administrative machinery to answer to Duverger's definition of a mass party as one with a bureaucracy and different layers of committed followers and hangers-on.[25]

By 1958, TANU claimed 200,000 card-carrying members, but subscriptions were not always paid. It was easier to raise funds for special drives than to collect subscriptions on a regular basis. This is so for a number of reasons:[26] scattered

[22] Bennett, op.cit., p. 25.

[23] Martin Lowenkoph, "Political Parties in Uganda and Tanganyika," Unpublished Master's thesis, London School of Economics, 1961, p. 75.

[24] Ibid., p. 36.

[25] Lowenkoph describes the transition as one from a cadre to a mass party, using Duverger's terminology. Cf. Maurice Duverger, Political Parties (London: Methuen and Co., 1955), esp. pp. 63-71.

[26] Bennett, op.cit., p. 26. William Friedland, Unions and Industrial Relations in Underdeveloped Countries, Bulletin 47 of the New York

population and poor communications make collection hard; most of the rural areas do not have banks and the farmers, whose incomes are usually seasonal, must be reached when cash is on hand; immediate officials are sometimes distrusted. Furthermore, funds do get channeled to individuals and are often spent foolishly because party discipline is too weak to enforce and supervise collection. And because the money does not come in, a dependable staff is not created which might in future collect funds efficiently.

TANU never had a stable source of finances before independence. Money was a constant worry to the leadership, who found it difficult to attract people to full-time party work when the salaries they could offer were so meager. In 1961, a TANU branch secretary received less than a domestic servant; he could not have existed without additional allowances (*poshos*) and aid from self-help schemes in building his house. Like the branch chairmen, they sometimes received a percentage of the subscriptions brought in; this still occurs, but it blurs the distinction between "paid" secretaries and "unpaid" chairmen at the branch level. A district secretary received less than a good copy typist,[27] although he was a full-time employee. Provincial secretaries were paid much more, but even their salaries were far below the standard for white-collar workers.[28] Officials could increase their income

State School of Industrial and Labor Relations at Cornell University (Ithaca, 1963), pp. 28-30, remarks on this phenomenon in Tanganyika trade unions. Special drives are more dramatic and the benefits from payment, for example, to send Nyerere to the UN, may be more tangible than keeping up dues.

[27] Colin Leys, "Tanganyika: The Realities of Independence," *International Journal*, XVII (Summer 1962), 258-59. A branch secretary received $14.00 a month; a branch chairman of TANU was not paid a salary, but received 10 per cent of subscriptions collected; a district secretary received $75.00 a month, and the district treasurer (now the deputy secretary) got $30.00 a month; a district chairman received an honorarium allowance of $21.00 a month. The salary scales are based on reports of TANU district secretaries at Kivukoni College.

[28] A provincial secretary was paid around $57 a month and a

by using their posts for private ends. But this practice certainly did not contribute to the construction of a bureaucracy on the basis of stable wage-payments.

The decision to create a permanent professional staff of organizers was difficult to implement. Although regional and district officials were appointed in 1956, it was not until 1958 that steps were taken in earnest to create this staff.[29] Nineteen fifty-eight was a critical year because candidates were to be chosen for the legislative council. National Headquarters wanted to be able to impose candidates for the elections of 1958-59 and later on for 1960. And since many of TANU's concerns revolved around getting funds, recruiting members, and passing out information from the center to candidates who were running for office, the central officials were in a strategic position to influence matters. But National Headquarters had to have officers in the field who could be relied on to capitalize on this potential leverage.

Prior to 1958, there was often little difference in the way that provincial/district secretaries and chairmen of TANU came to office. Although the secretaries were supposed to be appointed officials and the chairmen elected ones, many of the pre-1958 secretaries were elected by TANU provincial committees. Frequently, they were co-opted to the job. For example, a regional secretary of TANU, who was also a civil servant, was threatened with dismissal from his government job unless he gave up his TANU post. He chose to leave TANU, and another man was co-opted into the vacated office. It was all done among a few people.[30] Sometimes a man

provincial treasurer $50. A provincial chairman received $50 a month allowance.

[29] At that time Edward Kisenge was Acting Secretary General of TANU; he later referred to his job as "just like running a ministry only with less well-paid staff and longer hours." (Reported by Joseph Nye, Jr., "Political Parties in East Africa Since Independence," to be published by Boston University Press.)

[30] The man co-opted, S. Maswanya, later became the Minister for

would start a branch or even a district organization and name himself as secretary; or an old secretary of the local TAA branch would convert himself and his organization into TANU. Thus both chairmen and secretaries of TANU prior to 1958 were often locals. It was also not unusual for a district secretary to be a recent inhabitant of the district rather than a native. Procedures were not regularized. Some chairmen were kept on by their people when they left the province to become secretaries in a different province.[31]

In some districts, a limited number of men were available who could or would handle the post of TANU secretary. When TANU National Headquarters began to appoint secretaries and to post men from one district or province to another, it increased the available pool for any one district. Furthermore, the distinctions between TANU secretaries and TANU chairmen at the district and provincial levels became sharper. The appointments of secretaries from the center strengthened the center and increased the power of both the administrative officials of TANU and the members of the central committee who made these appointments. Salaries, as well as appointments, came from the center at Dar es Salaam; this made the secretaries financially independent of the local elected chairmen and the TANU elected committees.

The strategy adopted by central leaders in the 1950's was designed to facilitate central control. Nyerere stressed that the tactics of independence must not be based on local demands, not only because these demands would threaten TANU's unity, but also because this strategy would strengthen the paid officials of the center vis-à-vis the elected officials who were supposed to represent local demands. Nyerere wanted to confront the colonial administration with the one

Agriculture. The man who gave up his post is once again in TANU, as deputy district secretary.

[31] Interview with Mr. A. S. Mtaki, junior minister of Commerce and Cooperatives and former TANU provincial chairman and secretary, Spring 1965.

major demand: independence.[32] But there was a built-in tension between this policy and the realities of Tanganyika because TANU was using local issues to increase its membership; the secretaries were supposed to contain local demands by stressing countrywide interests.

Perhaps the most crucial difference in the backgrounds of elected and appointed officials was in the realm of their respective educations.[33] In 1958, it was determined that only people with at least Standard VIII education (two years of senior secondary school) were supposed to serve as district or provincial secretaries. These qualifications were not always fulfilled because of a scarcity of educated TANU people. Nonetheless, the nature of the recruitment of secretaries was fundamentally changed and the relationships between the TANU center and its provincial and district organizations were altered when the educational criterion was established. Despite the appointment of district and regional secretaries after 1958, there was simply not enough time for TANU to become a centrally directed, tightly organized party between 1958-61. And since a major organizational effort was not required to defeat the opposition to TANU in the elections of 1958-59 and 1960, retrospectively, it is not surprising that by 1962 TANU was still unable to call out even a majority of the potential electorate.

With the advent of independence in December 1961, it appeared that TANU was running down after having achieved its major goal.[34] The turnout for the elections in independent Tanganyika was poor; meetings called by TANU both in Dar es Salaam and elsewhere were less well attended than they had been prior to independence; difficulties in collecting dues were even more apparent than they had been during the

[32] Stahl, *loc.cit.*

[33] Interview with Mr. Edward Kisenge, former Acting Secretary General of TANU and Parliamentary Secretary in the President's Office, Spring 1965.

[34] Leys, *loc.cit.*

struggle for independence. The argument was made that TANU's influence had been achieved during a period when the heterogeneous elements of labor, peasant farmer, or herdsman and the fragmented ethnic and tribal communities were unnaturally united by the cry of *Uhuru* (Independence).[35] Some observers stressed the decline of TANU, others felt that independence simply revealed TANU's inherent weaknesses, which had previously been mistaken for strength.

This argument misses the point. Relative to its major problem before independence, TANU was quite strong; otherwise it could never have become the spokesman for Africans' demands. But this strength was based on non-organizational factors to a large extent, and in many cases these factors ceased to operate after it became clear that TANU would bring Tanganyika to independence. For example, TANU leadership's attitudes toward tribal groups and chiefs had changed markedly by 1961. Tribal unions and the neutrality of the chiefs had been very useful while TANU was challenging the colonial administration; when TANU found itself leading an independent government, it could no longer tolerate neutrality from group leaders. In 1960, Julius Nyerere called attention to the new situation by making it very clear that he did not envision a place for the chiefs *qua* chiefs in central government:

> We tell the Chiefs quite frankly that their authority is traditional only in the tribes, which were traditional units. Tanganyika is not a traditional unit at all, and if the Chiefs want to have a place in this thing we call Tanganyika, they have got to adapt themselves to this new situation. There is nothing traditional in the Central Government of Tanganyika today.[36]

[35] George, *loc.cit.*
[36] Julius Nyerere, "Tanganyika Today: The Nationalist View," *International Affairs*, xxxvi (January 1960), 43.

He later added that, although no major changes would occur immediately, the chiefs' status would inevitably decline as the people enjoyed an increased participation in their own affairs. He qualified this with the following:

> If an instrument of government is doing its work properly, there is no need to do away with it or replace it with another instrument. I believe that if the Native Authorities of Tanganyika need polishing up they will be polished up so that they can do their work properly.[37]

When the new Tanganyika government was formed in October 1960, local governing bodies were put under the jurisdiction of the Ministry for Local Government and Housing. The Minister, Rashidi Kawawa, announced that it was the government's policy to have a majority of directly elected councilors in all of the 2,800 rural councils.[38] There was no immediate firing of chiefs, although certain chiefs who had strongly opposed TANU were removed. In 1962 and 1963, chiefs, sub-chiefs, and headsmen were removed as officials of the Native Authority systems. The Native Authority system was abolished, but under the new system many chiefs were appointed as executive officers of local government at the district, divisional, and village levels[39] because there was a scarcity of trained administrative personnel or, in some cases, because local people insisted on former chiefs as executive

[37] Julius Nyerere, *The Month in Tanganyika* (Dar es Salaam) (July 1960), p. 5, cited in Taylor, *op.cit.*, p. 208.

[38] Taylor, *op.cit.*, p. 206.

[39] Act No. 14 of 1962, a local government amendment, empowered the Minister of Local Government to transfer the powers of Native Authorities to another person or body. Act No. 13 of 1963, An Act to Repeal the African Chiefs Ordinance, abolished the Native Authority system. The act of repeal did allow for chiefs who had been appointed as members of councils or boards by virtue of their executive offices to remain in those positions by a decree of the Minister for Local Government. Cf. Ministry of Local Government Circular No. 16/63 of February 28, 1963.

officers. A number of chiefs went into central government as civil servants where their administrative abilities could be used on civil service boards, marketing boards, et cetera. Some became elected or appointed officials.[40]

In 1961, tribally affiliated organizations were also subjected to attack by TANU.[41] Whether or not a tribal union was progressive or traditionally oriented, the very fact that it was organized on some base independent of TANU, and particularly on a tribal base which was by its nature a parochial point of reference, was enough to cast it beyond the pale; for such a group could potentially raise demands which would be "tribalistic" and threaten national unity.

TANU reacted similarly toward religious organizations which had been useful to it during the terminal colonial pe-

[40] Chief P. Marealle became chairman of the Local Government Service Commission; Chief Adam Sapi Mkwawa became speaker of the National Assembly; Chief M. H. Abdiel Shangali was chairman of the National Tourist Board; Chief Erasto Mang'enya was minister of Community Development and National Culture and was formerly head of Tanganyika's Mission to the United Nations; *Mwami* Teresa Ntare was parliamentary secretary to the same ministry; Chief M. Lukumbuzya was principal secretary (permanent secretary) to the Ministry of External Affairs; Chief John Maruma was chairman of the Transport Licensing Authority; Chief Mbeyela was an area secretary (civil service head of a district).

[41] Glickman, *op.cit.*, reports that in 1961, out of 48 replies from African members of the National Assembly only 3 listed their former occupation as chief; 13 Africans noted some chiefly connection. Source: Guy Hunter, *New Societies of Tropical Africa* (London: Oxford University Press, 1962), Tables 13 and 14, p. 285. At one time, 5 MPs were listed as chiefs. In the list of Tanganyika Information Service in October 1961, Chiefs Mhaiki, Mang'enya, Ziota, and Fundikira were elected members. Chief Mbarnoti was a nominated member. Chief Mhaiki resigned from TANU and Parliament in 1964 when he complained that people were being detained without due cause. Chief Ziota is a regional commissioner and at least one other commissioner as of January 1965, was a chief, S. K. Rugaba. Chief Mybeyela had been an area commissioner until the end of 1964. He is now a civil servant area secretary. Anna Gwasa was an area commissioner and the sister of *Mwami* Teresa Ntare, former parliamentary secretary, who is of chiefly lineage.

riod. TANU had links with Muslim religious-cultural organizations centered on the Coast and with Christian groups also. But as independence approached, TANU issued a warning to all religious organizations to stay out of politics. The All-Muslim National Union (AMNUT), formed in 1957, had never put itself forward as a political party; but it did act as a Muslim pressure group. It was critical of TANU for not supporting Islamic education, and was generally conservative toward social changes, such as the emancipation of women and secular education. TANU threatened to ban it on a number of occasions. When elements within TANU put forward "Muslim" demands, TANU leaders quickly reacted. An Elders Section within TANU was provided for by the TANU Constitution. It has been dominated by the coastal and Islamic sections of TANU centered in Dar es Salaam and Tanga. The first head of the Elders, Sheikh Takadir, was expelled from TANU for doubting that there were enough Muslims on an election slate.[42] Takadir was expressing a demand very familiar to the American pattern of maintaining ethnic and religious groups' political allegiance. President Nyerere himself always takes pains to point out that he is influenced by Catholic, Protestant, and Islamic ideas and individuals; he includes among the main influences in his life a Catholic priest, a Protestant missionary, and a Muslim religious leader. But when religious-based demands were made within TANU, Nyerere quickly moved against those who voiced them.[43]

TANU could no longer tolerate the parochial demands of

[42] Glickman, op.cit., p. 11. Sheikh Takadir's expulsion for "mistakes and misbehavior" has been mentioned in a short history of TANU by the then Deputy Secretary General, Edward Barongo, *Tanganyika African National Union* (Swahili) (Dar es Salaam: Thakers Ltd., 1962), p. 2.

[43] Sheikh Takadir was ostracized by his former colleagues. It is reported that TANU leaders would not have appeared at his funeral had it not been for the personal intervention of Nyerere.

the primordial groups which had facilitated its rise to power, because they now threatened to prevent the central leadership from exerting that power. Asserting authority over a widely scattered and heterogeneous peoples would be difficult under the best circumstances; organized representation of special groups might make it impossible. Thus non-TANU organizations were regarded *ipso facto* as divisive and challenging to TANU. And factionalism within TANU was perceived as equally iniquitous.

Conclusion

The Tanganyika African National Union went from dominant mass movement to ruling party as Tanganyika moved from colony to independent state. Since the context of the rise of TANU has been outlined, it should be possible to avoid an exaggerated notion of the need for a tightly organized, disciplined party, to achieve this result.[44] It was fairly easy to assume the mantle of power; but the degree of control that TANU could exert was conditioned by the legacies of the colonial period. The entire range of social, economic, political, and physical inheritances were constraints on the building of a new society in the image of the new leadership. Chief among these inheritances was the organization of the national movement itself, which became another constraint on TANU as a ruling party.

TANU has lived from its inception with an internal difficulty which is shared—in varying degrees—by ruling groups in all new states: the problem of establishing strong ties between the center and the periphery, which are sensitive enough to persuade a favorable response from each link to the messages from the center. Specifically, the difficulty involves two

[44] Aristide Zolberg, "The African Mass-Party State in Perspective," Paper delivered at the annual meeting of the American Political Science Association, Chicago, Illinois, September 9-12, 1964, has sketched a framework for making more realistic appraisals of mass parties in Africa.

major relationships which emerged in the pre-independence period and are still central to politics in Tanganyika: the relationship of TANU as a "Swahili" organization with the tribal-traditional areas; and the relationships among leaders —to each other within their own echelon, and to leaders at other levels. Much of the rest of this study is concerned with these relationships.

PART II

Organization, Recruitment, and Ideology

CHAPTER III

Elected TANU Officials in the Regions and Districts

STUDIES of one-party systems often begin with an examination of central party bodies and then move to sub-national and primary party groups. This tendency to emphasize central party structures stems from a belief that the one-party system is a one-party system by virtue of the fact that a strong political power center has been able to dominate or abolish party politics. Thus even when the sequence is reversed, moving from primary party organizations to central and controlling party bodies, the major focus is usually on presidiums, central committees, control committees, secretariats, party conferences. Much of the literature on the Communist Party of the Soviet Union, for example, has been about the "inner" bodies,[1] and greater attention has been paid to central institutions than to local ones. In some instances, there may be justification for this, since it is the highly centralized nature of decision-making and control which is being stressed.

However, much of the writing on one-party states in new nations has been devoted to describing central party structures with much less justification. It is hard to escape the conclusion that for many writers the difficulty of doing research in districts and sub-district levels has led them to concentrate on central structures. But unless we know the nature

[1] See, e.g., Merle Fainsod, *How Russia Is Ruled* (Cambridge: Harvard University Press, 1957); Kenneth Whiting, *The Soviet Union Today* (New York: Frederick Praeger, 1962), pp. 121-33; Derek Scott, *Russian Political Institutions* (New York: Frederick Praeger, 1961). Most textbooks on the Soviet Union devote much more attention to central party bodies than to primary ones: e.g., G. Carter, A. Ranney, and J. Herz, *Major Foreign Powers* (New York: Harcourt Brace and Co., 1952), chap. xxxix.

of district, regional, and branch party organizations, we cannot see how the party functions and how the different levels interrelate; we are left with a network of formal organizations but little idea of how they operate. Note that in studies about American political parties, the obvious absence of articulated central party structures has forced students to begin with an examination of party functions and then look for structures.[2] Micropolitical studies must often proceed from functions in formulating structures because there may be no well-articulated structures at local levels.[3]

It is necessary to look at both central and regional/district organizations in order to understand the way TANU works. Discovering which TANU institution was responsible for making particular decisions at various territorial levels entails finding out where and in what manner authoritative allocations are being made.[4]

Insofar as there is a TANU center—that is, a locus of decision-making—it is not synonymous with any one specific TANU institution within the formal pyramidal organization of the party. A small number of individuals make up the TANU center in that they consult with the President on policy decisions and are usually "in on" major appointments. In the recent past, these have included the members of the TANU Cabinet:

[2] See, e.g., V. O. Key, *Politics, Parties, and Pressure Groups* (New York: Thomas Y. Cromwell and Co., 1958); A. Ranney and W. Kendall, *Democracy and the American Party System* (New York: Harcourt Brace, 1956).

[3] On the whole, political scientists who have dealt with Africa have shown much less concern for micropolitical studies than they should. Until very recently, this realm has been left to anthropologists.

[4] For a discussion of "authoritative allocations of values" see David Easton, *The Political System* (New York: Alfred Knopf, 1960), and *A Framework for Political Analysis* (Englewood Cliffs: Prentice-Hall, Inc., 1965), pp. 47-57, where a political system is identified as "a set of interactions, abstracted from the totality of social behavior, through which values are authoritatively allocated for a society."

Julius Nyerere—President of TANU and President of the Republic

Rashidi Kawawa—Vice President and Second Vice President of Tanzania

Oscar Kambona—Secretary General, former Minister of External Affairs, and Minister for Regional Administration

Isaac Bhoke-Munanka—Financial Secretary, Minister of State in the President's Office for Establishments

Nsilo Swai—National Treasurer, Minister of State for Development and Planning, and Minister of Industries, Power, and Mineral Resources.[5]

Other ministers played important parts in the Cabinet though they held no TANU posts. In fact, ministers without TANU positions are sometimes considered to be more powerful political figures than those who are also high TANU officeholders:[6] the latter may play an important role in appointments, but are not involved in policy decisions.[7] These judgments about powerful ministers are readily forthcoming from fellow researchers, university students, and civil servants; but it is not easy to get Tanganyikan political leaders in Dar es Salaam to join in the game. Their hesitancy implies more than simply an unwillingness to reveal the inner relationships of the party to an outsider; it reflects a strong disinclination of elite members to view interrelations among the political elite in terms of hierarchy. There is strong commitment to viewing both society and the political elite as cohesive and

---

[5] As of September 1965.

[6] E.g., the former Minister for Home Affairs and now Minister for Communications, Mr. Lusinde, and the Minister for Labor who is also Secretary General of the National Union of Tanganyika Workers, Mr. Kamaliza, are considered to be more powerful than Mr. Swai or Mr. Bhoke-Munanka who hold both ministerial and high TANU posts.

[7] When the post of TANU Deputy Secretary General was held by John Nzunda, he was consulted on many appointments but did not come into government policy-making.

psychologically homogeneous, even if ethnically and socially heterogeneous. No doubt, it is the very consciousness of national leaders that society as a whole is socially heterogeneous and separated from the elite by huge gaps in wealth and status that makes for this insistence that power is shared equally among the elite and that the elite itself is a custodian of the power inherent in the people.[8]

Julius Nyerere for one has provided us with an image of a democratic society that is essentially devoid of politics—that is, devoid of power relationships and party politics.[9] His statement that developing countries cannot afford party politics can be translated to mean that the political leadership of developing countries must try to convince the populace that social differences are without political meaning:

> The dilemma of reconstructing a society where important decisions must be made about the distribution of scarce resources and limited benefits while not attaching political meaning to such decisions is quite evident.[10]

In the regions and districts, there is much more willingness to look political distinctions in the face. Perhaps one reason is that the middle-level elites in the regions and districts get a great deal of enjoyment from speculating about who is up and who is down in Dar es Salaam. Another reason is that here the political culture is not continuous: the middle-level leaders in the regions and districts do not share the commitment of national leaders to espousing political homogeneity at all costs. They know where they stand vis-à-vis

[8] These strains were evident in many interviews I had with national leaders in Dar es Salaam.

[9] See Julius Nyerere, *Democracy and the Party System* (Dar es Salaam: Tanganyika Standard Ltd., 1963), chap. vi.

[10] Douglas E. Ashford, *The Elusiveness of Power: The African Single-Party State* (Ithaca: Cornell University, Center for International Studies, 1965), p. 25.

high- and middle-level elites in Dar es Salaam, and do not seem to feel the need to blur the distinctions between themselves and the people. Thus politics in the regions and districts is more realistically talked about and conceived of.

Some indices of power can be established independently of the rankings made by members of the political elite themselves. I have suggested that dual TANU and government officeholding is important but not necessarily crucial. Being "in on" appointments and policy decisions seems an operative definition. Another useful indicator is which of the ministers ran unopposed in the recent September 1965 election for the National Assembly—Second Vice President Kawawa;[11] the then Minister for Foreign Affairs and Secretary General of TANU, Oscar Kambona; the then Minister for Home Affairs, Job Lusinde; the Minister for Labour and Secretary General of the National Union of Tanganyika Workers, Michael Kamaliza; the then Minister of Local Government and Housing, Ausin Shaba; and the Junior Minister for Labour, F. V. Mponji. The nature of the ministerial post is important too;[12] but this is rarely an independent factor, as a minister of Foreign Affairs may be simply a spokesman for the President.

One important variable is whether national figures have their own political base. This involves looking at networks of influence—family, tribe, or regional ties, patronage appointees who owe loyalty and/or continued tenure to individual leaders. For national political figures in Tanganyika

[11] The Second Vice President is appointed by the President and he has his own portfolio. The Second Vice President is an elected Member of Parliament. The First Vice President, Sheikh Abeid Karume, did not stand for election as he is an appointed leader and a Zanzibari. Zanzibar did not hold elections for the National Assembly in 1965.

[12] Thus when Job Lusinde was moved from Home Affairs (security) to Communications, or when Oscar Kambona was moved from Foreign Affairs to Regional Administration, this might be seen as a relative decline.

have neither tribal/regional nor patronage bases of power; and neither command of a ministry nor command of TANU National Headquarters provides an organizational base for power. Thus, despite the staying power of individual leaders in high TANU and government posts, national political leaders do not have their own power bases to give security of tenure. Julius Nyerere's personal popularity is widespread, but it cannot be assumed that other national leaders are known and revered throughout Tanganyika.

Once we get beyond what TANU looks like on an organization chart and begin to examine the way various TANU institutions work and interrelate, we find that it suffers from problems of integration just as Tanganyika does. The gaps in Tanganyika's society are reflected in the gaps in communication between various levels within TANU. The fact that national leaders are without their own political bases is an expression of the lack of organizational development at the center and the lack of political development in the regions and districts. While in one sense the absence of strong regional and district political groupings bodes well for future national integration, it also means that the building-blocks for national unity are weak and fragile. Thus the strengthening of TANU central political organs and of regional, district, and local ones must take place simultaneously. But the TANU center is not itself strong enough to determine the process of political change outside the capital; and the national leaders, who are neither spokesmen for regions and districts nor party bosses who control regional organizations, cannot create a political center from local alliances.

TANU then is a national institution which is not controlled from a central party headquarters. It is rather like a tree with many roots and branches: in certain places the roots strike deep; in others they can find no soil in which to grow. And while the trunk of the tree is always clearly visible, some of the roots and branches have strayed so far and become so entangled in brush that their relationship to the main trunk may appear tenuous, if visible at all.

We have already seen that a major theme in TANU's history has been the relationship between national leaders and the TANU organizations outside Dar es Salaam.[13] This relationship has been described as one between the leader and the masses.[14] But it may be more precisely described in terms of a number of relationships: between national leadership and regional and district level leadership; between the national leaders and the basic village units, with which there are some intermittent but direct ties (for example, when leaders make tours up-country); between the various regional, district, and branch organizations, both vertically—as orders flow down and information and requests flow up—and horizontally—as different geographic units meet at the same level of the hierarchy. There are also three sections of the party: the TANU Youth League (open to those who are between the ages of 6 and 36); the Women's Section (to which all women belong); and the Elders Section. These sections are organized at branch, district, regional, and national levels; section organs interact with other TANU organs, and section representatives sit on TANU committees and come to TANU conferences at the various levels. At present there are three organizations affiliated with TANU: the National Union of Tanganyika Workers, the Cooperative Union of Tanganyika, and the Tanganyika African Parents' Association.

The Constitution of TANU

In 1965, major constitutional changes were made in TANU. Prior to 1965, TANU had been defined by *T.A.N.U., Sheria na Madhumuni ya Chama* (literally, Law and Intentions of the Association). The constitutional arrangements for the party had been essentially the same since 1954, al-

---

[13] See chaps. i and ii.   [14] Bennett, *op.cit.*, p. 25.

though the intentions of TANU as stated in the Preamble to the Constitution had been modified after it was clear independence would be granted.[15]

TABLE 1

Formal Links Between TANU and Government

1) The leader of the party is both President of Tanzania and President of TANU.
2) All Members of Parliament are delegates to the National Annual Conference and members of regional and district executive committees of their constituencies.
3) The President and members of the National Assembly constitute a Standing Committee of the TANU National Annual Conference.
4) Regional commissioners (appointed by the President) are *ex officio* TANU regional secretaries. They act as:
   (a) *Ex officio* Members of Parliament.
   (b) Members of the National Executive Committee.
   (c) Delegates to the National Conference.
   (d) Chairman of the regional development committee.
   (e) "Proper Officer" for supervising the district councils.
   (f) Responsible for sending official reports to the various ministries.
5) Area commissioners are TANU district secretaries, chairman of the district development committee, and non-voting delegates to the National Conference.
6) The TANU district chairman is chairman of the district council.
7) The TANU branch chairman is chairman of the village development committee.

The organization of TANU has been based on territorial units (see Fig. 1). However, functional or "place-of-work" TANU branches also exist, and are increasing in numbers. Policemen have joined TANU as a police branch; TANU branches have been started in the military; and there are TANU branches that are coterminous with pilot agricultural projects.

TANU has both elected and appointed officials, and differ-

[15] Nyerere is said to have modeled TANU's first Constitution along the lines of the Constitution of the Convention People's Party in Ghana. Bennett, *op.cit.*, p. 17.

Fig. 1: The TANU and Government Pyramid

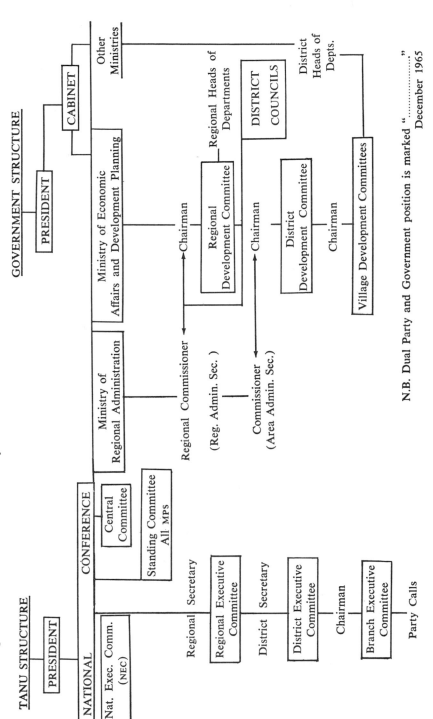

GOVERNMENT STRUCTURE

TANU STRUCTURE

N.B. Dual Party and Government position is marked "..........."
December 1965

ent TANU organs are made up primarily of elected or appointed members. The National Conference with its elected President and Vice President, and the National Executive Committee (NEC) are elected bodies, though both have *ex officio* members; the Central Committee and the National Headquarters members are appointed or *ex officio*; regional, district, branch, and cell organizations have both elected and appointed members.[16] The distinction between elected and appointed TANU officials is an important one, which existed even before TANU formed the government.[17] From the moment TANU began appointing officials in the regions and districts (1958-59), the elected and appointed hierarchies became potentially competing systems of political power. However, there is no simple bifurcation here: some individuals hold both elected and appointed posts; some elected as well as many appointed officials hold both government and TANU jobs; some elected and some appointed TANU people operate only at the districts and regions, whereas others also come to national institutions and take part in deliberations in Dar es Salaam. For example, in the past, one man could be district secretary of TANU and thus an area commissioner and head of government in his district; at the same time, he might be a regional chairman of TANU and come to the NEC in that capacity. There are a number of possible overlappings, and thus the relationships between elected and appointed officials cannot be neatly drawn in terms of two separate parallel hierarchies.

TANU Organizations at the Regional Levels

When we speak of a regional or district chairman of TANU, we refer to the chairmen of the TANU executive committees at those levels. The chairmen of the executive committees are elected by the Annual Conference of the regions and dis-

---

[16] Cells have been a very recent innovation in TANU. They are considered in chap. x.

[17] See chap. ii.

tricts. Membership in the regional conference is given in Table 2.

TABLE 2

Membership in the Regional Conference

Regional chairman
Regional secretary
Members of the regional working committee (These include the aforementioned regional chairman and regional secretary plus 4 people appointed by the regional chairman. Usually the regional secretary is equal to or more important than the chairman in the appointments. The TANU deputy regional secretary is often a member of the working committee.)ᵃ
All Members of Parliament resident in constituencies in the region
All members of the National Executive Committee resident in the region
All district chairmen in the region
Five delegates elected from each districtᵇ
A representative from each of the affiliate organizations
A representative from each of the party sections
Members of the regional executive committee (The regional executive committee includes all members of the regional conference except the 5 delegates elected from each district to the conference. It also includes all district secretaries of TANU in the region—that is, the area commissioners—and one person from each district who is elected at the regional conference to be the elected regional executive committee member.)ᶜ

ᵃ The appointed working committee members have no vote. They are the only representatives now specifically designated as being without the vote. In the past, MPS and MNES who were on the conference by virtue of their residence in the region had no vote unless they were also elected delegates.

ᵇ Prior to the 1965 changes, 2 members came from each district.

ᶜ In the past, district secretaries were listed as regional conference members in their own right. Now they are included by virtue of their membership on the regional executive committee. They have no vote at the regional executive committee meetings. Working committee members are without vote there too.

The size of a regional conference varies depending on the number of districts within the individual region. There are 17 regions altogether, most of which have 3 or 4 districts, but Mtwara Region has 6 and Mara Region has 2 at the extremes. The regional conference now meets in ordinary session once every two years immediately before the National Conference's own session, and its business consists largely of electing the new regional chairman, nominating an MNE who must be approved by the National Annual Conference, and electing the regional executive committee. These elections are supposed to take place at the same time throughout Tanganyika; but in 1964-65, the regional officers for 1965 were elected over a period of almost a month as different regional conferences met from December through January.[18] The regional conferences consider the report of the regional secretary on TANU work done in the region—on ministerial programs as well as on work carried out by TANU organizations in self-help programs or on TANU literacy or recruitment drives. Although the TANU policy and program for the year is supposed to be laid down here, little formulation of developmental programs goes on, though schemes for local projects—largely of self-help variety—may be introduced for consideration.

The regional executive committee is supposed to be convened four times a year. It is made up of all *ex officio* members of the regional conference plus a delegate elected at the regional conference to be an executive member for each district. The four members elected from the district to sit on the regional conference are not members, but aside from them, the membership is the same as the regional conference. As an executive body, the regional executive committee is too scattered to play a major role in TANU or government affairs. TANU work in the regions is handled by the regional working

[18] In 1965, the regional conferences were supposed to meet from July 26 to 31 to elect new officers. Changes in the TANU Constitution led to convening new conferences before the year was out. But some regional conferences did not take place until the first week in August.

committee and the district executive and district working committees. The regional executive committee's major function involves determining the candidates for TANU regional offices—that is, most of its energies go into electing a chairman, a new executive committee, and an MNE. (In this respect, the regional TANU bodies function more like American constituency parties than like the *oblast* party organizations of the Soviet Union's Communist Party.) Though the stipulated functions of the regional executive committee include the administration of TANU affairs in the region, and the planning and implementation of governmental policies,[19] these duties are in fact handled by the regional commissioner, the working committee, and by government civil servants. But when it comes to selecting men for regional TANU offices, the executive committee truly comes to life; what may be a sleepy TANU office for most of the days of the year then becomes a beehive of activity.

The regional conferences are involved in handling representation and succession functions. Just as American national parties come to life as national entities—and in fact identify themselves as existing at the national level—when they choose candidates, so the TANU regional party organizations come to life and identity. This parallel can be carried even further. With some few exceptions, the strongest American party organizations exist as party machines in urban areas. These machines were based originally on ward organizations, and it was precisely at this level that the most frequent elections were held for the most numerous offices. Similarly in Tanganyika it is at the district level—not the regional or branch level—that TANU organizations are most vigorous and visible. And it is at the district level where the

---

[19] The executive functions of the executive committee are stipulated in the TANU Constitution. The governmental functions have been stipulated by national leaders' speeches and directives to TANU offices. These functions have been formalized through a hierarchy of development committees.

most numerous elections take place, both in terms of number of offices to be filled and in terms of frequency of elections.

If the example of American parties is suggestive for Tanganyika, we should expect to find TANU to be non-policy oriented, at least outside the capital. To say that a party is non-policy oriented does not mean that policy issues never arise, but rather that cleavages within the party are not over policy issues; the party's central function is not to frame or to discipline its members in the framing of the policies of government. I shall argue that although the NEC is supposed to frame the policies of the TANU government, in fact it has not done so over a range of important issues. Nor has TANU been successful in disciplining its members in the framing of policies of government. Furthermore, division over policy questions plays very little part in elections for district, regional, and national offices. TANU officials in the regions and districts never discussed politics with me in terms of major policy issues.[20] And I have often been told they do not discuss major policy issues with each other.

Of course, individuals may differ over the location of a well or hospital; but larger issues—agricultural versus industrial development, foreign policy—do not characterize politics in the regions and districts of Tanganyika. Rarely is there policy disagreement about the way policies should be implemented. Some individuals may be more willing to use strong-arm methods than others to put across a program; but such differences are seen as personal idiosyncrasies, not as fundamentally opposed approaches to implementation of programs. Thus when a regional commissioner began putting recalcitrant citizens in jail for not supporting his programs, he became known as a "tough"—among the milder epithets. Expatriates in Dar es Salaam might refer to him as a radical

[20] There has been one major exception in the past: policy disagreements have arisen over the place of non-Africans in Tanganyika.

(presumably because he was willing to use force), but TANU leaders did not view him as having different policy orientations. Nor did the commissioner see himself in any kind of disagreement with a stated policy for implementing programs. Policy did not come into it at all.

TANU is a non-ideological party in the regions and districts, in the sense that outside Dar es Salaam neither TANU members nor TANU officials are concerned with the issues as they have increasingly been put within elaborated ideological frameworks at the center.[21] That politics in Dar es Salaam can become more ideological—that is, carried out in a special language where specific policies are related to theories of development—but that the regions and districts are not affected by this attests to the decentralized nature of TANU.

National TANU bodies do not determine the individuals who hold elective TANU office in the regions and districts. Prior to 1965, candidates for the National Assembly were nominated by district organizations. Although the NEC could disapprove them, it did so only once in the 1960 election. In 1965, the NEC intervened to disallow one of the two candidates selected by a TANU district conference primary for nomination as TANU candidate for National Assembly in 15 cases out of 91 constituencies (or 182 opportunities).

There is one regional TANU office which is elected at the National Conference rather than the regional conference itself. This is the post of MNE or elected member from the region to the NEC.[22] Each TANU regional conference nominates a man to represent it at the NEC, but the Territorial Conference is not bound to accept that nomination. In fact, any TANU resident can come to Dar es Salaam to stand against the regional conference nominee. The regional conference

---

[21] See chap. vi.

[22] Regional chairmen and MNE used to be elected for one year, but they are now elected for two years under the 1965 constitutional changes. District chairmen are still elected yearly.

nominee has a great advantage, however, since he is proposed and argued for by the regional chairman, the regional secretary, and the members from the region who are attending the National Conference as district delegates. If this group is not itself divided, it can prevail over an outsider. But votes are taken and opposition is expressed. When the Annual Conference met in March 1965, and elected the MNEs, the press reported that "although quite a few had opposition in these posts, they were elected."[23] The elections for these regional leaders are contested and there is turnover of regional chairmen and MNE which can be seen in Tables 3 and 4.

The Tables show that some individuals have been very successful in perpetuating themselves in office. Furthermore, not all turnover is a result of electoral defeat; some of the regional chairmen and MNE have been appointed to government posts and did not stand for reelection.[24] Appointment to government posts did not automatically disqualify one from holding elective TANU office. Some of the regional chairmen and MNE tried to keep their TANU posts even after they became commissioners. They were able to be both chairman of MNE and commissioners as long as they resided within the region where they were elected to TANU office. However, in practice, a regional chairman or an MNE would hold his post although he became a regional or area commissioner outside his region.[25]

[23] *Tanganyika Standard*, March 9, 1965. The TANU paper, the *Nationalist*, March 9, 1965, stressed that most of the candidates were elected unanimously. Before the 1965 constitutional changes, the National Conference was called the Annual Conference.

[24] Thus regional chairmen P. S. Muro, S. Mtaki, and R. Tambwe became regional or area commissioners in 1962 and did not run for TANU elected office.

[25] E.g., as of September 1965, 2 MNE were area commissioners: H. Kiluvia and M. Kalemaga. The former was posted outside his region, the latter within it. As of March 1965, 3 MNE were area commissioners; all 3—Kissokiy, Laicer, and Kalemaga—were within their

In 1965, the Presidential Commission on the Establishment of a Democratic one Party State recommended that area commissioners should be unable to stand for regional chairmen, and that an elected member of the NEC should be required to resign his post of area commissioner if he held both.[26] This recommendation, which was subsequently adopted, resulted not from a worry over a conflict of interest or heavy work load, but from a concern that MNE and regional chairmen who became area commissioners would put the regional commissioner in an embarrassing position: these men would be his formal equals in the TANU hierarchy but subordinates within the regional administration.

When we consider the nature of the regions themselves, it may seem surprising that individuals can have long tenures as regional chairmen or MNE. Regions are entirely artificial, administrative demarcations. Under the colonial regime, 9 provinces had been set up; the independent Tanganyika government first restyled these provinces as regions, and then in 1962-63 increased the number of regions to 17.[27] This increase in number was designed to make administration more efficient and rule from a regional center feasible.[28] It was

---

regions. Kissokiy is an interesting case: he has been an MNE and a six-time TANU regional chairman. He moved out of Mbeya Region for a short period in 1964 when he was an area commissioner of Iringa District. This district is contiguous to districts in Mbeya Region. He retained his chairmanship even when he was out of the region (the residency requirement was not strictly applied, apparently), but returned shortly thereafter to Mbeya Region and became area commissioner of Mbeya District.

[26] *Report of the Presidential Commission on the Establishment of a Democratic one Party State* (Dar es Salaam: Government Printer, 1965), p. 28. Hereafter this document is referred to as *Presidential Report*.

[27] The original regions of Tanganyika were: West Lake, Lake, Northern, Tanga, Central, Western, Southern Highland, Southern, and Eastern. The 17 regions are now called West Lake, Mwanza, Mara, Kilimanjaro, Arusha, Kigoma, Tabora, Tanga, Dodoma, Shinyanga, Coast, Mtwara, Morogoro, Iringa, Ruvuma, Mbeya and Singida.

[28] Staff Circular No. 5 of 1963 stated that in increasing the number

TABLE 3

TANU Regional Chairmen

Regions		1961	1962	1964
Arusha				K. R. Maro
	Northern*a	P. S. Muro	K. R. Maro	
Kilimanjaro				O. Lema
Tanga		Z. Shemshanga	Z. Shemshanga	A. Chombo
Mwanza				J. Tosiri
	Sukumaland*	S. Yusufu	J. Tosiri	
Shinyanga				F. Lukinga
West Lake			K. Karuandira	J. Songoro
Mara		C. Nyakasangani	C. Nyakasangani	M. Mazubesi
Dodoma				K. Feruzi
	Central*	S. Mtaki	S. Mtaki	
Singida				L. Nkindwa
Tabora				R. Chiriamkumbra
	Western*	R. Tambwe	R. Tambwe	
Kigoma				K. Omari
Mbeya				E. Mwangoka
	Southern Highlands	M. Kissokiy	M. Kissokiy	
Iringa				M. Kissokiy
Ruvuma				D. Kambanga
	Southern*	L. Mhina	L. Mhina	
Mtwara				L. Mhina
Coast				O. Londo
	Dar es Salaam*	O. Londo	O. Londo	
Morogoro				L. Mwinyikondo
	Eastern*	L. Mwinyikondo	L. Mwinyikondo	

a The starred regions were the larger regions before they were broken up in 1962. The lists of 1961, 1962, and 1964 are from personnel rosters in the TANU central office.

necessary to make the regions governable in size, since it was hoped that the regional heads of government would be effective agents of the center. Given the great distances involved within regions and the poor communications network, it was logical to increase the number of regions. Decreasing the size

of regions the intention was to improve the political oversight and leadership of the government services and development programs in the rural areas.

ELECTED *TANU* OFFICIALS

TABLE 4

TANU Members for the National Executive in the Regions

Regions	1961	1964	1965 (March)	1965 (August)
Arusha		A. Laicer	A. Laicer	H. Amiri
Northern*a	A. Laicer			
Kilimanjaro		R. Saidi	R. Saidi	R. Saidi
Tanga	E. Kisenge	A. Sembe	A. Sembe	R. Abdallah
Mwanza		M. Majaliwa	T. Ambrose	C. Mboneja
Sukumaland*	S. Mohamed			
Shinyanga		S. Salum	S. Salum	S. Mwangangalu
West Lake	L. Kuluture	H. S. Kayamba	H. S. Kayamba	H. S. Kayamba
Mara	A. Chambiri	F. Hosea Irungu	F. Hosea Irungu	F. Hosea Irungu
Dodoma		I. Kajembo	C. Hussein	C. Hussein
Central*	A. Mkamba			
Singida		S. Msindai	D. Misano	D. Misano
Tabora		(Mrs.) M. Ramadhani	M. Ramadahani	(Mrs.) A. Maufi
Western*	M. Rehani			
Kigoma		M. Rehani	H. Hamisi	H. Hamisi
Mbeya		A. J. Mponda	M. Kissokiy	(Mrs.) F. Mwashambwa
Southern Highlands*	N. Chelula			
Iringa		S. Masasi	S. Masasi	S. Masasi
Ruvuma		H. Kiluvia	II. Kiluvia	II. Kiluvia
Southern*	M. Kalemaga			
Mtwara		M. Kalemaga	M. Kalemaga	M. Kalemaga
Coast		(Mrs.) T. Mzee	T. Mzee	T. Mzee
Dar es Salaam*	M. Mzee			
Morogoro		(Mrs.) H. Swedi	H. Swedi	H. Shango
Eastern*	H. Swedi			

a The starred regions are the larger ones before they were broken up in 1962. Source: the 1961 list is from the *Tanganyika Standard*, February 14, 1961, p. 1. The 1964 list is from the TANU central office. The March 1965 list is from the *Tanganyika Standard*, March 9, 1965, p. 1. The August 1965 list is from the *Nationalist*, August 7, 1965. New elections were held in August 1965 under the new arrangement.

93

of the regions made it further unlikely that any one region could pose a threat to the center by virtue of being a strong political and economic unit. This was not likely to begin with because the regions were so large and diversified, and political leaders in the regional centers—which are towns of anywhere from more than 50,000 (e.g., Tanga) to less than 10,000 people (e.g., Musoma)—cannot exert control over their regions.

The regions, as drawn, are not natural economic demarcations. While many have a large majority of one particular tribe, all regions are multi-tribal.[29] Furthermore, we have seen that Tanganyika tribes are not centralized political entities. Thus tribal/regional leaders do not characterize Tanganyika's political life, as they do Uganda's.[30] The regions do not provide a base for national political power. Individuals find it hard to consolidate political power at the regional level. Factionalism within TANU at the district and sub-district levels affects elections for regional leaders because of the way delegates to the regional conference are chosen. Thus not only does the dual hierarchies of elected and appointed officials give two bases of support, but it is difficult for individuals who have achieved high electoral position to dominate the electoral process in the future. Within a region, there are a number of bases from which individuals can try to influence the selection of elected regional TANU officers. This can be seen by looking again at the membership in the regional conference (see Table 2). The list itself does not

[29] E.g., although Kilimanjaro Region has many Chagga and Mwanza Region is predominantly Sukuma, both regions include many non-Chagga or non-Sukuma.

[30] There are leaders in Uganda who claim, with some success, to represent not only their own tribe but also other tribes. They are "Northern" leaders. The fact that Uganda is divided into districts and kingdoms in a federal-type structure has given such leaders a framework to operate within. And the framework has called forth tribal/regional leaders.

tell us whether or not the different categories of membership constitute viable power bases. In practice, they do.

From 1961 to 1965 many of the MPs felt that they had an independent political base by virtue of being already elected to office. Until 1965, it was not known how "open" an election could take place for a new National Assembly. MPS mended fences but primarily they looked to the NEC and the President for approval of their performance. As it turned out, the district TANU conferences were crucial to the continued holding of office by MPs because the TANU district conferences nominated two candidates and most of the nominated candidates were approved by the NEC to stand as the only legal candidates under a TANU banner for the 1965 election. But immediately after independence, MPs felt secure in the local political positions.[31] Increasingly, they were appointed to government posts: at the beginning of December 1964, 37 out of 98 MPs held office as ministers or junior ministers; in addition, 10 MPs were regional commissioners, 3 were area commissioners, and 1 was Deputy Speaker. Others served on or were chairmen of bodies like the Mwanachi Company which was linked to TANU, or the Worker's Investment Company which was linked to government but were not state concerns.[32] Prior to 1965, these government officials looked to Dar es Salaam, not to their constituencies for continuation in office.

The regional chairman has his own base of support, as does the MNE. The regional chairman resides in the regional center and the MNE may not, so the latter exerts less influence in the politics of the regional center. Both men cultivate the members of the regional executive committee and the

[31] I refer to the African MPs and not the Asian and European MPs who were elected under the tripartite system in the 1960 election.
[32] William Tordoff, "Parliament in Tanzania," *Journal of Commonwealth Political Studies,* III (July 1965), 90-91.

other members of the regional conference. In the past, one man was elected from each district by the district conference to be on the regional executive committee. If an aspiring regional leader had antagonized a particular TANU district organization, he found a formidable array of delegates ranged against him. More often, each district TANU team split its allegiance for regional leaders. The district chairmen of TANU and the district secretaries (the area commissioners) as well as the regional secretaries all want a say in the election of the regional chairmen and the MNE.

How then can we explain the success of certain regional leaders? The first thing to note is that these leaders are not "regional bosses" who dominate the politics of their regions. As we shall see, they do not have the patronage available to become bosses; whatever patronage exists is at the disposal of the regional commissioner. The elected long-tenure leaders are often those who were among the founders of TANU in their region. They have not received a salary for their elective posts. Thus a few regional chairmen have even accepted fairly low-level government posts in order to have a salaried job. (This has outraged some TANU people who think these low-level government posts are beneath the dignity of a regional chairman.) The elected leaders have been farmers or traders and active in transport enterprises.[33] They have not aspired to play national roles and their relatively low education—low as compared to the early TANU-appointed regional and district leaders and the younger generation coming out of Kivukoni College or the University College—would hinder their entering into ministerial or junior ministerial posts. Some have been able to become area commissioners; few became regional commissioners.[34] Even

[33] E.g., K. Karuandira, former regional chairman of West Lake (1963) has long been an entrepreneur in the West Lake Bus Service whose headquarters are in Bukoba.

[34] And as we shall see, the elected leaders have had decreasing success in becoming commissioners.

the long-term elected leaders play a role subsidiary to that of the regional commissioner.

Thus part of the answer to the question—why their success?—is that younger and better-educated men offer little competition.[35] When some of the regional chairmen, MNE, and district chairmen ventured forth to run for the National Assembly in the September 1965 elections, they were beaten very badly by challengers who had been less prominent in the regional organizations or even latecomers to TANU.[36] But as long as they stay within their TANU regional conference, they have electoral success. They are brokers between factions in the TANU regional organizations, and they try to straddle the factions. Whereas the regional commissioners try to get above the factions, the elected officials can manipulate from within. This is particularly true of the regional chairmen who reside in or near the regional center and are involved daily in TANU affairs.

Regional and district chairmen, often men in their early forties or younger, are usually older than area and regional commissioners. But they do not project themselves as the *wazee* (elders) who stand out so sharply in TANU affairs in Dar es Salaam. Nor do they appear to be the "take-charge guys" as many area and regional commissioners do. And they lack the business-like detachment of civil servants. The chairmen can also be distinguished by their dress. Unlike the *wazee*, with their flowing white gowns (*kanzus*) and Muslim hats, the commissioners usually wear the Tanganyika national costume of gaily patterned shirts (*vitenge*). Ministers and TANU National Headquarters officials favor status sym-

---

[35] The *Presidential Report* suggested that members of the NEC who are not MPs should be paid the same salaries as MPs. This would mean that MNE and regional chairmen would all hold salaried posts. Competition for their jobs would increase. Still, the August 1965 MNE elections showed no more turnover than previous ones, and the MNE have proved to be hard to dislodge.

[36] See chap. xiii for the 1965 elections.

bols—like walking sticks—while the chairmen prefer to blend into their surroundings by dressing like many others around TANU headquarters in a region or district. They seem to make a deliberate effort not to appear as an elite. Perhaps this is one secret of the success of those long-term regional chairmen.

TANU Organizations at the District Level

Before the 1965-66 changes in the TANU Constitution, the functions of TANU district executive committees were not defined beyond a general instruction to implement the plan of work approved by the annual area conference. The functions of the branch organizations were listed in more detail:[37] to publicize TANU, identify problems of citizens and inform the area office about them, watch out for mischief, and educate members in administrative affairs. Today branch and district executive committees are described in the same way, without specific functions being attributed to either. The former characterizations were misleading because the district executive committee has been the most active of TANU committees outside of the center, and it plays the most important role of any TANU functioning body outside Dar es Salaam. The regional executive committee, which meets once every four months, is difficult to convene on other occasions because of the distances involved in getting members from the districts to the regional center. This is one reason why the regional executive committee is not a constant force in either making or supervising policy.

Much of the work at TANU regional headquarters falls to the regional working committee. But the regional working

[37] The earlier TANU Constitution referred to sub-branches; the new one refers to branches. The terminology had been confusing because sub-branch was sometimes meant to correspond to sub-divisions of districts which are larger than the branches which corresponded to villages or clusterings of villages. Sometimes TANU branches referred to the organizations which existed in function units (e.g., the police or communal farms).

committee cannot easily deal with TANU affairs outside of the region's main town and its immediate environs. Thus the district executive committees receive instructions from National Headquarters via the regional headquarters, but they are free from close regional supervision.

Also, the regional headquarters are staffed with government officials from the various ministries. The actual work of government is done by these officers in conjunction with the regional commissioners and their own administrative staff. There may be no representatives of some ministries in the districts. The central ministries do not have enough trained personnel to post officers to each of the 60 districts. Because of this lack of a developed government staff in the districts, TANU district executive committee members have a wider scope of action. This is a crucial point for understanding TANU's roles in Tanganyika: because of the weakness of the state apparatus, it has fallen to TANU organizations to handle many tasks which, in developed countries (including the Soviet Union), are considered government rather than party concerns. A traveler going from one district center to another may find regular TANU members manning a road block, making sure that paddy or grain is not illegally moved from one district to another, or checking to see that individuals have paid their district taxes; they may even try to collect taxes on the spot, though taxes are supposed to be paid only to government tax collectors of the district councils. These duties are devolved on TANU organizations not because TANU is trying to encroach on the preserves of constituted civil service authorities, but because these authorities simply are not there to do it themselves. At a meeting of government servants and TANU officials, the difficulty of collecting taxes sometimes comes up. It may be suggested that a member of TANU help in collection, and that member is not always an elected or appointed TANU official; he may be a civil servant.

Until 1965, the TANU district executive committees operated separately from the major institutions of elected local government—the district councils. But the membership of the district executive committees (see Table 5) and the district councils overlapped and the workings of the two bodies in any district were in fact closely linked.

TABLE 5

Membership of TANU District Executive Committees

TANU district (area) chairman

Members of the regional executive committee who live in the district

Members of the district working committee which is composed of the area chairman, the area commissioner, who is the TANU area secretary, the deputy secretary, and 3 appointed members

Delegates from the Women's, the Youth, and the Elders' Sections

One delegate from each of the affiliate organizations

Ten members elected at the district conference[a]

---

[a] Note that sub-branch chairmen and secretaries do not sit on the district executive committee like the area chairmen and secretaries sit on the regional executive committee. The sub-branch chairmen and secretaries do come to the district conference. The members of the district working committee, with the exception of the chairman, have no vote.

The 10 elected members constitute the elected element of a district executive committee. Each branch of TANU (or in TANU terminology, each sub-branch), now elects 2 representatives to come to the district conference. They vote for nominees who stand for district executive committee. Since every district has 10 elected members of the committee, while the numbers of divisions and sub-divisions and the number of TANU branches within a district varies, an elected member does not represent a specific branch or division. However, branch conferences of TANU do nominate candidates for district executive committee membership, and they put this man forward at the district conference. (Some branches even send a special candidate—called the *sauti* (voice)—to oppose the official nominee; but this is not a common practice. Members of some district executive committees had never heard of it and were puzzled by the procedures; and there is no stipulated rule about it in the TANU Constitution.)

The existence of a local government body at the district level works to enhance the importance of the TANU district executive committees. In 1962, elected district councils became the local government authorities, replacing Native Authorities throughout Tanganyika. When Tanganyika achieved "responsible government" in 1960, 2,800 rural councils existed; they were placed together with the urban councils under the Ministry for Local Government and Housing. The new government's policy was to have directly elected councilors in all the rural councils, rather than only in the lower-level village councils. Until the early 1950's the pattern of local government was such that rural areas were governed by Native Authorities established under the Native Authority Ordinance, and urban areas by township authorities under the Township Ordinance.[38] The Local Government Ordinance of 1953 provided for the gradual replacement of Native Authorities by autonomous district councils which were to be largely independent of central government. The county councils that this ordinance provided for were not established; however, district and town councils were created.[39]

[38] For development of elected local government see J. Gus Liebenow, "The Chief in Sukuma Local Government," *Journal of African Administration*, XI (April 1959), 84-92; J. Gus Liebenow, "Tribalism, Traditionalism and Modernism in Chagga Local Government," *Journal of African Administration*, X (April 1958), 71-82; Hans Cory, "Reform of Tribal Political Institutions in Tanganyika," *Journal of African Administration*, XII (April 1960), 77-84; K. E. Shadbolt, "Local Government Elections in a Tanganyika District," *Journal of African Administration*, XIII (April 1961), 78-84.

[39] Only one county council was established and it was dissolved in 1959. A summary of local government developments can be found in

The Local Government Ordinance with its amendments provides for the establishment of town and district councils with instruments made by the Minister for Local Government and approved by the National Assembly. Such instruments provide for the area of jurisdiction of the council, its compositions and functions. Councils can issue bylaws, with the approval of the Minister for Local Government; and they can regulate their own procedures by means of standing orders, though they have in practice adopted model standing orders issued by the Minister for Local Government.[40]

Very few of the elections for district and town councils have been contested. Usually TANU candidates are unopposed; the effective election of candidates has already taken place in the nominating process. When the TANU area executive committee comes to nominate candidates to stand for the district council, electioneering does go on: individuals who wish to be nominated often canvass for support throughout their district. Although council membership is usually determined in the TANU district executive committees, there have been exceptions; individuals have run as independent candidates against the official TANU nominees. One such case had far-reaching effects on the formal relationship between the TANU district executive committees and the district councils. It also hardened the attitudes of many middle- and high-level TANU officials against holding completely open elections in Tanganyika, and gave impetus to

J.S.R. Cole and W. N. Denison, *Tanganyika* (London: Stevens and Sons, 1964). There are 60 administrative divisions at the district level but only 58 councils because Mbozi district division lies within the Mbeya Council and Mufindi district lies within Iringa Council. Two separate councils, Arusha and Meru amalgamated on January 1, 1965, and the Buhaya Council split into Bukoba and Korogwe councils on that date. In 1965, there were 13 town councils and 2 municipal councils.

[40] William Tordoff, "Regional Administration in Tanganyika," *Journal of Modern African Studies*, III (1965), p. 77.

the law that TANU candidates be the only *de jure* candidates in all elections.

In 1963, the official TANU candidates lost their majority in a district council election in Bukoba,[41] West Lake Region. The national leadership asked itself: Was it worth losing control of an important council where there were allegations that tribalism and religious issues had been injected, in order to give public proof of the essentially democratic nature of TANU-dominated Tanganyika by upholding an open election? Most of the national leaders did not think so.

The central TANU government was not afraid that the Buhaya Council would carry out policies inimical to the center's own policies; the statutory powers of the central government are very great vis-à-vis the elected councils. In fact, elections to the district councils are really advisory to the Minister of Local Government. Act No. 3 of 1962 (Regulation of Elections to the District Councils) was intended to bring formal elections. But rural councilors were in law appointed by the Minister for Local Government, following the holding of an informal election.[42] An official in the Ministry for Local Government has said that the Minister for Local Government has never put into effect formal elections for "confidential reasons."[43] Obviously, government wanted the Minister for Local Government to retain control. The Minister of Local Government was not bound to accept the councilors indicated. Even if he did accept a council, he could then dismiss it. He could appoint new members or a commission that has the powers of the council. The central government can regulate and conduct the business of the councils and inspect their work. This is done through commis-

---

[41] The district council was the Buhaya District Council.

[42] Now the Local Government division is part of the Ministry of Regional Administration.

[43] Personal interview with official in Ministry of Local Government, 1963.

sioners, through local government officers who are central officials of the division of Local Government, and via special trips made to councils by central leaders. The Minister of Local Government could appoint the area commissioner as chairman of the district council even though the area commissioner was not a member of the council. The regional commissioner is the proper officer for district councils and this gives him power to advise dissolution, approve certain appointments, and check finances.

In the Buhaya case, there was no contention between the independents and the regular TANU candidates over governmental policy issues. The struggle was one over jobs, power, and personalities. Both camps were for "development" and for attracting industry to Bukoba; both supported national TANU policies; and both called themselves TANU. However, many of the independents were teachers and many were Catholics.[44] While they ran as independents, most were TANU members at the time of election. Though charges were made that they injected religious issues into the contests, most of these charges were not convincingly supported.[45]

There was one issue which emerged as a major bone of contention. After the election, when the independents had a bare majority, they were joined by some candidates who had run as official TANU candidates and by *ex officio* chiefs. These men refused to accept the TANU whip in the district council. When the Minister of Local Government dissolved the council—or more accurately never accepted the advisory election —he claimed that the TANU nominees had betrayed the people by running under a TANU banner and then turning rene-

[44] Bukoba is the largest Catholic diocese in Tanganyika and the seat of Laurean Cardinal Rugambwa. But it is also an area of Lutheran and other Protestant missionary work.

[45] My remarks are based on interviews with many of the independents, including the chairman of the independents. I also interviewed the official TANU councilors, the area and regional chairman, and the Ministry of Local Government officials involved.

gade. The fact was that these men would no longer obey the TANU district executive committee. The chairman of the opposition who formed a majority of the council said that the issue in question was the right of councilors to create policy in the council chamber rather than in TANU headquarters.[46] These councilors did not want to accept dictation by the TANU district executive committee. National leaders soon became involved in this district imbroglio. Both factions appealed to leaders in Dar es Salaam with whom they were personally connected. Those who shared Nyerere's attitudes did not think that any challenge to TANU was *prima facie* treasonous and must be ruthlessly smashed, but they did think that any dissidence might be the germ of future disunity which would hamper the development effort. The district and regional leaders on the spot and the middle-level leaders in Dar es Salaam were much more inclined to see any challenge to constituted TANU authority as a basic challenge which must be firmly put down.[47]

The effect of the absence of a tradition of legitimate opposition in Tanganyika politics was manifested by the Buhaya example. The independent councilors were seen as obstructive because they were a group that would not go along with the regular TANU organization. This is not unfamiliar in one-party-dominant states. The TANU local organization and the TANU regulars on the council could not adjust

[46] He said that when the Minister of Local Government had once come to Bukoba he had told the councilors that they ought to make a policy in the council chamber and not outside of it. Personal interview with Gaspar Rutagwelera, 1964.

[47] There are exceptions to this description of regional leaders, too. In a discussion with a then area commissioner who was passing through West Lake, I said that TANU had been responsible for the Bukoba Council situation because it had not laid down the boundaries which were acceptable for dissent nor had it established any specific criteria for TANU affiliation. The area commissioner replied: "A little ambiguity is a good thing in a single party." My own experiences lead me to believe that this is a fairly unusual point of view among area commissioners.

to a situation where they were not dominant. The council was fairly evenly split; and quorums became difficult if the TANU regulars who were in a slight minority left. They were obstructionist to the hilt and acted as they imagined their opponents would have acted if they had been a significant minority. This is the only example we have of the way an "opposition" has acted in Tanganyika in an elected body since independence—albeit, a TANU opposition.[48]

This does not mean that the acceptable district councils— councils composed of members who were nominated and elected as official TANU candidates—are disciplined arms of central government. One good example of the contrary situation can be seen by looking at the workings of the Buhaya Council which replaced the dissident one. In 1965, government wanted the Bukoba District Council (there was a change of names in 1964) to abolish a land tenure system in its district which was called the *nyarubanja* and which was considered in Dar es Salaam to be a semi-feudal, and thus inequitable system. The Bukoba District Council could not agree on how to do this or whether to do it at all. Government finally had to pass a bill in the National Assembly to outlaw the system.[49]

[48] There have been a few individuals who have been oppositionist MPs, though all but one have returned to the fold. A few seats on district councils have also been held for a while by non-TANU parties. More significant has been the operation of independents on the district councils. There were a number of independents on the Kilimanjaro District Council in 1963, though they did not apparently function as a bloc. Still with a quarter of the councilors independent, TANU formed an elected members organization to agree on matters before council meetings.

[49] This is only one example among many of district councils refusing to comply with the wishes of central government. Ministers have accused individual councilors, including council chairmen, of being factional with each other and with TANU's regional office. Councils have been warned to mend their ways or be dissolved. And there have been dissolutions because of misappropriation of funds (Newala and North Mara).

Difficulties with councils have been tolerated because the councils that have been "regular"—that is, officially TANU —though not amenable to discipline, are not perceived as threatening TANU hegemony even where there may be local insubordination to an area chairman or area commissioner. But after the Buhaya uproar, sentiment within TANU hardened against allowing anyone to stand as a candidate for elective office. A system of preselection was instituted in 1965 for candidates at both national and local levels. The TANU district conference now holds a "primary" for selecting two candidates to contest district council elections as well as elections for the National Assembly.[50] Furthermore, the Buhaya case revealed the necessity to rethink the relationship between the TANU district executive committee and the district council. The new Constitution of 1965 established that members of the district executive committees of TANU would be *ex officio* members of the district council. When this procedure was first recommended it was pointed out that local authorities have legislative functions in the making of bylaws but that these functions are of less consequence than the business of administration. The conclusion was that the TANU district executive committees ought to be incorporated into the district councils.[51] The fact that the TANU district executive committees were carrying out administrative duties and trying to determine the legislative programs of the district councils was left unstated. A May 1965 joint session of the NECS of TANU and the ASP determined that the area chair-

[50] For elected local government contests, the process begins at a sub-branch or ward level. All nominations are presented to the sub-branch or ward conference (the *Presidential Report* suggested that sub-branch executive committees make the first preselection, but the National Executives of TANU and the ASP modified this so that it is the sub-branch conferences that do so). Then the full list is submitted to the TANU district conference which has the final say. The NEC of TANU delegates its own authority to the district conference, but the NEC can step into the selection process if it so desires.

[51] *Presidential Report*, p. 25.

man of TANU—that is, the chairman of the district executive committee—should be the chairman of the district council *ex officio*. Thus the *de facto* influence of the TANU district executive committees on the district councils has been given formal expression.

This *de facto* influence went beyond determining nominees for the district council. District executive committee members themselves serve on district councils and important committees of the councils, particularly the finance committee. Because the district executive committees and the district councils have operated on the same plane, the former have been able to play legislative roles that are not open to TANU committees at other levels and to dispense patronage throughout the district councils. Election to government bodies still holds many prizes.

District and town councilors are not paid officials; they receive an allowance during the time the council is in session. The chairman receives a monthly stipend and a somewhat larger allowance, but none of this amounts to large sums. Yet competition for TANU nomination to council seats is keen in many places. The explanation is partly that these relatively small wage payments may not be entirely negligible to the farmers, traders, and schoolteachers who have usually filled the council seats.[52] But more important than the money received directly is the possibility of getting ahead: being a councilor means that one is "in on" projects under consideration in the district. The benefits can be substantial if one is a councilor and has some connection with building or supply-

[52] Schoolteachers may no longer stand for the district council. The Ministry of Education now prohibits this. The Ministry claims that since district councils now employ teachers, the teachers would thus be their own employers if they were on the district councils. The Ministry also claims that too much time was being spent away from classes when teachers traveled to district council meetings. It was not irrelevant that teachers were prohibited from standing after the independent candidates beat official TANU candidates for seats on the Buhaya District Council. Most of the independents were teachers.

ing for local government. It is my impression that many government complaints about misappropriation of district council funds come about because some district and town councilors think they are entitled to kickbacks. While downright embezzling has occurred, it is probably more common for district councilors to get remunerations for favors done or anticipated. The district council has the power to rebate school funds and allow nonpayment of tax in hardship cases. These are areas where members of the finance or education committee are able to feather their own nests. Being a district or town councilor also confers status. Particularly in rural areas, life can be much more exciting if one is a councilor: instead of farming, time is spent in the towns— talking, arguing, being in on things. For the more ambitious there is the possibility of getting ahead by attracting attention and perhaps subsequently running for a seat in the National Assembly.[53]

Local politics in Tanganyika is very much concerned with who will get a government job. District councilors and TANU district executive committee members are in a position to influence the hiring policies of the district councils, though they were recently stripped of some patronage powers when the Ministry of Local Government was given the right to appoint divisional officers of the district council and the Ministry of Community Development began to appoint assistant community development officers.[54] In special cases, the district council has power to compensate individuals: for example, a 1965 Act of Parliament gave the Buhaya District Council powers of compensation for landlords who are expropriated.

[53] Many MPS elected in September 1965 had been district councilors.

[54] The district council itself had made these appointments in the past. Many TANU activists were made divisional executive officers and community development assistants. In the September 1965 elections, a number of winning candidates had been divisional executive officers of the district council.

Much of local politics in Tanganyika is still a matter of settling old, pre-independence scores. Being a district councilor or a district executive committee member provides leverage for fighting battles over land rights or debts owed. Thus local office is important, and the way in which TANU chooses its candidates for elective offices is crucial to local politics. In the 1963 Territorial Annual Conference, Oscar Kambona said that TANU regional and district elections tended to perpetuate leaders, and individual members from the districts were complaining that they had no say. The chairman of the Conference, Mr. Kawawa, stressed that elections would be conducted by secret ballot. Mr. Kambona said that regional and area commissioners and MNE would direct the elections of local and district and regional leaders. However, the appointed leaders have their own vested interests in seeing leaders elected whom they can work with. And as we shall see, appointed leaders are involved in determining candidates for district council seats and for TANU elected posts.

Conclusion

The TANU elected organizations in the regions and districts constitute political oligarchies that have had a good measure of success in perpetuating themselves. The very nature of elections to regional and district executive committees is oligarchical in that an annual conference which is dominated by outgoing executive committee members controls the electoral process. Now the electorate will get a chance to decide between two official TANU candidates for district council seats, but the preselection process will still take place in the TANU district conference, and the conference will be dominated by the district executive committee. But this does not mean that the candidates will not reflect real divisions within the TANU oligarchy: the struggle for jobs, power, status goes on within the TANU district and regional organizations, and there are independent bases of power within the hierarchy of elected officials. As we turn our attention to the recruitment to TANU appointed posts, we shall get another perspective on the elected positions in the regions and districts, and we shall see that the appointed officials themselves make alignments with various elected officials as they try to consolidate themselves in their own offices. Discussion of appointed officials will confirm rather than contradict the image that has been presented of a loosely knit oligarchical structure.

CHAPTER IV

Appointed TANU Officials in the Regions and Districts

TANU had to rule the newly independent Tanganyika without the aid of a tightly organized staff of paid, appointed officials in the regions and districts, who were directed from Dar es Salaam. Though there were important distinctions between the backgrounds of elected and appointed officials—particularly in the realm of education—appointed officials were often "locals" too, and movement from one hierarchy to another was common. There were many shared values between them and great similarities in the way they carried out their tasks. In fact there was, and still is, an overlap of tasks so that the categories of elected and appointed TANU officials are not functionally distinct in practice. Appointed officials too have representative functions, and they are involved in problems of succession to office. Not only do they try to affect the outcome of elections for TANU office but they themselves move into elected posts. Moreover, as there is a rapid turnover among the individuals who hold specific appointed TANU posts, the members of the TANU appointed hierarchy who are supposed to bring TANU rule to the districts and regions as legitimate delegates of central TANU authority are also involved in a crisis of continuity. Finally, appointed officials act as if they too were subject to election: in the main they are politicians, not administrators. But they are not politicians of a party bureaucracy which can take for granted their acceptance no matter where they are dispatched. Nor are they agents of a patronage machine which can rely on its own largesse to gain acceptance for them. They must worry about their popularity; they have constituency concerns. And they have little to offer in the way of goods and services with which to ingratiate themselves. Nor do they have a coercive apparatus at their disposal with which to intimidate those who live beyond the immediate environs of the town where the district and regional appointed TANU officials operate. We will see later on how the appointed and elected officials relate when it comes to implementing programs. At this point, the characterization of the appointed officials in the regions and districts must be drawn.

TANU Secretaries Before Independence

A decision was made by central leaders sometime in 1958 to establish a hierarchy of appointed officials who would work outside Dar es Salaam. These officials would be beholden to National Headquarters and the central committee, and would not have to rely on the good will of district and regional TANU organizations. Despite this intention to have appointed secretaries and deputy secretaries in the regions and districts before 1960, secretaries were often recruited in the same way as the elected district and regional chairman. Both were usually co-opted into office by TANU officials who were leaving because they needed more money; and on occasion, deputy secretaries and secretaries were even elected into office. As late as 1960, a treasurer of a district TANU office was elected to his post.[1] His background was similar to that of many TANU chairmen and MNE, who were often farmers, businessmen-traders, or lorry drivers. They were men with local status and more than average means, who performed valuable services and at the same time furthered their own ends.

It is true that between 1958 and 1960 more secretaries were recruited from ex-colonial government employees, clerks, typists, veterinary assistants than were chairmen. But these backgrounds could be found among the chairmen also.

---

[1] Before 1962, not all treasurers were deputy secretaries. There were separate treasurer posts. After 1962, the deputy secretaries were also the TANU treasurers.

And some of the secretaries, particularly those who got in on the ground floor, had a post more in common with the local farmer-traders than with the clerk-typists.

Just as there were no clear and continuous distinctions in recruitment to TANU posts for secretaries and chairmen, the process of dismissal from these posts was sometimes similar. The secretaries were supposed to be dismissed or removed only by National Headquarters. But as late as 1960, a district secretary was "voted out of office" by the district TANU committee because he had complained that district committee members did not bother to read central instructions, and he had not supported the local TANU organization on a land tenure question. His refusal to go along on a local issue indicated that he was not a "true nationalist—not for independence of Tanganyika." According to TANU procedures, the local TANU people had no right to do such a thing, and the confused secretary was advised by the district commissioner, an expatriate, to "hang on there."[2] He persevered and was able to maintain his position. This occurred in a district where there was a great deal of internal squabbling. The various TANU factions appealed to Dar es Salaam for support. Nyerere himself tried to avoid taking sides in local issues, and while Dar es Salaam wanted to maintain the principle of control over the appointed officials, it was not willing to go all out in support of individuals in order to do this.

The fact that a local TANU organization would try to dismiss its secretary shows that the secretary was not considered to be outside its reach. The principle of appointed secretaries subject only to TANU National Headquarters had not taken hold in two years.

In other words, up to 1960, the distinction between appointed and elected officials, though made in principle, had not been clearly marked out through the process of recruitment and dismissal in practice. One important effect of this

2 Interview with the ex-district commissioner, 1965.

was that all did one another's job. Competition was based on local factional and personal struggles and not on different organizational commitments. Another important effect was the great deal of movement from elected to appointed posts that took place between 1958 and 1960. What distinguished different TANU officials was the length of time they had been with TANU. In this connection, it is interesting to note that one TANU official offered the opinion that the men who were committed to TANU early, both chairmen and secretaries, were the Tanganyika equivalents of the Soviet *apparatchiki.* He saw commitment to TANU as the one thing which distinguished chairmen and secretaries from others—not any special talent for organization or any special functions that they performed.[3]

However by 1961, the distinctions between elected chairmen and appointed secretaries had become clearer in practice. Two interrelated factors caused this: secretaries were given specialized tasks which called for different talents than those demonstrated by elected officials or secretaries theretofore; and TANU was able to recruit better-educated men as it became clear TANU would lead Tanganyika to independence. The bandwagon effect was at work. TANU could call on men with clerk-typist skills to keep party files, process communications, and build an organization on a more permanent basis than the *ad hoc* calling of meetings and gathering of subscriptions. When these men began to operate as appointed secretaries, treasurers, and deputy secretaries, they defined their jobs and distinguished their roles from those of the elected officials.

Despite the existence of the elected TANU committees and chairmen, district secretaries started to see themselves as "men alone." One secretary said in 1961: "In fact, the Sec-

[3] Interview with Mbutta Milando, Summer 1964. Mr. Milando is now personal secretary to President Nyerere. He was then area commissioner for Ngara District.

retary is the sole representative of the Union in the public [*sic*] and it is only through his activities that the Union can command the confidence of the people." He expressed the idea that party administration and discipline were the responsibilities and prerogatives of the secretaries and that this "double coincidence of responsibility represents a lot of complications to determine the Secretary's efficiency [*sic*]." In other words, it was hard to administer the district TANU organizations and to ensure a disciplined organization. He implied that one of the reasons for this difficulty was the very existence of officers with an elected base, who were somewhat, though not entirely, independent of the secretaries.[4] Another secretary described himself as "independent in matters of organization and in matters of policy working under the working committee and the district executive committee."

National Headquarters tried to make clear the distinction between secretaries and chairmen. Its formula, however, did not go very far toward clarifying the relationship between them. A TANU memorandum of January 1959, said that secretaries would be responsible for organization and policy and the chairman would be responsible for policy and organization.[5] If one makes any sense of this formula at all, it would seem to order priorities rather than to stipulate different concerns for the two categories. The central leaders were reluctant to be more precise for fear of creating a gulf between appointed and elected officials.

The same secretary who felt himself the "sole representative of the Union in the public," expressed the difficulty of his job and implied his reliance on others:

> If you take into consideration the number of problems requiring attention of the district secretary, you will see that for one man alone it is too much. This leaves no time

---

[4] I was able to read a number of short reports written by TANU district secretaries about the way they saw their jobs.

[5] Lowenkopf, *op.cit.*, p. 154 reports this memorandum.

to rest, no time to think properly, always he is involved in traveling, visiting and organizing in the branches. . . . And because there are no hotels in the rural areas he [the secretary] meets with problems of good nourishment and healthy accommodation.

The secretaries do have a very exhausting job. But one of the reasons why they saw themselves stretched too far was because they were acting as advisers to cooperative societies and local TANU literacy or adult education programs, and were involved in a host of other social and economic programs sponsored by TANU. Though the secretaries saw their need to rely on others, there was little division of labor whereby they delegated tasks, voluntarily, to other TANU officials. There were many reasons for this: the secretaries were often unsure of the people they were working with when they came into a region as strangers; they were afraid that if they delegated authority to other district officials it would be used to undermine them; district secretaries felt they could not delegate authority downwards to branch secretaries and chairmen because such people were often unreliable. One secretary said:

Even though branches were more responsible for the collection [of funds for the general election], it was only the district secretary who could present the case clearly before the public. Therefore, it is so difficult for one man to cover the district.

He was referring to the fact that people would often not respond to lower-level officials' request for funds unless the district secretary was present.

The secretaries found themselves involved in all TANU activities because the functions of the party were very extensive and the relationships within TANU had not had time to develop along functionally specific patterns. By 1961, the secretaries felt they were clearly responsible for TANU organization and administration in the region or district where they worked. But they interpreted organization and administration to mean "TANU affairs." They were concerned with problems of organization, with getting people to meetings, with feeding out information, with mobilizing support for TANU projects, and with supervising the collection of branch subscriptions (among other things). Obviously the size of their district and their ability to get around it was crucial. Here the importance of Tanganyika's geography cannot be stressed too much. In order to stay in touch at all with the branches, the district secretaries had to be constantly in motion. But they were often as unwilling to delegate the running of the district TANU headquarters office to the TANU treasurers and deputy secretaries as they were to leave the countryside to elected TANU officials.

The solution was ingenious but not very efficient. Everyone would travel at once and often together. Since the different roles of chairman and secretary were not clearly defined before independence, it was not surprising that tasks were not parceled out. Sometimes the territory of a district or region was broken up and the chairman would be in one spot while the secretary traveled to another. But as often as not, the "TANU team"—secretary, chairman, perhaps some members of the district executive committee and MNE—would travel around the district together. And they did much the same thing on their trips. They were on the platform together, making essentially the same speeches, exhorting people to achieve the goals set by leaders.

Why did the TANU district leaders cluster so much as they traveled around the district? In part, I think it was a feeling of safety in numbers; they reassured each other by their presence. If the secretary was new to the district, he felt that he needed the chairman and the executive committee members along as familiar faces. Also, no one liked to be left out of these *safaris*; not being on stage could be construed as a loss of status. And because there was fragmentation of TANU authority, it was probably necessary for both the chairman and secretary along with some committee members to be on hand before people were convinced that the TANU organization was serious about a particular matter.

While some of these patterns are still in evidence, a major change occurred in 1962 with the appointment of area and regional commissioners. The appointment of these commissioners changed the nature of the relationship between elected and appointed TANU officials in the regions and districts; and the way that these relationships changed depended a great deal on the process of recruitment to the posts of the commissioners.

Appointment of Area and Regional Commissioners

In October 1961, the TANU "responsible government" announced that area and regional commissioners would be created as heads of government in the regions and districts of independent Tanganyika.[6] The first Legislative Act of 1962 established political officers as heads of districts and regions.[7] There were two interrelated reasons for the appointments of regional and area commissioners. Nyerere and other TANU leaders at the center were very much aware of the problems involved in exerting central control over local TANU units and of imposing governmental authority throughout Tanganyika. When regional and area commissioners were appointed in early 1962, TANU asserted that it was the government. Since the commissioners became TANU secretaries on appointment, and since, as we shall see, they were

[6] Taylor, *op.cit.*, p. 207; John Smythe, "Political Projects," *Spearhead* (November 1961), p. 6.

[7] Act No. 1 of 1962 was "An Act to amend the Constitution of Tanganyika to make provision for Regional Commissioners and Area Commissioners," February 22, 1962.

recruited from former TANU secretaries and chairmen, the TANU government asserted that the TANU organizations in the regions and districts would play an important role in the development of independent Tanganyika. Secondly, as the commissioners were appointed by the center, and as they were recruited more often from former secretaries than from former elected TANU officials, the TANU center was making it clear that it would try to impose its wishes on local TANU organizations.

The aim was to make the commissioners the dominant representatives of the TANU government. By making the new heads of regions and districts heads of government and TANU secretaries concurrently, the TANU leaders hoped that the commissioners would be able to bring the authority of the TANU government to regional, district, and local levels. The commissioners would command the ministerial representatives in the regions and districts; they would have their own staff of civil servants in regional administration; and they would command the TANU organizations at their own levels. Their authority would be supreme because it would rest on an amalgam of state and TANU legitimacy.

Reaction to the Colonial Pattern

When TANU leaders made it clear that Tanganyika was led by a TANU government, they were among other things reacting to the colonial experience of government by civil servants. Because they were new, the TANU leaders felt the need to assert the primacy of TANU; and they had come to their exalted positions as heads of government in a new state by virtue of being TANU leaders. But when they stressed that TANU now ruled Tanganyika instead of a colonial regime, they were also stressing that political rather than administrative officials were governing. The break with the old provincial administration and with government by administrator was emphasized when the Act No. 2 of 1962 changed the name of the administrative units from provinces to regions at the same time that certain statutory functions were transferred to regional commissioners.[8] This break was stated quite clearly by the Minister for Local Government and Administration when he moved the second reading of the Bill which provided for the new commissioners:

> In the past officers of the Provincial Administration have been obliged to carry out numerous political functions in their capacity as chief Government spokesmen in their provinces and districts. They have, in practice, in the eyes of the people, been the Government. In an Independent Tanganyika with a popularly elected Government, such a state of affairs is no longer appropriate. Although officers in the public service carry out ministerial policies as a matter of course, it is most desirable that the mass of the people should realize that these policies are those of the Government of the day, and this can be done only if, in provinces and districts, explanations of Government policies are made by political representatives, and if the political functions of civil servants are carried out by political representatives.[9]

In order to understand this reaction, we must say something about the pattern of administration in Tanganyika under British rule.

The United Kingdom, as the United Nations Trust Territorial Government, had the overall responsibility for maintaining law and order, encouraging political development,

---

[8] "An Act to restyle the Provinces of Tanganyika as Regions, to transfer certain Statutory Functions to Regional Commissioners and for matters incidental thereto and connected therewith, to amend the Interpretation and General Clauses Ordinance, the Official Oaths Ordinance and the National Assembly [Disqualification] Ordinance and to repeal the Deputy Provincial Commissioners Ordinance," February 22, 1962. Act No. 2 of 1962.

[9] Quoted in Cole and Denison, *op.cit.*, pp. 65-66.

and coordinating all government activities throughout Tanganyika. These responsibilities were discharged by the provincial administration, which also had responsibility for day-to-day administration of the provinces.[10]

The provincial administration was the basis of the colonial government, and was involved in all plans for the advancement of the territory. The central government's authority was concentrated in the person of the district commissioner, who was the focal point of local administration. He was the head of the district team, and was responsible for law and order, the proper functioning of the government's executive machinery, and the promotion of social and political development in his district. He was both the adviser and the supervisor of the Native Authorities (local government bodies), and was supposed to be the principal medium through which public opinion—particularly African public opinion—was conveyed to government.

While the government of Tanganyika was highly centralized at the center and determined much of what would in some countries fall within the scope of regional or local units (for example, education, police, roads), the administration of policy was in fact decentralized.[11] Since communications and transportation were inadequate, discretionary powers of policy formulation as well as execution devolved on the district commissioners.

As independence approached, the role of the district commissioner was greatly modified under the impact of a ministerial system. Government activity became more specialized as the pace of development increased after World War II and as the British administration took a greater interest in eco-

---

[10] F. J. Glynn and John B. Seal, Jr., unpublished report, "Job Analysis Report on the Regional Administration." This report has relied on *Appointments at the Senior Levels in the Civil Service* (Dar es Salaam: Government Printer, 1958), pp. 46-52 for material on the provincial administration.

[11] Young and Fosbrooke, *op.cit.*, p. 169.

nomic development. Senior officers were established in Dar es Salaam who worked to central ministries. Regional agricultural, veterinarian, education, and police officers were appointed. As this occurred in the 1950's, regional administrative officers exercised less power in initiating policies, and became primarily coordinators of the district or provincial development effort.

But the evolution of the colonial administration notwithstanding, British rule remained rule by civil servants. The shift from general administrators in the provincial administration to technical civil servants from the ministries did not alter this fact. In part, it was as a response to this situation that the TANU government established political officers as heads of districts and regions.

The provincial and district commissioners and officers (the district officer worked to the district commissioner) were the most exposed of all the British administrators in Tanganyika because they had such wide scope of action and were in such close touch with Africans. Towards the end of the 1950's, the district and provincial administrators came into increasingly close touch with TANU leaders in the districts and regions as TANU had to register branches and as its organizations acted as pressure groups. Some ex-district commissioners have said that they were not very aware of TANU leaders in their districts even as late as 1958 or 1959;[12] but TANU leaders were very much aware of them.

Furthermore, the colonial district and provincial administrators were not Africanized extensively before independence; Europeans filled these important positions before, and after, independence. When Nyerere became Chief Minister in 1960, he promised that half of the then 58 districts would have African district commissioners by 1961. But before the change to political heads of regions and districts in 1962, less than half of the districts had African district commissioners,

[12] Interviews with a number of ex-district commissioners.

and none of the provinces had African provincial commissioners.

The TANU government had to replace the expatriate civil servants as heads of districts and provinces if it was to establish its rule outside of Dar es Salaam. But who could replace them? African civil servants were not desirable from the point of view of TANU leaders at the center and in the regions and districts, nor in fact were they available. In 1960, there was not a single African judge or magistrate, nor any African permanent secretaries or principal assistant secretaries. In 1961, there were only 1,170 Africans holding senior- and middle-grade civil service posts out of a total 4,452 such posts.[13] Neither the civil service nor the educational system had been geared to an early independence.

The Africans who had taken over as district officers and district commissioners between 1960 and 1962 were sent to Dar es Salaam as permanent secretaries and assistant secretaries. Since the African civil servants in regional administration moved to the center, it was impossible to immediately Africanize all the civil service posts in the regional administration without suffering a sharp decline in administrative services. Thus expatriate civil servants in regional administration were asked to stay on. Some ex-colonial provincial commissioners moved into central ministries; others stayed in regional administration with a new title of administrative secretary. They became the chief civil servants in the region. The commissioners became their political bosses. Trained civil servants were so scarce in the regions that it was only at the end of 1964 that all administrative secretaries were Tanganyikans.[14]

[13] *Report of the Africanization Commission of 1962* (Dar es Salaam: Government Printer, 1962).

[14] Another example of the scarcity of people available for high level civil service jobs in the regions occurred when the regions were increased in number from 9 to 17. The aim was to make the regional commissioners visible political heads by not giving them too huge

The political leadership was committed, in any case, to having political heads in the regions and districts. Before independence, when Nyerere was Chief Minister, he sent out a circular letter to government departments, taking up the question of the relation between the public, civil servants, and politicians.[15] It stated that since a people's government now existed, there could be no future justification for referring every complaint to civil servants. He made it clear that civil servants were to keep out of the political arena, and politicians were not to be drawn into matters relating to the public service or to individual civil servants. Since civil servants were enjoined to enter TANU in 1965 (it had been opened to them in 1964), we must be very clear about the factors which governed Nyerere's Circular Letter of 1960.

The decision to keep civil servants out of politics in 1960 reflected the central leadership's desire to demonstrate that a TANU government was ruling. But it was also aimed at insulating the civil service from local TANU interference. Nyerere revealed this when he said: "I would remind you that policy is decided by the central government and not by local party representatives. Political party organizations are not concerned with the execution or implementation of policy."[16] Local TANU organizations were neither to make nor to execute policy. One realm was the prerogative of the central government, the other the responsibility of the civil service. Nyerere was showing his fear not only that local TANU organization and TANU members of the Legislative Council might try to enforce their will on civil servants, but also that the local organizations would deflect the will of the TANU cen-

---

a territory. But the supporting staff for the commissioners was stretched very thin by an increase of 8 regions.

[15] Circular Letter No. 1, 1960, reprinted in *Transition*, I (December 1961), 23-25.

[16] *Ibid.*

tral government. To some extent, the British norm of a neutral, apolitical civil service free from the interference of politicians was making its presence felt.[17] Also, Nyerere felt that civil servants would execute central government policy faithfully; he seemed less sure about the local TANU organizations.

This does not mean that a transformation of the politics of Tanganyika towards bureaucratic norms was taking place. There was no suggestion that the civil service should rule, no evidence that a no-party rule was coming about. Quite the contrary, the appointment of regional and area commissioners underlined the TANU-ness of the system. Of course, even if commissioners were to be selected as political appointees not subject to civil service criteria and regulations, civil servants could have been recruited to political posts. But very few of the first commissioners were civil servants. The TANU government wanted to bring a TANU presence to the regions and districts. The fact that from August 1953 onwards a colonial ordinance prohibited Tanganyikan civil servants from belonging to political parties meant that TANU had not recruited its active members from African civil servants. Civil servants had been active in the TAA; but this ruling debarred them from membership in TANU. Some, like Nyerere and Kambona, did give up their jobs;[18] but many who relied on a steady salary ceased to play a part in TANU.

However, the lack of participation by civil servants in

[17] Nyerere welcomed the establishment of a Public Service Commission which would strive for an impartial civil service. Nyerere did not suggest that civil servants should be executives of policy and nothing more. Though he felt that judging by experience elsewhere that is what they were likely, in the long run, to be. "But at the present stage of our development, I trust that they will continue to be guides, philosophers and friends to all and sundry; they must not now or in the future be the targets of antagonism."

[18] They were teachers and the ban fell on them as government employees.

TANU between 1954 and 1962 can be exaggerated. African civil servants helped TANU covertly if not in the open, and many people who worked for the colonial government also participated in TANU. Most of these were clerks, veterinary assistants, and medical assistants. Former expatriate district officers have said that the colonial government was not always assiduous in rooting out people it knew participated in TANU.

Many future TANU commissioners and ministers or parliamentary secretaries held these low-level government posts. A number of TANU leaders important today participated in the anti-colonial movement while holding higher government positions in the colonial period, particularly executive local government jobs. Many men now prominent in TANU joined in the late 1950's; but they held government jobs until then, thereby providing a connection between TANU and African civil servants (though these men were not identified as "civil servants" in 1962 but rather as TANU people).

While some civil servants resented the fact that less-educated men were taking precedence over them, and some TANU members were ill disposed to civil servants whom they saw as collaborators with the British, it is incorrect to say that the civil service was an incipient opposition to the TANU government.[19] The antagonism that existed was largely between district and regional TANU officials and the better-educated African civil servants who had risen in the civil service. These civil servants were moved to the center where they served under ministers and parliamentary secretaries who in most cases were intent on cooperating with their civil servants.

[19] As George, *op.cit.*, has argued, there were too few African civil servants in high position to constitute an educated elite in opposition to TANU. As one Tanganyikan, Mwakawago, *op.cit.*, p. 18, put it, the absence of a highly educated elite influenced the smooth development of nationalism.

Recruitment of Area and Regional Commissioners

Civil servants were not going to be the pool from which to recruit political heads of regions and districts; the commissioners were recruited almost entirely from TANU appointed and elected regional/district officials. Secretaries and chairmen were the obvious choices once civil servants were eliminated from consideration: they had worked at these levels and had already established themselves in TANU organizations, they had struggled for independence and could now be rewarded with salaried jobs; and they fulfilled the criteria of political commitment and loyalty to TANU. Moreover, they brought the TANU presence to government outside Dar es Salaam. This was important in 1962 when people still distinguished between TANU and government. As time went on, the distinction between party and government blurred for many local people.[20]

From the leadership's point of view, of the two categories —chairmen and secretaries—the latter were the logical choice to staff most of the commissionerships. The TANU secretaries would, presumably, share the commitment to exerting central control over local TANU organizations since they were agents of the center. (We shall see that this assumption was not always correct.) And since, by 1962, secretaries were appointed who had better educations than the chairmen, they would be more efficient administrators. The secretaries had been posted from place to place in pre-independent Tanganyika because central leaders considered them less parochial and more adaptable to new conditions.[21] On these grounds, it was presumed they could get along better

[20] Norman Miller ("Village Leadership in Tanzania," Paper delivered to the EAISR Conference, Makerere College, December 1964), says people in the village where he worked did not distinguish between TANU and government.

[21] Interviews with a number of central TANU and government officials.

than the chairmen with representatives of the ministries with whom they would have close contact. And finally, the TANU leadership was committed to filling the commissioner posts on non-tribal grounds. Commissioners would be moved from region to region, from district to district, and from the center to the regions; and the secretaries were already functioning in this way.

The original TANU Constitution did not specify the way in which regional and district secretaries should be appointed. (The 1965 Constitution gives the President the power to appoint regional and district secretaries; branch secretaries are appointed by the Central Committee.) However, during the last two years before independence, they were appointed from Dar es Salaam; but it was not the National Headquarters operating as a central personnel and appointment bureau which dominated the process. There was no central filing system where the names of potential candidates could be consulted; appointments were made on the suggestion of a number of TANU officials. In short, the process was very unsystematic.

National Headquarters officials—that is, administrative secretaries and the Acting Secretary General himself[22]— would put forward names for appointment, as would the President and Vice President of TANU and members of the Central Committee. Regional chairmen, and MNE sometimes sponsored candidates for appointment. At this time the central TANU officials were also passing on candidates for the TANU nomination for National Assembly. Central Committee approval was necessary before National Assembly candidates were confirmed, but deputy secretaries could be promoted to secretaries and new appointments could be made to secretary without formal confirmation by the plenary Central Committee. Administrative officials in National Headquar-

[22] The Secretary General, Oscar Kambona, was not in Tanganyika during most of 1958-59.

ters could suggest these promotions and appointments which would then be considered by the Establishments Committee of the Central Committee. Nyerere prevailed if there was conflict over appointees.[23] But neither he nor other central leaders tried to dominate completely the appointment of secretaries; they would sponsor men with whom they were personally connected, but no one central leader tried to see that all such appointments were "his men." No one man, including Nyerere, could even call on enough men in 1958-60 to fill the district and regional posts. Thus even when the secretaries began to be appointed from the center, this process did not lead to a network of regional and district secretaries who were beholden to one man for their appointment. If the secretaries gave Julius Nyerere allegiance, it was because he was the admired leader of TANU and not because he was their sponsor in every case.

After 1962, the appointments of commissioners had to be cleared through Nyerere, though not every commissioner was his personally sponsored candidate. In 1962, regional administration was part of the Ministry of Local Government. Thus commissioners were, and are, part of the regional administration division, working under the Minister of Local Government. After the presidential system was established in December 1962, regional administration was in the office of the Vice President; in July 1964, it was moved to the President's office. The transfer of regional administration to the President's office emphasized what was already a fact—that the regional and area commissioners were appointed by the President.[24]

[23] Lowenkopf, *op.cit.*, relates an episode where Nyerere prevailed over three officials in National Headquarters who tried to impose their own candidate for an Asian seat in the Legislative Council elections. Nyerere prevailed over Sijaona, Bhoke-Munanka, and Maswanya. All three are now ministers.

[24] Once again regional administration was reshuffled when a new Cabinet was formed after the elections of September 1965. A Min-

The President wanted to be in closer touch with regional administration, and he wanted to be seen as the fountainhead of authority for appointing and supervising the commissioners for two reasons. First, the Directorate of Planning was moved to the President's office after having been an independent ministry; it thus became logical to move regional administration and the central establishments division, which had both been in the Vice President's office, in order to integrate more closely civil service planning and administration with planning as a whole.[25] Perhaps more significant, the very factors which recommended that the planning body be put under the President, that important new steps had to be taken, also argued for reallocating the direct responsibility for regional administration. The President felt that only his own authority would be able to see the measures through. If a number of area and regional commissioners were to be fired —as turned out to be the case—and if people were recruited from civil service posts to staff new openings among the commissioner's posts, the President felt he must be directly responsible.

Nyerere had always been consulted before a commissioner took his post or was transferred. Though the commissioners were TANU secretaries, TANU National Headquarters as such was not involved in their appointment; neither the Central Committee nor the NEC has had any authority for the ap-

---

istry of Regional Administration was created with Oscar Kambona as its head. The minister, who is also TANU Secretary General, now commands the commissioners in their TANU and government hierarchies. However, it is certain that the President still passes on appointments. In 1965, Local Government became part of a Ministry of Regional Administration, completely reversing the 1962 relationship.

[25] Central Establishments Division is headed by a civil servant, Mr. M. C. Othman. There is a minister of state who is responsible for establishments. Establishments are divided into sections for: personnel, common cadres, central recruitment, localization and establishment, staff relations, central training, staff inspection, and job analysis.

pointment of commissioners. The pre-1962 pattern persisted in that a number of men were involved in the process of selecting commissioners aside from Nyerere. Oscar Kambona and Rashidi Kawawa were consulted, as well as other important TANU ministers, individual members of the Central Committee, and members of the NEC.

When the central leaders travel, they look over possible future commissioners. They also inquire of regional and district leaders how present commissioners are doing, and hear requests for new commissioner appointments. But they never ask regional and district leaders if they will accept a regional commissioner. The central leaders will inform the districts and regions who is being sent, and they will consult regional commissioners about a new appointment of an area commissioner. But the regional and district officials have no veto over appointments.[26]

I have used the term "TANU center," which really means this small group of high-level TANU ministerial leaders who make these appointments. The NEC is not part of the TANU center thus defined; and, as we shall see, the National Headquarters staff is too underdeveloped to function as an important central institution. The Central Committee along with the TANU Cabinet (President, Vice President and Secretary General, Deputy Secretary, Financial Secretary, and National Treasurer) are the only institutions that can be considered the TANU center in an unqualified way.[27]

[26] Interview with Second Vice President Rashidi Kawawa, April 1965.

[27] The Deputy Secretary General of TANU has been involved in commissioner appointments on both the TANU and government sides. John Nzunda was concurrently Deputy Secretary General and Parliamentary Secretary in the Vice President's office when regional administration was under the Vice President. Nzunda was the man most concerned with deputy regional and district TANU secretaries. These men do not hold government posts but they can be promoted to commissioners. After regional administration was moved to the President's office, Bhoke-Munanka and Edward Kisenge had responsibil-

The decision to appoint commissioners was the first major legislative act of the independent TANU government. Recruitment to the posts revealed the materials that the regime had to work with, and the values of the leaders with respect to the agents it chose to rule in the name of TANU. And since the commissioners were to head the party and state machinery in the regions and districts, their abilities and values became crucial variables in the operation of the TANU government.

The TANU leaders in Dar es Salaam preferred to make provincial TANU secretaries into regional commissioners; thus provincial chairmen became lower-ranking area commissioners. In 1961, there were 10 listed provincial chairmen and 11 listed provincial secretaries. (See Table 6.)

The provincial secretaries who became regional commissioners had many similarities in background. They usually became provincial secretaries in 1958-59 when TANU began to institute paid secretaries on a wide scale. Far from being discriminated against because of their relatively late commitment to TANU, those who became regional commissioners were prized for the administrative experience they had acquired in government or business, in clerical and/or managerial capacities. Thumbnail sketches of the secretaries show their similar backgrounds:

> John Nzunda, who was to become Deputy Secretary General of TANU, was born in 1922 at Mbozi. He was educated at Malangali and Tabora government schools (1932-41), and took a diploma in journalism at Transafrica College in South Africa. He had been a postal clerk and telegraphist at the age of 20 (1941-42), an accounts and correspond-

---

ities for regional administration. The former was a Minister of State for Regional Administration and at the same time TANU Financial Secretary. The latter was Parliamentary Secretary for Establishment in the President's office and former Acting Secretary General. Thus men familiar with TANU Headquarters work and holding high posts in TANU were always involved in commissioner appointments.

133

APPOINTED *TANU* OFFICIALS

TABLE 6

Careers of Provincial Officials

| | By 1964 became | | |
	Regional Commissioners	Area Commissioners	Other
10 provincial secretaries[a]	6[b]	3	1
10 provincial chairmen	2[c]	5	3[d]

SOURCE: A pamphlet on the history of TANU entitled *Tanganyika African National Union* printed by Thakers Ltd., Dar es Salaam, n.d., gives the holders of posts for provincial and district chairmen and secretaries and for provincial members of the NEC during 1961. We can therefore tell from which of these categories the first commissioners were appointed.

[a] There was no chairman listed for West Lake Province in 1961, but the 1962 West Lake chairman became the chairman of the Bukoba town and district councils.

[b] Six of the provincial secretaries became regional commissioners in the first batch of 1962 appointments: John Mwakangale, Richard Wambura, John Nzunda, Samuel Luangisa, J. Abdallah, S. J. Kitundu. The first 3 later became parliamentary secretaries.

[c] The 2 provincial chairmen who became regional commissioners were S. P. Muro and S. A. Mtaki. Mtaki was to become an area commissioner and then a regional commissioner. In 1964, he became a parliamentary secretary. He had served as a provincial secretary before becoming provincial chairman. Muro was made ambassador to Sweden.

[d] Two provincial chairmen did not move into government jobs at all. One became an executive officer of a district council that operated within his province.

ence clerk in the provincial administration (1942-48), a clerk in a business firm (1949-50), the secretary to a rural council in Mbeya (1951-52), a public relations assistant in South Africa (1952-55), and an administrative assistant in a British firm (1956-58). Nzunda became a provincial secretary of TANU in 1959.

134

Richard Wambura was born in 1927 in Musoma and became a provincial secretary in 1958. He was educated privately in Musoma and Kericho, Kenya, and attended Kivukoni College for one year. He had been a clerk in the Overseas Food Corporation, a chief storekeeper for the Tanganyika Cotton Company Limited, and later a shop assistant. He also worked at B. Nicholas and Company Limited. He was a Member of Parliament for Maswa since 1960.

Two men who joined TANU at its beginning also had administrative experience:

R. J. Abdallah was educated at Tabora Secondary School in 1941, and became a provincial secretary in 1958. He had been a government employee between 1941 and 1952, and had joined TANU in 1954.

Selemani Kitundu, who was born in Musoma in 1927 and educated at Mwisenge School (1934-38), had been secretary of the Tanganyika African Association branch at Musoma (1951-54), a member of the Musoma township authority (1950-58), and a member of the South East Lake County Council (1955-56). He was provincial publicity secretary of TANU (1955-59), and became a provincial secretary in 1959.[28]

The only provincial secretary who became a regional commissioner without having worked previously in executive or administrative capacities was atypical of the provincial secretaries:

Samuel Luangisa had been chairman of the Buhaya District Council before becoming a provincial secretary. He

[28] The biographical data presented has come from different sources. Newspapers, personal interviews, and *Who's Who in East Africa, 1963-64* (Nairobi, Marco Surveys, Ltd., 1964).

was from a prominent Haya family and the brother of a chief. He had local connections and elected position rather than administrative experience.

In these respects, Luangisa had a background more characteristic of TANU chairmen. However, it is incorrect to assume from this that provincial secretaries were administrators only. Kitundu also served as a representative on elected bodies as had Luangisa, and 3 of the 6 provincial secretaries who became regional commissioners were MPs at the time of their appointments in 1962: Nzunda, Mwakangale, and Wambura all had been elected to the National Assembly in the general election of 1960. They had been chosen to stand as TANU candidates because they were considered competent, and they were to be rewarded for services rendered, although they had not been elected representatives on local government bodies before standing for the National Assembly. Nonetheless, it should be kept in mind that they did serve as representatives, and were not related to their constituencies simply as secretaries of TANU who were appointed from the center.

The fact that experience in executive or administrative capacities was a major qualification for appointment as regional commissioner is underlined when we look at the backgrounds of the 4 men who became regional commissioners in 1962, but had not been provincial secretaries at the end of 1961. (One man had been a provincial secretary in the past and had served in a number of administrative posts in TANU before he became a regional commissioner.)

Edward Barongo was born in 1928 at Bukoba. He served in the East African Army Medical Corps until 1950, and was a district and then, in 1957, a provincial secretary of TANU. He was one of the founders of the West Lake TANU organization and was elected provincial chairman of TANU in 1958. Prior to his appointment as regional commissioner, he had been the Deputy Secretary General of TANU. He was an MP as well.

A. K. Sykes was a TANU founding father. He was born in 1926 in Dar es Salaam and educated at government secondary schools. He was a long-standing member of the Central Committee, had been a general secretary of a union in 1950, and had served in the army.

Sheikh Amri Abedi was born in 1924 in Ujiji and educated at the Tabora Secondary School (1937-41). He did postal work training (1942-43) and Islamic missionary training (1944-53). He studied at Rabwah College in Pakistan (1954-56). He was first elected as an MP in 1959, and was elected mayor of Dar es Salaam (1960-61).

Army service or enrollment in a training school set men apart in Tanganyika; it is no exaggeration to say that a man who had been to the army or had attended some training course, even for a short time, qualified for an executive post. Many of the elected TANU officials could not boast of such qualifications. Simply having worked as a salaried employee was a qualification for one who had been in continuous touch with the modern wage sector.

The provincial chairmen were more likely farmers and traders than salaried employees.[29] Whereas the provincial secretaries all spoke English and had at least some secondary school education, the provincial chairmen generally had little formal education.[30] The only provincial chairman who went

[29] E.g., Lila Mwinyikondo and M. N. Kissokiy, 2 provincial chairmen who became area commissioners, are listed in the *Who's Who of East Africa* as "farmer and trader" and "businessman" respectively. In other words, they had worked neither as government clerks nor in some administrative/clerical capacity.

[30] Mwinyikondo's formal education ended when he was eight years of age; Kissokiy's before he was twelve.

directly to appointment as regional commissioner in 1962 had an atypical background:

> S. P. Muro was born at Kilimanjaro in 1927, and educated at government secondary schools (1942-47). He took a pharmacy course and became a compounder for the Overseas Food Corporation during the groundnut experiment at Kongwa. He later returned to Chaggaland, his home, and became divisional magistrate of the Chagga local government (1952-60). He founded and was managing director of the Muro Brothers firm, and was active in the cooperative movement. Between 1960 and 1962 he served as chairman of the Tanganyika Coffee Board, vice chairman of the Moshi Town Council, and Vice President of the Kilimanjaro Native Cooperative Union.

Although Muro's background was similar to that of other TANU chairmen in that he held elective posts and was important in local commerce or farming, he had also been outside of his home district and had executive experience.

When it came to staffing close to 60 area commissioners posts, TANU quickly ran out of provincial secretaries and chairmen, and had to turn to district secretaries and chairmen. During 1962, 57 area commissioners were named. I have been able to trace the backgrounds of all but 17 of them (see Table 7).

Since the original 57 appointments to area commissioners, there has been turnover, but no one category has been eliminated: ex-district secretaries remain the largest single category; elected TANU officials still become area commissioners. The NEC can be a springboard for appointment as the MNE and the regional chairmen make contacts at the center and develop their connections.[31] But on the whole, TANU regional

[31] As of March 1965, 3 out of 17 MNE were area commissioners: A. Laicer, M. Kissokiy, M. Kalemaga. Being a commissioner does not appear crucial to maintaining oneself as either MNE or regional

TABLE 7

Backgrounds of the First Area Commissioners

40 area commissioners—

    from TANU posts:

        15 district secretaries
         5 provincial chairmen
         4 district chairmen
         4 regional MNE[a]
         3 provincial secretaries
         3 officials from National Headquarters[b]
         1 chairman of the Central Committee

        35

    from local government:

         2 chiefs
         1 executive officer of a district council[c]
         1 teacher and school supervisor

         4

    from trade-union movement:

         1 full-time official[d]

SOURCE: A list of TANU officers for the end of 1961 gives the names of 56 district secretaries. In addition to the 15 secretaries who were made area commissioners in 1962, at least 2 others were to become area commissioners in 1963-64. Two of these 17 became regional commissioners in time and 1 of these 2, Martin Haule, became a parliamentary secretary.

[a] Actually, 6 of the 8 MNE listed in 1961 became area commissioners in 1962. One has already been listed as a district chairman; another is listed as a provincial secretary.

[b] T.A.K. Msonge, a former Deputy Secretary General, became an area commissioner as did Mbutta Milando who was at various times district secretary, National Youth League secretary, an assistant publicity secretary, a sub-editor of the TANU newspaper *Ngurumo*.

[c] One man listed under district chairman became executive officer of a district council for a very short time before his appointment as area commissioner.

[d] Others listed under different headings had involvements with trade unions but they were not full-time officials.

chairmen and MNE have had decreasing success in becoming commissioners since the first appointments were made in 1962. At that time, 7 out of 10 provincial chairmen of 1961 became either area or regional commissioners. Of the 17 regional chairmen in 1964, 11 were new men compared to 1961 regional chairmen.[32] Only 2 of these 11 have ever been area commissioners, and none have been regional commissioner. Of the 17 MNE listed in 1964, only 3 were listed in 1961; 2 of these have been commissioners.[33]

On occasion, district chairmen and regional chairmen still become commissioners: one district chairman became a deputy secretary of TANU. But it is much more likely that the district chairmen who are promoted move to regional chairmenships, to MNE, or to membership on regional water or sanitation boards in non-executive capacities.

Vacancies in area commissioner posts are sometimes filled by appointing TANU deputy regional secretaries. Some of these deputy regional secretaries are former district secretaries who did not become commissioners in 1962. But if a man who had been a district secretary was not appointed area commissioner during 1962, his chances of making it at all were slight:[34] many of the commissioners appointed in 1962

---

chairman. Of 6 long-tenure chairmen, 3 have been commissioners; and of 3 long-standing MNE, 2 have been area commissioners.

[32] Of the 10 regional chairmen listed in 1961, 4 were still regional chairmen. However, since new regions were created after 1961, I have counted 2 1961 district chairmen who are now regional chairmen as if they were 1961 regional chairmen. Neither man has ever been a commissioner. See Table 3 for lists of regional chairmen.

[33] By 1965, 12 names appeared who were not MNE in 1961. None of them had ever been area commissioners. See Table 4 for lists of MNE.

[34] The TANU district secretaries of 1961 almost never stood for regional and district TANU elected office. I know of 1 out of 57 who became a district chairman. I have not been able to account for 30 of the 57 district secretaries in 1961: 15 became area commissioners in 1962; 2 others became area commissioners later on; 1 was a deputy regional secretary as of 1965 and 8 were deputy district secretaries as

stayed, and the center avoided relying on the old district secretaries.

In December 1964, 34 of the area commissioners who had been appointed between May and December of 1962 were still on the job.[35] The new area commissioners had not been recruited from any one dominating pool as had occurred in 1962;[36] reliance on district secretaries for new appointments was over.

Movement of Commissioners

Tenures in each district were very short and the rate of movement from one district to another was high. This indicates that individuals had difficulties in their districts. Although 20 commissioners did not move at all during 1964, 38 moved at least once;[37] thus for half of the area commissioners, tenure at one post was only six months or less. This was true for regional commissioners too. Moreover, some commissioners had moved twice in 1964 and 2 of them had moved three times. (See Table 8.)

---

of the end of 1963; 1 became chief clerk at National Headquarters. I have been told that some district secretaries did become divisional executive officers, but have no data to substantiate it.

[35] Of the 23 drop-outs, 4 became regional commissioners; 3 became parliamentary secretaries; 2 were in the civil service—one as an administrative secretary, the other as an area secretary; 1 was in preventive detention, being incarcerated for his part in the January 1964 mutiny; 1 was the personal secretary to the President. Of the remaining 12 commissioners, 4 were still commissioners as of January 1964, and 3 were area commissioners as late as August 1964. The other 5 fell by the wayside shortly after 1962.

[36] Fifty-nine area commissioner posts were listed as occupied in the December 1964 Government Directory. Of the 25 new commissioners, I have been able to establish the backgrounds for 14 men: 4 had been civil servants, 3 of high rank at the district or regional level (1 had been an administrative secretary, 2 were local government officers, and 1 had been an employee of a district council at lower rank), 3 had worked at TANU National Headquarters; 2 were MPs; 2 had been TANU district secretaries in 1961; 2 had been TANU district chairmen in 1961; 1 was from the trade-union movement.

[37] One post was vacant in December 1964.

TABLE 8

*Area Commissioners Tenure in Office
as of December 1964*

Commissioners	Period Post Held (Months)
5	1
4	2
6	3
8	4
4	5
1	6
2	7
6	10
2	11
38	

The pattern of movement indicates that non-locals had less success in operating as commissioners than those who were from the district where they were commissioners. Localism rather than tribalism is evident here: those commissioners with comparatively long tenures were often individuals who were active on the local scene before appointment to commissioner and had held elected as well as appointed TANU posts;[38] they were not necessarily from the major tribe in the district.

Three regions in particular have had relatively few commissioners. Two of them—Coast Region and Mtwara Region—are coastal regions.[39] The district headquarters are often located in coastal towns (for example, Dar es Salaam,

[38] Of the ten commissioners who held their posts for two years or more, 1 was an MP; 1 was a district chairman of TANU; 1 was a regional chairman of TANU; 3 were MNE in their regions; 2 were the first TANU district secretaries of their district.

[39] The third region is Singida. I am unfamiliar with the region and can offer no explanation for the pattern there.

Bagamoyo, Mafia, Kilwa, Lindi, Mtwara). In both regions, the commissioners have moved among the different districts, but have stayed within the region. They are either from the Coast or have spent much time there, particularly in Coast Region; and are usually Muslims, with ties to the TANU elders. (For example, S. A. Kandoro, area commissioner for Bagamoyo, who is from Ujiji-Kigoma on Lake Tanganyika, has been chairman of the TANU Elders Section. He fits into the pattern of the TANU *mzee* or elder.) These men are effective political heads for coastal and coastal-type districts.[40]

Frequent movement of commissioners is a good index of difficulty in operating as a political head and a reflection of Tanganyika's localism in politics. Almost all the commissioners I interviewed admitted the factor of localism while denying that movement was itself a reflection of difficulty. One of the reasons given by the commissioners themselves for frequent movement is that the government wishes to acquaint them with different parts of Tanganyika and to break down tribalism and localism. There is also an awareness of the possibility that commissioners who have been in one place a long time may form "family circles" and insulate themselves from local and central criticism. It is true that the longer a commissioner stays in one place, the more he tends to dominate local TANU organizations; frequent movement prevents him from consolidating his position to such an extent. And some commissioners feel that the center does not want them to consolidate their position.

This last view in particular runs counter to my understanding of why commissioners were appointed in the first place. They were instituted because the TANU center wanted to be able to dominate the regional and district organizations; toward this end, commissioners were given extensive powers. And yet as soon as a man begins to know his district, he may

[40] What constitutes an "effective political head" is discussed briefly at the end of this chapter and more extensively in chaps. x and xi.

be moved to a place far removed geographically and with very different social patterns. Many of the commissioners I questioned about this replied that they could not confidently respond because they were new to their districts, when in fact many had been in their district for six months—a relatively long tenure. Many of the commissioners feel insecure in their knowledge of local conditions, despite the attitude of some of them that as commissioners and TANU district secretaries they are well aware of the powers and duties of their positions by virtue of service in other districts. Those commissioners who move right away to take command of a new situation on the basis of their previous experience in another district are not always successful. Conditions may differ so widely that patterns of rule which work in one district are untenable in another; civil service officials are often new men who cannot always be relied upon. The area and administrative secretaries circulate a great deal too. Thus the commissioners are thrown back on the district and regional TANU officers, in particular the chairmen and the deputy secretaries. But these latter also move around: as paid officials of TANU National Headquarters they are posted from place to place—from Dar es Salaam to the districts and regions—and attend brief courses to further their education. And as we shall see, the chairmen and the commissioners are not always easy partners. If the center aims at controlling local organizations, anything which makes the commissioners dependent on the chairmen works against this aim.

The center realizes that frequent transfer of commissioners is inefficient. How then can the frequent movement be accounted for if the center has a vested interest in stability of tenure which allows for greater efficiency and greater control of district and regional TANU organizations? There is something in the notion that frequent movement does not allow certain commissioners to consolidate their positions. While the center wants central control of up-country TANU organizations, and while it hopes to use the commissioners as the main instruments to achieve this control, not every commissioner is a reliable instrument of the center. Some commissioners consolidate control and then use it for their own purposes which are not always harmonious with those of the center. For example, one commissioner was devoting much of his time to personal enterprises—bars and places of prostitution; these entrepreneurial activities were not what the center meant by fostering economic development in the districts. Another commissioner had intimidated civil servants and TANU officials and was using his personal discretion to have people beaten for disobedience to him. A third was deeply involved with his own relatives' political interests in a district.

Now it is not uncommon for political bosses and commissars the world over to be involved in vice, to form—literally and figuratively—family circles, or to bully citizens. If anything, Tanganyika's commissioners have been accused relatively rarely of these sins. And only on one occasion has a commissioner been involved, or had his involvement come to light, in a political plot against the regime.[41] Commissioners have not even been accused of deliberately going against orders from the center; they have not overtly set themselves up politically against the center.

However, sins of political omission or commission are serious in Tanganyika, yet difficult to bring to light because the center does not have a staff for inspection and control. It may be that the infrequency of accusation against commissioners is due to the weakness of the center's own mechanisms for bringing such affairs to light. Grumbling about TANU practices in the districts does not always reach Dar es Salaam because communications are intermittent and the very chan-

---

[41] The aforementioned area commissioner who was put under preventive detention in 1964—Mr. Hongoli, was area commissioner for Kahama.

nels of communication are those individuals who would be accused of malpractice. As long as a district oligarchy can remain fairly solid, it can dominate the flow of information to Dar es Salaam.[42] Leaders in Dar es Salaam are aware of this,[43] and find one response in moving commissioners when they suspect them of violating central directives.

A commissioner may cease to function as an arm of the center and may begin to act as if he were himself a local. All commissioners must rely, in various degrees, on their elected TANU organizations; if they try to become a part of the elected organization in order to win its support, which is necessary for putting across development programs, they may compromise themselves as agents of the center. Commissioners will sometimes support programs which are of no interest to the central planning and development office simply because they are important to local TANU organizations. In one district headquarters, for example, the commissioner was spending a great deal of time soliciting funds to build a new hotel, despite the fact that the *Five Year Plan* made no provision for such a place. Because of the enthusiasm of town TANU leaders, the commissioner embraced the program, even to the neglect of centrally established projects.[44]

Why not simply sack a man who has fallen prey to local pressures or is suspected of feathering his own nest? Answers are made at two different levels of response; the first has to do with political ethics. No central leaders overtly condone commissioners acting in a self-interested way. In fact, there is little tolerance of "family-circle" activity because it smacks of clanism and localisms which are anathema at central lev-

[42] TANU has appointed traveling commissioners to check on abuses for just this reason.

[43] This became clear in interviews I had with central leaders.

[44] Another example occurs where the regional commissioners must be responsive to locally initiated agricultural development projects although they are enjoined to devote their time and local resources to the support of centrally initiated pilot farm schemes.

els. There is less open tolerance among national leaders in Tanzania than in the United States for what might be called in America normal patronage politics. The rhetoric of politics is more puritanical. National leaders stress self-sacrifice for the nation, action for "pure" motives, African Socialism with its collectivist rather than individualist ethics. Nyerere sees something almost insidious about the give and take of politics in terms of interest and conflict, though he is personally tolerant of different viewpoints.[45] Tanganyikan leaders have a narrow rather than a broad conception of corruption.[46]

However, national leaders recognize that it is essential for commissioners to come to terms with local pressures. The feeling is that a man who makes a bad job of it should be moved rather than sacked because his job is, after all, a difficult one. In the past, TANU leaders felt an obligation to people who had struggled against the British administration; leaders preferred to move old comrades rather than fire them. But the decisions to transfer instead of fire had a more basic cause than comradely feelings: The prospects of replacing one poor commissioner with a better man were not promising. Thus TANU kept shuffling the same men around in the hope that improvements would result. Nothing relevant could be done to change the situation given the decision to recruit from TANU officials. But the organizational muscles were flexed just the same.

Recruitment from the Civil Service

After 1964, TANU began to recruit commissioners from the civil service in greater numbers, in hopes that, with their ad-

---

[45] See chap. vi.

[46] For a narrow or "moralistic" approach to corruption see Ronald Wraith and Edgar Simpkins, *Corruption in Developing Countries* (New York: W. W. Norton and Co., 1964). For a critique of Wraith and Simpkins see Colin Leys, "What Is the Problem about Corruption," *Journal of Modern African Studies,* III (1965), 215-30.

ministrative and executive abilities, civil servants could strengthen the regional and district TANU organizations. On July 10, 1964, the Second Vice President, Mr. Rashidi Kawawa, announced to a meeting of over 1,000 civil servants in Dar es Salaam:

> We want civil servants to join TANU so that they can help us in our struggle against poverty, disease and ignorance. ... Civil servants are the most educated people in our country. We cannot afford to leave them aside in important discussions concerning the country of which they are a part.[47]

The theme that all should participate in the national movement had been sounded by Nyerere even when he had maintained the distinction between civil servants and politicians in 1960. And in *Democracy and the Party System*, Nyerere rejected the

> . . . present artificial distinction between politicians and civil servants—a distinction desirable only in the context of a multiparty system where continuity of public administration must not be thrown out of gear at every switch from one "party" government to another. . . . In a political movement which is identified with the nation, participation in political affairs must be recognized as the right of every citizen, in no matter what capacity he may have chosen to serve his country.[48]

Civil servants were told they could join TANU and, more than this, they could be politicians. "It would be sheer hypocrisy," said Mr. Kawawa, "to refuse government employees the permission to become a politician and at the same time to rely on them to prepare political speeches to be delivered by ministers."[49]

[47] *Nationalist*, July 11, 1964, p. 1.
[48] *Democracy and the Party System*, p. 26.
[49] *Nationalist*, July 11, 1964, p. 4.

Although this was the official opening of TANU to civil servants, in the past, at least one high-level TANU figure—a parliamentary secretary—had become a permanent secretary and had not given up his TANU card (though he did give up his seat in the National Assembly). At the local levels, civil servants had joined TANU before now. In fact, one regional trade union secretary complained in an interview in 1963 that a district TANU chairman was forcing local government servants to join TANU and pay dues. He had complained to the regional commissioner, and had received no reply. The regional commissioner, when asked about this, said that civil servants would probably be able to join TANU someday; he could not allow them to do so now since it was illegal.[50] He did not deny, however, that a TANU district official was exerting pressure on local government officials. The issue was not resolved as far as I know until the July 10 announcement which in this case regularized the *de facto* situation.

In this announcement, the Vice President made it clear that government wanted civil servants to criticize TANU from within it if they had criticism to make. On July 21, the *Nationalist* reported that 90 per cent of the civil service had either registered or applied for TANU membership. (The customary procedure was for civil servants to march in procession to TANU offices where they bought their membership cards and thanked the government for allowing them to join TANU.) The Minister for Finance, Mr. Bomani, pointed out that there were 48,296 civil servants in Tanganyika, and if all joined, their annual subscriptions would amount to almost $40,000. But the party did not recruit civil servants primarily for this reason; their talents would be useful, and their presence within TANU would mean that no sector of the population was outside the national movement and thus felt to be outside the nation-building process in the most immediate

[50] Interview with Oswald Marwa, regional commissioner of West Lake, November 1963.

149

sense. Mr. Oscar Kambona warned that if civil servants, military men, and police were excluded from TANU they would begin to think of themselves as different and would demand special consideration. "Now is the time to annihilate such mentality so that everyone can think of building the nation of which he or she is a part."[51]

The Parliamentary Secretary to the Second Vice President and Deputy Secretary General of TANU, Mr. John Nzunda, stated that government's decision to admit civil servants did not mean that civil servants would be allowed to constitute new policies contrary to those of TANU.[52] This was both a warning to civil servants and a reassurance to TANU members. Government wanted the civil service to refashion itself in the image of a "Tanganyika way":

In Tanganyika and the United Republic we are faced with problems, traditions and ways of life peculiar to our countries; it is obviously expedient to adapt our civil service to meet those conditions and control them. We can do this by retaining what is best from the past and adapting it to the future. . . . It would only be odd if we persevered with a civil service tradition alien to our heritage. . . . There is a vast difference between countries with long-established civil services and the new developing countries like our own, which have to build up their administrative systems from scratch. . . . We have complete freedom of choice, and we are under no obligation whatsoever to copy any other country.[53]

[51] *Nationalist*, July 30, 1964, p. 1.

[52] Speech made to civil servants at Moshi, July 27, 1964. *Nationalist*, July 28, 1964.

[53] Speech by Amon Nsekela, Secretary of the Presidential Commission and Permanent Secretary to the Ministry of Industries, Mineral Resources and Power, to a seminar of administrative secretaries on August 4, 1964. This speech was printed in full in the *Kivukoni Newsletter*, Dar es Salaam, September 10, 1964, pp. 2-9. This passage is on pp. 3-4, and p. 6.

The distinction between civil servant and politician is seen as one which can only hinder the government in its implementation of the Development Plan.[54] The urgent actions that are required call for a local civil service which identifies civil service with the policies of government and the needs and aspirations of the people. The permanent secretary argued that identification could only be achieved if the civil service was allowed to enter the political arena.[55]

This idea and the specific decision to expand recruitment of commissioners from the civil service came from President Nyerere. In a speech made in August 1964, President Nyerere said:

> Responsibility cannot be entrusted to people for sentimental reasons, or left with them once they have failed because they are nice people . . . these are circumstances which call for the use of every person who can be obtained and whose skill or experience contributes in any way to movement in the desired direction.[56]

This speech was followed within two months by an increase in the number of commissioners from civil service backgrounds. And for a few men the game of musical chairs, whereby commissioners moved from district to district but were never fired for incompetence, came to an end.

In September of 1964, the post of regional commissioner of Mbeya was filled by the former permanent secretary to the administrative division of the President's Office, Mr. Mwakang'ata; a civil service administrative secretary, a civil service area secretary, and a local government officer all became

[54] Editorial in the *Nationalist*, August 5, 1964, p. 4.

[55] Nsekela, *op.cit.*, p. 6.

[56] Speech by President Nyerere at the opening of Dar es Salaam University College Campus, August 21, 1964. Issued by Information Services Division of Ministry of Information and Tourism, Dar es Salaam, 1964, p. 14.

151

area commissioners.[57] This was the largest number of ex-civil servants serving as commissioners at one time since 1962, though there had been civil servants who had been appointed commissioners in the past. There were never more than 3 or 4 civil service commissioners at one time,[58] until December 1964, when there were at least 7 and the prospect is that more will be appointed from administrative grades.

It is important to distinguish between recruitment of commissioners from high and middle rather than lower grade civil service for two reasons: not only are the training and abilities of the grades different, but low-level civil servants, particularly from local government, have often been TANU people originally who came into the civil service as patronage appointments. Civil servants from the administrative grades —administrative secretaries, area secretaries, local government officers (all of whom operate in the regions and districts), and permanent or what are now principal and assistant principal secretaries of the central ministries—bring to their commissioner jobs skills that many of the early commissioners do not possess. They have an ability to work with written communications, to fathom statistics, and to participate in some of the more administrative and technical work of implementing the *Five Year Plan*. However, some of the first commissioners have stayed on and have learned the skills appropriate for trying to put across the *Five Year Plan*. The reason TANU secretaries were more suited than the elected chairmen in the first place was that they possessed some administrative abilities and experience.

[57] There were rumors in Dar es Salaam that civil service area secretaries would become commissioners in large numbers, these rumors did not materialize.

[58] When a civil service commissioner was to be added, another civil service commissioner was retired from the ranks. E.g., Mr. M. P. Mazinga was made regional commissioner in 1963. He returned to the civil service as principal assistant secretary in the Planning Office. He was replaced by another civil servant, H. C. Mgone, a former administrative secretary. Mgone has now returned to civil service also.

Continuity and Change in the Relationships
Between Elected and Appointed Officials

The appointment of civil servants does promise a greater understanding of the economics of development and the laws within which the commissioners must work. Often in the past, the general ineffectiveness of commissioners and the consequent high rate of transfer was due as much to a failure to appreciate the necessity of doing things to enhance the prospects of economic development as to gross violations of law. But appointing a man from the civil service to be a commissioner does not automatically guarantee his success. He must first master his local TANU organization; he must work within TANU frameworks and understand TANU values and goals. It is too soon to judge whether the civil servants brought into these positions will be able to do this. While some of the TANU district secretaries who moved into commissionerships felt they had "been there before," they were actually involved in completely new tasks and they were dealing with a wider circle of people—ministerial representatives and non-Africans. Yet they did have the confidence that their TANU background gave them, and they shared with the TANU chairmen a sense of being TANU people. Even if many chairmen and secretaries have a hard time specifying what being a TANU person means they have made specific commitments to TANU. They may see these commitments in different lights —the chairmen stressing TANU supremacy and the secretaries/commissioners stressing the unity of the TANU government—but they are still TANU in a way civil servants cannot be at this juncture, whatever the attempts of central leaders to proclaim the identity of a "new" civil service inextricable from TANU, and whatever the attempts of individual civil servants to become more "TANU" than other commissioners.[59]

[59] At an international conference in Nairobi, one civil servant,

Furthermore, movement between the hierarchies of elected and appointed officials, has helped contain the potential conflict which is built into the dual structure of TANU district and regional organizations. Usually there has been at least coexistence and often cooperation between the elected and appointed officials in district and regional TANU organizations. If many more civil servants are recruited to be TANU secretaries/commissioners the relationships between elected and appointed officials could change.

At the present time, the commissioners as heads of government and TANU secretaries can usually prevail within the regional/district TANU organization. But they attempt to reach a consensus because they recognize that they must get the cooperation of the elected officials if they are to succeed. Many of the pre-1962 patterns of relations between elected and appointed officials persist. Though there are representatives of the central ministries with functional responsibilities, the commissioners too are involved in soliciting support for ministerial programs; they still go out on *safari* with groups of TANU officials, and in some places rely on the elected chairmen to get support for programs. However, the presence of a commissioner is now usually sufficient to put across a sense of purpose and TANU government commitment to an undertaking.

The commissioners are still stretched very thin. Population remains scattered. Authority within a district or regional TANU organization remains diffuse. Tasks are not easily sepa-

---

turned commissioner, raised a great cry when he thought something unfavorable to TANU had been written. He was the most vocal of all the TANU personages at the conference. Individual civil service/commissioners have been very successful at becoming "TANU." Ministers and parliamentary secretaries speak of civil servants who became commissioners and who have done excellent jobs. But they are still very conscious of the civil servant origins of such people. In the regions and districts also such consciousness still persists.

rated and this, in conjunction with scarcity of trained personnel, makes for little division of labor.[60]

Earlier patterns persist in other respects too. Regional commissioners have had votes of "no confidence" passed on them by the TANU regional organization and have been requested to move on. True, this is not the same thing as being "voted out of office." Regional TANU people now realize that commissioners cannot be treated this way, but attempts are still made to influence the selection of the commissioner. Rather than pass a "no confidence" vote it would be more likely for a local organization to undermine an unwanted commissioner by making life difficult for him. District and regional organizations have appealed to national leaders visiting them or have sent emissaries to Dar es Salaam to complain about a commissioner. The tendency has persisted for Dar to avoid direct confrontations with local TANU organizations by transferring commissioners if their positions become very difficult.

There has been one factor in particular which has worked to bolster the position of the elected chairmen in the face of the new powers of the secretaries/commissioners. Some powerful MPs, MNEs, and junior ministers who were once regional chairmen (as well as regional secretaries) are still committed to the idea that within the regional and district TANU organizations the TANU chairman remains paramount.

[60] The NEC insisted in 1964 that there should be a more rational distribution of time and men at least as concerns meeting visiting dignitaries. In the past, when an important visitor arrived in a region from Dar es Salaam, whole district teams traveled an entire day to greet the visitors at TANU regional headquarters expending scarce petrol, using scarce landrovers and their own time and energy. In the latter part of 1964, the NEC passed a decree ordering travel from the districts to the regional headquarters to cease unless the President or Vice Presidents were on hand. The NEC also said that holidays ought not to be declared for visiting ministers but only for the President and the First Vice President. President Nyerere prompted the NEC to issue these decrees.

Many people I interviewed strongly disagreed with this point of view. Vice President Kawawa pointed out that a chairman of a district or regional TANU executive committee does not have a position analogous to the President of TANU because the latter has executive power both in that capacity and as President of the United Republic of Tanzania. Some went so far as to see the regional chairmen as supernumeraries in the TANU organizations, and called for their abolition.[61] In contrast, men who felt the regional and district chairmen *should* be vital factors not only thought that they were important in their organizations but that they "gave orders to commissioners" and "could have him [the commissioner] transferred." Mr. S. Mtaki, a junior minister, expressed the opinion that the chairman was superior in TANU affairs but had no role in government;[62] he said that the commissioners were there to coordinate TANU and government activities and were after all "only secretaries before [becoming commissioners], doing administrative work."[63] (Another man[64] spoke of the "regional chairman and *his* working committee"; "the chairman can go through the TANU minutes and give orders to the commissioner and the deputy secretary.") When I mentioned to Mr. Mtaki that some chairmen accepted fairly low-level government jobs, the junior minister replied: "Those are giving up politics." And when I asked if district/regional organizations did not get paralyzed if co-equal chairmen and commissioners differed over conducting TANU business, he answered that the importance of the chairmen was a crucial aspect of democracy in TANU. He said that the system was democratic. "It may not always be best but this is the democratic way. If a commissioner is stymied, he is stymied."

[61] I do not associate Vice President Kawawa with the view.

[62] Interview with S. Mtaki, Junior Minister for Commerce, April 1965.

[63] *Ibid.*

[64] He did not wish to be quoted.

Those who see the chairmen as equal or even superior to the commissioners and stress the former's role in TANU affairs see a dichotomy between TANU and government; the commissioners are seen as coordinators of the two spheres. Those who state that the commissioners are clearly paramount and hence the chief officials of the TANU government in the districts and regions, recognize no such distinction; no separate component of TANU affairs is explicitly admitted.

A partial explanation for this difference of perception is in the different backgrounds I have described. Many of the men who felt that the chairmen were still so important were former chairmen. My own conclusion is that the chairmen were important if one took a compartmentalized view of TANU affairs in the regions and districts: for they do have a great deal to say about when meetings will be held, and who will speak; and the commissioners do need their support. Some chairmen are co-equals with the commissioners on matters of a strictly local concern. But on matters which pertained to central policy, chairmen are much less frequently involved; the commissioners are the interpreters of the center to the regional and district organizations.

We can now approach TANU's central bodies keeping in mind the patterns of recruitment and membership in the regional and district organizations, since these central institutions are in large part composed of regional and district officials.

CHAPTER V

TANU at the Center

WE MUST differentiate the TANU national organs—that is, those responsible for party affairs as a whole (Cabinet, Central Committee, NEC, National Conference, National Headquarters)—because they do not function as a compact unit which imposes central will or policies upon regional and district organizations. Certain officials operate at the center itself—Dar es Salaam; others come to Dar es Salaam periodically to constitute central organs—the NEC and the National Conference—which are made up largely of representatives from the district and regional TANU bodies. While they all meet at the center to discuss national policy, they are themselves organs of the national rulers only intermittently. In order to understand this it is necessary to take up each of the TANU national institutions in turn, looking at their membership and their functioning.

The President of TANU

The President of TANU stands at the apex of the party. It is difficult to speak about the "Presidency of TANU" since Julius Nyerere has been the only President and, because of his historical position, the presidency as a governing institution is inseparable from the man himself.[1] He is the Father of the Nation—the *Baba Ya Taifa*; thus his power does not depend on his position in TANU. Rather, TANU derives strength from Nyerere's own personal popularity and from his historical

[1] There have been two Vice Presidents of TANU. The present Vice President, Rashidi Kawawa, a founder of TANU and one-time leader of the Tanganyika Federation of Labour, was elected in 1960. Formerly, John Rupia was Vice President. Rupia is still an appointed member of the Central Committee, although he was defeated in 1965 in his bid for a National Assembly seat. The Vice President is elected annually by the Annual Conference and is Chairman of the Central Committee when the President is absent.

role as *the* national leader. Thus the constitutional arrangements which define the presidency are less important than Nyerere's character and ideas in determining the role of the President within TANU affairs.

Briefly, the constitutional arrangements are as follows: the President serves without salary, although he receives an allowance of about $70 a month from the party. He is elected by the National Conference for a period of five years, and can be removed by a two-thirds vote of the National Conference. Periodically, the suggestion is made that Julius Nyerere be made the President of TANU and of Tanganyika for life, but Nyerere has always rejected this idea.[2] He has accepted an honorary life membership in TANU—quite a different matter.

The President is Chairman of the Central Committee and appoints its members. But in theory, he is not an administrator for TANU affairs;[3] administration is the function of the Secretary General. In fact however, Nyerere is involved in all major TANU promotions and appointments; in many ways, he is the TANU center. Up to 1964, Nyerere monopolized the articulation of a national political culture in Tanganyika and defined TANU to its members, the country as a whole, and the outside world.[4] Insofar as policy initiation came from non-expatriates at the national level, it came, literally, from the head of Julius Nyerere. But this does not mean that Nyerere

[2] In a National Assembly debate of June 1965, Second Vice President Kawawa replied to the suggestion that the National Assembly declare Nyerere life President of Tanganyika by saying "every person in Tanzania had that desire." But he could not see why a law should be passed. "If a law was passed, then we shall be creating a monarch. We do not want a monarch; nor will he agree to be made one." *Nationalist*, June 10, 1965, p. 4.

[3] In the 1950's there was a chairman of the Central Committee who was elected from among the members of the Central Committee. Even at that time the President had the right to appoint Central Committee members.

[4] See chap. vi for a description of ideology in Tanganyika.

has been successful in implementing his policy choices. Both as TANU President in internal TANU affairs and as President of the Republic in national affairs, he has often been markedly unsuccessful in carrying his party with him and in implementing decisions made at the national level. Nyerere's relations with his National Executive Committee were exposed immediately after independence when Nyerere resigned from the prime ministership, thus revealing the paradox of the national hero who is not always able to carry the day although he is always able to make himself heard and to influence TANU policies.

"Probably few emergent countries have suffered such a drastic revision of their overseas 'public image' as Tanganyika soon after achieving independence."[5] For on January 22, 1962, after only forty-four days in office as Prime Minister, Nyerere resigned to "return to TANU." To the outside world, Nyerere not only spoke for his country, he was equated with TANU and Tanganyika. Thus his resignation as Prime Minister and the circumstances of that resignation provoked widespread dismay abroad.[6]

In the May-June 1961 meeting of the Tanganyika Legislature (the first meeting under the new title of National Assembly), a number of backbenchers showed impatience with some government policies: more rapid Africanization was called for; middle-level leaders were impatient to see the fruits of independence. If economic development could not

[5] Leys, *op.cit.*

[6] I suggest that the overseas image of Tanganyika changed very radically in the first year of Tanganyika's independence because a power and cohesion was attributed to TANU which it did not have and did not need in order to monopolize the politics of independence and become the national movement which led Tanganyika to independence. While foreign observers were aware that the tasks of ruling would be different from those of mobilizing for *Uhuru*, perhaps many of them failed to understand that the anticipated strains would be the greater because of the organizational form which had evolved during the anti-colonial struggle.

be brought about quickly, at least Africans should replace Asians and Europeans in government and commercial jobs. TANU leaders in the regions and districts were also feeling the frustrations of organizing after independence: meetings were harder to organize, and crowds were more difficult to marshal; enrollment of new members had ceased.[7] At the same time, groups in Dar es Salaam and in the regions were making demands on the TANU leadership: trade unions wanted wage rises and other benefits; some unions, among them the teachers' and medical workers' union, threatened strikes. Nyerere said that the country could not meet these demands and he threatened to dismiss all government workers who went on strike after their demands had been considered. This statement called forth criticism of Nyerere by union leaders.[8]

It was against this background that the TANU government had to make a number of policy decisions. The demand for *Uhuru* was achieved; it was now necessary to spell out what *Uhuru na Kazi* (Freedom and Work) would mean. During August and September, Cabinet members toured the districts explaining the objectives of a new *Three Year Plan* and promulgating the slogans *Uhuru na Kazi* and *Uhuru na Jasho* (Freedom and Sweat). But the issues which dominated attention revolved around the place of non-Africans in the new Tanganyika. Economic demands were couched in terms of equalization of income among the races. The racialism that was manifested was largely an expression of frustration and discontent associated with the depressed economic condition of Africans relative to Asians and Europeans.

It was in this context that government's proposals for Tanganyikan citizenship were published and discussed in October 1961. One of the provisions of the Citizenship Bill was that anyone who was a citizen of a Commonwealth country and had lived in Tanganyika for a period of five years would be eligible to obtain citizenship by registration after Decem-

[7] Bennett, *op.cit.*   [8] Taylor, *op.cit.*, p. 203.

ber 9, 1961—Independence Day. This provision provoked anti-Commonwealth and racialistic sentiments among TANU members in the National Assembly.[9] One MP, who was to become both a regional commissioner and a parliamentary secretary, said:

> I think 75 per cent of the non-African population still regard an African in Tanganyika as an inferior human being. Why is it so? It is because the white population has been dominating us, both economically and politically, and their neighbours, the Asians, have been economically dominating us, we Africans. . . . Do you think the individual African forming the vast majority of the population will agree to have equal rights with the Europeans and Asians? My answer is no. . . . All foreigners who are living in Tanganyika now and have transferred their money to their home countries or to other countries should within this period of five years bring their money back. I repeat . . . they must bring it back. From now on those foreigners who are rich . . . should contribute at least 15 per cent of their money to us, the Tanganyika National Fund.[10]

Other MPs expressed similar sentiments.[11]

Earlier in October 1961, many of the men who were later

[9] Debate on the Citizenship Bill can be found in *Tanganyika Assembly Debate, Hansard,* 36th Session, 5th meeting, September 17-18, 1961, columns 303-20, 324-74.

[10] This peroration was cut short by the speaker after Mr. John Mwakangale claimed that "they are bluffing us, cheating us, doing all sorts of things showing that they are our friends—but I know . . ." Mr. Nyerere rose in reply to say: "There cannot be a bigger difference between the speakers [for others took a similar line] and this Government here. Discrimination against human beings because of their color is exactly what we have been fighting against." These remarks were published in Leys, *op.cit.,* pp. 260-61. They are found in the *Tanganyika Assembly Debates, op.cit.,* pp. 329ff.

[11] National Assembly members Tumbo, Msindai, Mtaki, and Wambura expressed similar opinions. Msindai was to become an area commissioner in 1962. Mtaki and Wambura became regional commissioners and are now junior ministers.

to speak up in the National Assembly attacked the government's and Nyerere's position in the NEC.[12] They persisted with these attacks in another NEC meeting of January 1962, during which Nyerere made up his mind to resign. (He was to say in January that he first considered resigning in October 1961, after the National Assembly debates.[13])

By then, the pressure from middle-level leaders—regional/district secretaries and chairmen, MPs, MNE, administrative secretaries in National Headquarters, and trade union leaders—had become very great. When the Citizenship Bill was presented to the National Assembly in October 1961, Nyerere said he would resign unless he carried the House with him. Under this threat, the Bill was carried overwhelmingly, but dissidence was not ended within TANU over racial issues which fed on economic imbalances. Throughout the last two months of 1961 unrest persisted, and Asians were periodically threatened in various parts of Tanganyika. The TANU leaders, busy during these months in trying to master their new government jobs, were out of touch with the middle-level leaders and the rank and file. When the NEC was again convened in January 1962, it had the air of an emergency meeting.[14]

According to one account, when Nyerere went to the NEC he wanted to convince it to open TANU to non-Africans.[15] If this is true, he must have been very much out of touch with NEC sentiments, which had already been expressed at the October meetings. But perhaps Nyerere had been overly reassured by his ultimate carrying of the day on the Citizenship Bill. Instead of obtaining the opening of TANU to non-Afri-

[12] *Spearhead*, November 1961, p. 2.

[13] Leys, *op.cit.*, p. 262; Helen Kitchen, "Why Did Julius Nyerere Resign?" *Africa Report*, VII (February 1962), 7.

[14] See William Friedland, "Tanganyika's Rashidi Kawawa," *Africa Report*, VII (February 1962), 7-8.

[15] This was later done by a decree of the NEC and subsequent approval by the Annual Conference in 1963.

cans, which was the only way of actually giving equal political rights to non-Africans, Nyerere once again faced demands for an end to the prominent role of non-Africans in Tanganyika. These demands were put in terms of calling for the abolition of reserved seats for minorities in the National Assembly; a demand for more rapid Africanization of the civil service, and the establishment of a republic—this last aimed at decreasing British influence and struck at the symbol of connection with Britain; a demand for faster development (understood by some to mean Africanization of economic life), and for a more centrally directed attempt at economic and social change. Cases of alleged discrimination against Africans were discussed during the NEC meetings. The first of a number of expulsions was announced on the first day of the NEC meeting.[16] Nyerere announced his intention of resigning on the second day, and the meeting accepted his decision on the fifth day.[17]

Nyerere was not forced to resign; in fact he had to persuade the NEC to accept his decision, and called a special session of the elders to explain his decision.[18] Nyerere was able to appoint his successor, Rashidi Kawawa, TANU Vice President and Minister for Local Government. Kawawa referred to Nyerere as "the commander in chief." "We are his troops. He is the Father of the Nation to whom we will continue to go for advice."[19] Kawawa's appointment was not a concession to the trade unionists who had been putting forward

[16] Apparently before the NEC met, Nyerere signed expulsion orders for 1 Swiss and 4 British subjects accused of racial discrimination. In at least two cases, high government officials were involved in making accusations: Mr. Namfua, a trade union leader who became parliamentary secretary, and Sheikh Abedi, Mayor of Dar es Salaam and later a regional commissioner, subsequently a minister.

[17] Leys, *op.cit.*, p. 263.

[18] In October 1961, Nyerere called the elders to hear him out in the controversy over citizenship. Bennett, *op.cit.*, p. 29; *Spearhead*, November 1961, p. 2.

[19] Taylor, *op.cit.*, p. 228, citing *African Daily News*, Salisbury, February 2, 1962, p. 10.

demands for more rapid Africanization and couching these demands in racist language. To many of them he was a pariah because he argued for cooperation with government and for moderation of the demands for Africanization.

However, if Kawawa's appointment was not itself a concession, Nyerere did make concessions. At Kawawa's first press conference, he confirmed that the NEC had requested the government to initiate steps towards making Tanganyika a republic.[20] Nyerere had not seemed in a hurry to do this.[21] While Kawawa insisted that Tanganyika would not leave the Commonwealth and that racial tolerance would continue to be a guiding principle,[22] there were further expulsions of Europeans.[23]

When Nyerere resigned, he said he would devote himself to full-time work in TANU. In his announcement of resignation, he called attention to the need for an able, elected government which would have the full support and cooperation of the people:

> It is also necessary to have a strong political organization active in every village, which acts like a two-way all-weather road along which the purposes, plans and problems of government can travel to the people at the same time as the ideas, desires and misunderstandings of the

[20] *Ibid.*, p. 229.   [21] Leys, *op.cit.*, p. 264.
[22] Kitchen, *loc.cit.*

[23] The then Minister of Home Affairs, Oscar Kambona, was not very convincing when he replied to a question in the National Assembly as to whether full verificatory procedures had been used in the investigation of the alleged discriminations. Another concession was the resignation of Sir Ernest Vasey, former Kenya Minister of Finance, who had been invited by Nyerere to come to Tanganyika as Finance Minister. Vasey was dropped from the Cabinet on the grounds that he was not eligible to become a Tanganyikan citizen. Being a Kenyan European was certainly one factor against him. (Derek Bryceson, another European but from Tanganyika, and Amir Jamal, an Asian, were retained in the Cabinet.) Vasey was regarded as conservative on economic affairs and represented continued European influence in the Tanganyika economy.

people can travel direct to government. This is the job of the new TANU.[24]

Nyerere saw the need to restore top-level contact with the people and with the TANU district and provincial organizations—contact which had become slight while TANU leaders were occupied with their ministries. He recognized that government could not put across its development program without efficient local TANU organizations, and he could not rely on middle-level leaders as intermediaries. Another important consideration was that, in turning to TANU, Nyerere could postpone a direct clash with opponents both in the NEC and in the Tanganyika Federation of Labour. At all costs, he wanted to avoid splitting TANU and forcing opposition elements into making common cause with the existing splinter parties. There was a real danger that just this might happen, because the feelings dissident TANU members were expressing differed little from those of Mtemvu and the ANC.[25]

Though the controversy within TANU went very deep, the party did not split. TANU retained the loyalty of its middle-level leaders for a number of reasons: Nyerere commanded a great deal of personal loyalty from the very men who opposed him on racial questions; and Nyerere was willing to discuss these opposing views in the NEC. One of the most important functions of the NEC was, and is, its "safety-valve" function. Thus, the TANU leadership remained solid. If factions emerged among the top leaders at this time, they never came to light.

I have recounted this episode in some length because it revealed a pattern which was to recur on other occasions between 1961 and 1965.[26] Nyerere would propose; the NEC

[24] *Kenya Weekly News* (Nakuru), January 26, 1962, p. 6. Also Tanganyika Information Services, Press Release, January 23, 1962, cited by Bates, *loc.cit.*, p. 431.

[25] The publicity secretary of the ANC, a Kenyan, was expelled from Tanganyika for exploiting racial differences. Taylor, *op.cit.*, p. 202.

[26] In 1963, MPs strongly opposed a bill to make men responsible

would resist; Nyerere would compromise rather than risk splitting TANU. Nor would he try to purge TANU of those who opposed him. When he resigned as Prime Minister and "returned to TANU," he traveled throughout the country making speeches; but he never stayed in any district long enough to alter its organization. He did not threaten the National Executive members or the members of the National Assembly who had opposed him. Quite the contrary, many of these men became junior ministers in 1963-64. Nyerere did not try to achieve a uniformity of views within TANU. Nor did he try to mobilize the Central Committee against the NEC.

On the other hand, the challenge of the middle-level leaders was not pushed to the extent that Nyerere's resignation was called for, although pressure from NEC members and MPs was indeed a challenge to Nyerere's authority—whether or not it was intended as such. But given the solidarity at the top of TANU, middle-level leaders were not willing to risk their own positions by making common cause with splinter groups. Furthermore, they were convinced that a unified TANU was essential for modernizing Tanganyika. And they were committed to Nyerere as the leader of TANU. (There has never been a serious possibility of replacing Nyerere by a TANU electoral process.[27])

Thus Nyerere's position as President of TANU was revealed in 1961-62 to be that of the unchallenged leader but not the leader unchallengeable. Furthermore, 1961-62 revealed a gap between Nyerere and the middle-level leaders who operated in central TANU institutions, the NEC, and the Tanganyika Parliamentary Party.[28]

Nyerere offered disgruntled TANU middle-level leaders the

---

for the illegitimate children they sired, although the bill was eventually pushed through after the NEC was persuaded.

[27] I do not include the possibility of a coup such as the army mutiny of 1964 threatened to become (see chap. xii).

[28] The National Assembly was, in effect, the Tanganyika Parliamentary Party since all but one member was under the TANU whip.

possibility of reinvigorating TANU's—and thus their own—position when he resigned from his government post. At the same time he was emphasizing his own commitment to TANU. Nyerere did not wish his resignation to be interpreted as his recognition of a distinction between TANU and government. Yet some were making this distinction.[29] Nyerere's own desire to avoid drawing this distinction makes it misleading to say that he saw the dissension in the NEC as a challenge to the authority of the government's Cabinet.[30] Nyerere had said, and would say again, that since TANU had formed the government, the NEC was the policy-making organ in Tanganyika. He did not labor this point precisely because he led a TANU government. The challenge was a challenge to the top leaders by middle-level leaders located in the NEC. Nyerere's resignation would have led to a crisis if he had seen a dichotomy between TANU and government: he no longer held a government post but would be consulted on every major issue. His resignation would have undermined the Cabinet's authority if he had not seen government as the TANU government which worked within the ultimate authority of the NEC and the Annual Conference. On a day-to-day basis, ministers have to be free to make their decisions. But many of these ministers are members of the TANU Central Committee. Nyerere has never come out for Cabinet autonomy vis-à-vis the NEC.

One problem for Nyerere was that not all the middle-level leaders in the national TANU bodies and not all the regional and district middle-level leaders could be given government jobs. A gap was opening up between full-time paid TANU

[29] One reporter wrote that Nyerere made up his mind to resign when members of the NEC began to talk of what government rather than party should do during the January 1962 meetings of the NEC. Clyde Sanger, "The Changing Face of Tanganyika," *Africa Report*, VII (July 1962), 3.

[30] Ronald Segal, *African Profiles* (Baltimore: Penguin Books, 1962) has posed the crisis as one of Cabinet versus NEC.

officials of regional, district, and National Headquarters organizations and the TANU-elected chairmen of district and regional organizations, on the one hand, and those TANU people who had moved into government posts as MPs or ministers and junior ministers, on the other. As we shall see, a major step was taken when regional and district TANU secretaries became regional and area commissioners—heads of government in their respective regions and districts. The person who received a government post benefited from the salary and prestige that went with it. But not all the middle-level TANU leaders could get the fruits of independence. Thus, a racial and economic dissatisfaction existed that could be exploited by individual middle-level leaders, including those who had received government positions.

The NEC and the TANU National Conference

The category "middle-level" leaders is a very broad one. The NEC and the National Conference, made up of both middle-level leaders and the inner ruling group, are national TANU organs with a strong preponderance of regional/district representatives. Thus it is during the meetings of the NEC and the National Conference (referred to before 1965 as the Annual Conference) that middle-level leaders who operate in the regions, the districts, and in Dar es Salaam have a chance to confront their national leaders as a group. As we have just seen, these confrontations are not marked by docility on the part of the middle-level leaders.

Observers have paid much more attention to the NEC than to the Annual Conference, because it has been assumed that the NEC is where TANU "makes" its decisions. The Annual Conference was described as the "sovereignty of TANU" because its constitutional functions are to approve, amend, or reject the policy and program of TANU as drafted by the NEC, and to approve the functional report of TANU. It was supposed to confirm or amend the decisions carried out by the

169

NEC, but was usually dismissed as being too weak and un-
wieldy a body to be involved meaningfully in discussion,
much less in policy-making.[31] This assumption was not entirely correct. Although the Annual Conference delegated its
power to the NEC between its own meetings, and although it
confirmed the NEC's decisions, the meetings of the Annual
Conference were themselves important and not very different from those of the NEC. Its significance is manifested in
the calibre of its debates, the kinds of speeches leaders directed to it, and the qualifications for membership.

In the past, two kinds of delegates attended the Annual
Conference: those elected specifically for the Conference,
and *ex officio* delegates. The elected delegates were from the
districts and affiliated organizations. The TANU Constitution
had not specified a limit to the number of delegates to be
elected from each district. In 1964, all the area chairmen of
TANU came to the Annual Conference, along with two elected
delegates per district. In 1965, the area chairmen did not
come. Each TANU district annual conference elected two representatives to the Territorial Annual Conference. (At one
time, the Elders and the Women's Sections elected a representative to the Annual Conference,[32] but they no longer do
so.) Along with these elected members, all the members of
the NEC came as *ex officio* members. Associated organizations
like NUTA usually sent the same delegates to the Annual Conference that they sent to the NEC.

In 1965, after the Presidential Commission's Report was
amended by a joint sitting of the TANU and ASP National
Executives, a new TANU National Conference came into being. The National Conference now meets every two years instead of annually. Its membership categories have been al-

[31] Bates, in Carter, *op.cit.*, p. 452. George, *loc.cit.*
[32] The original TANU Constitution called for the branch where the
Territorial Annual Conference was to be held to elect a Women's
and Elder's representative. Now the Conference is always held in Dar
es Salaam.

tered, but the basic dichotomy between members elected to the Conference and *ex officio* members remains. (See Table 9.)

TABLE 9

Membership in the National Conference

The President, Vice President, Secretary General, and National Treasurer.

2 elected delegates from each district (120 members).

All Members of Parliament (including 107 elected members, 15 appointed members, 17 regional commissioners who are *ex officio* MPs, and the members of the Zanzibar Revolutionary Council).a

17 regional chairmen.

60 district chairmen.

60 district secretaries.b

17 members of the National Executive Committee elected by the National Conference.

Members of the Central Committee appointed by the President (usually around 10 to 15 people).c

One delegate from each affiliate organization.

---

a MPs are a new category. They have the right to vote at the National Conference and they constitute a Standing Committee of the Conference, replacing the old Tanganyika Parliamentary Party and its 4 representatives to the Annual Conference. At the first meeting of the National Conference after its redesignation, 3 Zanzibar regional commissioners and the members of the Zanzibar Revolutionary Council came. Since the members of the Zanzibar Revolutionary Council are members of the Tanzanian Parliament, they can attend the National Conference; but since they are not TANU members, they cannot vote.

b Without a vote.

c Without a vote.

Total membership in the National Conference is more than 400 people. In the past, a little over 100 had voting rights; now over 300 can vote. However, it is not clear that voting rights are important. Non-voting members could always participate in discussions and exert influence; and most

171

issues were decided by determining a "sense of the meeting" rather than by taking a vote. (The election of regional members for the NEC was the one issue where a vote was always taken.[33]) Today voting rights matter even less because the Conference has been turned into a much larger, congress-like body which is primarily a forum for the leaders, and serves to confirm decisions already made elsewhere. This was true to some extent before the National Conference was created. Any TANU member could come as an observer to the Annual Conference. At the opening of the 1965 Annual Conference on March 4, thousands of people thronged the Msimbazi Community Center to hear President Nyerere open the Conference; members of the ASP and representatives of the various liberation movements which make their home in Dar es Salaam attended as "official observers"; members of the diplomatic corps and private citizens also came. Obviously policy was not being made in front of all these people. The President used the Annual Conference as a forum from which to make important statements on foreign policy,[34] and to warn TANU leaders who were abusing their positions. In the afternoon, the participants, including non-Tanganyikans who were officially recognized observers, broke up into committees to discuss questions of health, education, and economic development. The committees functioned to inform members of official policy, and to encourage support for proposed initiatives, rather than to frame policy.

The Annual Conference served to acquaint delegates with new TANU procedures and to inform them if the existing procedures were not being complied with. In 1963 for example,

[33] After the first session of the National Conference, the Conference became an electoral conference which was attended by delegates from the ASP and which selected the candidates for the presidential election. The NEC selected the candidates for the parliamentary election.

[34] Relations with West Germany reached a crisis over the establishment of an East German Consulate in Dar es Salaam. American-Tanzanian relations were also reviewed. *Tanganyika Standard*, March 5, 1965, pp. 1, 4.

the Secretary General had to spend a good deal of time—necessitated by confusion and misunderstanding—explaining to delegates that election of district, regional, and village leaders ought to take place at the same time for each level of election. Leaders stressed that these elections should be carried out by secret ballot, and that the time of office would be the same for all leaders.

The agenda for the March 1965 Annual Conference was determined by the NEC which met directly before the Annual Conference. The March Conference passed a number of resolutions to the effect that individuals should use 5 per cent of their income to buy government bonds; government should seek all possible ways and means of exploiting more fully the wealth of the country; the words and thoughts of every Tanganyikan citizen should be guided by TANU regulations because these were the foundation of the nation. And a resolution was passed which established a committee to look into the conduct of TANU members. This particular Conference is reminiscent of a Soviet Communist Party Congress, where the leaders use the Congress as a sounding board and as a way of educating delegates to government policy; but the minutes of other Annual Conference meetings convey quite a different impression.

Not all the Conference meetings were large and public; some were confined to the official delegates. The Annual Conference would be convened at a time of crisis, as it was after the mutiny of the army in January 1964.[35] The minutes that I have seen of the NEC and the Annual Conference are quite similar, both in the kinds of topics discussed and in the approach. Questioning of ministers on government policy and practice was wide ranging in both bodies; both have taken up the question of the speed and extent of Africanization, the poor quality of some local leaders, the problem of TANU finances, and the relations of government to TANU.

---

[35] The Annual Conference was disrupted when the mutiny broke out. It was reconvened a month later.

173

TANU delegates have proposed that government contribute money for TANU salaries (Nyerere opposed this as being self-consideration). In the January 1963 Annual Conference, members raised complaints that the government was being too difficult in giving out loans to TANU farmers.[36] This same question had been raised in the July-August 1962 meeting of the NEC, when the operation of the Agricultural Credit Agency came up for discussion.

Since the Annual Conference was usually convened just after the NEC meeting, there was a great deal of continuity between them.[37] (Now that the National Conference meets every two years, this will not be possible.) The Annual Conference did not question the work of the NEC, in part this was because their memberships overlapped. Also the NEC was not thought to be responsible for formulating government policy, despite the claims of ministers that it was a policy-making organ. However, the Annual Conference and the NEC made ministers and parliamentary secretaries defend their policies before them. If a minister or a parliamentary secretary was not a member of the TANU bodies, he could be called before them.

Cabinet members or their junior ministers handled questions much as if they were on the floor of the National Assembly during question time. While some of the questioning was irrelevant, some was critical and useful. One minister said: "Don't underrate the delegates to the Annual Conference; they are often businessmen or farmers and have a serious concern with economic matters."[38] Evidence of this con-

---

[36] I have been able to look at minutes of the Annual Conference meeting that took place at Msimbazi Community Center in Dar es Salaam, January 1963, and minutes of various NEC meetings and Central Committee meetings. Many of the above topics were also discussed at Central Committee meetings.

[37] There is no fixed date for convening the Annual Conference. The place and time are fixed by the National Executive. The Secretary General notifies all branches of TANU two months before the date fixed.

[38] Interview with Nsilo Swai, TANU National Treasurer and a Cabinet Minister, April 1965.

cern can be found in the minutes: while most concerns are specific, they are not necessarily parochial; often they appear in various places throughout Tanganyika (for example, the question of what is government's program for the farming of cotton and tobacco). General questions concerning agricultural matters were promptly answered by the parliamentary secretary to the Ministry of Agriculture; to more technical questions—default on loans, for example—he might reply that the matter should be put to government, or to village, regional, or district development committees for consideration.

Surprisingly enough, the Annual Conference was not dominated by the *ex officio* members. The January 1963 minutes show that during one long meeting as many as 40 people raised their voices from the floor, only 13 of whom were members of both the NEC and the Annual Conference; many were merely district delegates to the Conference; some were TANU district chairmen as well as district delegates. There was no difference in the tone or content of the questions asked by NEC members and district representatives; outspoken "backbenchers" appeared in both groups. This is less likely to be the case in the future. The recent changes in the Annual (now National) Conference will work to distinguish the NEC and the National Conference. Debate and questioning will fall to the NEC, and the Conference will confirm and legitimate, and will be used as a forum. It is unlikely that the National Conference will be a place where middle-level leaders can confront ministers and TANU Cabinet members.

The NEC itself has been variously described as the "soul and conscience of the Party,"[39] the "political power station"[40] of Tanzania, and the policy-making organ of TANU. Insofar as TANU organs make policy, the NEC, rather than the National Conference or the Central Committee or National

[39] *Presidential Report*, pp. 16-17.
[40] Clyde Sanger "Tanzania's Presidential Commission Report," *East Africa Journal* (June 1965), p. 21. Sanger said the NEC is being established as the national power station.

175

Headquarters, is the place where important TANU decisions are made. However, it does not follow that most of the day-to-day decisions about governing Tanganyika are taken in the NEC. In fact, policy for the TANU government is usually made by the President in consultation with key ministers; rarely does the Cabinet as a whole play an important role. Important ministers sometimes speak out without presidential approval, feeling perhaps that they are expressing the sentiment of the NEC, even if they have had no formal consultation with it.[41]

It was in the NEC and the Annual Conference rather than in the Central Committee that the issues surrounding the place of non-Africans in Tanganyika were thrashed out. The decision to admit non-Africans to TANU was made in the NEC and then ratified by the Annual Conference. Similarly, the resolution that Tanganyika should become a one-party state was first passed by the NEC in January 1963 and then approved by the Annual Conference at its sitting a few days later. This has been the pattern: the NEC agrees and the Annual Conference ratifies. And in this sense, the NEC is the place where important decisions are taken. But TANU and government policy rarely originate in the NEC. Rather, TANU government leaders bring to it formulated policies for approval. If resistance is met, the leaders will try to persuade the NEC; they may even drop an issue entirely rather than push against the NEC. And yet to my knowledge, when the NEC has rejected a policy put to it, it has never put forward an alternate policy of its own. The chief function of the NEC, therefore, is to veto or approve proposals; it can also force leaders to postpone or modify their policies. But it does not propose and establish its own policies.[42]

[41] E.g., when Oscar Kambona condemned American policy in Tanzania on the basis of what appeared to be forged documents and President Nyerere took a markedly different tone.

[42] These judgments are based on interviews with members of the NEC. Most NEC members I spoke with said that the NEC "made"

A given NEC meeting often considered a whole range of important domestic issues in Tanganyika, although prior to 1965 it had little to do with economic planning per se, and has never been deeply involved with foreign policy issues.[43] (See Table 10.)

TABLE 10

Agenda for NEC *Meeting of January 10, 1963*

1. To read and approve the minutes of previous meetings.
2. Consider matters arising from the minutes.
3. Hear the report from the Secretary General.
4. Hear reports from various departments: the Elders, the Women's Section, Youth League, Publicity.
5. The relationship between TANU and the government to be discussed.
6. The government being disrespected for consideration.
7. The picture of the President's garb for consideration.
8. Problem of lack of food in the country to be discussed.
9. The selling of food in Tanganyika.
10. Life members.
11. Disgraceful games and dances which undermine the reputation of the nation.
12. Permanent secretaries and administrative secretaries of ministries.
13. Difficulties of school children getting into standard IX.
14. Misappropriation of finances.
15. Difficulties in obtaining scholarships.
16. According respect to Tanganyikans.
17. Dissatisfaction with magistrates.
18. Difficulties with European settled farms.
19. Financial statement.

The NEC is composed of the top central TANU officials—the President, Vice President, Secretary General, and Treas-

policy. But as the interviews proceeded, it became clear that they meant the NEC must agree to policy or at least not overtly oppose it.

[43] When foreign policy issues reach crisis proportions, the NEC may give the government, and Nyerere personally, a vote of confidence. It did this in 1965 when relations with West Germany had reached a crisis over the status to be accorded East Germany. But on the whole, TANU organs do not become involved in foreign policy, which is left to the President and the Ministry of Foreign Affairs. At present, TANU has no division of foreign affairs in its secretariat.

urer—the members of the Central Committee appointed by the President, and top regional officials—MNE, regional chairmen and secretaries. One delegate from each of the affiliate organizations and two delegates from the TANU Youth League are also included. The new TANU Constitution added the Secretary General of NUTA, the Principal Secretary to the President, a civil servant, and the Attorney General or Solicitor General, provided they are members of TANU.[44]

A critical question is whether the NEC functions as a national body vis-à-vis local, district, and regional TANU organizations, or is itself primarily a body dominated by regional leaders who put forward regional interests vis-à-vis elected and appointed TANU officials at the center. In other words, is the NEC really analogous to a Communist Party Central Committee, which is primarily a mechanism for central control rather than a forum for regional interests?

Regions are not entities to which people have strong attachments. And there are neither strong regional party organizations which dominate the countryside,[45] nor powerful regional TANU leaders who come to the center and operate there. However, TANU dissidents did make themselves heard in the National Assembly and the NEC in 1961-62. The outspoken backbenchers in the National Assembly included not only elected members of the NEC, but also regional secretaries of TANU.[46] Thus, Nyerere was faced with opposition

[44] Without vote are: members of the Central Committee, the regional secretaries, the Principal Secretary to the President, and the Attorney General.

[45] This will become clearer in chaps. x and xi when implementation of the *Five Year Plan* is discussed.

[46] Of the 50 African MPs in 1960, there were 4 provincial and 5 district TANU officials. Thirteen members of the Central Committee, plus 4 TANU Cabinet members were also MPs. (Lowenkoph, *op.cit.*) At the end of 1961 only one regional chairman was an MP, and only one MNE was an MP; 2 regional secretaries were MPs. In 1962, however, 5 regional commissioners were MPs after one regional chairman who was an MP became a regional commissioner and after

from his appointed members on the NEC as well as from elected ones in the National Assembly and the NEC. This is not very surprising in view of the relative lack of differentiation between regional-appointed and regional-elected TANU officials in 1961-62. The regional secretaries after all had representative functions; they could not succeed without the support of their local organizations. But we do not have to argue that the TANU activists in the regions and districts were pressuring them; they had the same biases, values, complaints as the regional TANU organizations they headed.

One commentator on Tanganyika at the end of 1961 grouped the regional officials together when he observed that Tanganyika regional officials were unhappy with the size of their representation in the National Assembly and identified with spokesmen for "radical" discontent.[47] Another has implied that appointed officials were agents of the center while elected officials made demands on the center.[48] I have sug-

---

2 more MPs were appointed regional commissioners.

Special Acts of Parliament have made MPs eligible for appointment as commissioners. Of the first 56 appointments for area commissioners, 3 were MPs; 5 of the 11 first regional commissioners were MPs. In March 1965, 10 out of 17 regional commissioners were MPs and 5 out of 60 area commissioners were MPs.

Between 1962 and 1965, over one-half of the regional commissioners and about 10 per cent of the area commissioners have been MPs at any one time.

[47] Martin Lowenkopf, "Outlook for Tanganyika," *Africa Report*, VI (December 1961), 6.

[48] Colin Leys, *loc.cit.*, stated that before independence, TANU's primary function was to mobilize support for *Uhuru Kamili* (complete independence). At this time, central officials and appointed regional and district officials fed out information and organized TANU membership drives. TANU activity centered around organizational questions. After independence, policy questions came to the fore and thus the elected officials within TANU were strengthened since they were supported to make policy and the appointed officials were supposed to administer it. The TANU Constitution does stipulate this by denying the right to vote to appointed officials on the NEC. The pressure Nyerere faced at the end of 1961 and the beginning of 1962 is ex-

gested that appointed officials also pressured the center and that the ostensibly central organ—the NEC—became the battleground for a confrontation between dissidents and leaders. But the problem cannot be so easily resolved in favor of a regional/national dichotomy.

For one thing, while it is true that some of the most outspoken dissidents in 1961-62 were regional commissioners, their views were shared by officials at National Headquarters in Dar es Salaam. Representatives elected to the NEC from the associated organizations and the Tanganyika Parliamentary Party (TPP) also put forward "extreme" Africanist demands on citizenship and economic issues.[49] For another thing, there was no specifically regional content to any demands: regional leaders neither presented themselves as regional leaders facing the center nor did they make specific demands for their region.

Thus, neither the "regional/central" nor the "elected/appointed" distinctions explain TANU dissent in 1961-62. What does explain it is the distinction between middle-level and high-level leaders. Elected and appointed middle-level leaders at both the center and the regions wanted higher status, more material benefits, and more security. Regional officials pressured to become MPS, and MPS were made commissioners; TANU secretaries wanted to become elected as well as appointed officials, and elected chairmen wanted to become commissioners.

Membership in the National Assembly gave status to commissioners despite the relative insignificance of that body itself. For regional chairmen and MNE it meant getting a higher

---

plained by the increase in the scope of elected officials as policy questions dominated over questions about administration of TANU.

[49] An example of a party "bureaucrat" who was a dissident was Roland Mwanjisi, editor of the TANU paper *Uhuru* and TANU Publicity Secretary, later a parliamentary secretary. Examples of elected representatives from associated or integral institutions include Peter Siyolvelwa, area commissioner and TPP delegate.

salary. As it turned out, the strong-minded, outspoken men who did not push things to a break with TANU had the best chance of moving up. Many of the dissidents were made parliamentary secretaries,[50] and found themselves defending the government policies they had once assaulted. Furthermore, most of the attacks on government from regional leaders came before commissioners were appointed. We can conjecture that the TANU center hoped to make the NEC a more reliable organ by making the secretaries into commissioners, thus changing their own attitudes and giving them the possibility of entering government themselves. These government heads of regions would owe their appointment to central leaders, and their attitudes would be tempered by ministerial considerations and made more responsible by their new perspectives and contacts.

If the regional secretaries had been truly disciplined agents of the center in 1961, and if they had dominated their regional organizations, they would have been able to dominate the NEC and make it a pliable tool of the center. But this was not the case. Perhaps then, central leaders hoped that one of the main by-products of instituting commissioners would be to turn the NEC into a central TANU organ. For although the decision to have commissioners must have been taken before the opposition in the National Assembly and the NEC came into the open in October 1961 and January 1962, central leaders knew that the NEC was not controlled by the

[50] The center has been anxious to give an increasing number of men experience in Dar es Salaam in ministerial work and then to move them to the regions as commissioners. The jobs are on a par in salary and are equivalent in rank. By moving commissioners to the center, the ministries are, hopefully, infused with first-hand knowledge of the regions. When parliamentary secretaries become commissioners they can bring the authority of a ministerial post and the prestige of close contact with central leaders to their regional posts. Although the ranks are on a par, many people do prefer to live in Dar es Salaam or travel abroad as junior ministers. But there has been a readier acceptance by TANU officials to go back "up-country" than in other African counties.

TANU center. It could be influenced and at times even dominated by central leaders—Nyerere in particular—but it was not a pliable instrument of the TANU center. One way to make it more amenable to TANU's national leaders was to advance middle-level leaders in status and material benefits. This could not be done for all middle-level leaders because a small pie could be sliced just so many ways. Thus district TANU chairmen and area commissioners have not done as well as regional chairmen, MNE, and regional commissioners. But it was primarily the regional leaders who were most vocal, and, by virtue of their membership in the NEC, in a position to be difficult. Giving them a position in government has had an effect similar to making vocal backbenchers into parliamentary secretaries. The meetings of the NEC and the Annual Conference after 1963 still show independent questioning, but there is general deference to ministers and TANU Cabinet members. Questions on delicate subjects—for example, government loans to farmers, the number of new schools being built—may be raised, but they are not usually pressed.

The dissident middle-level leaders were well aware of the scarcity of trained personnel and knew that they could not easily be replaced. Furthermore, an MP or a regional chairman had a base which was not subject to assault by the center; even regional secretaries could count on tolerance for their views. There was little fear of being purged by Nyerere because this was not the way he operated. When Nyerere "returned to TANU" at the beginning of 1962, he did not occupy himself with the reorganization or restaffing of the districts, regions, or National Headquarters. Within ten months, he was elected President of Tanganyika, and—given the state of TANU's organization at National Headquarters and the lack of close control over regional and district organizations —could not possibly have carried out any purge.

Since 1961-62, there have been no issues which created such an intra-TANU crisis as those racial/economic issues which concerned the place of non-Africans in Tanganyika and the pace of Africanization. These issues have reared their heads from time to time since then—we shall meet them again in connection with the army mutiny of 1964—but have been partially superseded by questions of economic development. These economic questions have been largely removed from the day-to-day considerations of middle-level leaders and all but a few top leaders who decide about them in conjunction with their foreign advisers. Because the middle-level leaders have been isolated from economic decision-making (at least until 1966), and because these leaders are less insecure as they gain experience, racial issues have for the most part been successfully separated from economic issues. After all, these issues *are* linked in Tanzania. But their relationship has been kept in perspective: racial tensions have not been allowed to dominate economic decisions. As we shall see, there has been some opposition to economic policies; but on the whole, the central government machinery has monopolized consideration of economic issues largely through its expertise which depends on its ability to call on experts from abroad.

New concerns have arisen over foreign policy and the Union of Tanganyika and Zanzibar. On foreign policy issues there is little discussion beyond the highest levels of the TANU government. The relation of the two parts of the United Republic, Zanzibar and mainland Tanganyika, has affected the evolution of TANU but, as far as I know, has not created a crisis situation in the NEC.[51]

Nor has the issue of East African Federation created a problem for TANU's leadership as it has in Uganda and Kenya where backbenchers and middle-level leaders have been outspokenly critical of their leaders' failure to negotiate an East African Federation. Nyerere has taken a staunchly pro-Federation stance, even though many of the policies Tanzania

[51] See chaps. xii and xiii.

has carried out have worked to lessen the chances for Federation.[52] The middle-level leaders have also been rhetorically committed to Federation; but they have espoused an economic nationalism and a more militant, ideologically "socialist" position on domestic and foreign affairs than Kenya and Uganda are willing to accept.[53]

It is in this realm—of ideology and style—that the middle-level leaders have differed from Nyerere personally. But no clear distinction between middle-level and high-level leaders as such can be made here, because many of the most important TANU leaders are closer to middle-level leaders than to Nyerere when it comes to ideology and political style— though not necessarily when it comes to making hard choices on concrete issues. (I will explore these differences in ideology in the next chapter.)

The important point here is that the NEC is not a tool which can be easily manipulated by Nyerere or other high-

[52] Ali Mazrui, "Tanzania Versus East Africa," *Journal of Commonwealth Political Studies*, III (November 1965), 209-25 has argued that Tanzania has in fact worked against East African Federation, albeit unconsciously.

[53] Middle-level leaders have been much less enthusiastic about Federation in the past than many now claim to be. In 1960, Nyerere declared his willingness to ". . . postpone the celebration of Tanganyika's independence for a few months and celebrate East Africa's independence in 1962 rather than risk perpetuating the Balkanization of East Africa." (Julius Nyerere, "Freedom and Unity," *Transition*, IV [1964], 48.)

Though Nyerere expounded a strategy which would have led to Tanganyika pulling the other East African countries up to *its* early date of independence and not really delaying Tanganyika's own date, his declaration produced a storm within TANU. The fear of a Kenya-dominated East African Federation was still strong whether the Kenya in consideration was to be white-settler dominated or not. For Kenya had better-educated middle-level and Cabinet-level leaders, and by virtue of its more developed economy could be expected to have the greatest weight in an East African Federation. It has been reported that Oscar Kambona fought against the dissidents in the NEC in 1960 when Nyerere was abroad. See *Vigilance Africa*, I (December 1964), 2.

level TANU leaders. On a central question concerning TANU's evolution, the NEC rejected Nyerere's proposal that candidates be allowed to run under a TANU rubric without any preselection process by the party. This never became an issue because Nyerere had no support, even among high-level TANU leaders, and he never confronted TANU with a choice between his person and his idea.[54]

The Central Committee and the National Headquarters

When Nyerere faced opposition in the NEC, he could not call on the TANU Central Committee and the National Headquarters for support, even though the Central Committee is composed of several high-ranking TANU officers and presidential appointees. The newest Central Committee, appointed in October 1965, included the President, Vice President, Secretary General, and Treasurer, *ex officio*. The Financial Secretary and the Deputy Secretary General of TANU were appointed, not *ex officio*, members. Table 11 shows that many Central Committee members hold high government positions.

Thus, 3 of the 9 appointed members and all 4 of the *ex officio* members hold high government posts.[55] The President

[54] See chaps. VI, VII.

[55] In the previous Central Committee (1964) there were 19 members. Nyerere, Kawawa, Kambona, and Swai were on it in *ex officio* capacities, and they all held high government posts. The then Deputy Secretary General was John Nzunda who was also a junior minister. Both he and Bhoke-Munanka, the Financial Secretary and a minister for state were on the Central Committee. Three other ministers were members: Sheikh Amri Abedi, who died in October 1964; T. Tewa, who became an ambassador and lost his seat on the Central Committee; and M. Kamaliza. There were 4 junior ministers: Bibi Titi, Lucy Lameck (another Women's leader), and Roland Mwanjisi. Joseph Nyerere, the President's brother was administrative secretary for the Youth League as well as Junior Minister for Culture and Youth, but gave up his seat when he was appointed regional commissioner and moved from Dar es Salaam. Mr. Kitundu was regional commissioner

TABLE 11

Central Committee, October 1965

President of TANU, Julius Nyerere (President of the Republic)[a]

Vice President of TANU, Rashidi Kawawa (Second Vice President of Tanzania)[b]

Secretary General, Oscar Kambona (Minister for Regional Administration)

Treasurer, Nsilo Swai (Minister for Industries, Mineral Resources and Power)

Members appointed by the President:
John Rupia[c]
Bibi Titi Mohamed,[d] TANU Women's Leader
Rajabu Diwani
Dossa Aziz
Mwinyijuma Mwinyikambi
M. M. Kamaliza (Minister for Labour and Secretary General of NUTA)
I. Bhoke-Munanka, Financial Secretary of TANU (Minister of State in the President's Office for Central Establishments)
Selemani Kitundu (Regional Commissioner of Coast Region and recently appointed Colonel of the People's Defence Forces— the political commissar of the army)
Dr. Wilbert Klerruu, Deputy Secretary General of TANU.

---

[a] The President of TANU is chairman of the Central Committee. This was not stipulated in the original TANU Constitution. Mr. Iddi Faizi Mafungo was at one time chairman of the Central Committee. Mr. Mohamed Kihere, MP for Tanga town and an area commissioner, was chairman for some years, until the National Executive decided before independence to make the President the chairman. Barongo, *op.cit.*, p. 2.

[b] The First Vice President, Abeid Karume is President of ASP.

[c] Mr. Rupia was Vice President of TANU before Mr. Kawawa became Vice President in 1960. Rupia was defeated in the September election for Parliament, winning 6,393 votes to his opponent's 15,019.

[d] Bibi Titi was formerly a junior minister. However, she lost her seat in the National Assembly in the September election, winning 7,343 votes to her opponent's 18,145.

usually appoints about 10 people to the Central Committee.[56] Residency in Dar es Salaam is a prerequisite for appointment because the Central Committee is supposed to meet in permanent session once a week and must be easily convened. The President has chosen to appoint a number of men not prominent in government affairs who have held neither appointed nor elected TANU posts outside of their Central Committee seats. These individuals—Diwani, Mwinyikambi, Aziz —are the *wazee* or elders of TANU, and are usually coastal Muslims prominent in the Elders Section of TANU.[57] Their prominence in the Central Committee may account for the view of one commentator that the "Swahili old residents" in Dar es Salaam have been given a disproportionate role on the Central Committee by the "Christianized nationalist leaders from the hinterland" as a "stratagem to ensure effective political influence in the capital city."[58] The appointment of such men to the Central Committee is a reflection of the importance of the *wazee* in TANU activity, not only in Dar es Salaam but also in other coastal towns such as Tanga, Pangani, and Bagamoyo. A Swahili political culture exists in those inland towns which have cultures similar to the Coast —for example, Kigoma-Ujijii—and in other Tanganyika

---

for the Coast in 1964 and 1965. Rupia, Klerruu, Mwinyikambi, and Diwani were all in in 1964. Aziz has replaced A. Sykes.

[56] It is not clear whether the Central Committee of 1964 was larger because the President appointed more individuals or because the Financial Secretary, the Deputy Secretary General, and the Publicity Secretary served as *ex officio* members. The Youth League administrative secretary and the Women's secretary (Bibi Titi) may also have served *ex officio*.

[57] Sheikh Takadir was the first chairman of the Elders Section. Mwinyijuma Mwinyikambi took over the chairmanship and sat on the Central Committee as an appointed member. When Sheikh Takadir was expelled, S. Kandoro, who had been a TANU administrative secretary from 1954 to 1962, was made administrative secretary of the Elders Section and sat on the Central Committee by virtue of holding this post.

[58] Coleman, *op.cit.*, p. 274.

towns which are not so pronouncedly coastal and Muslim—for example, Musoma. Thus, TANU is not only characterized by green-shirted youths who hang around TANU offices doing odd jobs, keeping order at meetings, manning roadblocks, et cetera; its style is also influenced by the *wazee*, who were among the founding fathers of TANU.

I think it is a mistake to pose a clear distinction between Christianized leaders of the hinterland and the coastal Swahili elements since both share the TANU/Swahili political culture. There is certainly no sharp Muslim/Christian split on the Central Committee itself,[59] which houses both appointed and *ex officio* members who are not originally from Dar es Salaam or even from the Coast, but who are Muslims—for example, Vice President Kawawa. These men bear little resemblance to the *wazee* in demeanor or political style. It is largely in terms of style that the *wazee* distinguish themselves. They stand for elder values—respect for age, commitment to the Swahili language, and to the *baraza* or meeting where people talk together "until they agree." They may wear traditional garments and take Islam very seriously. But there is no evidence that they have constituted a bloc either on the Central Committee or within TANU itself by acting as an Islamic interest group on religious/political issues:[60] they have voiced no opposition to non-Islamic education or to the principles of the secular state in general.

Some Muslim leaders in Tanzania have taken "Muslim" positions; Mr. Kawawa has himself warned against Muslim parochialism. But so far, TANU has been able to encompass religious differentiation. The prominence of the *wazee* among appointed Central Committee members, and their virtual monopoly of those seats designated for individuals who are not government or TANU officeholders, is not a response to any organized Muslim pressures, but rather a rec-

59 Professor Coleman did not pose such a split.
60 The aforementioned Sheikh Takadir was a definite exception.

ognition of the importance of the "old residents" in Dar es Salaam and the importance of the *wazee* within TANU. Also, elders are respected and valued for their wisdom in TANU and within Tanzania as a whole.

The Central Committee is given broad powers by the TANU Constitution. It is the organ concerned with day-to-day administration of party affairs, and is empowered to take all measures deemed necessary to enforce decisions laid down by the NEC. The Central Committee is "to review major trends, formulate tactics and strategy for the guidance of the NEC; and in the event of an emergency to assume full responsibility to safeguard the Union and its functions."[61] It has the power to appoint and remove from office all TANU officials except those elected or those appointed by the President.[62] The Central Committee can establish National Headquarters departments, raise levy for special purposes, and consider names of candidates for local government election—provided that it delegates this power to annual district conferences.[63] Whereas the NEC meets approximately every three months, the Central Committee is convened much more frequently, and is scheduled to meet weekly.

But what does the Central Committee do? Does it make policy, despite the TANU Constitution's stipulation that the NEC should be the policy-making organ for TANU?

The broad outlines for TANU affairs are provided by a few leaders at the top and must be approved by the NEC; the Cen-

---

[61] TANU Constitution, Article 4, Section 7, "Functions of the Central Committee"; and also TANU Reference PR/II/9, 1964.

[62] This is a recent stipulation. The Central Committee may establish a Service Commission which shall exercise such functions on its behalf. See *Nationalist*, October 7, 1965, p. 1. The Central Committee could remove a deputy secretary of TANU but not an area or regional commissioner since these would be presidential appointments.

[63] This power then simply calls attention to the Central Committee as the authority under which the annual district conferences received *their* authority to name candidates. Presumably, the Central Committee can step in and disallow a candidate as the NEC can do for parliamentary candidates.

tral Committee makes policy for day-to-day TANU affairs. But day-to-day TANU affairs do not require a continuous re-working of policy for the party. The executive functions of TANU are assigned to various departments at National Head-quarters which are under the leadership of the Secretary General.[64] The Secretary General is elected by the NEC for a two-year period and is responsible to the President for the overall supervision of the party. This supervision is supposed to be undertaken through the executive departments of the National Headquarters which are charged with implementing NEC policy under the supervision of the Central Committee. But at no time has there been a large, well-organized staff which could either supply the Central Committee with its own administrative machinery for gathering and processing information or which could direct the paid TANU officials in districts and control the elected TANU officials. Regional and district party secretaries and deputy secretaries have not op-erated under the close supervision of the Central Committee. The National Headquarters staff simply is too thin to control TANU personnel from the center. (As late as 1961, one ob-server reported that he could find no one who knew how many workers were on the TANU payroll.)[65]

A 1961 TANU pamphlet shows six sections in the central staff: administration; publicity, press, and foreign affairs; fi-nance; Youth League; Women's Section; Elders' Section. Each of the sections had a secretary.[66] At the beginning of 1963, five sections were listed: administration;[67] finance; publicity; press; refugees. The administrative section em-ployed 18 people; this included the Deputy Secretary Gen-

[64] The present Constitution makes no mention of National Head-quarters. The former one provided for it in the statutes.

[65] Leys, *op.cit.*, p. 253.

[66] Barongo, *op.cit.*, p. 3. At one time in 1961 there was a section for local government and social affairs; publicity and press were in one section, but foreign affairs and provincial affairs were in another.

[67] The NEC abolished the post of Administrator General in 1961.

eral but not the Secretary General. The financial section and the publicity section had 4 and 7 people respectively; and the press and refugee sections had 8 and 2 people. Clerks, typists, messengers, and drivers were included in the 18 people under the heading of administration; only about 5 or 6 were actually doing administrative work.

Obviously, these few people cannot hope to keep a close watch over the activities of thousands of TANU officials. There are approximately 1,500 TANU branches, each with a chairman and a secretary; 60 districts, each with a secretary, a deputy secretary, a chairman, and district executive committee members; and 17 regions, each with a secretary, a deputy secretary, a chairman, MNE, and regional executive committee members. It would be very difficult to watch over the activities of the paid TANU officials alone. (In 1961, Kasela Bantu, then the Publicity and Press Secretary of TANU, estimated the number of officials who receive a salary at around 750 and those who receive a living allowance at around 500.[68])

Three major bottlenecks stand in the way of building a strong central staff at TANU Headquarters. First, the finances are not available for locating, hiring, and training TANU administrative personnel. Money collected by TANU district offices and sent to National Headquarters is supposed to be the major source of TANU's central funds. However, the Financial Secretary warned the TANU Annual Conference in January 1963, that the districts were spending much more than they had estimated and not sending money to the center. More than half of the districts did not send any money for the last six months of 1962, including such important districts as Dar es Salaam, Moshi and Arusha. In the case of Moshi, mishandling of finances was alleged, and the National Treasurer warned that criminal charges might be lodged against the Moshi TANU Treasurer. One delegate claimed

[68] Bantu, *loc.cit.*

that all available funds in his district were being spent on constructing a building; but he asserted that the *balance sheet* was being sent every month.

All this occurred after independence, when TANU had lost some of its momentum and subscriptions were declining. The Financial Secretary warned that the Central Office might not be able to continue fulfilling its duties;[69] and the National Treasurer described the state of party finances as "bad and shocking." A total of approximately $19,000 had been collected in the last six months of 1962 from 26 districts, including one contribution from Northern Rhodesia. Some of these districts sent as little as $70.00 and one of them, Maswa, contributed one-third of the total.[70]

The National Headquarters does not have to rely entirely on the districts for funds. A list of its income and expenditure for July-December 1962, showed that it received almost $18,000 from rental of its offices to the University College, $3,850 in contributions from MPs, and small amounts from the Elders Section and Youth League. There were also direct

[69] TANU reference No. Fin/Corr/11/4, January 12, 1963. The Financial Secretary is a paid official who received 425 shs. a month. The present Financial Secretary, Mr. Bhoke-Munanka, is a prominent TANU official and a minister for state in the President's office in charge of establishments. The former Financial Secretary was Gaspar Whaya. The Financial Secretary does more paper work and spends more time on TANU funds than the National Treasurer. But since Mr. Bhoke-Munanka has an important government job, the Financial Secretary is not now a fulltime TANU official. The Financial Secretary asks the district and provincial committees for estimates; he may do this in February and ask for estimates by April. He prepares the Budget in May. The Financial Secretary prepares the estimates for debates. The Treasurer presents the Budget for debate. The Financial Secretary presents the Budget, once approved by the NEC, to the Central Committee which then authorizes the Deputy Secretary General to send circulars of instructions on the approved Budget. The Financial Secretary does most of the work, but the Treasurer makes himself available also.

[70] I have not been able to compare districts for other years to determine whether one or a few districts again provided such a large share.

sales of TANU cards, other rents, sales of books and newspapers. The total income from all these non-district sources was about $63,000. National Headquarters' expenses for the half-year equaled income.[71] Over $17,000 per month went for employees' salaries. More than one-third went to the administrative section.

The supplementary funds from rentals, contributions, and direct sales are not enough to put finances on a firm footing. Thus TANU officials have had to ask government to come to their aid and support National Headquarters' activities.[72] For example, the Publicity Secretary of TANU, claiming that government was not supporting the TANU newspaper *Uhuru* with advertising, asked the TANU Annual Conference to request a grant from government to cover costs of publication and to give the publicity section transport privileges.[73] Government has responded on some occasions: it has given privileges to the Mwananchi Development Corporation (a TANU

[71] These figures are not indicative of what TANU spends in the course of a year. In a document—*TANU, Makadira ya Mapato ya Mtumizi* (Account of Revenues and Expenses) the approved estimates for 1962-63 (June-July) totaled around 1½ million shillings or over $200,000. Of this amount, almost one-third was spent on building projects tied into the *Three Year Plan.*

[72] TANU officers also have asked government officials to help check TANU accounts both at National Headquarters and in regional offices. One regional commissioner preferred to let his government officials keep charge of the accounts of a TANU fund-raising drive because he did not trust the competency of the TANU treasurer.

[73] The weakness of the publicity section on its own was demonstrated when the printing order for *Uhuru* was cut back from 50,000 to 10,000 and then to 5,000. The Financial Secretary ordered this cutback. The Publicity Chairman accused TANU branches of contributing to the decline by not even trying to sell the paper. Newspapers were piled in corners and in some places nobody had bothered to open the packages sent. In addition, many TANU offices never forwarded money obtained from sales. The publicity department decided to look for commercial agents who know how to deal with this business and ceased relying on the branches. *Taarifa Ya Idara Ya Utangazali*, January 11, 1964, Report of the Publicity Section.

commercial enterprise); and it gave a grant to start the *Nationalist*, an English language TANU newspaper.

The second bottleneck in building an administrative staff at National Headquarters is the high turnover of administrative personnel at the center. Even the Secretary General post turned over frequently before independence, and the Deputy Secretary General's office continues to be occupied by one person only for a short time.[74] The same was true for the TANU Treasurer's office until recently.[75]

There has been little stability of tenure in the lesser administrative and clerical positions at National Headquarters either. These lower ranking officials in National Headquarters have been appointed by the Establishments Committee, which was a sub-committee of the Central Committee. The Deputy Secretary General and the Financial Secretary were *ex officio* members, and there were 7 others from the Central Committee elected out of its own membership. The Establishments Committee considered applications for employment and handled promotions at the advice of the Secretary General. The Central Committee must approve appointments to

[74] Oscar Kambona has been the Secretary General of TANU since its formation, and as such he has been responsible for running TANU National Headquarters. However, since he was abroad so often as Foreign Minister, his duties devolved on the Deputy Secretary General. And Mr. Kambona did not function as Secretary General during an important period in TANU's history. When he left for study in England in 1956, his functions devolved on Messrs. Gitagino and Mtemvu (later the leader of the African National Congress). Later on in 1956, Mr. Stephen Mhando was nominated by Mr. Nyerere in conjunction with the Central Committee as the Acting Secretary General. After Mr. Mhando, Mr. Edward Kisenge became Acting Secretary General in 1957. Mr. Kisenge was sometimes referred to as Organizing Secretary General. Mr. Kambona returned from England and took up his post again in 1959, but he was away from Tanganyika during the first years when TANU was trying to develop a network of paid officials.

[75] The National Treasurer post has been held by John Rupia, I. Bhoke-Munanka, Idii Faizi Mafungo, and the present Treasurer, Nsilo Swai, all within ten years.

administrative posts. These posts are sometimes filled by district and regional TANU officers. The turnover is high because men prove unable to work efficiently at the center. It is these appointments to National Headquarters along with appointment to deputy regional secretary and deputy district secretary which are the prerogative of the Central Committee.

The third bottleneck in building a strong central staff is the opposition to such a staff in certain TANU quarters. This opposition stems from a number of factors. The leaders of government are themselves TANU leaders, deriving their authority in part from having been leaders of the independence movement, but also from being the inheritors of the colonial rulers. They ascend to the control of government machinery, receive salaries appropriate to their status, and monopolize the symbols of power—State House, large automobiles, titles. It is very important that they are the *first* inheritors. Since the new leaders moved into what is the first attempt at indigenous rule over the whole territory, they have more scope to monopolize symbols and more freedom to try to create new institutions in their own image than future rulers will have. Thus, control of a government ministry is a peculiarly important source of authority and power because for the first time an African minister can put his stamp on the ministry. Furthermore, he has a staff of civil servants to feed him information and to process his orders; expatriates may still be working under him. The Central Committee does not have such a staff at its disposal. Few individuals are in a position to derive power and status solely from a high place in the TANU hierarchy. Few Tanzanians, even politically conscious ones, could say who the appointed members of the Central Committee are.

This does not prove that membership on the Central Committee does not reflect and/or convey political power. But since the Central Committee and the National Headquarters do not set out policy guidelines for the TANU government (insofar as this is done at all by a TANU organ it is done by the NEC), they would have to govern day-to-day TANU and government affairs in order to be considered ruling political bodies. Neither send instructions to the ministries; neither determines promotions or appointments to governmental agencies. They cannot even govern TANU affairs in the regions and districts because they have no direct channels of communication to and control over these TANU organizations.

It is important to be clear on these matters because the terms of description—Central Committee, NEC, Administrative Secretaries, and Secretary General—can conjure up images of a communist party where secretaries of the party are powerful political figures. But secretaries in the Secretariat of the Communist Party of the Soviet Union (CPSU), for example, have administrative cadres they can manipulate; a TANU administrative secretary does not. Furthermore, a Secretary of the CPSU does not have to hold a government job in order to be recognized as an authoritative political figure; but the full-time TANU secretaries and the members of the Central Committee who do not hold government jobs have neither the status nor the income of men who wear a government and a party hat. That high TANU position alone does not convey great authority is an indication that there are important values in the system which do not attach to TANU institutions; not all images of authority and power are formed in terms of TANU. One important inheritance from the colonial power is the attachment to symbols and to concrete institutions of state—government posts convey authority and prestige in the system, since, after all, these posts were held by the British administrators themselves. And government officials, not TANU secretaries, travel abroad and are seen with foreign leaders. Thus all the prestige of being an actor on the international stage is accorded to individuals in their governmental capacities.

Many of those who are already government ministers and TANU officials are not eager to see the development of a central staff of TANU officers, if this means that a new locus of power and authority will come into being. For the leaders of TANU and government are leaders by virtue of their personal qualities and their historical roles as founding fathers of TANU and first ministers of the state. Furthermore, since Tanzania is not characterized by strong tribes or pronounced regionalism, these leaders do not have a tribal or regional base. They are particularly vulnerable to the development of new leaders who would base themselves on the loyalty of and control over administrative cadres. On the other hand, it is difficult for any one leader to rely on any TANU administrative hierarchy without first building himself an administrative staff at the center. The Secretary General would normally be in the best position to attempt this (and in fact Oscar Kambona has been accused of trying to do this), but Kambona has not been at all a constant presence at TANU Headquarters. Whatever his personal loyalties to Nyerere, he would have a formidable task in attempting to build and then lead the National Headquarters as a power bloc.[76]

There are others who are not enthusiastic about the creation of a strong National Headquarters' Secretariat working under the Central Committee. Both the elected TANU officials in the regions and districts and civil servants have interests which run counter to such a development. Many elected TANU officials are represented on the NEC. While some of the members of the NEC—especially those who do not hold government as well as TANU jobs—would like to see the principle of TANU supremacy firmly established, they do not interpret this to mean the supremacy of the National Headquarters over them. Thus, members of the NEC are not en-

[76] It is not clear whether his appointment as Minister for Regional Administration will facilitate doing this, presuming he has a mind to do so.

tirely committed to the strengthening of the administrative staff at National Headquarters; for it is precisely the absence of this staff which prevents the emergence of a Central Committee that could dominate the other TANU organs as well as government machinery.

Constitutional Changes in TANU's Central Institutions in 1965

The Presidential Commission on the Establishment of a Democratic one Party State called for a number of changes in the central organs of TANU. And in the course of 1965, the NECs of TANU and the ASP amended the *Presidential Report,* and brought about changes in membership and powers of the NEC and the Annual Conference. The Central Committee was not affected and the National Headquarters was touched very little.

If anything, the NEC has become a more important organ than it was before 1965: its scope and power have increased, and it has begun to function in governmental capacities. The NEC preserved its small size while the National Conference expanded. It assumed the power to name candidates for the National Assembly. In the past, the NEC had the right to approve candidates who ran for office under a TANU label. Yet the National Headquarters rather than the NEC had been the one to intervene in the very rare case where an MP nominated by a district was unacceptable to national leaders.[77] In the 1965 election for Parliament, it was the NEC who made the final decision as to who would stand from the districts. The Presidential Commission had suggested that the joint NECs of TANU and the ASP also nominate the President of the Republic. However, a joint session of those NECs modified

[77] Mr. Sarwatt of Mbulu was rejected in 1960 only to run and win as an independent. He was the nominee of his district TANU organization but was rejected at the center. National Headquarters officials had disagreed with Nyerere before independence over a candidate for an Asian seat. The NEC did not come into the quarrel.

this so that the National Conference reconvened itself as an electoral conference to nominate the single candidate for President. The National Executives decided that it would be more democratic to have a joint meeting of the Territorial Conferences of the two parties establish a nominee, and not the National Executives. This does widen the nominating process, but it is unlikely to alter the dominance of the National Executive in choosing a presidential candidate.

The Presidential Commission recommended that the President of TANU be able to remove officials of TANU National Headquarters:

> TANU is a national political movement and its principal offices should have so far as possible a representative character. For this reason we consider inappropriate the existing provision in the Constitution [of TANU] that the Secretary General, the Deputy Secretary General and the National Treasurer cannot be removed from office except for misconduct. We recommend that the Constitution should provide that the holders of these offices may be removed by the President of the Party, who should be required in the event of exercising this power to report on the circumstances to the next meeting of the National Executive Committee.[78]

When the NEC amended the *Presidential Report*, it put itself in the place of the President as the final judge of the National Headquarters officials:

Instead of the President having the power to remove from office the Secretary General, the Deputy Secretary General and the National Treasurer, he should have the right to suspend them from office, whereupon he would be required to report to the next meeting of the National Execu-

[78] *Presidential Report*, p. 29.

199

tive on the circumstances leading to this action and the National Executive would finally decide on the matter.[79]

The recommendations of the Presidential Commission vis-à-vis the President and the NEC make it clear that the Commission did not see the NEC and the President as alternating balances of a scale. On the contrary, implementation of the Commission's recommendations should lead to an increase in the power of both at the expense of TANU National Headquarters officials,[80] the MPs, and middle-level leaders who will not attain the heights of command of regional elected and appointed TANU hierarchies.

The President has become independent of Parliament in that he is now directly elected instead of being elected by MPs who constitute an electoral college.[81] The NEC is given the privilege of summoning witnesses, taking evidence, and ordering the production of documents. The NEC also has the benefit of trained civil servants, in that the principal legal advisor of the government, the Attorney General, and the President's Principal Secretary are among its members. This, of course, adds to the numbers of appointees the President makes to the NEC.[82]

The *Presidential Report* also suggested that members of

[79] *Nationalist*, May 7, 1965, p. 2. All the NEC's amendments to the *Presidential Report* were made in the first week of May 1965.

[80] The Secretary General, Deputy Secretary General and National Treasurer get two short paragraphs in the *Presidential Report*. Nowhere is the National Headquarters staff mentioned. This may be, as it has been said, because the *Report* deals with constitutional matters, and the development of the central staff is an administrative matter. (Interview with Vice President Kawawa, April 1965.) But the central staff might have been involved in constitutional changes also.

[81] No presidential election was even held under this procedure although the Republican Constitution called for it. The election for the presidency in 1962 was a direct election because an election for Parliament had taken place in 1960 and there was no wish to hold another.

[82] The NEC approved a suggestion of the Presidential Commission to this effect, but insisted that these appointees be TANU members. It rejected the majority view of the Presidential Commission that they have the right to vote on the NEC.

the NEC who are not MPs be given the same salaries and allowances as MPs.[83] This proposal meets a major demand of the middle-level, unsalaried regional leaders—the MNE and the TANU regional chairmen. When the proposal takes effect, their salaries will be less than that of a regional commissioner, but the gap will be relatively small in comparison to former days. No longer will a regional TANU chairman try to get a job as a divisional executive officer, a post which is far below a number of TANU officials in status, in order to have a salaried job.

Another important change has already been made in the position of regional commissioners: they have become *ex officio* members of Parliament within a new category of National Members.[84] These are members free from constituency concerns. The Presidential Commission felt that the regional commissioners were a vital link between government, the party, and the people, and as such, have an important role to play in Parliament. This recommendation flies in the face of the opinion that commissioners already spend too much time on safari rather than in their offices; commissioners who were elected MPs were criticized on the grounds that they were in Dar es Salaam too often. Now, within the NEC the regional commissioners are distinguished by being members of the National Assembly and the NEC. Membership in the National Assembly confers status still, though it adds little to the powers and prerogatives of the regional commissioners.[85]

[83] The NECs did not amend this proposal. However, it had not yet become law at the time of writing.

[84] Another new category of National Member for Parliament included 15 people to be selected from the National Assembly from a list of candidates submitted by the National Executive. The National Executive receives nominations for this list from the Cooperative Movement, NUTA, University College, the Association of Chambers of Commerce and other institutions designated by the President.

[85] For regional commissioners, the desire to be MPs can in part be attributed to the continuing influence of symbols and institutions surrounded by the authority of the ex-colonial power. These symbols have taken root in the soil of the independent country; although they have been adapted, they still retain many of their old connotations.

The NEC has increased its prerogatives, and its members have increased their personal privileges; the NEC has distinguished itself markedly from the National Conference. But it has not assumed control over TANU. Whatever its eventual say on questions of economic policy, TANU affairs, foreign policy, the NEC has no mechanism through which it can control the TANU regional, district, and local organizations. This lack of a central TANU apparatus which can be used as a tool has forced the NEC to exert itself by virtue of the fact that its members are important in the regional TANU organizations. But the TANU regional chairmen, the regional secretaries/commissioners, and the MNE do not consistently act in unison in any one region, much less as spokesmen for the NEC vis-à-vis sub-national TANU units. Furthermore, the regional heads cannot impose their wills very far outside the regional headquarters.[86]

Little pressure is being generated to build a central TANU bureaucracy.[87] And failing to have such a staff, TANU cannot become a "mobilizing" or a "revolutionary-centralizing" party. However, there are those who would like to see TANU function as a revolutionary party: Nyerere himself wants a TANU which can revolutionize Tanzania by mobilizing society; but he wants to hold on to certain traditional values, and he is not willing to sacrifice democratic spirit and procedures within TANU. Others are less reluctant to abandon the open party: they stress the centralizing aspects of a revolutionary party; they would like to create a TANU modeled on Leninist parties. We must now confront these different images of TANU held by various TANU elites.

In this connection, to be an MP is a desired thing in its own right even if no new material or political benefits accrue.

[86] This will be seen when implementation of the *Five Year Plan* is discussed.

[87] University students are being brought into the civil service, not into TANU National Headquarters. There has been some talk of bringing them into a research division of TANU, but there is little enthusiasm for having them man some central administrative bureaucracy.

CHAPTER VI

Ideology and Commitment

ELITES IN NEW STATES consciously try to devise formulas by which they can justify their positions and through which they can bridge the gap between themselves and non-elites.[1] Ideologies are created to legitimize rule and also to integrate traditionally and non-traditionally oriented communities. Elites who are indeed oriented towards economic development must find formulas which will act as an ideology for development.[2] When a radical transformation of society is undertaken, extraordinary claims are made on the population. The norms of state bureaucracy are insufficient to provide an "ideological grease" for development in a society which has integrative problems and which must undertake a big push in order to overcome backwardness.

In Tanzania, a battle of ideas has begun over the components of the ideology for development, despite TANU's claim to being a monolithic party. There are some who believe that Nyerere's ideas will not facilitate integration and development. While these individuals do not comprise a clearly defined group openly opposed to Nyerere, they do articulate—with varying degrees of explicitness—a different kind of socialism than Nyerere: he speaks of African socialism, they of scientific socialism. Since Tanzania has neither a consistent, all-embracing national tradition nor strong parochial traditional units, Nyerere does not see tradition as always and everywhere threatening development. He wishes to retain the bonds of traditional community—so long as they do not conflict with economic development and social

[1] Cf. Binder, *loc.cit.*

[2] Alexander Gerschenkron, e.g., has noted thrusts of development in Russia, Germany, and France accompanied by specific sets of ideas about the cause and cure of backwardness. Cf., *Economic Backwardness in Historical Perspective* (Cambridge: Harvard University Press, 1962), pp. 22-26.

change—in order to use traditional patterns to bring about modernity; and he envisions TANU as the carrier of both traditional and modern values. (This is one reason why he has not been anxious to revise TANU's decentralized nature.)

Others within TANU insist that traditional communities must be broken via a strong party; they believe that only through social conflict will the problems of backwardness be solved. Nyerere's ideas seem to them gradualist and therefore unsuited to rapid social and economic change; they demand more vigor, dynamism, and drama than Nyerere's formulations provide. And the political aspirations of newcomers to power—Zanzibaris and middle-level elites in particular—lead them to search for their own formulas to legitimize their aspirations and provide them with ideologies to attract followers.

The challenge to Nyerere has so far been made on ideological rather than personal or organizational grounds. And the challengers cannot be neatly grouped as a counter-elite or an emergent elite on the basis of some social differentiation or even on a position in the TANU hierarchy, for there are middle-level leaders who accept Nyerere's ideas. Receptivity to Nyerere or to scientific socialism in Tanzania probably depends on career lines and personal experiences that cannot be broadly characterized—travel abroad, experience of racial discrimination associated with colonialists, self-conception and motivation all of which are amenable to psychological as well as sociological analysis.[3]

In view of TANU's structure, it is impossible for any one "TANU" ideology to reflect the whole organization. No central institution exists which can impose such an ideology, and insure its acceptance among all who identify themselves as "TANU"; there is no mechanism through which all TANU

[3] I have found very useful Morris Janowitz's, "Sociological Notes on the Analysis of Military Elites," in *The Military in the Political Development of New States* (Chicago: University of Chicago Press, 1964), pp. 107-25.

members can be kept constantly in touch with a political ideology as it changes to meet new needs and situations; and there is no means for TANU leaders to institutionalize their view of reality and enforce it within their own organization.

Often in a particular culture certain values are widely shared; they can be translated into political strategies and presented in formal ideologies—in "schematic images of social order"[4]—and remain widely and easily shared. This situation, however, is seldom found in a new state. The very concern to change the old patterns of society calls forth attempts to provide new ways of thinking about social problems. Whatever the content of new programs, some people will resist new conceptualizations because they are new and must be adapted to. Furthermore, social change affects people unequally, even in a relatively homogeneous society. People anticipate these changes, whether accurately or not. Thus there is no reason, a priori, to believe that people either in TANU or in Tanzania at large would spontaneously embrace a political ideology simply because it was promulgated by new leaders who were the first indigenous leaders for the whole country.

And yet, people have written about Tanganyika and about TANU as if the ideas associated with one man—Julius Nyerere —were the belief system of a whole society. There has been a narrower, but equally mistaken tendency to equate the ideology of TANU with Nyerere's ideas. This has occurred because Nyerere is often equated with Tanganyika on the world stage; and is concerned with promulgating his thoughts at home and abroad.

However, it would not be entirely accurate to assume that all published statements about the past, present and future of Tanganyika were the work of Nyerere alone. Several news-

---

[4] To borrow a phrase from Clifford Geertz, "Ideology as A Cultural System," in *Ideology and Discontent*, David Apter (ed.) (Glencoe: The Free Press, 1964), p. 63.

papers existed, before and after independence, which did not mouth Nyerere's views. Among them were the English language newspaper, owned by British interests and printed either in Tanganyika (*The Tanganyika Standard*; circulation about 10,000 as of 1962) or in Nairobi, Kenya and brought into Tanganyika. There were also Gujerati papers and papers in tribal dialects; and Swahili papers which were not TANU organs (the daily *Ngurumo*, for example, owned by Thakers Ltd. and with a circulation of 12,000). Catholic and Protestant Missions printed their own papers in various languages (for example, *Kingozi* owned by the College of Catholic Bishops and with a circulation of 26,000). And TANU's own weekly, *Uhuru* (circulation: 15,000) was edited by Roland Mwanjisi who expressed many of the attitudes of the middle-level leaders who had opposed Nyerere in 1961-62.[5] Thus *Uhuru* sometimes expressed racialistic views that Nyerere did not condone.[6]

With this said, it is still true that Nyerere presented an image of Tanganyika to the outside world. Undoubtedly, this was less true for those who read the Swahili and vernacular press. But even for these readers, it was Julius Nyerere who dominated the presentation of issues at the national level. This is no longer the case. Now various attitudes and positions at variance with Nyerere's are more or less explicitly held by a number of TANU middle- and high-level office-holders. Since Nyerere occupies a special historical position in Tanzania, and since the commitment to unity within TANU is widely shared by the great majority of middle- and high-level leaders, Nyerere's definitions of issues and his characterizations of the present and future society are not contradicted in public. Instead, those who put forward different

[5] The circulation figures are from the *Tanganyika Press Directory* (Dar es Salaam, 1962).

[6] Another major Swahili paper was *Mwafrika*, edited by R. Makange as a TANU paper. It was first a weekly and then a daily.

ideas simply by-pass Nyerere's own formulations; they do not confront them head on. We cannot say that a dialogue is going on in Tanzania.

Furthermore, those who hold ideas at variance with the President's are not formed into hard and fast factions. Individuals are bidding for personal influence by espousing ideological lines. And they are trying to influence policy within TANU and the ministries by making these lines public. But groups have not formed around ideological orientations within TANU. It is not even accurate to speak of cliques within the TANU elite which explicitly differentiate themselves from other cliques and from TANU as a whole. And personal friendships still crosscut ideological boundaries.

At one point, it might have been useful to group a wide spectrum of implictly non-Nyerere views under the heading of a "Nationalist Group." For the *Nationalist*, an English language daily and a TANU organ,[7] not only served as the mouthpiece for individuals who differed from Nyerere's positions, but it also articulated the feelings of individuals and served to identify them and the ideas and interests they held in common. From the middle of 1964 until the middle of 1965, the *Nationalist* put forward the views of these individuals in editorials, in news articles, and in coverage it gave to various people. In the middle of 1965, the *Nationalist* began to take a much more moderate tone and is now less identified with "non-Nyerere" views.[8] However, the individuals who were enthusiastically supported in its pages are

[7] The *Nationalist* is the first English daily owned by Africans in East Africa. It is published by the Mwananchi Publishing Company, Ltd., a TANU subsidiary; but nowhere on its letterhead is the *Nationalist* called an official organ of TANU. It has received a subvention from government. It began printing in the spring of 1964.

[8] During this year, the *Nationalist* was edited by a Ghanaian, James Markham, and there was a European on the editorial staff. Since then the editor has been replaced and the Englishman, Richard Kisch, was told to leave Tanzania on twenty-four hour notice. The *Nationalist* does not publish a list of editors with each issue.

still identifiable as holding positions derived more from the pages of Lenin and Mao than from the pages of *Ujamaa* and *Democracy and the Party Systems*.[9]

These individuals include men from Zanzibar who, since the Union of Tanganyika and Zanzibar in April 1964, brought to their government posts a new language, a new rhetoric. They have infused a distinct ideology into the mainland. Disagreement is also evident among middle-level leaders in Dar es Salaam—among junior ministers and administrative officials at TANU National Headquarters, a few regional and area commissioners—many of whom should have composed Nyerere's closest audience if his own ideas were to take hold. But Nyerere's more gentlemanly, individualist, and essentially gradualist doctrines did not suit them; they wanted something more systematic, more "logical," more dramatic. Many trade union leaders with official positions in TANU also objected to Nyerere's policy.

The trade union movement in theory is organically related to TANU.[10] And in fact, the TFL was the major association linked to TANU. They had organized for each other, and many trade union leaders occupied important TANU positions from its inception. But the TFL housed leaders who shared many of the nationalistic and racist views expressed in 1961-62 by central and regional TANU officials. I noted that C. K. Tumbo, leader of the People's Democratic Party, had been leader of the Railway Workers Union; he and other trade union leaders acted as spokesmen for trade union pressure groups in 1961-62 and tried to form alliances with the TANU dissidents.

The central administrative organization of the TFL was

[9] I do not mean that such people necessarily have read Lenin or Mao.

[10] Nyerere has always referred to TANU's relation to the Tanganyika Federation of Labour (TFL), which embraced all trade union affiliates, as being organically linked.

weak: it faced many of the same problems in exerting central control over affiliates that TANU faced vis-à-vis its territorial organizations, and it suffered from similar financial and personnel difficulties. Consequently, the affiliated unions had a good deal of autonomy, and TANU could not control the trade union movement simply by controlling the central TFL institutions. Instead TANU had to governmentalize the trade union movement by a series of Acts of Parliament which culminated in the National Union of Tanganyika Workers Act (No. 18 of 1964).[11] The National Union of Tanganyika Workers (NUTA)[12] is explicitly affiliated with TANU and has representation on the NEC; its Constitution provides for organizational links with TANU. Thus government has been able to eliminate many of its old opponents within the trade union movement. (Some were put under preventive detention after the army mutiny.) However, while neither NUTA as such nor any of its constituent unions as yet make the kinds of demands that the TFL and its affiliated unions used to make in opposition to government policy, elements within NUTA are prepared to pressure private investors much harder than government. And some officers of NUTA's central administration, are committed to a socialism much more "scientific" than Nyerere's version.

Two high-level leaders not in complete accord with Nyerere have received extensive and enthusiastic coverage in the *Nationalist*: A. M. Babu, the Minister of Commerce

[11] This Act centralized all trade union organizations in one union which replaced the Tanganyika Federation of Labour. The General Secretary of the National Union and his Deputy Secretary are appointed by the President of the Republic. They hold office at the President's pleasure, though the term is set for five years. Assistant general secretaries are appointed by the General Secretary. The first General Secretary was the Minister of Labour, Mr. Michael Kamaliza, who retains that post.

[12] The abbreviation for the new trade union organization should be NUTW. But this would neither make a very nice sound nor would its rearrangement spell "TANU."

and Cooperatives, a Zanzibar leader who entered into the Tanzanian government at the ministerial level after the Union; and the Secretary General of TANU and Minister for Foreign Affairs, Oscar Kambona. Kambona has taken much more outspoken and anti-Western positions in foreign affairs than Nyerere; Babu operates within a very different framework from Nyerere, consistently giving a Marxist-Leninist-Maoist analysis of society. Although both men have been accused of harboring ambitions to be President of Tanzania,[13] each has stated his unswerving loyalty to the President.

Neither Mr. Rashidi Kawawa, Vice President of TANU and Second Vice President of Tanzania (Mr. Sheikh Abeid Karume is the first Vice President of Tanzania but he, unlike Mr. Babu, stays in Zanzibar), nor President Nyerere himself received as much attention and glorification in the pages of the *Nationalist* as did Mr. Kambona. In fact, President Nyerere would not permit the kind of hyperbolic flattery that Kambona got in the *Nationalist*. Insofar as a personality cult was being built in Tanzania, the *Nationalist* was constructing one around Mr. Kambona.[14]

That the *Nationalist* made its pages available to all these men[15] does not mean that it did not fully report President

[13] See e.g. the November 26, 1964 issue of *East Africa and Rhodesia* and also the *Economist*, November 21, 1964 for reports of allegations against Mr. Kambona especially. Mr. Kambona sued one British newspaper which had called him a communist agent and won damages in the British courts.

[14] A recent trip made by him to Morogoro was reported by the *Nationalist*'s correspondent in the following terms: "Fantastic? Yes . . . His arrival caught the public attention almost to the exclusion of every other consideration that day. I [the reporter] stood stiff-necked struggling with the incredible truth that a force of personality could whip up excitement to such a pitch of hysteria." This may have been everyday fare, even understatement, in Ghana, but it is not the way people talk about Nyerere in Tanzania. *Nationalist*, June 1, 1965, p. 6.

[15] The *Nationalist* also made itself available for various factions within the Congolese anti-central government movements and for

Nyerere's speeches and hail him as the great leader of Tanzania.[16] However, Nyerere was challenged in the *Nationalist* on the issues he himself had set out: African socialism, one-party democracy, and the nature of economic policy in Tanganyika.

Nyerere's Thought

Julius Nyerere is most commonly referred to in the press, in TANU hand-outs, and by other leaders as *Mwalimu* which is translated as *The* Teacher—the giver of truth.[17] President Nyerere is also referred to as *Baba Ya Taifa*—Father of the Nation,[18] a title usually reserved for ceremonial occasions. For example, if Nyerere is returning from abroad, both the Swahili and English language newspapers will herald the return of *Mwalimu*. But in an article commemorating the founding of TANU or the anniversary of Nyerere's election as President of TANU or President of Tanganyika, he is almost always referred to at least once as *Baba Ya Taifa*. Both these appellations call attention to Nyerere's special historical position: he is the first leader of independent Tanganyika and he is the leader who brought Tanganyika to independence.

---

particular factions in the Southern Rhodesian and South African nationalist movements.

[16] For that matter, the fortnightly *Vigilance Africa* or *Macho* which was unrestrainedly committed to Chinese positions also hailed Nyerere as the leader of Tanzania. This paper published a number of issues toward the end of 1964 and the beginning of 1965. It was English language on one page and Swahili on another. It claimed to stand for "Marxist-Leninist ideals, scientific socialism, and African unity." Editorial in I, No. 10, February 18, 1965, 2.

[17] Similarly, the Swahili word *mzee* or old man, when used in addressing a leader, conveys more than a generalized deference or respect; Kenya's President Jomo Kenyatta, e.g., is called *Mzee*—a very special title meaning *The* Old Man.

[18] Swahili has only one word for Father—*Baba*. *Baba* includes the Victorian sense of respected and stern Father and the sense conveyed by "Daddy." Nyerere, as *Baba Ya Taifa*, is not the respected but distant George Washington—Father of the Nation—but a mixture of the *pater familias* and familiar "Dad."

Nyerere has provided ideas and symbols through which others can understand the society in which they live and imagine the society of the future. While he has been the most ideological of the East African leaders in that he has tried to formulate his ideas systematically and provide symbolic frameworks, Nyerere is suspicious of creeds and dogmas,[19] and thus has been disinclined to create a blueprint for the new society. And, he has not very successfully married his ideas and symbols to programs for action. Several things have contributed to this. For one thing, many of the programs of the TANU government are designed by expatriates, who, while often sensitive to Nyerere's values, are largely unconcerned with providing a new symbolic framework. Economic constraints also operate in Tanganyika to undermine many of Nyerere's ideas about social and economic equality. In trying to take account of these constraints, Nyerere has made his formulations more pragmatic and less persuasive to those who must be his closest audience: the TANU middle-level leaders.

Thus Tanzania has a leader whose writings appear in all the anthologies on "ideology in the new states" under the headings of "African Socialism," "Pan-Africanism," and "Democracy." But neither the programs of the TANU government nor the definitions of TANU itself have been forged completely in the crucible of Nyerere's own ideals. Though it is true that Nyerere has stamped his style and some of his ideals on aspects of Tanganyika's social and political life and on aspects of TANU's operation, we shall have to account for the fact that new streams of thought have entered Tanganyika and are bidding to become the components of a new TANU ideology.

African Socialism

Ujamaa: The Basis of African Socialism is one of

---

[19] Nyerere, *Democracy and the Party System*, p. 24.

Nyerere's most important pieces.[20] *Ujamaa* is literally translated as "Familyhood" or "Brotherhood." In *Ujamaa*, Nyerere is concerned with socialism and traditional African society, and problems of stratification in society. Nyerere writes about the foundation and the objectives of African socialism, and presents his vision of a future Tanganyikan society. Socialism—like democracy—is construed by Nyerere to be an attitude of mind. It is this attitude of mind, rather than a rigid adherence to a standard political pattern, which "is needed to ensure that the people care for each other's welfare."[21]

African socialism is distinguished from capitalism which seeks to build a happy society on the basis of exploitation of man by man; and it is equally opposed to doctrinaire socialism which seeks to build its happy society on a philosophy of inevitable conflict between man and man.[22] The foundation and objective of African socialism is the extended family. All men are regarded as brethren—as members of an ever-extending family.[23] It was not only the anti-colonial struggle which taught the need for unity, Nyerere says; traditional African society expressed a socialism which recognizes society as an extension of the basic family unit. Nyerere has elsewhere said that the ideal is community, not communacracy.[24] The attitudes of traditional African socialism must be regained and applied to the new societies being built.[25] With this statement, Nyerere recognizes the existence of elements

[20] *Ujamaa: The Basis of African Socialism* (Dar es Salaam: Tanganyika Standard Ltd., 1962); hereafter called *Ujamaa*.

[21] *Ibid.*, p. 2.   [22] *Ibid.*, p. 8.

[23] Nyerere calls attention to the first article of TANU's creed: *Binadamu wote ni Ndugu zangu, na Afrika ni moja* (I believe in Human Brotherhood and the Unity of Africa).

[24] Nyere, "Will Democracy Survive in Africa?" *African Special Report*, v (February 1960), 3-4. "Community is of a genuine community or brotherhood; commune is an artificial unit of human beings."

[25] *Ujamaa*, p. 6.

in African society which are opposed to traditional African socialism. He says that capitalist attitudes of mind and capitalist methods were brought into Africa by colonialism. The use of the word "worker" in the sense of "employee" as opposed to "employer" reflects this frame of mind.

Neither the man who aspired after personal wealth nor the idler were known to traditional society. Acquisitiveness for the purpose of gaining power and prestige is unsocialistic: apart from the anti-social effects of the accumulation of personal wealth,[26] the very desire to accumulate is an expression of insecurity, and must be interpreted as a vote of no confidence in the social system. It is the way in which wealth is distributed that distinguishes the socialist from the capitalist society.[27] A fair share must be fair in relation to the whole society; if it is greater than the country can afford without having to penalize anyone, then it is not a fair share.

Nyerere's understanding of the past provides the basis for his views that Tanganyika should have as few stratas as possible within society and the minimum of differences between them. He is, however, well aware of the difficulties of creating an essentially egalitarian society under prevailing conditions.

[26] Nyerere states that it is not necessary to read Adam Smith or Karl Marx to understand that neither land nor tools alone produce wealth, but that labor is required. He distinguishes between *intrinsic* and *artificial* value. Certain groups by virtue of the "market value" of their particular industry's products, *will* contribute more to the nation's income than others. But the others may actually be producing goods or services which are of equal, or greater intrinsic value although they do not happen to command such a high artificial value. For example, food produced by the peasant farmer is of greater social value than the diamonds mined at Mwadui. But the mineworkers of Mwadui could claim, quite correctly that their labor was yielding greater financial profit to the community than that of the farmers. If, however, they went on to demand that they should therefore be given most of the extra profit for themselves, and that no share of it could be spent on helping the farmers, they would be potential capitalists. *Ibid.*, p. 7.
[27] *Ibid.*

For Nyerere, *Ujamaa* is African socialism. He has recently said that there are different ideological roads to African socialism,[28] but he has never accepted Marxism-Leninism as a creed to be embraced in Tanzania. Although no one in Tanzania has openly accused Nyerere of being a bourgeois nationalist because of his refusal to opt for scientific socialism, the *Nationalist* did publish a series of articles in June 1965, attacking the Kenya White Paper, *African Socialism*.[29] These articles, entitled "Kenya's African Socialism," were signed by "A Critic," who insisted that he was an African and a socialist, though it did not follow "that the combination of both qualities entitles one to define oneself as an "African Socialist"—even by Kenya's definition.[30] "A Critic" claimed that the Kenya White Paper was against socialism and for capitalism; and was particularly indignant at the phrase, "both Marxism and Laissez-Faire Capitalism have been failures."[31] (Compare *Ujamaa*: "Ujamaa . . . is opposed to Capitalism . . . and it is equally opposed to doctrinaire Socialism.") The Kenya paper was also attacked for its alleged statement that feudal institutions were the strongest heritage on which to base the essence of African socialism. The word "feudal" was never used in the Paper to describe the institutions it wanted to preserve; and it had urged the preservation not only of specific institutions (independent farms, for example), but of traditions as well—the very same traditions in fact which Nyerere had stated as the basis for African socialism in *Ujamaa*. Tom Mboya, head of the Ministry of Planning and Development which drew up the Kenya White Paper, had been very much influenced by *Ujamaa*. He drew

---

[28] Seminar for TANU Deputy Secretaries, *Tanganyika Standard*, May 1, 1965, p. 5.

[29] This paper has been published as a pamphlet, *African Socialism* (Nairobi: Government Printer, 1965).

[30] "A Critic" articles were published in the *Nationalist*, June 28, 1965, p. 6, and June 29, 1965, p. 6.

[31] *Ibid.*

heavily from it in his own book, *Freedom and After*,[32] which, in turn, was referred to in writing the White Paper. In effect then, "A Critic" was actually attacking *Ujamaa*.[33]

A few days before this particular critic of the Kenya Paper held forth, the *Nationalist* published an article by "A Contributor" who rejected the very idea of an African socialism.[34] He outlined the evolution of society from a primitive stage to socialism. He noted that Lenin, "the founder of modern Socialism," had believed that principles would be modified in particular circumstances and adapted to national and national/state differences. Lenin's analysis "surely demolishes the myth that the scientific socialist theory is one and the same solution for all situations and for all time." The author argues, nonetheless, that there is no distinctly African or Asian socialism "from a purely realist point of view"; the very diversity of states within Africa prohibits the inclusion of all under any one label. Yet socialism as a form of social organization is universal. "A Contributor" takes up one of Nyerere's main points in *Ujamaa*: Do classes exist in our African societies? Here the proponent of Lenin's scientific socialism hedges his bet by saying that it is possible to have a society without classes, but they will arise if capitalism is allowed free development. This statement did not contradict Nyerere's version of traditional, classless African societies; and Nyerere himself had admitted that capitalism had already brought attitudes of mind associated with classes. There is, however, an inherent contradiction between Nyerere's view of African tribal society as essentially without

[32] Mazrui, *op.cit.*, pp. 225ff. has made this point.

[33] I have said that "in effect" the author was attacking *Ujamaa* because I cannot prove he was consciously doing it. Polemics in East Africa are fairly rare and an esoteric language of communication is not all that common. Nonetheless, the audience for "A Critic" would be familiar with both *Ujamaa* and *Freedom and After*. I am personally convinced that "A Critic" saw the connection.

[34] Remarks of "A Contributor" were published in the *Nationalist*, June 18, p. 6, and June 19, 1965, p. 6.

class and therefore without class conflict,[35] and Marxism-Leninism, which is a theory of class conflict. "A Contributor," reader of *Left-Wing Communism: An Infantile Disorder*, knew this. But rather than oppose *Ujamaa* head-on, he merely said that labels—African, European, or other—ought not to be placed before socialism.

Not all who desire a socialism more "militant" than Nyerere's embrace scientific socialism so heartily. Some middle-level leaders differ with *Ujamaa*'s formulations more in political style than in content. And middle-level leaders who speak in a Marxist jargon never used by Nyerere also recognize a "Tanzanian way."[36] Nyerere has admitted, sorrowfully, that there will be difficulties in building a society with a minimum of differences between strata. Others have spoken with relish of these difficulties because they show that Tanganyika has undergone and will continue to undergo the evolution that history has in store for it. It is almost as if certain leaders know they are historical actors because they can participate in an indigenous class struggle.

Economic Policy and Nationalism

TANU had not worked out a program for development before independence. The single aim was *Uhuru*—Freedom, the only slogan *Uhuru Na Umoja*—Freedom and Unity. After *Uhuru* had been achieved, Nyerere wrote:

All we were saying [before independence] was "Let us

---

[35] Nyerere wrote in *Ujamaa*: "Indeed I doubt if the equivalent for the word 'class' exists in any indigenous African language; for language describes the ideas of those who speak it, and the idea of 'class' or 'caste' was non-existent in African society." He has said that in Tanzania, "in the short run there was always the problem of inter-community conflict about the division of national wealth between all the citizens." *Tanganyika Standard*, March 25, 1965, p. 3. But he still avoids a class analysis.

[36] The *Nationalist* editorials have noted Tanzania's "own way to socialism." See, e.g., April 29, 1965, p. 4.

unite and once we have achieved *Uhuru* the rest will take care of itself." . . . We deliberately refused to answer questions as to what we would do after *Uhuru*, because the moment we had started to do that we would have got our forces divided about future plans and that would have been wrong. . . . It is only now after the political problem has already been settled, that we can start grappling with the economic problems of developing our country.[37]

Thus Nyerere, because of his firm commitment to unity, consciously decided to avoid putting forward a specific program for development.

When it became clear that *Uhuru* would be granted, new slogans replaced the old—*Uhuru Na Kazi* (Freedom and Work), the "war against poverty, ignorance, and disease." And Nyerere's promise that the focus would shift to economic problems was fulfilled, as evidenced by the amended TANU Constitution in which the aims and objects of TANU are set forth. The first (1954) version of the Constitution states that:

> TANU will work to encourage cooperatives and trade unions; urge that producers get the best price and that consumers buy in the best market; help Africans establish an increasing share in the running and owning of business; establish a minimum wage and a system of assisted farming; and oppose alienation of land.[38]

The commitments of TANU were to social policies which would ameliorate economic hardships and lead to greater Africanization of the economy. There was no explicit statement of development policies which would change the structure of the economy; nor was there a concern with development per se.

[37] Stahl, *op.cit.*, pp. 7-8.
[38] Martin Lowenkopf has reproduced the articles of the TANU Constitution in his *Political Parties in Uganda and Tanganyika*.

The amended version (1961) listed under "aims and objectives of TANU" the elimination of poverty, disease, and ignorance, and the insurance of a decent standard of living for all citizens.[39] A section was devoted to increasing the country's wealth by establishing collective control of the means of producing national wealth, including national resources and the media for disseminating and receiving information. Cooperative functions would be encouraged; and private enterprises run for the benefit of the whole country would be promoted. All these measures were to be carried out by a "democratic and socialist form of Government." The linking of "democratic and socialist" expresses the connection that Nyerere sees between political independence and economic development. He has said that, "therapy for a country's political ills lies in involving every citizen in the program for rapid economic development."[40]

Between the attainment of independence and the new 1965 TANU Constitution, Nyerere seemed unwilling to define more explicitly than he had in *Ujamaa* what he meant by "socialist." The first TANU Constitution provided merely a set of guidelines for a program of development, but they did not add up to a program itself. The 1965 Constitution stipulates that in order to ensure economic justice the state must have effective control over the principal means of production; it must intervene in the economic life of the country to ensure the well-being of the citizens, to prevent the exploitation of one person by another; and it must prohibit the accumulation of wealth to an extent which is inconsistent with a classless society. Thus, government is to participate wherever possible in the economic development of the country to effectuate collective ownership of the means of production.

[39] TANU Constitution, Dar es Salaam: Mwananchi Publishing Co., Ltd., n.d. (English translation, from TANU National Headquarters, mimeograph).

[40] Julius Nyerere, *TANU Na Raia* (TANU and the Citizen) (Dar es Salaam: 1962).

While this is not in itself a departure from anything in *Ujamaa*, it is more specific.

TANU leaders see the present *Five Year Plan* as a statement of TANU values and goals first set forth at the 1959 Annual Conference and promulgated in the 1965 TANU Constitution. When Nyerere recommended the *Five Year Plan* to the National Assembly he stressed the importance of guarding Tanganyika's inheritance—its values and traditions. Change should not sweep away all that has gone before:

> Perhaps the most important of all, we must also retain the values of brotherliness, of familyhood which our fathers had. This, in fact, is the purpose of all our work and all our plans; the creation—through African Socialism—of a country in which we can all live proudly as brothers.[41]

When Nyerere stressed the values of traditional society in *Ujamaa*, he did not take an anti-industrial position. He rejected two modern industrial creeds: what he called capitalism and doctrinaire socialism; he rejected class warfare and acquisitiveness for the purpose of gaining power and prestige. But he never rejected the benefits of industrial wealth, or equated agrarian wealth with some higher value. For Nyerere, industry is associated with modernity and dignity; to be forever agrarian is to be forever backward.

> Tanganyika must end her absolute reliance on the prices of primary commodities. We must have an industrial base to our economy. Only when we have achieved this will our future be to some extent safeguarded.[42]

However, Nyerere has not equated economic development with heavy industry; nor has he understood the *Five Year*

[41] Julius Nyerere, Address to the National Assembly, May 12, 1964, reprinted in the *Tanganyika Five Year Plan for Economic and Social Development*, I (Dar es Salaam: Government Printer, 1964), xv. Known as the *Five Year Plan*.
[42] *Ibid.*

Plan as a document which calls for it. And while he has favored communal farming schemes and collectivized pilot projects, he has not insisted on communal or collective farming; in fact he has often praised the virtues of the yeoman-farmer.

Other voices have been raised which go much farther than either Nyerere or the present version of the TANU Constitution and which differ markedly from Nyerere on the subject of economic development and industrialization.

The *Five Year Plan* was formulated before the Union with Zanzibar, but was not commended by Nyerere to the National Assembly until May 1964, after the Union had taken place. By the time various ministers could present the National Assembly with the duties and expectations they had for their ministries, Zanzibaris headed important economic ministries. Among them, Mr. A. Babu was made a Minister of State in the Directorate of Planning and later became Minister for Commerce and Cooperatives; Mr. Kassim Hanga, one of the leaders of the Zanzibar Revolution and onetime Vice President of the Zanzibar Revolutionary Council, became Tanzanian Minister for Industries, Mineral Resources, and Power. Mr. Hanga, in his address to the National Assembly introducing the industrial development program of the *Five Year Plan*, expressed an idea of development very different from anything which had been propounded before in Tanganyika.[43] Mr. Hanga's interpretation of the *Five Year Plan* was at variance with both the facts of the *Plan* and Nyerere's conception of it. Furthermore, Hanga utilized a Marxist-Leninist ideological framework, and a rhetoric distinctly Stalinist in style and content, which had never been stated so boldly in Tanganyika, though it had been in vogue for many months in Zanzibar itself.

[43] Address to the National Assembly of the Minister for Industries and Mineral Resources, Mr. Kassim Hanga, printed in the *Nationalist*, July 2, 1964.

Hanga's style and his ideas echoed the Soviet Five Year Plans of the 1930's. Mr. Hanga stated that the establishment of heavy industry was the overall basic policy of his ministry: "Unless we build up heavy industry, we shall not be able to build up any industry, and without that we shall be doomed as an independent country." The Minister acknowledged that investment in heavy industry required a "colossal amount of money," which he believed could be derived from increasing exploitation of agricultural resources by the state. Strict economy must be employed in order to get resources for heavy industry, and sacrifices would be required. Whatever the difficulties, the Minister for Industries continued, his ministry would do everything possible to see that iron and steel industries were established as soon as possible—"as iron and steel are the foundation of the industrial base of the country"—and to further his ministry's policy of having "a coal and metallurgy base in the United Republic." The Minister asked rhetorically: "What is the main link of our development plans? The main link in the development plan is heavy industry with machine building at its core." The way to overcome backwardness is to have a storm economy.[44] "We intend to build an industry that shall pour tens of thousands of tractors, harvester machines and other complex machinery into the countryside." He also connected the form of agricultural organization to the possibilities of development when he said: "Socialism can be built on the basis of largescale production"; "largescale farming can serve as a foundation of socialism, but not largescale private farming." And, referring specifically to Zanzibar, Mr. Hanga said largescale agriculture was the only way peasants could rapidly improve economic conditions in the countryside. "Smallscale independent peasant farms either decline and become impoverished or develop and give rise to capitalism."

[44] The word "storm" is mine, not Mr. Hanga's.

The theme of heavy industry was linked to that of sacrifice. In the past, heavy industry had always been considered in the context of an East African Federation, or at least an East African Common Market. But now Mr. Hanga stressed that Tanzania must be prepared to "go it alone" if necessary. The aim was to convert the United Republic from a weak, agrarian country dependent on the caprices of other countries to a powerful, industrial country, fully self-reliant and independent of exploiting countries.[45]

Economic nationalism has more and more dominated the tone of discussions about economic development in Tanzania and has already led to some major departures in economic policy. Nyerere himself has warned that the underdeveloped countries may have to organize themselves into a trading and aiding bloc in order to protect themselves against richer nations. But he wants to avoid this if possible, for he recognizes that the path to development will be much longer and more arduous if the poor nations cut themselves off in this way. Nyerere has said that development can and will take place in Tanzania but that help must be marshaled. Increasingly he has stressed self-sufficiency and self-sacrifice as aid from abroad is not so readily forthcoming.[46] And he has said that there is no disgrace in accepting aid as long as Tanzania is frugal and makes sacrifices herself. But Nyerere does not propound economic nationalism in the name of national independence and economic development.

Those who have employed a Marxist-Leninist framework have been the most aggressively nationalistic in economic policy. The Zanzibar ministers, Babu and Hanga, have stressed the conflict between the "have" and the "have-not" nations. They have been more insistent than Nyerere about

[45] Interview with Mr. Hanga, December 1964.

[46] Speech made at Tukuyu, reported in the *Nationalist*, August 20, 1964. Nyerere said Tanganyikans were governing themselves only a quarter. "Complete independence means being in a state of self-supportment."

the need for a bloc of underdeveloped countries to confront the West. At the same time, they have argued that Tanzania must build an independent national economy on the basis of self-reliance.[47]

In Tanzania, men who analyze economic conditions in Marxist-Leninist terms, who use a language replete with such words as "national bourgeoisie," "peasants" (Nyerere uses the word "farmer"), "feudal institutions," describe themselves as nationalists as well as internationalists.[48] And indeed, their economic positions are nationalistic.

Nationalism dictates certain preferences in economic policies: an emphasis on industrialization as the path to economic development; the choice of certain industries which are regarded as key industries at different stages of developments (for example, the insistence that a steel industry is the *sina qua non* of economic development); the preference for public enterprise over private enterprise; in the area of trade policies, the great emphasis on import substitution and self-sufficiency; and finally, the opposition to the investment of foreign capital and to the employment of foreign technical personnel.[49] The Marxist-Leninist-Maoists have expressed their commitment to all the preferences noted.[50] Their political philosophy has not stood in the way of economic nationalism. If anything, it has reinforced this nationalism by

[47] See A. M. Babu, "Tanzania Pointing the Way to Wealthy Economy," *Nationalist*, May 4, 1965, p. 5.

[48] Personal interviews. One man said to me: "I . . . am always called a communist but I am an African nationalist." He then went on to make it clear that he was an African nationalist, as well as a communist, in his own lights.

[49] Harry Johnson, "A Theoretical Model of Economic Nationalism in New and Developing States." *Political Science Quarterly*, LXX (June 1965), pp. 169-85.

[50] Babu, *loc.cit.*; Hanga, *loc.cit.* There has been no overt opposition to getting foreign investment or foreign personnel. They have stressed the need to be self-sufficient but they have been realistic about the need to import skills and capital.

providing categories in which to justify it at this stage of Tanzanian and world development.[51]

There are men who argue, in effect, that Socialism in One Country must be built. Here is the identity of socialism and nationalism. One consequence of this congruence of commitments has been a veiled attack on East African Federation by some of the proponents of this ideology of development. Letters to the editors of the *Nationalist* have appeared which argue that the formation of an East African Federation is desired by Western monopolists so that they can control a larger market. The desire to maintain a common East African currency is ascribed to British and Americans who will control East Africa through sterling and dollar control. Only a genuine East African Federation should come about. The duty of the Tanzanian people is to expose the sham Federation proposed by the imperialists. And behind all this is the idea that the present governments of Uganda and Kenya are not entirely free of imperialist control.[52]

Not all proponents of economic nationalism have expressed themselves in the language of Marx and Lenin. When Tanzania withdrew from the East African Common Currency Board, some MPs rose to denounce Kenya simply in nationalistic (and paranoid) terms.[53] One MP stood up in the Tanzania National Assembly and said:

[51] I have not related Johnson's analysis of the way in which nationalism in the economic field tends to direct economic development policy in certain specific directions. In some areas of preference, nationalism and Marxism-Leninism-Maoism are clearly congruent, e.g., favoring extensive state control and public ownership of enterprises. In other areas Johnson deals with, the congruences are not so clear. One preference may have to give way to another or be displaced or submerged in that larger identity of socialism in One Country.

[52] See S. S. Abdullah's letter to the editors, *Nationalist*, June 26, 1965, p. 4.

[53] The Minister for Finance, Mr. Paul Bomani, announced Tanzania's withdrawal when he presented the annual budget to the Na-

Our country has been turned into a mere market by Kenya for their manufactured goods. Even with regard to the East African Common Services, our country is an underdog. . . . Indeed I can only say that we are tired of exploitation.[54]

Another said:

Let no one use Tanzania as a scapegoat. For quite a long time we have sacrificed our development in favor of unity. All this is on record. And now Kenya wants to blame us; perhaps because they think they can continue to fool Tanzania.[55]

Julius Nyerere was in Nigeria when the storm broke. Thus his restraining hand was not evident, and some MPs went so far as to suggest that Tanzania reconsider its position in the East African Common Services Organization.

Another important theme which has been exploited is the myth of success. Nyerere has always maintained that development will take place and he points to what has already been accomplished.

Nyerere says the slogan for the *Five Year Plan* should be: It can be done; play your part. He stresses the long pull and the need to understand that, while percentage increases in per capita income may come about during the *Five Year Plan* period, Tanzania will still be very poor and underdeveloped. He wants to make people conscious of the statistics and aware of the *Plan* without making a fetish of figures and paper documents.[56]

---

tional Assembly on June 10, 1965. See the *Nationalist* and the *Tanganyika Standard* and the *East African Standard* of June 11, 1965.

[54] P. Mbogo, Mpanda and Area Commissioner in Biharamulo, quoted in the *Nationalist*, June 15, 1965, p. 1.

[55] Mr. Richard Wambura (Maswa), Junior Minister, Vice President's office and former regional commissioner, quoted in *ibid.*, p. 2.

[56] Speech of Julius Nyerere to a conference of regional commission-

The *Nationalist* has propagated the idea that success is assured if people become nation-builders, and that there already exists a remarkable record of progress:

> The United Republic of Tanzania enters her fourth year with a remarkable record of achievements, a steady progress, and a solidly determined and confident future. What has failed elsewhere or has been looked upon as a long-term target has found immediate success in Tanzania.[57]

Tanganyika's past is characterized as one of unawareness. Where Tanganyika was lethargical and tolerant, almost unaffected by the rising tide of Africanism, it is now said to have leaped into the mainstream and emerged as a center of activity. Speeches are made extolling the nation-builders. To be a nation-builder is to be a participator, one who gathers crowds, starts farming schemes, mans tractors, and does the work of ten in Stakhanovite fashion.[58] Nation-builders are also people who buy bonds and don't drink too much beer.

> Long live the Unity of the Peoples of the United Republic of Tanzania; Success to the Five Year Development Plan; Forward to a Socialist Society which will be able to rationalize and intensify its [the *Plan*'s] Development.[59]

Nyerere has said much this same thing, but in quite a different language.

Democracy, the Party, and the State

Perhaps the most important issue of all has revolved around the differing conceptions of the way TANU is to be

---

ers, October 26, 1964, reprinted in the *East Africa Journal* (December 1964), pp. 23-27.

[57] G. Likungu, "Remarkable Record of Progress," *Nationalist*, special *Uhuru* Supplement, December 9, 1964, pp. 13, 18.

[58] The *Nationalist* ran a series of articles in this style from October 13 through 18, 1964 on nation-builders written by Richard Kisch.

[59] From a *Nationalist* editorial.

organized and operated. And on these grounds a compromise which is weighted towards Nyerere's own views has emerged in the form of the *Report of the Presidential Commission on the Establishment of a Democratic one Party State,*[60] the subsequent amendments to the *Presidential Report,* and the new operating procedures contained in the TANU Constitution and the Interim Constitution for Tanzania.

Julius Nyerere has stated his conception of an operating democracy as a society which is essentially without factions. At first, when Nyerere was confronted with a de facto one-party situation after the elections for Legislative Assembly in 1960, he argued that a one-party system could be democratic. In a short article, he asserted that the two basic essentials of democracy were freedom of the individual and insurance that the government of a country will be freely chosen by the people. Nyerere affirmed his devotion to democracy:

> We are aware of the efforts and even the sacrifices people in new countries may be called on to make in the national interest in the process of consolidation of their newly won freedom through economic reconstruction. But even granted this, there should be no conflict between our commitment to freedom for the individual and the need for the national effort. In fact, these can work together harmoniously as long as the emphasis is on the national interest as implying the interests of the individuals who comprise the nation.[61]

Nyerere soon moved to a position in which he argued that a one-party system of government was even more democratic than a two-party or multi-party system. *Democracy and the Party System* attempts to provide the framework for an at-

[60] Published in April 1965.
[61] Nyerere, "Will Democracy Survive in Africa," *loc.cit.*

tack on organized disagreement in Tanganyika and a positive affirmation of democracy as Nyerere construes it.

Nyerere has argued that democracy "in its true sense" is a familiar phenomenon to the African.[62] Ideally, it is a form of government whereby *all* the people settle their affairs through open discussion. Nyerere maintains that the two-party system requires certain disciplines: (1) after the selection of official candidates, all party members must support the official candidates only; and (2) party candidates who have won elections and have taken their seats in Parliament must remain bound by the rules of party discipline. When the party is conducting its own internal business, fellow members may compete for offices or oppose one another. Those whose political thinking has been moulded by the Western parliamentary tradition have now become so used to this tradition that they cannot imagine democracy without it. But the question ought to be posed: How can you have democracy with a two-party system?—rather than: How can you have democracy with a one-party system?

Where there is one party and that party is identified with the nation as a whole, the foundations of democracy are firmer than they can ever be where you have two or more parties, and each represents only a section of the community. A two-party system can be justified only when the parties are divided over some fundamental issue; in any other circumstances, it merely encourages the growth of factionalism. To put it another way, the only time when a political group can represent the interests of a section of the community without being a faction is when that group fights to remove a grievous wrong from society. But then the differences between this group and those responsible for the wrong it fights are fundamental; and there can be no question of national unity until the differences have been removed by change. And "change"

[62] Following ideas from Nyerere, *Democracy and the Party System.*

in that context is a euphemism because any change in fundamentals is properly termed a "revolution." The reason why the word "revolution" is generally associated with armed insurrection is that the existence of really fundamental differences within any society poses a "civil war" situation, and has often led to bloody revolution.

If you have a two-party system where the differences between the parties are *not* fundamental, then you immediately reduce politics to the level of a "football game." "The politics of a country governed by a Two-Party system are not, and cannot be, *national* politics; they are the politics of groups whose differences, more often than not, are of small concern to the majority of people."[63] Given fundamental agreement, it would be more sensible if both sides were to disband their football teams and let the electorate choose the best individual from among them all. There could then be cooperation in getting the job done. "This is what we do when we elect party leaders—party policy having been agreed upon. And this is what *should* happen when we elect national leaders—national policy being agreed upon."[64]

Nyerere then repairs to an historical argument to reinforce his points. "In Africa politics must be taken seriously" (more seriously than under the conditions of the football-match politics). He calls attention to the origins of African political parties, which make them different from parties in Europe or America. European and American parties came into being as the result of existing social and economic divisions. African parties were not formed to challenge groups ruling their own people; they were formed to challenge the foreigners who ruled over Africa.

They were not, therefore, political "parties"—i.e. factions—but nationalist movements. And from the outset they represented the interests and aspirations of the whole

63 *Ibid.*, p. 7.
64 *Ibid.*, p. 11.

nation. Now that the colonialists have gone, there is no remaining division between "rulers" and "ruled," no mono-political power by any sectional group which could give rise to conflicting parties. The only reason for the formation of such parties, therefore, is the desire to imitate the political structure of a totally dissimilar society.[65]

In rejecting factionalism, Nyerere rejects parties whose membership is confined to an aristocracy, either of birth or of intellect, for aristocratic parties neither are, nor are intended to be, national parties.

They are sectional groups which seek to rule the rest of society by virtue of their own claim to superiority. And in all such parties—whether the factional parties of a two-party democracy or the vanguard aristocracies of an ideological dictatorship—it is the leaders who "elect" each other.[66]

The major tenets of *Democracy and the Party System* go beyond an attack on factionalism. They contain an anti-party ethic. *Democracy and the Party System* expresses a desire to abolish politics from society insofar as politics means organized disagreement. While Nyerere has not explicitly rejected the premise that diversity of opinion and individual dissent are necessarily harmful to the body politic, his concept of individualism is one where individuals are not identified by and with their own interests. This would be selfishness. To let individuals organize in their own interest would be to raise selfishness to a legitimate political principle. Individual interests must be identified only insofar as they replace collective interests.

Nyerere's conception of the *need* for unity in Tanganyika, and his idea that individuals ought not to disagree about the essentials *of* a good society *in* a good society have led him to accept a diversity of individual opinion as long as it has no

[65] *Ibid.*, p. 15.   [66] *Ibid.*, p. 21.

organized political expression. TANU is still the Tanganyika African National *Union* to Nyerere.[67] His commitment to the idea of political equality has led him to insist that TANU must not restrict itself by setting up narrow criteria for membership, but must maintain itself as an open political movement. He has argued for making Tanganyika *de jure* a one-party system so that TANU can become truly democratic by allowing it to dispense with the disciplines required in a multiparty system. "Then any member of the Movement . . . would be free to stand as a candidate if he so wishes."[68] He has almost been saying that until TANU is completely all-embracing, it cannot be simply identified with the nation. He has recognized that while some people may respond more to TANU than to an idea of the state, others must be brought to feel themselves part of the nation and they may have rejected entrance via TANU in the past. Nyerere's commitment to national unity has led him to talk in terms which make the national movement and the state coextensive. They both embrace the whole society.

Thus Nyerere has never accepted the view that TANU constituted an elite within Tanganyika, nor has he tried to define an operational code for party functionaries as distinct from other TANU members. Nyerere does not use the language of "cadres" and "party militants." The pledges a TANU member makes reflect this:

(1) All human beings are my brethren and Africa is one country.

(2) I will serve my country and all its people.

(3) I will personally volunteer to work for the eradication of poverty, ignorance, and disease.

(4) Bribery is the real enemy of Justice; I will neither receive nor give bribes.

[67] He does, however, refer to TANU as a party as well as a national movement.

[68] *Ibid.*, p. 25.

(5) An official rank is a responsibility. I will never use my position or that of other people for my own benefit.

(6) I will educate myself as much as I can and utilize my knowledge for the benefit of all the people.

(7) I will cooperate with all my fellow members in building our country.

(8) I will speak the truth and will never betray.

(9) I will be a loyal member of TANU and a good citizen of Tanganyika and Africa.[69]

These are not commitments to an elitist organization; TANU is only mentioned once.[70] The March 1965 TANU Annual Conference added a tenth pledge:

(10) I promise to be loyal and faithful to the President of the United Republic of Tanzania.

This is a specific political commitment: oaths of personal

[69] TANU Constitution (English), pp. 10-11.

[70] Compare some pledges a Communist Party member makes in the Soviet Union:

(1) To protect the unity of the Party might and main, as the chief requisite for its power and strength.

(2) To be an active fighter for the implementation of Party decisions . . . a passive and formal attitude on the part of Communists toward the Party decisions undermines the Party's efficiency and is therefore incompatible with continuance in its ranks.

(3) To observe Party and state discipline which is equally binding on all Party members. . . .

(4) To raise his level of political understanding and broaden his knowledge of the principles of Marxism-Leninism.

(5) To develop self-criticism and criticism from below. . . .

(6) To inform leading Party bodies, up to and including the central Committee, of shortcomings irrespective of person.

This is not an all-inclusive list of pledged duties. Nor have I given any of the rights of Party members. The list is taken from the *Rules of the Communist Party of the Soviet Union,* adopted by the Nineteenth Party Congress (Moscow: Foreign Language Publishing House, 1953), reprinted in Evanston, Illinois, 1959, mimeograph.

loyalty can be the basis for political creeds and elitist organizations. But TANU has no tests to prove this loyalty. Thus the pledge stands like an American pledge of allegiance to the flag.

Neither do the aims and objects of TANU, as they have been defined by Nyerere, bind the members into an elitist organization. They are in keeping with the idea of TANU as a national movement, a union of the people of Tanganyika.[71]

[71] Article Two of the Constitution of TANU. The aims and objects of "TANU" shall be:
(1) To maintain the Independence of our country and its People's Freedom.
(2) To ensure recognition of the inherent dignity of the individual in accordance with the Universal Declaration of Human Rights.
(3) To establish and to safeguard a democratic and socialistic form of Government, which would be devoted to—
    (a) consolidating national Independence and to ensuring a decent standard of living for every individual;
    (b) giving equal opportunity to all men and women irrespective of race, religion or status;
    (c) eliminating poverty, disease and ignorance by means of co-operation between citizens and their government;
    (d) eradicating all types of exploitation, intimidation, discrimination, bribery and corruption.
(4) To develop fully this country's means of wealth in order that the entire nation may benefit by—
    (a) owning collectively the principal agencies and factors of production, e.g., land, water, air, power and means of communication;
    (b) developing to the maximum the co-operative effort in the fields of production, distribution and exchange;
    (c) encouraging private enterprise where this is directed toward the benefit of the whole country.
(5) To cooperate with all political parties which are fighting for the Independence of Africa in order that the entire continent may be rid of colonialists and its Independence may be consolidated and preserved.
(6) To endeavour to bring about unity in Africa through cooperation with the other Independent African states.
(7) To endeavour to bring about peace and security in the world through the United Nations.

Nyerere's conception of TANU as an all-embracing movement left him open to the accusation that he advocated a no-party system for Tanganyika instead of a one-party system. The main line of attack was centered on his suggesting in *Democracy and the Party System* that candidates might run under a general TANU rubric and contest against each other (even for the Presidency). The TANU rubric appeared to be without content: Nyerere had not defined what it meant a TANU person to be, beyond swearing the pledges I have noted above; and he had not formulated a role for TANU, beyond saying that TANU would act "as a two-way, all-weather road along which purposes, plans, and problems of government travel to the people and, at the same time, ideas, desires and misunderstandings of the people travel to the Government."[72] Thus, the editor of *Spearhead* (a journal published in Dar es Salaam from 1961 to 1963, now defunct, and which Nyerere used as a forum) insisted that it was only within the limits of an established and accepted ideology that a one-party system could work. Otherwise, "idealism not based on realities would lead to a 'no-party' state and anarchy."[73] The editor maintained that Nyerere had crossed swords with the communists for making their policies a creed, but that there was a far greater pitfall in failing to establish a recognizable ideology, with certain fundamental and well-defined concepts, upon which policy should be based.

The Tanganyikan students of Makerere College responded to *Democracy and the Party System* by asking Nyerere if his open movement would not, in effect, lead to a proliferation of factions, tribally based perhaps, which all called them-

[72] This was the job of the new TANU as outlined by Mr. Nyerere in the Tanganyika Information Services press release, No. 1, January 22, 1962, quoted in Bennet, *loc.cit.*

[73] Frene Ginwala, "No Party State," *Spearhead*, III (February 1963). Colin Leys, "The Need for an Ideology," *Kivukoni Journal* (Dar es Salaam, 1961), p. 4, also felt that TANU and Tanganyika could not do without an ideology.

selves TANU. In a memorandum presented to Nyerere when he addressed the students at Makerere, they asked in what way TANU would be a party at all, if it was entirely open.[74]

These commentators were expressing the fear that in the absence of a narrower definition of TANU, the nation would itself be politically undefined. They feared the emergence of internecine fighting within TANU. These views were expressed in 1962-63 by people who were in sympathy with Mr. Nyerere's own attitudes. No voice was raised publicly by those middle-level leaders who had opposed him in the NEC. In fact, there has been no frontal attack on *Democracy and the Party System*, just as there has never been one on *Ujamaa*; but a number of views have been made known which have expressed very different sentiments and proposals than those contained in *Democracy and the Party System*.[75]

"A Critic's" article on the Kenya government's *African Socialism* includes the following passage:

> Para. 10 [of the Kenya Paper] makes the curious statement that "African Socialism does not countenance a party of the elite, stern tests, or discriminatory criteria for party membership." But you do not build socialism without socialists, and socialists must go through "stern tests" and discipline, since theirs is the task of leading the fight

[74] Memorandum of the Makerere Tanganyika Students "One-Party System by Law," mimeograph, 1963.

[75] Mention should be made of one short piece which supports Nyerere's position. Dr. Wilbert Klerruu, now Deputy Secretary General as well as Publicity Secretary of TANU, wrote a shorter version of *Democracy and the Party System* which he called *One Party System of Government* (Dar es Salaam: Mwananchi Publishing Company Ltd.), 1964. In his pamphlet, Dr. Klerruu argued that in a one-party system there is no need to subordinate freedom of opinion to party expediency, or national loyalty to party loyalty. He also argued for the maintenance of inter-party criticism. But he nowhere repeated Nyerere's assertion that "any member of the Movement [which in this context means any particular citizen, since it is a National Movement we are talking about] would be free to stand as a candidate if he so wishes."

against the well-entrenched, well-organized forces of exploitation and reaction.

Socialism must come from the people themselves, through their own party organization which is uncorrupted and uncorruptible by the machination of the forces of exploitation and reaction. That is why a socialist party CANNOT be a party of all the people. Can anyone seriously suggest that a reactionary, say like any leading Kenya settler, will automatically become an "African Socialist" once he takes a party membership card?[76]

Nyerere has always held that political redemption is possible. He would not say, of course, that anyone will "automatically" become an African socialist, but he has held out the possibility of all individuals becoming whole through identification with and participation in the political community. The aim of TANU is to make all citizens realize they are participants in the nation.[77] And the attitude of mind rather than the social origins or class position of an individual must define his place in the system.

Nyerere has never expressed the idea that the development of a one-party system in Tanganyika was somehow the outcome of ineluctable laws of history. His attitude has been that "in relation to the form of our future society, and in relation to our political institutions . . . we must grope our way forward."[78] He said that the establishment of a one-party state was the logical sequence to the establishment of TANU which, "when formed, received the overwhelming support of the people of Tanganyika."[79]

Compare this to the view expressed by the Parliamentary

[76] "A Critic," op.cit.

[77] TANU Na Raia, op.cit.

[78] Nyerere first said this in July 1961, and quoted himself in an address to the National Assembly on June 8, 1965. Reported in the Nationalist, June 9, 1965, p. 4.

[79] Ibid., p. 1.

Secretary for Commerce, MP for Mpwapwa constituency, and former regional commissioner and regional chairman, Mr. A. S. Mtaki:

> The laws of history teach that society travels from primitive communalism, feudalism, capitalism and then socialism which calls for the establishment of a one-party state. That Tanzania should be a one-party state is inevitable because we have reached the stage of socialism.[80]

Nyerere had never connected the establishment of a one-party system with socialism in this way because he has not defined the state as an expression of any class interest. He has never identified TANU as expressing the "real" or "higher" interests of the state. In fact, Nyerere does not write about the state either in *Democracy and the Party System* or in *Ujamaa*.[81]

The Presidential Commission

A Presidential Commission was convened to consider changes necessary in the Tanganyika Constitution, in the Constitution of TANU, and in the practice of government to bring into effect a democratic one-party state. The Commission was called after the January 1964 mutiny of the army had been put down and its members broken into three groups which toured the regions, soliciting opinions from the public at large.

One member of the NEC said that the membership of the Commission reflected a compromise between civil servants, political leaders, and technical personnel.[82] Since individuals

[80] Speech of Mr. Mtaki to the National Assembly, *ibid.*, p. 8.

[81] In the 25 pages of *Democracy and the Party System*, the word "state" appears twice. Nyerere refers to Disraeli describing a situation as "Two Nations within a State" (p. 8), and he refers to the "City States of Ancient Greece" (p. 1). In *Ujamaa*, the word does not appear at all in the English version.

[82] From personal interview.

were not representing interest groups on the Commission, it would be more accurate to say that Nyerere had thrown the net very wide in an attempt to get a mixed body of opinion on the Commission. He was not trying to have the Commission represent some assumed configuration of Tanganyikan political life.[83]

When President Nyerere announced the membership of the Commission, he recalled that on January 14, 1963 he had made public the decision of the NEC that Tanganyika should become a democratic one-party state *de jure*. Thus the President made it clear that the decision to have a one-party state, constitutionally, had already been taken in 1963. Furthermore, Tanganyika would remain a Republic with an executive head of state; and the Rule of Law and the independence

[83] At that time, the President announced that he had empowered the National Executive to appoint a Commission on the one-party state. The Presidential Commission consisted of: Vice President Kawawa as chairman; the Minister for External Affairs, Oscar Kambona; the Minister for Justice, Sheikh Abedi; the parliamentary secretary for Community Development, Miss Lucy Lameck; the then parliamentary secretary for Vice President's office, now Minister of State in the President's office, Mr. Bhoke-Munanka; Dr. L. Stirling, a European MP; Chief Marealle, chairman of the Local Government Service Commission; Attorney General, Roland Brown, an expatriate official; Deputy Solicitor General, Mark Bomani; Deputy Chairman of the Tanganyika Agricultural Board, Mr. H. Msefya; the then administrative secretary in the Ministry of Development Planning and now permanent secretary in the President's office (the civil service head of the civil service), Mr. J. Namata; a Mr. Mustafa; and the secretary to the Commission, Mr. Amon Nsekela, then permanent secretary to the Ministry for Foreign Affairs and now permanent secretary to the Ministry of Industries. Members included people associated with the TFL, the Cooperative Movement, TANU, the Elders, civil service and non-African citizens of the Republic. Sheikh Abedi died before the Commission's deliberations were completed, and four Zanzibaris were appointed after the Union with Zanzibar; Mtoro Rehani, Hamed Amir, Hamisi Masoud, and Ahmed Hassam Dira. Advisers from Guinea and Yugoslavia were not able to come to Tanganyika as planned; however, one member of the Commission went to Guinea and one went to Yugoslavia. Memoranda were submitted by interested parties in Tanganyika.

of the judiciary would be maintained. These principles were part of the original basic principles of republican Tanganyika.[84]

The President also instructed the Commission to observe the following principles: there shall be maximum participation by the people in their own government and ultimate control by them over all organs of state on a basis of universal suffrage; there shall be complete freedom for the people to choose their own representatives in all representative legislative bodies within the context of the law; there should be complete equality for all Tanganyika citizens, and maximum political freedom for all citizens within the context of a single national movement.[85]

Nyerere's instructions to the Commission were later amplified but they left entirely open the kind of socialist society that was to be built. They did not predetermine the question of whether or not TANU was to be a completely open political party.[86] The Commission wrestled with the very question that has been behind the hidden dialogue between Nyerere and other TANU leaders: Can a single party be a vehicle for nation-building in Tanganyika without turning into a Leninist party?[87] The balance to be decided on the level of intentions

[84] When the proposals for a republican constitution were first put forward in Government Paper No. 1 of 1962, Proposals of the Tanganyika Government for a Republic, four basic principles were stated: (1) as far as possible our institutions of Government must be such as can be understood by the people; (2) the Executive must have the necessary power to carry out the functions of a modern State; (3) Parliament must remain sovereign; (4) the Rule of Law must be preserved. See J.P.W.B. McAuslan, "The Republican Constitution of Tanganiyka," *International and Comparative Law Quarterly* (April 1964), pp. 508-66, for a discussion of these principles.

[85] *Presidential Report*, p. 2.

[86] In fact, a document titled "Guide to the Commission on a One-Party State" took up a range of questions on party/state relationships in a one-party system; the nature of TANU as an open party; criteria for candidates to stand for election, etc.; and posed these subjects as *questions*.

[87] I use "Leninist" to describe a militarily disciplined, centralized

is that between a militant, disciplined party and a free society. Of course, any decision to try and create a Leninist party would not necessarily be implemented in fact. And for those who shared Nyerere's idea of TANU the question arose: How can TANU be constituted so that anyone (or as Vice President Kawawa said, 99 per cent of the people)[88] can join and at the same time retain an identity and a value as a disciplined organization useful for implementing development plans.

The Presidential Commission answered the question— What then should be the character and the role of TANU as the single political party recognized by the Constitution?— by saying:

> In a One-Party State the threat, actual or potential, from an opposition disappears. This means that the party's survival no longer depends on mass membership or affiliation. From this it is sometimes argued that the party should see itself in the new context as an elite group, a minority ideologically dedicated who provide from above the leadership necessary to activate the inert mass of the community. Whatever practical advantage this may have in terms of dynamic leadership, we decisively reject this view of the Party and its role. We find it at variance with democratic principles and, in particular, with the principle of democracy as understood in traditional African society. We do not see TANU as an elite but as a mass party through which any citizen of good will can participate in the process of Government.[89]

The background for this statement was included in the very injunction to the Commission which was itself based on Nyerere's *Democracy and the Party System*. In fact, the

---

party with a powerful and authoritative party center which is unrestrained in its actions towards individuals and other organizations.

[88] Interview with Mr. Kawawa, April 1965.

[89] *Presidential Report*, p. 15.

Commission's Report quoted from this work immediately after the paragraph above:

> No party which limits its membership to a clique can ever free itself from the fear of overthrow by those it excluded. ... But a National Movement which is open to all—which is identified with the nation—has nothing to fear from the discontent from any excluded section of society, for there is no such section.[90]

Having rejected the idea of TANU as an elite group, the Commission still had to consider what TANU should require from a citizen applying for membership.

> To insist on narrow ideological conformity would clearly be inconsistent with the mass participation in the affairs of the Party which we regard as essential. ... On the other hand if membership involves no political commitment of any kind, TANU would become co-extensive with the Nation and cease to function as a political Party in any serious sense.[91]

Africans have always been able to join TANU simply by paying entrance dues (now two shillings or 28 cents American) and subscribing to the TANU pledge. Application is supposed to be made to a sub-branch secretary who submits it to the sub-branch committee for consideration. But membership cards have been issued freely, and even those who have

[90] *Ibid.*

[91] *Ibid.*, pp. 15-16. The *Report* thus echoed the reaction of the aforementioned Tanganyika students of Makerere College to Nyerere's idea that TANU would be open to every patriotic citizen without defining the criteria for "patriotic" and suggesting that every patriotic citizen would be allowed to stand for office. The Tanganyika students wrote in a "Memorandum on One-Party System by Law in Tanganyika": "The establishment of a national movement which is completely identified with the state but without the characteristics and functions of a normal political party might well be the setting for a proliferation of small factions based on tribal, religious, regional or class units."

not kept up their monthly dues (now 50 East African cents or about 7 American cents) are rarely disciplined and do not lose their membership.

By 1965, TANU was opened to all citizens without regard for race or occupation. After a decision of the NEC in 1963, Asians and Europeans were allowed to join.[92] The following year the colonial government's 1953 rule that civil servants were not allowed to join political organizations was revoked, and TANU was explicitly opened to civil service, army, and police. TANU had never held an ideology of exclusivism which put civil service beyond the political pale; thus during the struggle for independence, though civil servants were not in the forefront, they were never considered enemies of the national movement. Nyerere's emphasis on unity is attached to a concept of nation-building which conceives of unity by amalgamation, not unity by cutting off offending parts. The desire to be all-encompassing is so great that in 1964 TANU headquarters announced that non-citizens could be honorary TANU members as long as they contributed to nation-building.[93] To the question—"Should TANU be open to all citizens of Tanganyika regardless of their political opinion? If not, should a citizen be entitled to join if he accepts the principles of TANU as set out in the TANU Constitution?"[94]—the Presidential Commission answered that adherence to the principles of TANU as set out in the TANU Constitution should be a condition of membership. And it reported that this was one of the least controversial issues it was asked to consider: those who submitted memoranda usually did not feel it necessary to support this view; they took it for granted.[95] The Commission recognized that the TANU principles set out in

[92] A decision Nyerere hoped to obtain in 1961!

[93] *Nationalist*, August 28, 1964. Statement of the TANU Publicity Secretary.

[94] This was the first question in the questionnaire. *Presidential Report*, pp. 5, 7, 16.

[95] *Ibid.*, p. 5.

Article 2 of the Constitution are not narrow ideological formulations, but rather a broad statement of political faith.

A party based on these principles, and requiring adherence to them as a condition of membership, would be open to all but an insignificant minority of our citizens and would, we believe, be a truly national movement.[96]

President Nyerere mentioned in a press conference on April 7, 1965—the day the *Presidential Report* was published—that the Commission urges that the mass party have a political creed.[97] Nowhere in the *Presidential Report* are the words "political creed" used. It is political commitment to TANU that the President understands as a political creed.

As we have seen, political commitment to TANU is essentially unspecific and undefined. Nyerere sees his political creed as an umbrella under which he thinks all Tanzanians should be able to find shelter; others had a different view. The differences in viewpoints were apparent to me when I gave a seminar on the *Report* at the University College in Dar es Salaam which was attended by a number of TANU political figures and civil servants. I put forward the view that though the President mentioned political creed in his press conference, and the need for political commitment was stressed in the *Presidential Report*, these terms referred to things understood to be so diffuse in Tanganyika that they were without political content. And I suggested that perhaps the development of Tanzania required a more sharply defined ideology such as the *Presidential Report* had rejected. The reactions were vigorous: some argued that the commitment to a "democratic and socialist form of government" provided all that was required;[98] others thought that a specifically Marxist or Communist ideology would in time emerge and in fact had

[96] *Ibid.*, p. 16.
[97] *Nationalist*, April 8, 1965, p. 4.
[98] Second Vice President Mr. Kawawa expressed this view in a personal interview, April 1965.

244

been emerging,[99] and that the destruction of the distinction between the institutions of party and government would not indefinitely postpone the question of defining a political creed more explicitly.

Nyerere has maintained since the publication of *Democracy and the Party System* that TANU should be *de jure* the single party in Tanganyika in order to make TANU internally more democratic and in order to give people a chance to express a real political preference. They had to be allowed to reject an individual without appearing to reject TANU.[100] But when, in 1963, Nyerere suggested that TANU hold completely open election where "patriotic" individuals could run as TANU candidates, the NEC rejected his idea.[101] MPs, regional chairmen, regional secretaries, and MNE were against holding this kind of election;[102] those who were already "in" were worried that they might be put out. And we shall see that their fears were well grounded. In fact, many months before any new election could possibly be held, district and regional TANU organizations began to stir with activity. Individuals felt that Nyerere's position heralded an opening up of TANU to competition. The "ins" often construed this activity as "factionalism." The appointed officials were just as unfavorably disposed towards the idea as the elected officers were. Some of them, having been formerly elected officials, shared the attitudes of the chairmen and members of the dis-

[99] This was said to me after the seminar.

[100] Address to the National Assembly, reported in the *Nationalist*, October 13, 1965, p. 2.

[101] There has never been any public account of the NEC meeting at which the President raised his suggestion. But the rejection of open elections by the NEC was told to me by a number of people who were National Executive members or who had access to its meetings. I was not able to determine the date of the meeting; the topic undoubtedly came up in more than one meeting. Apparently, no vote was taken and the President did not propose his suggestion formally.

[102] This statement is based on interviews with more than 18 present and former commissioners, many MPs and TANU chairmen.

trict councils. All the commissioners with whom I spoke said they needed a disciplined, or at least non-fractious local TANU organization to work with, and they were afraid open elections would destroy the unity that did exist in branch, district, and regional organizations.

The solution was to hold elections after a process of pre-selection. Although preselection had always gone on, its form was now enshrined in the TANU Constitution and the Constitution of the Republic:

> The positive role of the Party cannot be sustained if it abdicates all right to influence the choice of candidates for election to Parliament. . . . We believe that it [a system of preselection] would help to sustain and strengthen the Party as a positive force in the politics of Tanganyika.[103]

The selected candidates are the only legal ones. Thus, although the Presidential Commission affirmed the idea of TANU as an non-elitist party, both the *de jure* one party and the system of preselection by the TANU district conferences and the NEC work to constitutionalize certain oligarchical tendencies in TANU. I am not arguing that for Tanzania as a whole the new arrangements do not provide wider choice than heretofore; they do.[104] But they also institutionalize a process of selection within a fairly closed circle. Thus, the view of the NEC rather than Nyerere's ideas of 1963 prevailed.[105]

[103] *Presidential Report*, p. 20. The *Report* noted that about half of those who answered their questionnaire on the subject of an entirely open contest were in favor of no preselection at all.

[104] The results of the parliamentary elections of September 1965 are discussed in chap. xii.

[105] I say Nyerere's ideas of 1963 because he seemed to have no difficulty in accepting elections contested by candidates who were preselected by the NEC and the district conferences. In fact, when the NEC's of TANU and the ASP amended the *Presidential Report* so that 2 instead of 3 candidates would stand for each parliamentary seat, Nyerere found this amendment to be an improvement.

However, the *Presidential Report* goes in different directions at the same time, because it is informed with the spirit of the President who constantly asks: How can we keep democratic feelings and institutions alive and growing in Tanzania? Nyerere believes in the "two-way street" actually going two ways. And his concern is shared by other national leaders, by some middle-level leaders, and apparently by many Tanzanians.[106] Nyerere appointed the Commission members. The membership was weighted toward technicians and civil servants to some degree. In part, this reflected the need to appoint people familiar with writing reports. And this brings us to a fact which cannot be lightly dismissed in Tanzania—the tyranny of the written word.

The President had given the guidelines. The commissioners had *Democracy and the Party System* before them (though they rejected one of its central premises). Most of the memoranda were presented by people interested in Constitution-making rather than revolution-making, for example, political scientists, members of the faculty of law of University College. The guidelines and the memoranda channeled the discussion to large degree. Since this was a new experience for many of the commissioners, it would not be odd if they were influenced by the documents directly before them. The *Report* notes "frank and open discussion" of the issues, when the commissioners toured the regions between March 16, 1964 and April 25, 1964.[107] Other commentators felt that the tendency was for a few people to dominate local discussions and for few views to be aired.[108] Publicity was given to the work of the Commission in the national broadcast

[106] One member of the Presidential Commission said he was struck by the widespread and deeply held commitment to free elections and an open party that were manifested when he toured the regions gathering information for the *Report*. Interview with Amon Nsekela, April 1965.

[107] Not all commissioners were on tour during the whole period.

[108] From interviews. I had no personal experience of such a meeting.

247

and the press. But the public debate on the *Presidential Report* after it was published never materialized.[109] Just as Nyerere was not attacked head-on over *Ujamaa* and *Democracy and the Party System*, there were no attacks on the views in the *Presidential Report* which were at variance with those expressed in the *Nationalist* at different times.[110]

The issues dealt with by the *Presidential Report* are by no means settled. Nyerere has called the *Report* a provisional statement rather than a final one.[111] And there have already been widely differing interpretations of it. For example, the *Nationalist* suggested that violations of party ethics be dealt with in "varying degrees of severity." It warned against pressure groups threatening TANU unity and singled out foreign enemies ("the wily foreign political merchant at our gate") intervening and using freedom of speech to promote disunity within TANU.[112] When Second Vice President Kawawa commended the *Presidential Report* to Parliament, he argued that freedom of speech was essential in a one-party state; a person should be listened to even if what he said "was foolish to another person."

People have to respect the government of their own free

---

[109] Sanger, *op.cit.*, p. 19. I was in Dar es Salaam when the *Report* was published and it created little stir among students of Kivukoni College where I was staying.

[110] The *Nationalist* greeted the *Report* by saying it was "ably written." But it was more enthusiastic about the subsequent amendments than the original document. ("There is no doubt that the amendments suggested constitute an improvement in making the original proposals put forward by the Presidential Commission more democratic." *Nationalist*, editorial, May 7, 1965, p. 4.)

[111] President Nyerere let it be known that another commission was to be convened to plot the Tanzanian way to socialism. When this book was in press, the NEC considered the Arusha Declaration which was drawn up by President Nyerere. The *Economist* reported that most members of the NEC were not even aware of the document's existence before meetings held in Arusha at the end of January 1967. *Economist*, February 18, 1967, p. 613.

[112] *Nationalist*, editorial, April 8, 1965, p. 4.

will and they should not be threatened so that they respect it. People should not fear their leaders, but they should feel free to confront them.[113]

Nyerere's impact on the *Presidential Report* was very great indeed. At the same time, it is evident that the Presidential Commission was conscious of the need to retain a party which could be useful for implementing development plans. It tried to find a balance between a party disciplined and effective enough to be useful for the development effort and a party decent and democratic enough to be, again, useful for the development effort and worthy to lead society. In this endeavor, the Presidential Commission was aware of the views of the emergent elite which emphasize unity and discipline. It would be grossly unfair to many TANU leaders who believe that a "tighter," "tougher," more militantly ideological TANU is required to ascribe these views to opportunism. Such views are not an unnatural response to the situation in which many a TANU leader found himself in Tanzania. It would be misleading to claim simply that all concern with democratic spirit is in Nyerere's hands and that all leaders who differ with him are obsessively absorbed with discipline and ideology. Nyerere himself seems to have moved to a recognition of the need for discipline as well as unity within TANU. And despite my characterization that Nyerere's sensibilities and ideas have fallen on relatively unfertile ground, many individuals who disagree with Nyerere when they propound their ideas are themselves affected by his tolerance, pragmatism, and moderation.

In TANU's early years, it might have been particularly rewarding to analyze those who differed from Nyerere in the NEC and the National Assembly in terms of personality traits. The willingness to coerce, to enforce discipline may still re-

[113] Vice President Kawawa, speaking in the National Assembly, reported in the *Nationalist*, June 10, 1965, p. 4.

flect predilections for gaining and using power. But now the analysis must come to grips with the real dilemma facing those at various levels of leadership in TANU: What kind of party can develop Tanzania? Individual perspectives must now be analyzed in terms of the roles people are called on to fill. The analysis must be an institutional one.[114] The conditions of development in Tanzania must be specified.

The Impact of Ideology

Before doing this, we must stress the importance of the style and content of ideology despite the fact of low literacy rates. For one thing, contact between the center and the districts is in good part a matter of discussion and speech-making. Many people are being brought into contact with the center for the first time. But the center is still very limited in the services it can provide and the tangible results it can bring to the people. Its relationships with the masses and the inter-relationships—vertically between TANU people at local, district, regional, and central levels, and horizontally from place to place—are in the realm of discussing problems and thinking about what can be done and the way to do it. Thus, the *way* in which problems are presented now is peculiarly important. The political development of Tanzania consists largely in the center establishing contact. The frames of reference for looking at the problems have a tendency to preempt the very political programs themselves.

The ideas that the leaders hold now will affect the way Tanzania develops in the future in a special sense. Obviously, it matters whether or not development is less important to them than identifying their country as *the* socialist state in East and Central Africa which takes its place in the sun by virtue of this identification rather than by virtue of its economic growth.[115] Decisions that are being taken will con-

114 If a concern with personality is retained, it is a concern for the political functioning of personality types.

115 When Tanzania broke relations with Great Britain in November

strain future economic decisions very much. This is particularly true because Tanzania is in a formative period. Its political institutions are new; the boundaries of the political system have recently been altered through the Union of Tanganyika and Zanzibar; cold war politics have come to East Africa with a vengeance; and very different ideas about political and economic development are for the moment coexisting in this highly volatile situation.

The people whom I have called middle-level leaders—the regional and district TANU leaders, leaders of organizations linked to TANU, MPS, TANU administrative officials, and the junior ministers at a higher level—may not make the policy for domestic and foreign programs. But they do more than influence the directions of these policies; they even do more than execute them. Their attitudes are as important as policies themselves because contacts between the center and the masses are intermittent, and government *means* the area commissioner, a few TANU leaders, and civil service representatives of the ministries. The ideas that the middle-level leaders hold about the nature of TANU and the way they perceive this process of economic development are crucial to the quality of life for the people that they rule. And where there are meager material and technical resources to change the way people live, the style and tone of existence is especially important when we characterize rule.

Thus, it is of great importance that the ideals Nyerere expressed in *Ujamaa* have not taken hold. *Ujamaa* has remained a statement of ideals; it has not been taken as a call to action. It is doubtful that

> *Ujamaa* has supplied a convenient and powerful ideology which is evolving into a comprehensible, flexible, and dignified ethic for programs and policies that spring from

---

1965 over Southern Rhodesia, it was clear that Tanzanian leaders sacrificed development for "purity" over Pan-African issues.

complex physical and psychological needs of an emerging and dynamic people.[116]

Ujamaa presents a statement of human values which is imprecise enough to justify many different government policies. But the tone has been much too soft to satisfy middle-level leaders. Marx, Lenin, Mao, Nkrumah have had "tougher" things to say.[117] Perhaps Nyerere is not enough of a reality-instructor for his immediate audience. Some find real difficulties in accepting *Ujamaa* because it is an attempt to synthesize old and new values. There are those who want nothing to do with the old, and feel that development must result in destruction of the small communities in which traditional African socialism is said to have been nurtured. For some, it is the pedigree of Marxist derivatives which impresses; Marxism-Leninism-Maoism has "worked" for them. One can list the psychological supports Marxism-Leninism has given to elites: certainty of success in the stream of history; justification for personal actions and for activism; a more elaborate and worked-out vision of the future than Nyerere has provided. Perhaps the greatest advantage of theories couched in Marxist language is that they are foreign. Nyerere is too close to home: he has tried to provide identity for Tanzanians in a changing world, to provide a framework for identifying with non-parochial institutions by looking to traditional patterns of behavior. At times he has seemed inconsistent, illogical, or even worse, anachronistic. Because he speaks in a language—literally and figuratively—known to his audience, he is easy to accept partially: he can be both agreed with and ignored. The foreignness of new ideologies has its own attractions: its very incomprehensibility and strangeness gives it an advantage with the middle-level leaders, who are often

[116] Fred Burke, "The Search for Ujamaa" in William Friedland and Carl Rosberg, Jr. (eds.), *African Socialism* (Stanford: Stanford University Press, 1964), p. 219.

[117] Individuals I interviewed expressed themselves to this effect.

semi-educated and open to *explicandums*. And the adoption of an ideology derived from outside Tanzania does not compromise the nationalist credentials of those who expound it. I have pointed to their nationalism and to the domestications of their ideology. Their predilection for a foreign ideology does not mean that they are not their own men. Whether they cynically or sincerely state their beliefs, Marxist-Leninists, Maoists, or some variety thereof can still be independent of any foreign power.[118] Nyerere, the African nationalist and the African socialist, is not seen by middle-level leaders to be any better a Tanzanian nationalist than Babu, who propounds Maoism. Insofar as Nyerere is more gradualist, more of a radical reformer than a revolutionist, he appears less nationalistic than the committed Marxist-Leninists and Maoists.

To those men and women familiar with *Ujamaa* and socialist theory, *Ujamaa* may provide a basis for, and a justification of, the African Revolution.[119] But it is not the African Revolution which needs justification in Tanzania; it is What IS To Be Done which is at issue. And here the evidence argues that *Ujamaa* has not taken hold among the elite of Tanzania. It has been reported that students at University College in Dar es Salaam (the only university in Tanzania) did not associate *Ujamaa* with the ideas Nyerere has attached to the concept; they did not relate *Ujamaa* to government policies or to the activities of TANU.[120] On the political hustings and in speeches justifying and explaining policy, Tanganyikan politicians are more likely to fall back upon slogans of neo-colonialism and imperialism than to resort to slogans of *Ujamaa*.[121] In one article devoted entirely to an exposition of *Ujamaa*, the author deplored the fact that *Ujamaa* had not

[118] I say "cynically" since some men do use a Marxist framework because it enables them to appear politically sophisticated as they bid for influence among middle-level leaders. It also associates them with powerful communist countries.

[119] Burke, *op.cit.*, p. 204.

[120] *Ibid.*, p. 200.   [121] *Ibid.*, p. 196.

been correctly perceived.[122] It would be more to the point to say that *Ujamaa* has been more often ignored.

We must be clear that the new ideological statements, and particularly the more elaborate Marxist varieties, are also largely ignored by the majority of area commissioners, TANU chairmen, and middle-level leaders outside of Dar es Salaam. The regional and district leaders speak in slogans rather than systematic ideological statements. They exhort people to work against "poverty, ignorance and disease," to be "unified" and "vigilant," and to obey TANU. Nonetheless, the language, style, and to lesser extents, the content of new ideological streams filters down. And while area commissioners and TANU chairmen are fond of dressing like Nyerere and clipping their moustaches like his, they do not emulate his way of thinking.

Still, Nyerere is admired by middle-level leaders who have opposed him on specific political issues and who have very different ideas about Tanzania's future. A man who has disputed with Nyerere in the NEC and National Assembly said that "*Mwalimu* knows all. . . . *Mwalimu* is of the proletariat. Though a teacher, he returned to the masses."[123] Because Nyerere stands above party and government, he can be universally admired. Furthermore, it is part of his political genius that he can stand for many things to many people. But because he is very much a part of his party and government and wants to lead them in fact as well as in title, he finds it increasingly hard to be all things to all people. However, the middle-level leaders who think differently than he does need him as he needs them: he is the man with the respect of the masses; his is the personal authority in Tanganyika.[124] Other

---

[122] *Ibid.*, p. 202. Burke reports that one Tanganyikan, in the newspaper *Mwafrika*, wrote an article, "The Policy of Ujamaa Must Be Explained Correctly," (Dar es Salaam), September 7, 1964.

[123] Interview with Saidi Mtaki, April 1965.

[124] He has been widely acclaimed on his visits to Zanzibar since the Revolution.

major leaders—Kambona, Kawawa, Lusinde, Kamaliza, Swai—are not nearly so well known or accepted throughout Tanganyika.

What of the local leaders—the village and sub-divisional leaders—and the masses themselves? They respond more to Nyerere than to any other man in Tanzania. He is cheered wherever he goes and is genuinely liked and deeply respected. However, this does not prove that his ideas have taken hold among the masses or whether those ideas were widely shared to begin with.[125]

Some of the most grandiose ideologies of development have taken hold in backward countries which started to undergo fundamental changes at a rapid rate.[126] But in Tanzania, backwardness has not yet been eroded enough. So far, Marxism-Leninism has not benefited from either mass-urban or mass-peasant support arising out of the pressures of a society undergoing rapid and dislocating change. There are not yet enough school-leavers, disgruntled clerks and petty civil servants, noncommissioned officers, or urban unemployed and disaffected youth piling up in the cities to provide the radical recruits to support the more radical ideologies being aired. The absence of large urban centers, the scarcity of large towns and densely settled rural areas has worked against the wide acceptance of even a popularized Marxism.

[125] It is not unreasonable to expect that Nyerere's less systematic, more personal and traditionally grounded ideas about social development are better received than the new streams in the thousands of small-scale communities throughout Tanganyika.

[126] Alexander Gerschenkron has shown how thrusts for development in different countries were accomplished by specific sets of ideas about the condition of backwardness. The greater the lag a country (e.g., Russia) experienced, the more radical and exalted were the theories which fired the effort to catch up. Cf. Gerschenkron, *op.cit.*, pp. 5-31. (Albert Hirschman, *Latin American Issues* [New York: Twentieth Century Fund, 1961], pp. 4-5, points out that Professor Gerschenkron's suggestive generalizations about ideology do not seem to hold in many of the countries that are today considered underdeveloped.)

Tanganyika has had migration from rural areas, but this migration has either gone abroad to the mines of Zambia and South Africa, or it has gone into pockets of people earning wages on sisal estates. Only in the last few years have people been coming to Dar es Salaam and the larger towns at a rate which is now alarming some political leaders. Unemployment has risen; measures have been taken to remove the unemployed and even to refuse emigration from regions into Dar es Salaam.[127] In few places in Tanganyika are there dispossessed peasants. Neither land hunger nor feudal relationships have characterized land problems in Tanganyika.[128] There has not been a great deal of land alienated to non-Africans. Thus the overwhelming majority of the people on the land have not been subject to conditions which radicalize and embitter.[129]

All this does not mean that emergent elite members must wait until their social support has been "created" before they can hope to see their ideology become dominant. The masses are essentially cut off both from the national leaders and from the regional and district leaders. The political complexion of Tanzania would change overnight if Nyerere were no longer President. A new ideology could be raised on high. But this would not mean that radically different policies

[127] Nyerere has begun to exhort people to go back to the land. The productivity of the farmer and his contribution to nation building are contrasted to the uselessness of the city loiterer. But this is not a real "back-to-the land" ideology because Nyerere has not implied that rural values are intrinsically better than urban ones or that rural work is a higher form. It is the city loiterer who is criticized, not the city worker.

[128] There are exceptions, of course. There has been land hunger on the slopes of Mount Kilimanjaro, and a few densely settled areas. And in West Lake Region there has been a land tenure system which bears resemblances to feudal systems. It is called the *Nyarubanja* and has now been legally outlawed by an act of Parliament (No. 1 of 1965).

[129] Zanzibar presents a different story: non-Africans there were large owners over a much greater proportion of the land than in Tanganyika.

could be *implemented* in Tanzania. For the implementation of policies depends not only on the structure of TANU but on the environment in which TANU operates; and this environment is much more resistant to change than the leadership of the country or the political arrangements within TANU. TANU's functioning depends not only on the values it promulgates and the internal arrangements that characterize it but also on the level and structure of economic development within Tanganyika. And it is the level and structure of economic development, examined in Part III, which will determine the material and human resources at TANU's command and thus will affect the internal arrangements and the values held.

257

PART III

TANU and the Economy of Tanganyika
Conditions, Apparatus, and Goals

CHAPTER VII

The Economy of Tanganyika

ALL POLITICAL STRUCTURES—parties, for example—must operate within environments which limit the possible forms of party development. It is tautological to say this, just as it is tautological to say that economic factors always work as a set of constraints on political forms. In order to get beyond such statements, we must show how the material conditions of a society do affect party development. I do not maintain that economic factors determine political development; and I have tried to show how TANU has been a product of anti-colonialism, cultural factors, Tanganyika's heterogeneity, and Nyerere's personality. Nonetheless, it is necessary to focus on economic factors—fairly narrowly defined—in order to understand the constraints on TANU's possible evolution.

The structure of the Tanzanian economy (agricultural/industrial balance, subsistence/monetary sector proportions), the level of resources (physical output in gross and per capita terms, GDP and per capita income) and productivity (of labor, capital-output ratios) have worked against the formation of a disciplined and centralized party, and have precluded the possibility of a totalitarian or "revolutionary-centralizing" system.

In order to make the connection between economic factors and TANU's organization and operation explicit, we must see what the party is doing to change the economy, and what changes, if any, are taking place in TANU as it organizes to achieve economic development. In this way we can perhaps avoid treating economic data as a set of givens which determine political development. It is important not only to detail the kind of political organizations that can and do live in certain economic settings, but also to see the interaction between political organizations and the economy in order to build toward dynamic conceptions of political development.

TANU exists to develop Tanzania: this has become its most generally formulated *raison d'être* since independence. But this does not mean that all TANU people understand development in terms of economic criteria, nor that TANU leaders always order their priorities in terms of economic development. The development of Tanzania is understood at the national level to mean an increase in the well-being of Tanzanians and an increase in the status and dignity of Tanzania in Africa and throughout the world; leaders believe that the well-being of Tanzanians includes a psychic well-being which depends on national dignity and independence. Thus Nyerere breaks relations with Britain over Britain's handling of the Rhodesian issue, seriously jeopardizing the *Five Year Plan* which depends on British financial and technical assistance, in the name of African freedom; thus Tanzania insists on its right to recognize an East German consulate in Dar es Salaam and loses West German aid; thus it insists on maintaining close relations with China, incurring American displeasure and lack of whole-hearted American support for the *Five Year Plan*.

These foreign policy decisions greatly affect the country's economic development because of Tanzania's heavy reliance on foreign aid and foreign investment. Domestic decisions also indicate an order of priorities where economic concerns are not always primary. A decision is made to avoid increasing taxation on small incomes substantially for reasons of equity and because government prizes its popularity—which, of course, may be a very rational decision; taxes may not be diligently collected at the district level because leaders may recognize the strain this would impose on district TANU organizations.

Issues which affect leaders at the center are not always perceived as crucial by regional, district, and local leaders. Nyerere does not have to worry about dealing with traditional leaders every day, as does a TANU area commissioner or a branch secretary. A traditional leader may be able to put across a development project more easily than a TANU leader; but by delegating responsibilities to traditional leadership, the TANU leader risks losing not only status, but sometimes even control over the program.

Despite the above, central leaders have generally retained a concentration on economic issues. They have been aware of the consequences when they have opted for foreign policy choices which have sacrificed economic development goals. And at the regional and district levels, TANU leaders do spend time and energies trying to achieve economic development. The domination of economic considerations over more general political and social considerations is often evident in Tanzania, but it needs to be shown. It cannot be assumed here or in any other country simply because the rhetoric of development is a rhetoric of economic development.

How can we relate political and economic development in Tanganyika? One possible interaction of a ruling party with its economic environment is for the party to become increasingly centralized and bureaucratized as it undertakes economic tasks, to become an agent for economic change and growth as it undergoes changes in organization and personnel. The system as a whole moves in one direction because the party can affect the economy.[1] In Tanzania, major changes in the patterns of rule are unlikely because TANU cannot really affect the economy: TANU is too weak and loose and has too few resources to tackle developmental problems, and the country is so poor that resources cannot be easily borrowed or appropriated to strengthen the party. Yet without TANU as an agent for economic development, the present structure and level of the economy persists.

This vicious circle is stated in a somewhat exaggerated

[1] The Communist Party in the Soviet Union from 1917 to 1933 is an example of a centralizing and bureaucratizing party internally changing and altering the system as it undertakes economic tasks.

fashion. Tanzania is not doomed to be frozen forever as a society; economy and party will change. If TANU were the only agent of change, neither economy nor party could develop substantially in the foreseeable future. But as it is, there are other agents of change. There will be infusions of capital and technical assistance from abroad. Foreign aid and training of TANU personnel abroad are external factors which work directly on TANU. Perhaps most important, within Tanzania itself there are already cash-crop farmers and some private commerce and industry which operate independently of state and party.

We can see how TANU interacts with the economy by examining first the environment in which TANU lives, and then the formulation and implementation of the *Five Year Plan.* The *Plan* is a statement of intentions, but we can see the beginning of TANU's attempts to implement it. It is essential to understand what economic development means and entails in Tanzania in order to understand TANU itself in the proper perspective.

Economic Conditions

Mainland Tanzania is large, poor, and sparsely settled with a communications system which is underdeveloped even by East African standards.[2] These crucial facts become stark for any ruling party attempting to establish centralized political control, because the population of 10 million is concentrated on the peripheries of a country larger than France and Germany combined. The people of Tanganyika live in clusters which are widely separated from each other and from Dar es Salaam. Much of the south is cut off from the rest of the country for at least a few months of the year during the heavy rains. Most of the roads and even some of the

[2] I have summarized the physical, demographic, and economic conditions in Appendix I.

railroad lines are not all-weather.[3] Only 2.7 per cent of the people lived in towns of over 5,000 people as of the 1957 census (low by sub-Saharan African standards).

Death rates have fallen and population is now estimated to be growing at 2.1 per cent a year.[4] This means that almost 45 per cent of the population is under sixteen, and raises immediate political issues. The economy will have to expand in the industrial and cash-crop sectors if these people are not to be either unemployed workers in the cities or subsistence farmers. Many youths are migrating to the towns, producing a severe strain on social services.[5] Unemployed or semi-employed youth, loitering in the streets or waiting around TANU offices for small jobs, begin to be a political problem. Party leaders are aware of them; but haranguing against loiterers, telling unemployed youth to go and farm, and even restricting people's freedom to come to Dar es Salaam has not dissuaded youth from accumulating in the towns.[6]

Having such a large percentage of total population who are not yet adults raises severe political problems which stem from a shortage of educational facilities. There is little agreement as to where schools should be built, or how many should be built instead of building industrial plants or investing in other kinds of social overheads. The TANU government has so far opted for free secondary-school education. But primary school is not free because the aim is to avoid a large number of primary-school leavers who are not trained for

[3] During one rainy season, the major rail link between Tabora in central Tanganyika and Kigoma in the west went under water.

[4] Denis Lury, "Brief Statistical Background for East African Federation," Paper presented to the Second Conference on Public Policy on East African Federation, Nairobi, November 26-30, 1964.

[5] Dar es Salaam had 128,742 people in the 1957 census. It now is estimated to have more than 175,000.

[6] In certain regions, people can immigrate to Dar es Salaam only with the permission of their regional commissioner; and the area commissioner of Dar es Salaam is empowered to deport loiterers from the city.

even clerical or industrial worker duties. Thus, the number of people who can reach secondary school is limited, and secondary-school graduates, not to say university graduates, constitute a real elite.

In this situation, the maxim that the secondary-school leavers lead revolutions while the primary-school leavers make up the body of the revolutionists is not entirely irrelevant to Tanzania. However, the structure of poverty, on the mainland at least, has not yet produced revolutionary urban workers or revolutionary landless peasants. The pressures for change are not coming from below. There is no real evidence that a rising level of expectations is forcing leaders to formulate economic and social policies to meet grievances. In fact, the *Five Year Plan* was created almost *in vacuo*; this was possible because the most active pressure group is TANU middle-level leaders who do not have a social class underpinning. So far, they have been successfully removed from *Plan* formulation.

To point out that Tanzania's per capita income is around $59.00 a year does not go very far in establishing the nature of the economy. Tanzania is a poor country, among the lower third of African countries in per capita income.[7] African per

7 *African Report*, VIII (August 1963), 32, produced a "Comparative Survey of Per Capita Income in Africa" (based on current market prices in 1961). Source for this was *Estimates of Gross National Product*, Statistics and Reports Division, Agency for International Development, April 1963. Comparative figures for national income are unreliable; accounting procedures may be very different and statistics hard to come by. The difficulties of national income accounting have been outlined in the Tanganyika context in Alan Peacock and Douglas Dosser, *The National Income of Tanganyika, 1952-54* (London, HMSO), 1958. There are two problems which are relevant to Tanganyika accounting: simple accounts imply that all output is exchanged for money; but in two respects this is not true. Output in a given period may be produced, voluntarily or involuntarily, for stock and so some valuation of stock changes must be made. Also, part of the output total may be consumed by producers and not ex-

capita money income has been put at between $17.00 and $22.00. Africans, making up over 98 per cent of the population, have around 70 per cent of the GDP;[8] 97 per cent of the African wage earners make less than $100.00 a month.

Most people still devote the major part of their work hours to producing staple food crops for their own consumption. There are regional variations with the central and southern regions, Dodoma, Singida, Kigoma, Tabora, Ruvuma, and Mtwara having relatively little cash-crop activity. But even in regions which have a nucleus of cash-crop production and/or industry, most of the people fall within the category of subsistence producers. They may grow some crops for taxes or to pay school fees, and they may engage in some market activities; but their efforts are geared largely to feeding themselves through their own production of staple foods.[9]

The non-monetary sector or subsistence sector is still more than one-third of total GDP, or about $200,000,000 out of $600,000,000.[10] This non-monetary value cannot be reached

---

changed for money at all. This raises the question of valuation of the subsistence economy. How value the output of work done on *shambas* (household plots)? There is also the question of accumulating and translating statistics.

[8] Dharam Ghai, "Some Aspects of Income Distribution in East Africa," EDRP Paper 51, November 1964, p. 3. African share of GDP in Kenya is even less; Ghai puts it at 50 per cent and for Uganda he gives 76 per cent.

[9] In some areas—Masailand, Dodoma, parts of Mara Region—cattle are raised. But many of the cattle growers also fall into the subsistence sector since they raise cattle as a sign of status and wealth, but do not keep them to sell for cash.

[10] According to Brian Van Arcadie, "Gross Domestic Product Estimates for East Africa," *Economic and Statistical Review*, IV (December 1963), ix-xii. Tanganyika, compared to Kenya and Uganda, covers a wide range under subsistence sector estimates for domestic product. In particular, subsistence construction activity and some craft industry are included. All automobiles are also included in definition of capital formation.

267

by government. It cannot be translated into government revenue in the form of direct money taxes nor can staple food crops be taken in kind; the administrative apparatus does not exist to do this. And subsistence farmers do not pay indirect taxes because they do not make purchases in the market. Thus the taxable base of the economy is much smaller than the GDP implies.

Tanganyika's economy has grown in the last decade both in terms of real output and from price increases. In fact, Tanganyika's economic performance compares favorably with its East African neighbors. However, Tanganyika's substantial increases in domestic exports, in the manufacturing sector and in real GDP as a whole, do not correlate closely with increases in human welfare. Tanganyika's comparatively favorable performance has depended in part on buoyant prices for sisal. Although government receives taxes from the sisal plantations, these are not owned by Africans; and only 2 per cent of the total population is employed as unskilled labor on the plantations. There have also been rises in the export values of coffee and cotton, based on enlarged output. But the significance of these rises may be kept in perspective if we note that in 1954, which was the best year for coffee exports up to 1960, the net output of coffee was estimated to be not much higher than that of "native beer."[11] (The incidence of rainfall may be a better indicator of welfare than exports, since drought and floods cause higher prices for staple foods while they damage the crops of many producers.)

Tanganyika's dependence on agricultural exports is the salient feature of her money economy: 40 per cent of all money income is derived from exports. Eighty per cent of export earnings comes from agriculture and livestock products against 13 per cent for minerals. Coffee, cotton, and sisal have accounted for well over half of export revenues,

[11] Cyril Ehrlich, "The Economy of Tanganyika, 1945-60," Unpublished manuscript, pp. 2-3.

with sisal alone accounting for close to 25 per cent of export revenues.[12] Agriculture has represented 45 per cent of total product; and manufacturing industry has represented only around 7 per cent of total product.

While there has been a shift from a subsistence to a monetary economy since the 1950's, agriculture has remained dominant throughout. Subsistence activities represent between one-third and two-fifths of GDP; but in the monetary sector, agriculture alone (excluding livestock, hunting, and fishing) is one-third of the total output.

Cash crops grown for export account for most of the agricultural output in the monetary sector. Sisal, the major cash crop of Tanganyika, has been entirely a plantation crop. African small-holders only began farming it commercially in 1964; and production has been dominated by Asians and Europeans. Cotton and coffee are the two major export crops farmed by African small-holders. Cotton is almost entirely an African-produced crop near Lake Victoria and on the Coast. Coffee is African-produced in West Lake, where the major concentration is on *robusta*, and in Kilimanjaro District where *arabica* is grown. In the highland areas around Arusha and Mbeya, Europeans have farmed coffee also.

While most of Tanganyika's coffee and cotton had been

[12] On the whole, since the middle of the 1950's, exports have expanded at a faster rate than imports, hence there has been a steady growth of a favorable trade balance in recent years. The favorable balance of overseas trade has been reduced by deficits on inter-territorial trade with Kenya and Uganda. The United Kingdom has been the biggest market for Tanganyika goods. *Tanganyika Data Book: Commerce and Industry* (Dar es Salaam: Government Printer, 1961), pp. 22-23. Domestic exports as a per cent of monetary GDP were 45.8 per cent in 1954 and 42.8 per cent in 1961. Of total exports in 1954 of 81.6 million dollars, agriculture represented 77.1 million dollars. In 1963, out of a total export of 136.1 million dollars agriculture accounted for 78.1 million dollars or still over 75 per cent of total exports. Brian Van Arcadie and Philip Ndegwa, "Future Trade, Balance of Payments and Aid Requirements of East Africa," EDRP Paper 31 (May 1964), p. 23, Table 1 and p. 26, Table 2C.

produced by Africans, Tanganyika has not been characterized by the growth of an African yeoman farmer class which has accumulated wealth and is organized politically. The Buganda phenomenon of prosperous cotton and coffee farmers is less common in Tanganyika. In some areas, notably on Mount Kilimanjaro and in West Lake Region, wealth has been accumulated from coffee growing; and there are some successful African wheat producers in Arusha Region around Mbulu. But, whereas in Uganda many farmers who grow maize or millet for their food crops also grow some cotton or coffee, in Tanganyika a larger proportion of farmers do not grow cash crops.[13]

This means that, while government is disadvantaged in terms of revenues and Tanganyika is economically less developed, government does not face strong pressure from farmers demanding higher prices for market-controlled crops like coffee and cotton.[14] Cash-crop farmers are grouped into cooperatives. Coffee and cotton are grown by individual farmers who sell the crop to the cooperatives. In some regions, cooperatives play an active political and economic part. The politics of West Lake Region is bound up with the Bukoba Native Cooperative Union; similarly, the Kilimanjaro Native Cooperative in Chaggaland and the Victoria Federation of Cotton Cooperatives in Sukumaland are important political and economic organizations. Marketing boards have even given local cooperatives monopoly rights over collection and distribution of certain commodities, and the cooper-

[13] Africans derive slightly less than 40 per cent of their total cash incomes from sale of cash crops and slightly less than 50 per cent from wages.

[14] The British colonial government had established controls over cotton through a Lint and Seed Marketing Board set up in 1952. Sisal, the major export crop, was subject to bulk purchase by the Board of Trade until 1948 after which estate-owners established their own marketing cooperative. Coffee had not come under state marketing controls in the colonial period. After independence, the TANU government created marketing boards for coffee (1962) and sisal (1964).

atives have entered processing industries—particularly the Victoria Federation. Cooperatives are themselves the major economic groups in most districts, but they have not functioned as organized interest groups for cash-crop farmers. The leadership of the federated cooperatives, operating at regional level, is linked with the TANU leadership; and many cooperative leaders have entered national TANU politics. But where the cooperatives are being used to collect taxes and to buy crops at lower than market prices, they are not very popular and do not serve to represent farmer demands.

Similarly, the trade unions no longer have as their primary function the representation of worker demands. The trade union movement grew up in close contact with TANU: many organization drives were carried out as joint trade union/TANU drives, and many TANU leaders were early trade union leaders. However, as employment fell between 1958 and 1963,[15] relations between TANU and the trade unions became increasingly uneasy. The drop in employment—in large part a response to a rise in wage rates which forced employers to cut their labor force[16]—made the issue of Africanizing the economy all the more explosive. Those Africans who do work in the commercial and industrial sectors do so as wage earners, but less than 5 per cent (around 9,000) are in executive or professional wage-earning positions.[17] The largest category of laborers is agricultural rather than industrial.[18]

[15] The number of employed fell 15 per cent, or from 397,000 to 342,000.

[16] While the number of employed fell, the wage bill rose 9 per cent between 1962 and 1963, and average cash earnings rose 35 per cent. See the budget speech of the Minister of Finance, *Tanganyika Standard*, June 17, 1964. Domestic servants are not covered nor are seasonal workers in peasant agriculture in these employment figures.

[17] Glickman, *op.cit.*, p. 3. Citing Theodore Geiger and Winifred Armstrong, *The Development of African Private Enterprise*, Washington, D.C., National Planning Association, Planning Pamphlet No. 120 (1964), pp. 33-34.

[18] The chief employment areas outside of Dar es Salaam are the sisal estates of Tanga Region, and the pockets of industry along the

These agricultural laborers do not provide a stable base for trade unions. They are often "target workers" who remain in one place for a comparatively short time and then migrate. Trade union leaders began to conflict with TANU leaders after independence, when the former found they could not build a stable political base, and had to face demands for greater wages, more employment, and rapid Africanization. Trade unions made what the TANU government considered irresponsible demands for wages and other benefits and during 1963-64 they were governmentalized by legislation.[19] A new trade union federation was formed, the National Union of Tanganyika Workers, which is designed to promote production as well as to represent worker interests. It handles its representational duties within the framework of government economic policy.

Industrial activity in Tanzania still means primarily the processing of agricultural commodities either for export or for local consumption. Although there is some secondary manufacturing in Dar es Salaam and other towns, ownership of industries has remained largely in the hands of non-Africans. In 1961, there were 5,365 factories registered in Tanganyika;[20] most of the registered factories run by electricity are still owned by Asians or Europeans. Some cotton-ginning factories are owned by the Victoria Federation of Cooperatives, and other cooperative societies have shares in various processing industries. Government owns TANESCO, an elec-

---

Central Railroad line (Morogoro and Kilosa), some industry in Moshi and Arusha and Mwanza towns and in some coastal ports. The largest category of workers after agricultural (plantation workers) is government employees who are about 12 per cent of salaried employees. Construction workers are less than 10 per cent. The manufacturing sector employs less than 5 per cent of the wage earners— food, drink, and tobacco industries accounting for one-third of the total workers in the manufacturing sector.

[19] See chap. xii.

[20] From *Statistical Abstract, 1962*, Table L 1, pp. 84-85. About one-quarter of the registered factories did not have electrical power.

tricity company, having bought out private shareholders in 1964, and government has shareholdings through its development corporation (the National Development Corporation, formerly the Tanganyika Development Corporation) in a number of joint enterprises with foreign investors.[21]

Economic Policy

Public policy—both the way it is formulated and its overall effectiveness—is related to the level and structure of the economy. Low income levels and a scarcity of material and human resources impose constraints on the organization and operation of central political institutions. These same low levels may work to undercut any challenge from non-governmental organizations. Much of the weakness of opposition parties in Africa has stemmed from their inability to resist the onslaught of a governing party which can dispense patronage and harry its opposition economically. Unlike Nigeria and Uganda, Tanzania does not have large numbers of farmers with independent resources to finance non-governmental organizations. But neither does it have resources readily available with which to grasp the nettle of underdevelopment.

This was also true for the colonial government. But the colonial government's attitude toward underdevelopment in Tanganyika was very different from the TANU government's. For Tanzanian leaders, achieving economic development means becoming modern. Personal dignity is at stake in the development of their country; and their political control is directly tied to economic growth. Economic growth and

[21] The British had not gone in for much state-owned industry in Tanganyika, but they have been instrumental in permitting the independent Tanganyika government to enter into joint ownership with private investors. The British government supported the Tanganyika National Development Corporation by underwriting one-third of its capitalization through participation by the Commonwealth Development Corporation in Tanganyika development projects.

structural changes in the economy bring their own dislocations and dissatisfactions even when real benefits are accru-
ing to large groups of people. In Tanzania, some changes and
dislocations are already taking place. The point is whether or
not growth will take place quickly enough to provide new
jobs in the modern sector and also enable leaders to direct
social change.

Furthermore, if central leaders can successfully expand resources, they can exert leverage at local levels through distribution of patronage. Their influence may be felt at local
levels not through the construction of a disciplined party organization responsive to orders from above, but rather
through local political machines which respond to allocations
made from the center. Non-economic allocations cannot be a
substitute for economic benefits. At the present time, there
are few political offices and direct economic awards that can
be distributed from the center. Thus, while it is true that economic benefits have a high marginal increment, there is little
to go around.[22]

It is useful to compare the response of the TANU government and the colonial administration, since the strategic importance of government activity can scarcely be exaggerated
in Tanzania.[23]

The role of government in Tanganyika in the post-World
War II years was a function of what the British colonial
administration could and would undertake. This administra-

[22] I am aware that the center can allocate non-economic rewards,
e.g., honors, titles, etc. Political offices which are not financed from
the center are hard to allocate centrally. Locals insist on determining
positions if they are paying salaries; and if no salaries are involved
local people want to determine officials by local election or appointment. While I do not neglect non-economic rewards I am skeptical of
the possibility of building central influence on any other base than
an economic one.

[23] See Cyril Ehrlich, "Some Aspects of Economic Policy in Tanganyika, 1945-1960," *Journal of Modern African Studies*, II (July 1964),
265-77.

tion has been described as singularly inadequate for active government intervention in economic affairs.[24] In the immediate postwar years, Britain suffered from a shortage of skilled men for overseas service. Furthermore, the British were unwilling to make finances available; and this soon became the crucial difficulty. By the early 1950's, even British prewar expectations for Tanganyika had not been entirely satisfied: educational facilities were not sufficiently expanded; and the major development project, the Groundnut Scheme, originally undertaken by a statutory British government corporation—the Overseas Food Corporation—never came near the envisioned 3 million acres to be cleared and planted.[25]

Government expenditure prior to independence varied as a per cent of GDP, but after 1950 was always at least 20 per cent. Current account expenditure was heavily weighted towards general administrative services, while capital expenditures were overwhelmingly devoted to social overheads.[26] The colonial government carried out a number of planned projects in Tanganyika—some of which were planned in London, like the Groundnut Scheme—which were designed to allocate resources in advance for future capital development. But aside from inadequate projection into the future, there was no attempt to allow for the future impact of investment and recurrent expenditure on the changing economy.

Tanganyika was only one among many British overseas

24 *Ibid.*, p. 267.

25 For the saga of the Groundnut Scheme, with its colossal failures and modest triumphs, see Alan Wood, *The Groundnut Affair* (London: The Bodley Head, 1950).

26 Railroad construction took place. The Southern Province Railway was constructed in connection with the Groundnut Scheme and ran from the new port of Mtwara (created for the Scheme) to Nachingwea. This railroad survived the Scheme and was a real asset as a by-product. The greatest effort of the colonial government in capital expenditures was on the building of roads. While the provision of roads was essential, soaring costs curtailed what was projected. After 1955, according to Ehrlich, costs and standards were lowered.

responsibilities, and one of the least important considering its size, relatively unstrategic location, ostensible lack of resources, and lack of a significant European population. TANU leaders felt that the British paid too little attention to the economic growth of their country. (Almost every speech Nyerere has made on economic affairs includes the refrain that an independent government is *now* concerned with the economic development of Tanzania.)

When the TANU government took over, it inherited the *Development Plan for Tanganyika 1961/62-1963/64.*[27] The *Three Year Plan* was largely concerned with outlining projects rather than analyzing the economy and providing for structural changes. Although the *Plan* did not describe itself as a capital expenditure program, it was essentially a capital budget adapted from and expanding upon the proposals of the World Bank's *Economic Development of Tanganyika.*[28] It did not stipulate any rate of growth higher than had occurred in the recent past—about 5 per cent before population growth was subtracted.

The *Plan* stated that industrial development, though desirable, would continue to depend upon the growth of an internal market and thus, to a great degree, upon the development of agriculture. The recognition of this situation, it was said, was one of the focal points of the thinking behind the *Plan.*[29] Both the World Bank Mission and the planners felt that emphasis ought to be on laying the foundations for growth rather than on covering a wider field at the expense of slowing down the rate of growth. Thus, social overheads were stressed in the *Three Year Plan.* And in fact, about two-

[27] *Development Plan for Tanganyika, 1961/62-1963/64* (Dar es Salaam: Government Printer, 1962), p. 5. Hereafter known as the *Three Year Plan.*

[28] *The Economic Development of Tanganyika,* Report of the International Bank for Reconstruction and Development, November 1960 (Dar es Salaam: Government Printer), hereafter known as World Bank Report.

[29] *Ibid.,* p. 2.

thirds of public capital formation in the *Three Year Plan* period, 1961-64, was accounted for by expenditure on transport, communications (road- and railway-building), irrigation, rural and urban water supplies, and school-building. The *Three Year Plan* did not make major departures from past colonial economic policy. And TANU leaders saw it as the last document of the colonial government, another collection of ministerial programs that could have only a limited impact on Tanganyika. It was perceived as belonging to the period 1945-60, in which neither "a favorable environment, a fortunate combination of market forces, nor a determined and aggressive government policy had lifted Tanganyika out of its desperate poverty."[30] But the *Plan* was not scrapped even though it extended well into the new period of independence. TANU tried to inject enthusiasm for economic programs by launching a supplementary "People's Plan" for village development in the spring of 1962, which was based on development committees at the village level. While an important element of popular involvement was added, the "People's Plan" was not a plan for development but an idea for grass roots participation. The TANU government had to work with the *Three Year Plan* until it could gather its own foreign specialists to elaborate a new plan.

Meanwhile, government extended the range and scope of marketing boards. While it wanted to gain a measure of control in the monetary sector, the primary impetus was political: government wanted to Africanize marketing and, if not eliminate, at least diminish the dominant position of Asian middlemen. Government's commitment to planning and controlling segments of the economy led it to marketing monopolies. It was not that marketing boards forced increased planning so that government could have predictable revenues.[31]

[30] Ehrlich, *loc.cit.*

[31] It is true of course that government's dependence on primary

There was no debate as to whether or not independent Tanganyika should plan; the dominant attitude of the leadership was expressed by Mr. Nsilo Swai, former Minister for Development Planning:

[Planning is] . . . clearly the most effective method of achieving the desired result since it is essentially a means of organizing all human and material resources to achieve within a given period maximum development possible in accordance with the social and political aims of the country.[32]

Tanganyika leaders, like many leaders of new states, were committed to the idea of planning. "Socialist" objectives, it is thought, can best be implemented through a plan; control of the economy can best be gained through a plan; a sense of nationhood can best be conferred by a plan, which is a demonstrable intention to do something about underdevelopment. Furthermore the Soviet Union and China have been successful with such plans.

The *Three Year Plan* was rejected because it did not fulfill any of the emotional and political needs expressed above, not because its specifics contradicted development programs which TANU had constructed on the basis of its stated goals; no such programs had been worked out. True, the *Three Year Plan* had not been formulated under a TANU government, but the presence of foreign experts does not explain TANU's rejection (foreign economists had been called in for the *Five Year Plan*). It was its colonial origins which counted against it. TANU leaders realized that it was not a plan at all, but merely a collation of development projects. It did not

---

product exports for raising taxes leads it to want to plan for revenues. (In 1963, central government derived 46 per cent of its total revenue from customs and excise taxes.) But this is not the major reason for planning in Tanganyika.

[32] Nsilo Swai, *Address to the National Assembly*, reprinted in *Five Year Plan*, I, 1.

commit government to a fullscale onslaught against poverty; it did not call for structural changes in the economy; and it did not question most of the basic assumptions which had governed the colonial government's economic policies. The non-economic factors—for example, colonial policies which led to restrictions on trained manpower—were taken as givens.

There were two other major strikes against the *Three Year Plan*. First, it allocated virtually no resources to industrial development outside of social overheads. The goals and aims put forward by TANU before and immediately after independence were broad enough to accommodate a wide range of developmental strategies; but after independence, TANU leaders felt that some effort towards industrial development was a necessary sign of nationhood. In 1960, the World Bank Report had said that growth of manufacturing depended on the size of the internal market; and they conceived of this market as a private market. Thus the growth of manufacturing was tied to the growth of agricultural production. Rising monetary income was to be the critical variable, which would allow for increased demand for manufactures. The possibilities of import substitution, within a limit set by demand, were also noted. No mention was made of government demand, which might be a critical factor.[33] The World Bank Report ruled out the possibility of import substitution in machinery and transport equipment, but stressed this possibility for certain processing industries and manufactured food-

[33] The World Bank Mission was less negative than an earlier group which expressed themselves in the *East African Royal Commission Report of 1955*. This Commission not only felt that the government was not equipped to establish and operate new industries, but it also pronounced its moral condemnation of forced savings for manufacturing development. It doubted the efficacy of encouraging voluntary savings and saw forced savings as more costly than raising external loans. It considered price stabilizing schemes as an unreasonable burden on the producer. With this argument, Tanganyika would not finance development from internal sources.

stuffs.[34] The *Three Year Plan* adopted this thinking; and thus, it was not ambitious enough for the new leaders. While they were prepared to be realistic, these leaders insisted on a positive statement of the *idea* of industrial development, even if industrial programs were not grandiose. Hope of industrial development in the future had to be held out.

The second strike against the *Three Year Plan* was that it never called for a machinery of planning, which is thought to be another tangible demonstration of statehood and to give evidence of a commitment to modernity. Since TANU inherited no machinery of planning, it had to create one.

I shall now turn to the construction of a planning machinery in Tanganyika and to the *Five Year Plan* itself, for it is through an examination of the *Five Year Plan* that we are able to observe TANU's role in formulating economic policy. And we will be able to see the beginning efforts to implement *Plan* goals, the difficulties involved, and the responses of TANU to these difficulties.

[34] World Bank Report, pp. 130-32.

CHAPTER VIII

The Formulation of the *Five Year Plan*

THE PLANNING PROCESS in Tanganyika from which the *Five Year Plan*[1] emerged involved TANU in the following ways: at the center TANU leaders and technical planners discussed goals; the NEC reviewed the planners' work. At the village, district, and regional levels TANU's involvement was more pervasive and continuous because the planning bodies at these levels were development committees composed of TANU elected and appointed officials as well as civil servants.

The Ministerial System

When the independent Tanganyika government was established, its formal pattern was that of the British ministerial system: Julius Nyerere became the first Prime Minister and his ministers served under him. We have seen that one of the weaknesses of TANU at the center is a lack of a central staff to exercise effective control over district and regional TANU activities. The central government suffered from a similar lack: the Office of the Prime Minister did not have as much control over the government as the Chief Secretary's Office had in the colonial government; the Prime Minister did not have the staff with which to exercise control; the major portfolios of Finance and Establishments were delegated to ministers. In general, the new ministries had more autonomy than the co-

---

[1] Although the *Five Year Plan* was published under the seal of the United Republic of Tanganyika and Zanzibar, it refers only to Tanganyika as it was published in Volume I: General Analysis, and Volume II: The Programmes. As of this writing, the Zanzibar Plan was pending publication. Hereafter, the document for Tanganyika is referred to as the *Five Year Plan*. For a more detailed treatment of the goals of the *Five Year Plan* (ed.), see Warren Keegan, "Tanganyika's Five Year (1964-69) Development Plan," in *Financing African Development*, Tom J. Farer (ed.) (Cambridge: M.I.T. Press, 1965), pp. 11-40.

lonial departments had. Some of the ministers—Kambona and Kawawa in particular—were important political figures and TANU officers in their own right. Nyerere's failure to consolidate his power through close control of TANU appointments before independence, and his practice of devolving many tasks on other men created a perfect opportunity for individual ministers to exercise autonomy. His concern that Tanganyikans would lose sight of overall directions and goals led him to expend major efforts on keeping these goals before the people. Perhaps for this reason he was reluctant to get immediately involved in detailed administration. As the leader of a new state, he was forced to travel abroad a great deal; his Pan-African and international interests accentuated this tendency. And his colleagues, having become the first ministers in independent Tanganyika, could easily pursue the development of their own ministries.

Tanganyika became a Republic at the end of 1962. However, the ministerial system was not abandoned. Although the Prime Minister was replaced by a President, the National Assembly remained as Parliament; the ministers remained and were all Members of Parliament.[2] One legacy of British rule carried over into the presidential/ministerial system which had serious implications for planning efforts was the tradition of a powerful Treasury. In the presidential system, the Treasury does not have control over the civil service; the Establishments Office and Regional Administration are located outside the Treasury. But the Treasury has extensive responsibilities with regard to territorial establishments through budgeting processes. It also has responsibilities for revenues and total government expenditures and for foreign aid negotiations.[3]

[2] Fig. 2 gives the organization of the central government of Tanganyika as of January 1965.

[3] The Treasury had the lowest percentage of any ministry for localization of civil servants. Only 29.8 per cent of the Treasury's civil servants were Tanzanians compared to 95.1 per cent for the Ministry

Fig. 2: Central Government in the United Republic of Tanzania[a]

PRESIDENT

PRESIDENT'S OFFICE

Minister of State for Union Affairs   Ministry of Foreign Affairs   1st Vice President   Central Establishment   Finance

2ND VICE PRESIDENT'S OFFICE

Defence Forces   Justice Dept.   National Service

EXTRA MINISTERIAL DEPARTMENTS

Exchequer and Audit Dept.   Speaker's Office National Assembly

Local Govt. Service Commission   Civil Service Commission

MINISTRIES

Home Affairs   Economic Affairs & Devplan   Regional Administration   Information & Tourism   Community Development & Culture   Labour

Education   Health   Housing

Communications and Works   Agriculture Forest & Wildlife   Land Settlement & Water   Commerce & Cooperatives   Industries Mineral Resources and Power

ADMINISTRATIVE →

SOCIAL →

ECONOMIC →

[a] Zanzibar has many of its own ministries. The central ministries, in practice, function largely on the mainland.

THE *FIVE YEAR PLAN*

Since the *Three Year Plan* was a collection of ministerial programs, it could be formulated without any major innovations in the colonial economic apparatus. Overall economic responsibility was vested in the economic section of the Treasury. The *Five Year Plan* was to be worked out by a staff devoted to planning.

The Directorate of Planning

In March 1963, a Ministry of Development and Planning headed by Mr. Nsilo Swai (TANU National Treasurer) was created to formulate and direct a *Five Year Plan*. Technical experts were brought to Tanganyika to assess feasible objectives and draw up a strategy for arriving at them. A Frenchman, M. Faudon, was appointed Director of Planning.[4] French planning methods recommended themselves to Tanganyika for a number of reasons. The idea of a mixed economy where indicative planning would predominate was the Tanganyika leadership's choice, since a centrally planned and state-controlled economy never seemed a practical alternative; and the French had experience of planning in a market economy.[5] It was politically desirable to fill sensitive positions in the planning department with those who were neither tarred with the brush of the past nor politically vulnerable in the present; and the French were not involved in East African politics. It was hoped that Communist countries (especially Yugoslavia) as well as Western countries would supply technical personnel; but no planners were sent from

---

of External Affairs; 95 per cent for Community Development; 91.7 per cent for Information and Tourism; 84.4 per cent for the President's office; and 70.5 per cent for Home Affairs. Only Communications and Works also had less than 50 per cent localization. *Nationalist*, July 1, 1965, p. 1.

[4] He was an engineer trained in the school of Pierre Masse.

[5] Most leaders were not aware of the special characteristics of French planning. But Mr. Swai had familiarized himself with different planning techniques.

Communist countries. The UN, Israel, West Germany, Britain, and the United States sent people; but the number of technicians in the Ministry of Development and Planning never totaled more than 5 during the first six months of the ministry's life.[6] And the planners who were sent were opposed to establishing a fully planned, centrally directed economy on political as well as technical grounds.

The *Plan*'s formulation at the national level was the work of the Director of Planning and his staff of technical experts. The Director worked under the Minister of Development and Planning until the ministry was abolished in May 1964, and relocated in the President's Office as the Directorate of Development and Planning. The Directorate was headed by three Ministers of State,[7] to whom the French Director of Planning then became responsible. The Directorate of Planning, with its Ministers of State and technical director, was directly responsible to the President for carrying out the following functions:

(a) Drafting proposals in consultation with the ministries for consideration by the Economic Development Commission (now the Steering Committee).

[6] There were vacancies in the staff of the Ministry well into the formulation of the *Plan* and there still are. By January 1964, a number of junior planning officers had been appointed in the economic planning secretariat. There were still vacancies for sectoral experts. The manpower planning unit was staffed, but the implementation and central division showed vacancies in its three staff posts. Now junior planning officers exist in this division and an apparatus is operating for control over other ministerial activities through watchdogs and liaison officers.

[7] Mr. Swai, Mr. Jamal, and Mr. Babu were the first three ministers of state. Mr. Swai was the first minister. He had responsibilities for coordination with other ministries and foreign aid and *Plan* implementation. Mr. Jamal was responsible for liaison with the private sector and became chairman of the new National Development Corporation. Mr. Babu was a minister of state but he became Minister of Commerce and Cooperatives. Mr. Hanga was the third minister of state with responsibilities for the Zanzibar Plan. See Presidential Circular No. 4, June 1, 1964, and its supplement of June 18, 1964.

(b) Providing the necessary technical advice on which the decisions of the Economic Development Commission could be based.

(c) Initiating action in the ministries (and regional development committees) for the formulation of projects necessary for implementing the *Plan*.

(d) Coordinating action on projects between different ministries, regional development committees, the National Union of Tanganyika Workers and the Tanganyika Association of Chambers of Commerce.

(e) Reporting to the President on the overall progress of the *Plan* and the causes of any unforeseen delay or difficulty encountered in its implementation.

Before the Directorate was created, there were two major organs for inter-ministerial coordination—the Economic Development Commission (EDC) and the Permanent Secretaries' Coordinating Committee. The EDC was the Cabinet reconstituted as the top-level, policy-making body for economic affairs.[8] It was supposed to define long- and medium-term targets of economic and social development and formulate the appropriate economic policy for achieving these targets. More specifically, the EDC would determine priorities in the activities of the public and para-public sectors; assess regional contributions to the achievement of national targets; and prescribe measures apt to induce such a contribution. The adaptation of fiscal and credit policies to the needs of development was another responsibility of the EDC. This body was to consider and endorse the National Development Plan before its submission to the National Assembly, especially with regard to the ministerial programs and the relevant current and capital expenditure. And it was to exercise

---

[8] The EDC could call on senior civil servants, representatives of regional development committees and employer and employee representatives for consultation when necessary.

control over the implementation of the *Plan* and approve amendments to it.[9]

The Ministry of Development and Planning worked under the EDC and sent orders to sectoral experts, to the permanent secretaries coordinating committee, to committees set up on manpower and finance, and to development committees. This was the theory behind the planning organization. But some of the lines of command, in fact some of the bodies stipulated, remained a "chart phenomenon" for some time. Sectoral working parties which were supposed to bring the private sector into the planning operation were set up belatedly. The confrontation of all the chief decision-makers in the economy was supposed to take place in the consultative bodies of working sectoral parties and control committees at the center. However, staffing problems at the center and poor coordination of the private sector with government prevented these bodies from becoming the wide-ranging and effective consultation machinery that had been anticipated.[10] To this extent, the "consultative economy" or the "club-minded" approach in Tanganyika, where the state remains the president of the club but everyone has the chance to express his own view and be informed of those of his fellow members, was not functioning as outlined. (This does not mean that the private sector was not brought into government deliberations. There are not a huge number of large private investors in Tanzania; thus government is able to meet informally with representatives of the Dar es Salaam Chamber of Commerce who can inform government of their intentions and help coordinate programs.) The establishment of this machinery for cooperation in preparation of a program accept-

[9] The outline of the functions of the EDC was provided in a Supplement of the *Nationalist*, July 2, 1964.

[10] E.g., the financial control committee was created but without commercial bank participation.

able to all economic agents was thought to preclude an elaborate administrative machinery within the Planning Ministry.[11] It might be more correct to say that the impossibility of having an elaborate administrative machinery made it essential to develop the consultative approach.

Yet there is a real pressure to create a highly developed administrative apparatus to direct Tanzania's economy. A large sector of society is outside the monetary economy. Where the market economy is not identical with the economy as a whole and where commodity markets are imperfect, it is difficult to affect the subsistence sector by fiscal or monetary means. Even if indirect controls have economic effect, it may be necessary to exert direct controls to enforce them because a large segment of the population may not be reached or bound by indirect controls. The physical apparatus for collecting taxes may have to be disproportionately large in relation to the population, because of the difficulties involved in collection. If the whole array of duties and obligations that are associated with individual participation in a modern state cannot be taken for granted, an elaborate administrative mechanism may be attempted to substitute for self-regulating mechanisms of society. The traditional self-regulating mechanisms may be working against the fulfillment of the individual's obligations to the state.

However, a poor country like Tanzania cannot afford the operation of this machinery, and does not have the human or material resources to create it in the first place. This is one of the vicious circles of underdevelopment. Some states begin to break out of it by creating an elaborate administrative machine at great costs and then trying to recoup these costs by utilizing the apparatus for development. In Tanzania, the choice is to use market mechanisms and encourage private enterprise, and also to utilize planning with areas of state

[11] Interview with Mr. Swai, October 1963.

and cooperative control. Still, it is felt that a system of rigorous planning must exist.[12]

The planning staff was to remain small and to concentrate on the formulation and coordination of economic activities, leaving to the technical ministries the full responsibility for control over execution. However, there have been changes made in the theory and organization of the planning system in order to ensure the precedence and implementation of goals established by the planners. On the political side, the EDC was superseded by a smaller group, called the Steering Committee, which is composed of the President, the economic ministers, and ministers invited to attend when topics relevant to their work are being raised. There is also a National Economic and Social Council designed to institutionalize private sector participation in the planning process. It is presided over by the minister in charge of planning, and representatives of employees' and employers' organizations are *ex officio* members.[13]

The Directorate of Development and Planning was created and placed within the President's office in order to centralize decision-making in development policy and to strengthen the chain of command within the government between the President and the various ministries. The Central Statistical Bureau was moved from the Treasury to the Di-

[12] One reason now given for the commitment to planning is Tanzania's dependence on foreign aid. It is said that a system of rigorous planning must exist to initiate and supervise the formulation of development projects since provision of foreign aid is dependent on the presentation of carefully studied projects which are sound technically and which fit logically within the national economic plan. Nsilo Swai, "Administrative Machinery for Planning is Vital," Supplement to the *Nationalist*, July 2, 1964.

[13] Private persons may be nominated and Cabinet members belong too. The effectiveness of this body may be gauged by Mr. Swai's complaints that attempts to gather information by surveys on manufacturing and commercial farming had met with little success. Many private employers did not respond to questionnaires, fearing government would use information against them for tax purposes or licensing situations.

rectorate, and the Directorate was given responsibilities for formulating overall government policy toward private investors—both foreign and domestic—and for defining the conditions of government assistance or participation in their investments. It was given its own watchdog and information officers who operate in the regions. The original idea of leaving the execution of the *Five Year Plan* to technical ministries was thus modified by the appointment of regional representatives to the Directorate of Planning. These officials will operate in "economic zones," each one comprising two or three administrative regions.[14] The aim is to set up small-scale directorates of development and planning in the zones. Assistant directors of development and planning are to guide regional development committees and regional commissioners, advise district councils on financial aspects of regional programs, work with private persons to stimulate investment, and harmonize regional programs.[15] Before the appointment of regional officials from the planning office, communications from the Directorate of Planning had to be channeled through field officers of the ministries—usually the regional agricultural officer.

These changes in the planning organization are essentially

[14] This has been a return, for economic purposes, to the old colonial provincial boundaries which existed before the 9 provinces were extended to 17 regions. Some of the new regions have been "Cinderella" regions. For example, Singida Region which was created out of the old Central Region does not have as full staffing of ministerial personnel as Dodoma Region which was also created from Central Region. Dodoma town had been the capital of Central Region (province). The new zones will be more viable economically. Staff shortages also make the smaller number desirable.

[15] From a speech by I. Simba (Assistant Director of Development) given in November 1964, at Kivukoni College on "Regional Planning and Control." President Nyerere called the Assistant Directors "economic lieutenants in the regions." He was sure that the regional commissioners, as chief executives, would welcome the presence of skilled officers who can help development committees draw up internally consistent programs. Speech to the regional commissioners, *Nationalist*, October 28, 1964.

changes of form and intentions. The operating economy is not altering its direction because of these structural changes. Very often the staff cannot be found to fill new positions, as proved to be the case for assistant directors of planning for some time. Furthermore, reorganizations have not only been frequent, but they have begun to reproduce original forms. For example, President Nyerere announced that a separate Ministry for Economic Affairs and Development Planning had been re-created in September 1965. He said that planning had originally been brought into his office because its functions and its importance were not sufficiently understood; this was no longer true. But there is little evidence to support this contention. When the Directorate was within the President's office, powerful ministers still ignored its communications or went directly to the President. And there is surely no reason to believe that field officers in the regions and districts have suddenly understood the operation of the planning system.

The frequent alterations in the central planning machinery might have made the very formulation of a coherent plan impossible if there had been an elaborate machinery, or if there had been much communication between the center and the regions, or if there had been close connection between political and technical officials. But since the *Plan* was formulated, literally, by three or four people at most, its formulation was not adversely affected by these alterations.

Formulation of the Five Year Plan

On the whole, TANU values had not been expressed in specific economic policies before independence.[16] For the leaders, the gap between ideals and technical choices was not filled by any definite ideas about economic growth. Many

---

[16] There was one exception: the leaders were determined to abolish freehold tenure and to set conditions for leaseholding. This had already been accomplished by legislation before the planners came to Tanganyika.

Cabinet members were not interested in proposals which did not affect their ministries directly. Furthermore, if political leaders had vetoed proposals of the planners in the EDC, they would have been hard put to offer alternatives. And because of the nature of the situation where a plan had to be completed quickly, negativism by political leaders was hard to justify.[17]

While the Minister for Development and Planning had training in economics, most political members in the EDC found it difficult to come to terms with the growth targets and techniques set by the planners; they could not always translate economic aggregates into political and economic strategies. Thus one of the advantages which Minister Swai promised would accrue to government from a planned system was, and is, vitiated. Planning is supposed to "constitute for the government a means of assessing the probable consequences of a political and administrative decision on the pace of development."[18] But this presumes that political leaders are able to assess consequences of economic policy.

The structure of TANU itself and TANU's place in Tanganyika was another important factor which permitted the political leaders' openness to the planners' priorities. The national leaders of TANU were insulated from African economic interest groups. Although some came from the trade unions or the cooperatives, they were not spokesmen for cooperative or trade union interests and were relatively free to ignore specific group demands. The economic groups are themselves decentralized and their position within TANU is weak.[19] TANU's very looseness makes it hard for the center to

---

[17] The planners and the political heads of ministries had just over twelve months from the time the Ministry of Development and Planning was created to prepare a comprehensive medium-term plan. The President had instructed them to prepare the plan within that period.

[18] Mr. Swai's Address to the National Assembly, *loc.cit.*

[19] E.g., the cooperative unions throughout Tanzania do not stand shoulder to shoulder behind the central National Union of Coopera-

impose itself. But it also insulates the center against specific demands.

National leaders do not face demands constantly (except those which originate in the capital city), and may not even be aware of the demands of organizations outside the capital. And the fact that national leaders do not have regional bases nor interest group constituencies means that they are "free" in the sense that they are often unaware of demands. Since groups and localities are not able to enforce these demands or even articulate them as policy issues at the center, Tanganyika is perhaps better described as a pressureless cooker than as a boiling pot.[20]

One might have expected the middle-level leaders to process demands for African interest groups. But they are not essentially interest-group spokesmen and thus have not pressured national leaders on economic issues until recently— except for the important issue of Africanization. Yet while they are not representative of any pressure groups, they are themselves the major pressure group in Tanganyika. In the past, if an issue did not directly concern them, or if they could be removed from considering a complex of issues, the political leadership would be free to accept the planners' priorities. The middle-level leaders had narrower concerns than they do now. After the infusion of new ideological strands in mid-1964, it became difficult to isolate middle-level leaders from decisions on economic policy. Members of the NEC, for example, did not at first realize the political implications of different rates of growth or various agricultural/industrial balances, and thus were not overly concerned with being involved in the establishment of economic goals.

---

tives (NUC), which faces the same problem that TANU faces in imposing its wishes over constituent unions.

[20] On the other hand, leaders have to be very concerned about foreign investors and lenders and their own domestic "foreign" investors, the racial minorities.

Middle-level leaders have become increasingly sensitive to the political implications of economic decisions.

The alternatives that politicians are likely to pose to technical experts stem from a concern with their role as articulators and aggregators of interests. When this concern is absent, they, by and large, do not have alternatives to pose. This was the case in Tanganyika during the *Five Year Plan*'s formulation.

There were three phases in the formulation of the *Five Year Plan*, all of which were dominated by the technical experts in the Directorate of Planning. The first phase consisted of determining and analyzing long-term objectives. This involved the planners in studying past rates of growth and testing higher rates against available resources and likely world-market conditions. From this examination the first planners' report emerged, and was submitted to the EDC in August 1963. Long-term objectives were discussed with the President, who provided the planners with an image of the kind of society Tanganyika leaders wanted. The problem, however, was that political leaders did not know enough about how rates of growth and patterns of economy affect society to be able to determine whether their image of Tanganyika was being implemented by the planners' choices. Was *Ujamaa* being translated into economic policies by the planners? The political leaders could not tell.

During this phase of Plan formulation, people from TANU National Headquarters were invited to attend liaison meetings held under the auspices of the Ministry of Development and Planning in Dar es Salaam. The nominal response to this invitation is an indication of the lack of coordination between TANU Headquarters and the ministries. The NEC was not convened to discuss the long-term goals set by the planners; middle-level leaders were not consulted; and in general there was no discussion of plan goals thoughout Tanganyika.

The second phase consisted of determining intermediate

stages to be achieved by 1960 in progress towards 1980 targets. Sectoral production was tested against foreign and domestic demand. Resources for achieving 1970 targets were computed. Factors relating to the East African Common Market were taken into account, and policies were formulated for involving the cooperation of the private sector and for seeking assistance from abroad. This second phase led to the submission of a draft outline of the *Five Year Plan* to the EDC in January 1964. There is no evidence that the EDC played a significant role in modifying the outline; nor did TANU people play a part in drafting the *Plan*, either as members of the NEC or as MPs. The NEC was supposed to be convened in Dar es Salaam in January when the *Plan* was submitted to the EDC. But the January army mutiny occupied the members' attention, and the NEC had to be reconvened a month later. Members with whom I spoke felt that the NEC had delegated its authority to decide on economic questions to sub-committees, chiefly to the TANU Cabinet—that is, to the leaders of the TANU government.

The third phase in *Plan* formulation was the drawing up of specific and coordinated development programs within the framework of the outline and in finalizing the *Plan*. At the center, various ministries coordinated under the Ministry of Development and Planning worked out their developmental programs. The civil servants and technical personnel were, of course, working under their political ministers. But here again, no political body per se—neither the Central Committee, the NEC, nor the EDC—was involved in working out specific programs and policies.

The Five Year Plan

When President Nyerere introduced the *Five Year Plan* to the National Assembly on May 12, 1964, he made it clear that the *Plan* was not put forward as an infallible document.[21]

[21] Mr. Swai gave a more detailed account of the *Plan*'s targets a

Its formulators were well aware that five years is too short a time to carry out the desired structural transformations in the economy. Thus, while the *Plan* period is from July 1, 1964 to June 30, 1969, the *Plan* itself has a fifteen-year perspective. By 1980 the three main objectives of the *Plan* are to be reached:

(1) to raise per capita income from the present $55 to $126.
(2) to be fully self-sufficient in trained manpower requirements.
(3) to raise the life expectation from the present 35-40 years to 50 years.

The employment target is to raise the number of salaried workers from the present 340,000 to 800,000, an increase in the wage-earning sector of the population from 3.5 to 5.7 per cent. Half of the 800,000 are expected to find employment in the agricultural sector.

If the targets are reached, there will be a 50 per cent increase in average income by 1970.[22] Assuming an average population growth of 2.2 per cent per annum, this income target implies an annual growth rate of 6.7 per cent in the GDP, almost double the rate achieved in recent years.[23] These are ambitious goals.[24] However, they are not meant to be brought about by depressing present consumption levels; no crash programs are being implemented. Furthermore, al-

---

month later when he addressed the National Assembly; he too emphasized the conjectural character of the *Plan* given uncertainties in climate and in world economic and political conditions. Mr. Swai's address is reprinted as "Approach to Economic Planning," *Five Year Plan*, I, 1.

[22] *Ibid.*, p. viii.

[23] Dharam Ghai's "Reflections on Tanganyika's Five Year Plan," EADRP, June 1964. This 6.7 per cent is growth in both subsistence and monetary sectors.

[24] According to Keegan, *op.cit.*, pp. 30-31, they are based on optimistic assumptions regarding the productivity of capital.

though the *Plan* announces a commitment to maximize growth, large sums have been allocated to social welfare.

The means stated in the *Plan* to achieve these goals reflect the difficulties of financing new programs in Tanzania. Government does not have at its disposal the revenues needed to embark on a large-scale program of state investment. The bulk of the population pays taxes only to district councils, which levy an income tax of about 1 to 3 per cent on all adult males. But these taxes provided only about 25 per cent of the estimated 1963-64 current revenue of $98 million.[25] And because of the difficulties involved, district councils have to devote a tremendous amount of time and energy to collection efforts. Revenue officers, executive officers of district councils, local government officers, and even officials not directly concerned with tax collection—commissioners, visiting leaders, TANU officers—all spend time trying to get people to pay taxes.[26] If they are not spending time in this manner, government exhorts them to do so. Officials are told not to be friendly with people who do not pay their tax; and in fact district councilors are often accused of being the worst offenders on non-payment. Government offices have been emptied, and officers sent on tax-gathering missions. Sometimes TANU and government officers have resorted to extra-legal measures: road blocks may be set up and a person asked to produce his tax receipt; if he cannot, those who form the road block try to collect the tax on the spot, even if no bona fide collection official is present.[27]

[25] Around three-quarters of this direct local tax is derived from the local rate. The local rate structure is chaotic with some district councils having a graduated tax structure and no two having the same one. The remaining quarter of the local tax collected by the district councils is a tax on agricultural produce called the produce-cess.

[26] An estimated 15 per cent of all males escape registration for taxation, before official exemptions begin to operate. Eugene Lee, "Local Taxation in Tanganyika," unpublished manuscript, Institute for Public Administration, University College, Dar es Salaam, May 1964.

[27] Tax collection is officially done by executive officers of the dis-

It is harder to escape from central taxes. But, while central taxes bring government three-quarters of its revenue, they fall on only 2 per cent of the population; and income taxes make up only one-quarter of total revenue. The balance comes from export taxes and import duties.[28] In 1961, about 14 per cent of the wealth produced in Tanganyika was accounted for by taxes. In developed countries, 20 to 30 per cent of GDP is accounted for by taxes.[29] The reason why in Tanganyika the contribution of taxes to GDP is so low is because the subsistence sector of the economy is virtually outside the tax net. If only the monetary sector were considered, revenues received by government would be 24 per cent of GDP.

Since per capita income levels are already so low, any attempt to get increased revenues from direct taxation poses serious political problems. Similarly, taxes imposed on the subsistence economy would be virtually impossible to collect and politically explosive. The collection of such taxes is obviously a function of the local governments' and TANU organizations' administrative and police abilities. So far, they have not been able to carry out even their present obligations in this realm.

It is not surprising then that the least explicit portion of

---

trict council. At the village level, responsibility is in the hands of the village executive officers. These officials, aided by a tax clerk of the district council, do the tax collection. The village executive officer is a political appointee, and administration of the local rate has not been free of political concerns.

[28] There is an income tax and a personal tax. The former is administered by the East African Common Services Organization and falls on around 16,000 persons. The personal tax is administered by central government and is levied on approximately 165,000 persons; but the same 16,000 persons who pay income tax pay about one-half to one-third of the personal tax. *Ibid.*, p. 1. The revenue tax falls on incomes of $280 a year or more.

[29] *Ibid.*, p. 14 citing John Due's *Taxation and Economic Policy in Tropical Africa* (Cambridge: M.I.T. Press, 1963), p. 25.

the *Five Year Plan* is that which refers to additional domestic finance. The relevant section suggests that even with GDP growing at 8.5 per cent a year, tax revenues from the present system are likely to expand at the rate of 5 per cent a year. The tax policy which will overcome this problem is not spelled out;[30] increased efficiency and budgetary austerity are assumed to resolve the difficulty.

The *Five Year Plan* relies heavily on foreign financing. It calls for an expenditure of about $688,800,000 for investment in the monetary economy by both public and private sectors for the five *Plan* years. About 53 per cent of this is to be undertaken by the public sector, of which central government is to be responsible for around 43 per cent,[31] EASCO around 6½ per cent, and local governments 3½ per cent. The rest is to come from the private sector. Central government investment, however, is to be financed 79 per cent by foreign sources, 14 per cent by domestic borrowing, and 8 per cent through taxation. This means that more than 40 per cent of total expenditure (both from public and private) is to come from foreign sources. But the reliance on foreign financing seems even more pronounced when we consider that private investment is made in large part by non-Africans; to a large extent, it is made by non-citizens. If we consider the private sector as a "foreign" source, then most of the *Plan*'s financing is from "external" sources. Obviously, this dependence on foreign financing limits the flexibility of the planners.[32]

[30] Paul Clark, "Foreign Aid, Domestic Finance and the Development Plan," EDRP, 1964, p. 7.

[31] Of total central government development expenditures, about 70 per cent is on its own account and 30 per cent is to be made available through parastatal organizations for their own programs.

[32] Leaving aside questions of foreign political influence (which I have discussed in "Foreign Aid Versus National Independence," *East African Journal*, February 1965), dependence on external sources means that funds may not be available for projects government has counted on. In Tanzania, more than 90 per cent of foreign aid is tied

As short-falls in investment funds began to appear during the first *Plan* year, government released stock issues, sold savings bonds in small denominations—sponsoring regional competitions to boost sales—and started a national lottery despite some misgivings that national morality was being debased.[33] (The fact that money was going to football pools in Britain apparently was decisive.) Government's response, at first, was to increase import duties rather than widen the direct-tax net. Then in 1965, a 5 per cent levy was imposed not only on salaries but also on a wide range of crops which are not required for local food consumption.[34] This tax provoked discontent among farmers, and was a factor in the defeat of the Minister of Finance in the September 1965 elections.

These measures have been decided on by the planners in

to specific projects. However, around half of external aid is expected to be provided on soft terms so as not to require investment in projects with relatively high yields. See G. Karmiloff's paper, "Problems of Regional Development and Industrial Location in East Africa," which was presented to the Seminar on Problems of Economic Development in East Africa, Nairobi, September 1964, held under the auspices of the East African Institute of Social and Cultural Affairs. (Mr. Karmiloff was expressing his own views in this paper; he was not writing in his capacity as an official of the Directorate of Planning where he was the senior economist.) Because government must get support for programs project by project, it is difficult to plan in a concerted way over time. And the planners must constantly worry about servicing government borrowing. Reliance on foreign sources for funds was an important factor in Tanzania's reluctance to use deficit financing for the *Plan*. Tanzania also operates in an East African system where common currency arrangements restricted the scope for monetary policy as a developmental tool. Tanzania has withdrawn from the East African Common Currency Board, thus eliminating one source of constraint which it *could* eliminate.

[33] There was an overall short-fall of 28 million dollars or almost one quarter of what should have been invested in fiscal year 1964-65. Mr. A.Z.N. Swai, "The Problem of Local Costs and the Five Year Plan," *Nationalist*, July 3, 1965, p. 6.

[34] See speech of the Minister for Finance, reported in the *Nationalist*, June 11, 1965, pp. 1, 4, 8.

the Directorate of Planning and Development and by Treasury personnel, and approved by political ministers. Obviously, the decision to levy a 5 per cent tax on cash crops has political implications, and the TANU government recognized them. However, little modification of actual *Plan* programs has been made in the light of criticisms from middle-level TANU leaders. Political decisions to change these programs have not been made, despite the fact that the boundaries of the political system have changed and new men with different ideas about economic development have come into the TANU government.[35]

Criticisms of the Five Year Plan

Middle-level leaders have criticized the *Plan* for not attempting to equalize income among regions. MPs have argued that wealthier regions and districts were being favored at the expense of poorer ones.[36] One MP, Mr. Kapilima, who was also a regional commissioner, went so far as to accuse government of following in the footsteps of colonialism because it had no policy for upgrading the poorer regions. (Apparently such remarks were not penalized, as he is still a regional commissioner though in a different region). It fell to Chief

[35] The Minister of Finance, Mr. Bomani, announced the intention to earmark a little over $5½ million to the Zanzibar Development Program while Zanzibar was expected to contribute $1,400,000 to the Union budget. The minister did not state that any cutbacks in mainland programs would be made to finance Zanzibar's development. Zanzibar has been getting her own foreign aid funds for her Three Year Plan. The highlights of this Plan were published in an article by Abdul Aziz Twala, Zanzibar Finance Minister, "Zanzibar's Three Year Plan," *Nationalist*, January 22, 1965, p. 6.

[36] S. Mtaki, then a regional commissioner and now a junior minister, R. Wambura, also then a regional commissioner and now a junior minister, P. Mbogo, an area commissioner, P. Siyovelwa, an area commissioner, and C. Kapilima, a regional commissioner were all outspoken about what they felt was the short shrift their districts were getting. They were all from poor districts, and have always been outspoken in the National Assembly.

Fundikira—newly restored to grace—to defend government's policy by pointing out that it was logical for industries to be established where the earning capacities, and thus the buying capacities, were greater. This, he said, was an economic fact, not a result of government design.

Since discussion of the *Plan* had already been held in June 1964 in the NEC, the MPs who spoke up now were merely letting off steam and going on record for their constituencies. In fact, the NEC discussion itself took place after the *Plan* had already been formulated. Although the NEC met officially with the Tanganyika Parliamentary Party on June 12, 1964, the *Plan* had already been published with a limited circulation by April and had been introduced to the National Assembly in May.[37] When it was finally made public in June and discussed in the NEC, no changes were made in the original version: government continued to plan public investment so that there would be direct correlations between per capita regional GDP and per capita investment.[38]

The planners maintained that it was necessary to delay equalization of incomes among the regions. There does not appear to have been much debate about this among political leaders. No adjustments were made in the *Plan* to take account of the criticisms, though government spokesmen did tell the National Assembly that they would try to persuade investors by informing them of the advantages of underdeveloped regions. But no priority was accorded to programs designed to break the bottlenecks to rapid economic growth in specific locations which could otherwise be attractive to investors.[39]

[37] The President addressed the joint meeting of the TPP and the NEC, and then members formed committees to consider the *Plan* and to advise government. Economic, political, social services, and local government committees submitted reports to the TPP.

[38] Karmiloff, *op.cit.*, p. 2.

[39] Many reasons have been given for government's failure to distribute expenditure between regions so as to bring about a narrowing

This was government's position in 1964. In 1965, when the Minister of Industry, Mineral Resources, and Power presented his ministry's budget to the National Assembly, he assured the House that the next time allocation of industries was considered, the Southern Highlands—which include Ruvuma, Iringa, and Mbeya Regions—would receive priority.[40] The minister made this statement following heated arguments made by the MP for Iringa, Mr. John Mwakangala (who is also regional commissioner for Dodoma) and the former MP for Songea in Ruvuma Region, Mr. Otini Kambona. If government actually begins to give the least industrialized regions priority, this will be a sure sign that the middle-level leaders are indeed making themselves felt in economic decisions.

The *Five Year Plan* has also been criticized for not insisting on more state-owned industry and not emphasizing collective and cooperative forms of agricultural production. These criticisms have not been so loudly or frequently expressed in the National Assembly as those concerning regional allocation of resources, but they have been sounded from time to time. In Zanzibar, appropriation of Arab-owned land and enterprises has taken place. A number of middle-level leaders have asked why this has not been done to Asian- and European-owned concerns in Tanganyika. One of the main targets has been the coffee and wheat farms which are held by farmers of Dutch or South African de-

---

of present income disparities. The planners believe that when development is rationalized along lines of geographical specialization, in the long term the spread in average regional income per capita will be narrowed. Meanwhile, the strategy is to seek (except insofar as social overheads are concerned) the greatest and earliest return on public investment. Moreover, there is a reliance on market forces to determine the optimal locations of industries by private investors. And there is the strategy of allowing investment to concentrate around existing "poles" so as to make maximum use of external economies. Cf. *ibid.*

[40] Reported in the *Nationalist*, June 24, 1965, p. 1.

scent; irritation is directed particularly to those who have left Tanganyika and run the farms as absentee landowners. Tanganyika had already nationalized all the land through acts passed in 1962, when freehold was abolished. At the end of 1964, the government revoked the leaseholds on a number of farms in Arusha, Mboya, and Iringa Regions.[41]

On another occasion Mr. Kasambala, the former Minister for Industries, Mineral Resources, and Power, threatened industrialists who did not increase their output with seizure of their enterprises.[42] While this has not occurred, there was more talk of it in 1965-66 than there had been in 1963-64.[43] And it is becoming increasingly difficult to insulate the planners from middle- and top-level leaders; maintaining this insulation has become one of the major tasks of the President and his economic ministers.

Conclusion

The tasks facing Tanganyika in its development effort are formidable indeed. The *Five Year Plan* is a statement of the intentions of planners and political leaders; it contains objectives which have been determined by what they think they can do to change the structure and levels of the economy and the social structure of Tanganyika. (These intentions have already been deflated by the fact that investment has not

[41] Responding to events in Zanzibar, President Nyerere said very pointedly that Zanzibar was not the only place where housing could be nationalized. People were renting out houses in Dar es Salaam and making great profits on their rentals. They were also running "key" rackets in housing.

[42] At the June 1965 meetings of the East African Central Legislative Assembly in Nairobi.

[43] In early 1967, Tanzania nationalized the banks and began to nationalize private industry. It is too early to know how far this will go or what impact it will have on Tanzania's future development. Nor can one determine from this distance the influence of middle-level leaders on these events; for changes among central planners have occurred, and new expatriates may be more congenial to nationalization.

been as much as anticipated for the first *Plan* year.) The *Five Year Plan* did not address itself to any political changes that might be required in order to fulfill its objectives. The decision to finance the *Plan* through foreign investment and loans rather than through a program which would necessitate sharply rising taxation, involuntary savings, or a vast program of mobilized "voluntary" labor meant that the planners and politicians were trying to achieve *Plan* goals without making major transformations in TANU's operation. Of course, political leaders hoped that TANU organizations would become more efficient and thus better able to play a constructive part in the development program; but they did not count on it.

Even the *Presidential Report*, which did introduce changes in the institutional arrangements of TANU and in TANU's relation to the state, gave no evidence of the intention to create a more elitist, disciplined, monolithic political party. Neither did its subsequent amendments, which were published one year after the publication of the *Five Year Plan*, attempt to establish TANU as a vanguard party which would direct and control all aspects of development through its own mechanisms or via a tight rein over the state machinery.

Thus, there is a congruence between the type of party TANU is and the intentions spelled out for it in the *Presidential Report*, and between what TANU is and the *Five Year Plan* which does not call for total mobilization of Tanganyika's resources in a forced draft plan for development.[44] This does not mean that TANU has no place in economic development under the *Five Year Plan*; it has always had a vital

[44] It can be said that this solution is no more than a realistic appraisal of the resources available and the TANU organization and state machinery which exist to command resources. But not all underdeveloped countries have conceived of their revolutions this way. And as I have suggested, there are people in Tanzania who disagree with the *Five Year Plan* and the *Presidental Report* and see them as provisional at best.

role to play in this sphere. But, as President Nyerere has admitted, there has been some uncertainty as to the nature of this role and what it requires of TANU members and the party leaders.[45] The new arrangements try to integrate TANU and government machinery, to demonstrate that there is no conflict between the civil service and TANU, and to make clear that there will be freedom to choose TANU representatives within the party. These ends are themselves framed with regard to achieving economic and social development. Since TANU does play an important part in the development of Tanzania, any attempt to change the socio-economic structure—including one via an indicative planning system and a loosely organized, locally autonomous party organization—must involve TANU in its own internal changes. Although we cannot predict all these changes, a closer examination of the present functioning of TANU will reveal the conditions for change and the alternative patterns possible.

[45] Julius Nyerere, "Address to the National Assembly," reprinted in the *Nationalist*, October 13, 1965, pp. 1, 2, 6, 8.

CHAPTER IX

Government in the Regions and Districts

DEVELOPMENT in Tanzania involves more than the implementation of the *Five Year Plan*. TANU and state structures must carry out a variety of tasks in the regions, districts, and villages as well. TANU and the civil service are trying to create an administrative framework which can direct economic and social change. Many, though by no means all, of the functions performed by them are indeed economic ones; and it is largely through economic duties that an attempt is being made to strengthen, or build for the first time, state and party structures. Thus, while government in the regions and districts cannot be reduced to the implementation of economic goals, these goals have a special importance for the construction of administrative bodies.

One fact of political life is the concern to relate the administrative structures of government to political forces within society. This aspect of political development is manifested as a "problem" in newly independent states or, more generally, in societies characterized by elites who try to bring about rapid social and economic change.[1] That a problem exists is evident to anyone who has attended conferences on the functioning of civil services in Africa or, for that matter, any conference on foreign aid, planning, or diplomacy where civil servant/politician relationships are invariably discussed regardless of whether they are on the agenda. The relationship between administrators and politicians is in constant flux, and a matter of concern to both groups. Individuals are often new to their jobs be they ministers, party officials or civil servants. This is certainly true in Tanzania

[1] Lucien Pye, "The Political Context of National Development" in *Development Administration*, Irving Swerdlow (ed.) (Syracuse: Syracuse University Press, 1963), p. 31. See also Lucien Pye, *Politics, Personality and Nation Building in Burma* (New Haven: Yale University Press, 1962).

where Africanization of the civil service came about only in the last stages of the colonial regime. But individual relationships are only one aspect of this problem.

The process of conscious nation-building in colonial territories usually began with the establishment of the legal and administrative structures of modern government, but the colonial regimes paid little attention to how these structures might relate to political processes and thus make them responsive to political forces in society. "Independence" meant not only freedom from colonial rule, but aslo establishment of political rulers above administrative personnel.

The rhetoric of identity between party and state which is put forward in many African states, Tanganyika included (but not in Zanzibar where the ASP has been declared a supreme body over the Zanzibar government), should not inhibit us from asking where power and prestige actually reside in a political system. Nor should we fail to describe the specific organization and operation of party and state hierarchies simply because political leaders assert an all-encompassing unity for their polities within which distinctions between different structures are unimportant.

At independence, some of the structures which could be utilized for nation-building in Tanganyika were inheritances from the colonial government: the civil service, the defense establishment, and the Native Authority institutions of local government. TANU leaders were determined to transform them or abandon them. By 1965, the civil service had been transformed; the defense establishment had been entirely rebuilt after the January 1964 army mutiny; and the chiefs had been abolished as government agents.

Other structures had emerged out of the anti-colonial struggle, the most important of which were TANU and its auxiliary organs. TANU had not predetermined its role before independence, had not specifically defined itself in relation to the tasks before it. And while it was true that Tanganyika had a party whose membership and activities extended to villages throughout the country, the nature of the membership and activities varied tremendously from one area to another. It was simply not true that in 1962 Tanganyika had a "disciplined and dynamic party" whose machinery could be utilized to the maximum in achieving economic goals.[2] But whether dynamic and disciplined or not, the need was, and is, to rationalize TANU to meet pressing problems, not to abandon it in favor of rule via civil servants controlled at the top by political leaders.

TANU is essential for achieving economic goals because it is the only organization with the potential for reaching people, both to disseminate goals and to organize efforts. Furthermore, many people feel a strong allegiance to TANU— even though they may not always agree with their local TANU organizations—because of its role in the fight for independence: TANU defied the colonial ruler; it asserted the dignity of the African and his ability to rule himself.[3] Others feel that since TANU is the ruling party, government orders must be obeyed because government is a TANU government. TANU activists express this idea, but it is shared by many TANU members who play little active part in TANU affairs.

In other words, for at least some people and probably for many people, TANU provides an "ought" component to an order: it legitimates government rule. This attitude is shared by TANU leaders, who insist that they are popular and representative. They can justify their own orders as TANU orders;

[2] G. Karmiloff, "Planning Machinery and its Operation in Tanganyika," Paper presented to the University of East Africa Public Policy Conference, Makerere College, October 1963.

[3] I am basing my opinions here not on any systematic surveys; these are my impressions from talking to people in and out of TANU organizations. Such people include civil servants who had no particular reason to praise TANU and were even hostile to TANU district and regional leaders. They also include farmers, students, people working in religious institutions, and teachers.

their responsibilities are derived from their TANU positions or government posts given them by TANU. These feelings helped newly appointed government leaders to assume the responsibilities of their ministerial posts. If they were TANU leaders before independence, they could step into government jobs with confidence in their right to do so.

It would be a mistake to approach TANU's roles in handling development tasks primarily in terms of the administrative expertise or technical abilities that TANU organizations can provide. TANU's most important function is to establish political authority. However, it was necessary to refashion TANU's organizations at the regional and district levels so that they could cooperate with civil servants and at the same time be instruments of central rule. I have described what this meant in terms of recruitment to new posts and interrelationships among TANU elected and appointed officials. One of the most important steps taken was to create area and regional commissioners. It is necessary now to define the formal powers of the commissioners and to see how they operate in their regions and districts as officials of the TANU government.

Commissioners As Heads of Government in the Regions and Districts

As the principal representatives of government in the regions and districts, commissioners are responsible for the efficient conduct of public business, planned development, and peace and good order. It is their duty to supervise not only the work of the administrative staff and TANU regional/district headquarters, but also the activities of all departmental officers who are posted to their region/district.

While commissioners are usually the most powerful men within their own TANU organizations, they have been limited by two important factors. First, they have not been given a free hand vis-à-vis civil servants in the regional administration and from the central ministries. The central leaders were well aware that some commissioners did not have the ability to see a development project through its various phases. Though many of them had more administrative ability than elected TANU officials, they were less educated and had less administrative experience than the civil servants who had been in the colonial government; and they did not have the technical experience that the officials of the ministries possessed. Thus, the commissioners were charged with putting into effect only a fraction of the responsibilities of regional government.[4]

Before independence, central ministries in Dar es Salaam had been encroaching on the powers of the colonial district and provincial commissioners. Though the independent Tanganyika government appointed political officers to replace colonial civil servants, these political officers were told to refrain from interfering in the day-to-day workings of ministerial representatives.[5] As commissioners learn more about administration and economic development, central government may become less concerned to circumscribe their interference in the affairs of the ministerial representatives. But the appointment of special representatives of the Directorate of Planning in the regions implies an awareness that even as the commissioners become better able to deal with economic development programs on a technical level, the complexity of the requirements increases. Furthermore, national leaders expect more expertise. Thus, it is an increase in relative rather than absolute knowledge which is needed before the commissioners will be allowed to interfere with technical programs.

Another factor which constrains the power of the commissioners is the authority patterns in the societies over which

[4] Seal, *loc.cit.*, states that the regional commissioner was responsible for putting into effect one-fifth of the responsibilities assigned to the administrative division in the Vice President's office in 1963.

[5] Staff Circular No. 14 of 1962. Reference No.: EB. 20/04. Establishment Division, Prime Minister's Office, July 1962.

they are supposed to rule. Since some Tanganyikan tribes have no strong centralized institutions, some of the districts in which commissioners operate include so-called segmentary societies; and segmentary lineages regulate political relations.[6] The commissioners are supposed to be focal points within these societies. And in fact in some ways they have fulfilled this function. Many people appealed to them, often with complaints and disputes that should have been handled by civil service officers. The commissioners were beset with petitioners because traditional rulers had been removed from their government positions, and because people often did not trust lower-level TANU or government officials to handle their grievances. Commissioners could get little office work done, and eventually had to refuse to see such people. But they did so reluctantly because they realized that without local support they could not do their jobs. They also felt that it was proper for people to bring such complaints to them. After all, they had replaced colonial civil servants who had not served Tanganyikans at all, and were supposed to be responsive to the people. Furthermore, listening to complaints was something the commissioners felt they could do; they had had experience in listening, making promises, and soothing ruffled feelings.

However, the commissioners were not only supposed to hear grievances. They were called on to transmit orders and to rule over dispersed and small-scale settlements, just as had their predecessors, the colonial provincial and district commissioners. It was one thing to listen to people, quite another to get them to do government's bidding. The only tradition of obedience to the orders of district or regional officials was the colonial tradition; the only "central" rule known to the segmentary societies was that of the colonial civil servants.

[6] See M. Fortes and E. E. Evans Pritchard, *African Political Systems* (London: Oxford University Press, 1940), pp. 4-5. See also Aidan Southall, *Alur Society* (Cambridge: Heffner, 1956), pp. 250-51.

And TANU had called this rule into question and put it out of business.

Thus the commissioners encountered a very difficult situation. And because they were political officials charged with carrying out fundamental social and economic transformations, their roles created tensions that colonial officials had not had to face; what the colonial civil servants could let pass the commissioners felt they must take a hand with. In other words, because both the central TANU leaders and the commissioners assumed more responsibilities and attempted many things never before done by government in Tanganyika, the difficulties of ruling in a segmentary society as a regional or area commissioner and an agent of the center were multiplied. Furthermore, unlike the colonial officials, they purport to rule by consent of the ruled.

Formal Responsibilities of the Commissioners

The act which instituted the regional commissioners stated that a regional and an area commissioner shall exercise such functions as are conferred upon him by any written law and such other functions as the Prime Minister may from time to time direct.[7] Subject to the provisions that the Chief Executive can declare otherwise, the commissioners were to be the objects of any references in any written law to provincial commissioners, district commissioners, officers in charge of an extra-provincial district, and administrative or district officers.[8] No general legislation had specified the powers of

[7] Act No. 1 of 1962, February 1962, Section 6, Part 5. The change to a presidential system at the end of 1962 did not involve any change in the statutory position of the commissioners.

[8] Article 3 of Act No. 18, 1962 and Article 4 of Act No. 2 of 1962. Withstanding the provisions of these articles, the Governor General could declare that references to officers of colonial nomenclature could refer to persons other than the new commissioners. The President now has such power. The Governor General exercised it on advice of the Prime Minister in the past.

313

the colonial district and provincial commissioners. Following the British practice of proceeding empirically rather than codifying such matters, a wide variety of ordinances did vest legal powers (many of which dealt with the maintenance of law and order) in the provincial and district commissioners; and these powers were inherited by the regional and area commissioners.[9] Thus the commissioners do have specific powers and duties although their positions have not been clearly defined by law or practice. In summary, the statutory functions of area commissioners are:

(1) Consideration and approval of applications for the holding of public meetings and processions.

(2) Power to arrest and detain a person for 48 hours until a criminal charge is prepared.[10]

(3) Removal of undesirable persons from townships.

(4) Registration of marriages.

(5) Issue of immigration documents to Kenya Africans. Area commissioners have this authority in districts where the regional commissioner has made a delegation of it.

(6) Release of convicted prisoners to extra-mural labour.

(7) Chairmanship of district councils, where applicable.[11]

[9] The Constitution of Tanganyika does not make any reference to these administrative posts at all. Nor does the act which established the presidential system. Cf. Tanganyika (Constitution) Order in Council S. I. 1961, No. 2274, Schedule II.

[10] This power was conferred by Act No. 49 of 1963, an Act to Amend the Regions and the Regional Commissioners, and the Area Commissioners Act, 1962. One section reads: When the Regional/Area Commissioner has reason to believe that any person is likely to commit breach of the peace or disturb the public tranquillity, or *do any act that may probably occasion a breach of the peace* or disturb public tranquillity, and that such breach cannot be prevented otherwise than by detaining such person in custody, the Commissioner may arrest or order a police officer in writing to arrest such person. (Italics added.) This Act is a local version of preventive detention act.

[11] This is under legislation which provides that the Minister for

314

(8) Chairmanship of district loan committees.

(9) Issue of short-term rights of occupancy.

There are also duties which have been conferred on the commissioners by administrative direction. Again, some of these relate to law and order. The commissioner is chairman of the district intelligence committee; he makes recommendations for granting firearm licenses and for the registration of societies. Repatriation of destitute persons to their homes falls within the commissioner's jurisdiction.

The area commissioner has designated responsibilities in the realms of planned development and the supervision of public business. As chairman of the district development committee, he has been instructed to encourage nation-building projects and to assist village-settlement schemes. The area commissioner also has general responsibility for the district office—that is, the actual headquarters and staff of the district administration. He has general surveillance of departmental and local authority activities, though he is not responsible for monies allocated to district headquarters.[12]

In general, the stipulated duties of regional commissioners are similar to those of the area commissioners, and they also fall under three headings: maintenance of law and order in the region; insurance of the planned development of the region; coordination and supervision of public business.

Whereas the area commissioners do not have any legal authority over district councils (though they do have a great deal to say about district council appointments and the running of the council), regional commissioners are the "proper officers" for the district councils: they advise district councils, report on performance, make confidential reports on

Local Government may appoint an area commissioner as chairman of a district council even though he is not a member of that council.

[12] The civil service area secretary is the responsible warrant officer in the district administration.

senior staff, and exercise certain financial controls, such as approving the estimates of the district councils. Regional commissioners also approve officers hired by the district council.[13] However, despite the wide array of powers they have vis-à-vis the district councils, the final arbiter of district council affairs was the Minister of Local Government, and is now the Minister for Regional Administration.[14] The Minister approves bylaws of the councils; and while the regional commissioner can dissolve a council, his decision had to be approved by the minister responsible for local government. The regional commissioners are advised in the use of their powers over district councils by regional local government officers. These officials, though they work under the regional commissioner at his headquarters, are agents of the Director of Local Government in the Ministry of Regional Administration and report directly to him.[15]

Neither the area commissioners nor the regional commissioners have any legal jurisdiction over town councils, which are officially under the Minister of Regional Administration; but they do have a great deal of informal powers. They are

[13] The district council hires clerks, typists, messengers, and village executive officers. These are patronage posts. Formerly, divisional executive officers were hired directly by district councils but now they, like the executive officers proper, are appointed by the Local Government Service Commission. District TANU organizations have split over these appointments as leaders try to dispense patronage.

[14] In 1965, the Ministry of Local Government was abolished. A Minister of State for Regional Administration absorbed the rural and urban local government divisions. Now these divisions exist in the Ministry of Regional Administration.

[15] Local government officers were appointed originally on a provisional basis. Government hoped that many of these officers would resign from central government and apply for posts as executive officers of the district councils, that is, as local government employees. Few did so because working for local government is less attractive. Moreover, the poor quality of the functioning of the councils has made the provisional appointment of local government officers into a long-term prospect.

the chief TANU officials, and the town council is a TANU town council. The commissioners are consulted on town-council appointments and projects, and often have a veto over town-council undertakings.

Many of the commissioners' general responsibilities have been outlined in speeches made by the President and ministers rather than in legislation or specific administrative edicts. Short training courses have been established to familiarize commissioners with the provisions and implications of legislation and the requirements of the *Five Year Plan*. I have already mentioned the attempt to make commissioners more "statistics-conscious." Commissioners have attended courses sponsored by the Ministry of Community Development at Tengeru near Arusha or to the Mzumbe Local Government Training Center in Morogoro Region. They have also taken short courses at Kivukoni College, a school for adults which has played a major role in training both high- and low-level TANU personnel. Often it is during one of these courses that the commissioner learns of his responsibilities. Ministers, permanent secretaries, visiting lecturers, and the President himself have come to Kivukoni to speak with commissioners. Another major channel of communication between the commissioners and leaders in Dar es Salaam is the visits made by high officials and trouble shooters to the regions.

Commissioners and Their Civil Servants

The Prime Minister's office considered it unwise to issue more precise instructions as to the formal relationship between commissioners and ministerial representatives than those contained in Staff Circular No. 14 of 1962:

> The good sense of all concerned and their common devotion to the interests of the country may be trusted to evolve from these directives a satisfactory and efficient relationship.

317

There were good reasons why government did not want to predetermine what were essentially new relationships between commissioners and civil servants. Some of the civil servants in the regions were still expatriates, and the commissioners were themselves new men. One relationship that the division of regional administration at the center wanted to keep open in particular was that between commissioners and their chief servants in the regional administration—the administrative secretaries at the regional level and the area secretaries in the districts.

The civil-servant administrative and area secretaries[16] are supposed to advise and assist the commissioners in their statutory, administrative, and political duties. The administrative secretary is the senior executive officer of the regional commissioner. He directs and controls the actual office work of the regional administration's headquarters. In this capacity, the administrative secretary gives orders to clerical staff and to district officers, including the area secretaries, in his region. The administrative secretary is responsible for all money allocated to regional headquarters.[17] While he works under the regional commissioner, he must also report to the administration division in the Ministry of Regional Administration. Similarly, the area secretary works to the area commissioner but he also reports to the administrative secretary and takes instructions from him.

The administrative and area secretaries were originally told to be desk officers. In practice, this was never completely the case, as they did go out on safari, and visited district headquarters to check the work of the district staff of the regional administration.

[16] The area secretary is not to be confused with the area secretary of TANU.

[17] The administrative and area secretaries are the responsible warrant holders for funds which are expended at the decisions of regional and area commissioners. But they have not effectively restrained the spending of their political bosses.

318

The civil service secretaries served as secretaries to the development committees.[18] In the absence of the regional commissioner, they took the chair of the development committees. When the commissioners were out of their regions or districts, the secretaries often traveled outside of district or regional headquarters. At these times, they acted as deputy commissioners and performed political functions. Even before TANU was opened to civil servants, commissioners socialized and talked politics with them. An administrative secretary or area secretary who had been at his post for some time might not be at all reluctant to enter into local political squabbles.

Expatriate civil servants in regional administration also became involved in TANU politics. For example, once when a regional commissioner was absent and the regional TANU organization could not decide on the itinerary of President Nyerere who was visiting the region, an expatriate administrative secretary handled all the arrangements, even to deciding how much time the President would spend with particular elected and appointed TANU officials. Another expatriate administrative secretary was asked by the regional commissioner to settle a patronage struggle in a district council because he could be an impartial arbitrator.

No neat dividing line can be made between administrative/executive and political functions; and certain executive functions of the civil-service heads of districts and regions involve them in local politics—administration of famine relief or refugee resettlement, for example. Other executive powers conferred by law are relatively devoid of political content. Area secretaries have limited magisterial powers of granting bail, signing affidavits, committing prisoners to mental hospitals. Area secretaries also have powers delegated to them by their area commissioners, such as scrutinizing

[18] Executive officers of the district council have replaced the area secretaries as secretaries of the district development committees.

applications for citizenship or firearms, though the actual recommendation is made by the commissioner.

In recognition of the far-ranging tasks of the area secretaries, a decision was made in 1965 to appoint about forty new civil servants as assistant area secretaries. The aim was to staff certain districts with two area secretaries, allowing one of them to travel throughout the district familiarizing himself with village problems; for one of the major jobs of the civil-service secretaries is to ensure that regional policies are understood and constantly applied outside regional and district headquarters. The scope and variety of the secretaries' work depends less on statutory authority than on their personal relationship with their commissioners.

Staff Circular No. 14 of 1962 told the commissioners that they "exercise general supervision of public business," and that "it is upon the Regional Commissioner and his Area Commissioners and Administrative officers that responsibility rests for the progress and welfare of the people in their charge."[19] The Circular states also that "responsibility for the efficient rendering of technical services is vested in the appropriate ministries."[20] The commissioners are entitled to receive from departmental officers all the information and assistance they may need for the conduct of public business in their own office. And they may issue orders to ministerial representatives, though they are enjoined normally not to intervene in departmental matters.

Economic Responsibilities in the Regions and Districts

While government has seen fit to restrict the activities of the commissioners, it has now begun issuing central directives urging commissioners to become involved directly in economic development. The President and his ministers are

[19] Staff Circular No. 14 of 1962.
[20] Ibid.

constantly telling not only the commissioners but the elected TANU chairmen and TANU executive committee members that they must now do more than make speeches exhorting the people to work harder; they must learn about the economic conditions of their regions and have concrete things to say and do about development projects. At the same time, the commissioners have been warned off from interfering with ministerial representatives and they have not been given specific responsibilities in the *Five Year Plan*. Thus, a very real tension has arisen.

The *Three Year Plan* never mentioned the commissioners at all, as it was formulated before these appointments were made. The only projects that would have been likely to come directly under the commissioners were the office-expansion programs within the regional administration. The regional commissioners were coordinators for development projects designed by and under the control of the ministries, Operationally, there was no policy formulation and little execution which fell to the commissioners in connection with the *Three Year Plan*.

The *Five Year Plan* did not take account of the new political arrangements in the regions and districts either. Nowhere in the *Five Year Plan* are regional or area commissioners mentioned, not even under the heading of "Administrative Machinery for Planning and Implementing Development," which elaborates the central planning and administrative organs. With very few exceptions, neither the *Five Year Plan* nor the regional plans I have seen mention TANU at all. In one regional plan, under a section on "Methods-Technical" to achieve objectives, the TANU Youth League was suggested as a disseminator of information. Under the following section—"Methods-Psychological"—no mention was made of TANU.

As late as January 1964, Vice President Kawawa told a seminar of TANU deputy secretaries that government would send copies of major government policies to TANU district offices for dissemination. This had not been done previously by government nor by TANU National Headquarters. But it would be incorrect to conclude from this that TANU has played no role in formulating the *Five Year Plan*. And the lower down the hierarchy of administrative units, the more important TANU is in plan implementation.

District and Regional Development Committees

The commissioners do not closely supervise the work of the ministerial representatives, but if the education officer or the agricultural officer wants to put a project across, he will almost always consult the commissioner in order to get his cooperation. This consultation can take place informally at the district or regional headquarters where both men have offices in the *boma*, a highly compact grouping of offices. Departmental officers of the ministries will usually be within a hundred yards of the regional commissioner and his administrative staff. Area commissioners and the district departmental officers for that district headquarters which is located at regional headquarters will be at the same site or one close by.[21]

Formal consultation between the commissioners and departmental representatives is carried out at regional and district development committee meetings. It is via the development committees that TANU is supposed to come into the planning process. The commissioners chair the meetings of the development committees, and civil servants, elected TANU officials, and TANU district councilors are members.

Development committees existed before the *Five Year Plan* was even started. Historically, the development committee structure was set up to channel self-help schemes, and the committees were instituted in order to rationalize

---

[21] E.g., Bukoba is the capital of West Lake Region. The district headquarters for Bukoba District are at the regional headquarters for West Lake.

self-help efforts at local levels and to shift the emphasis away from voluntary, unintegrated self-help to nation-building organized nationally and reaching down to village levels.[22] The development committees were meant to provide both a central mechanism and a channel of communications between the center and the villages, by which local projects could be integrated into overall plans and objectives.[23]

Government's idea was that small communities ought to think for themselves and select projects as much as possible on their own initiative. But government was not willing to permit economic waste. It was one thing for the village development committees (VDCs)—made up of village residents—to identify important local needs, and another thing to plan at the local level. With approximately 7,500 VDCs in 1963, no central plan could possibly hope to coordinate all the efforts of local development committees. The personnel needed to feed information to the center did not even exist. Information about crops, population, et cetera, could come only from technical officers traveling through the rural areas. Much of the information might be gathered by TANU people, but it had to be processed before it could be sent to Dar es Salaam by the agricultural and community development officers.

During the course of 1963, it became increasingly important to have information channeled from the localities to the center because the central planners needed this data for *Plan* formulation. The VDCs obviously could not process information and send it on to the center much less "plan" local development: the funds available for their own projects are meager; and even schemes that can be financed completely

[22] Joseph Nye, Jr., "Tanganyika's Self-Help," *Transition*, III (November 1963), 35. I am indebted to the author for making available the unpublished materials upon which this article was based.

[23] See mimeographed extract of the *Policy Statement to the Budget Session of the National Assembly*, by the Hon. J. S. Kasambala, June 1963, p. 1.

from local sources must be sent up to the district development committee for approval. Recognition of the VDCs' limits led the Ministry of Local Government to urge the district development committee (DDCs) to plan and initiate schemes for village development when the VDCs were not doing their "duty";[24] these plans would then be carried out by the VDCs.

The DDCs do come into the planning process, though their efforts had little to do with the formulation of the *Five Year Plan*. They are one of the district council's functional committees, which include education, finance, public health, social services, communications and works. But, whereas the other committees are composed primarily of district councilors, the DDCs membership is not. (See Table 12.)

TABLE 12

DDC Members

The area commissioner who is chairman of the committee.
All members of the finance committee of the district council which consists of all the chairmen of the other functional committees of the council, including the chairman of the district council.
All departmental technical officers in the district—i.e., the agricultural extension officer, the education officer, et cetera.
The district chairman of TANU if he is not already a member of the finance committee of the council.
The executive officer of the district council.

In theory, the DDCs are supposed to consider village development proposals of VDCs after they have been submitted (on May 1 of each year) to the executive officers of the district councils. The executive officers then process the proposals and distribute them to the functional committees of the council. In turn, the functional committees decide on pri-

[24] John Mwakangale, the then Parliamentary Secretary for the Ministry of Local Government, in a policy statement. *Tanganyika Standard*, November 21, 1963. For village plans see Appendix III.

orities and draw up a program of development which is then submitted to the full meeting of the district development committees.[25] Then the DDC is to "review, coordinate and arrange priorities of all proposals received and form a development master plan for the district."[26] These master plans were supposed to be the basis for the regional plans which, in turn, were to be the raw plans for the central planners.

Needless to say, the process does not work quite this way; there are many irregularities in procedure at the district level. Nevertheless, the DDCs do gather information and send it to the regional development committees (RDCs). The compiling of preliminary targets and the sending of semi-processed information—these are the principal functions of the DDCs in the drawing up of plans. However, while they are critically placed in the development committee hierarchy with regard to watching over village plans and seeing that final plans are implemented, they are too local to be able to plan final targets, and must rely on the next highest level, the RDCs, to check the consistency of the VDCs' projects they approve. They are better able to fulfill their function of forming a master plan for the district than are the VDCs to form a master plan for the village, but once again DDCs rely on the regional officers to make district plans consistent. Even where a district has exceptionally good ministerial representatives, an able area commissioner and TANU leaders, the district "plan" is not a comprehensive or integrated document, but rather a set of agricultural targets based on past yields, acres sown, and future predictions.

The DDCs also frame estimates for development and capital works of the district council; and when funds for a project are to be raised within a district, the RDC is likely to approve a district proposal. But the overwhelming share of all projects that get *finished* are those financed through the central ministries.[27]

[25] From Local Government Circular No. 20 of 1963.   [26] *Ibid.*
[27] About $1.7 million was made available to local government au-

325

The area commissioner is supposed to "summon the members of the main District Development Committee who will meet to put into execution the approved development projects."[28] This implies that the DDC does somehow execute projects; in fact they do not, although they do meet for a few days each month. Individual members of the DDC—departmental officers from the ministries, commissioners, TANU chairmen—may carry out executive responsibilities, but they do so in their individual capacities, not as members of the DDC.

The role of TANU people in discussions on economic questions in the DDCs has undergone a marked change in two years. The minutes, particularly of the early meetings, indicate that an extraordinary variety of issues came under discussion. At first, talk centered around the proposals of the ministerial representatives—especially those of the agricultural officers.[29] Some TANU people and commissioners were not even present at these DDC meetings, and ministerial officers complained that TANU, for all the talk, was not interested in the "nuts and bolts" of development. This complaint is heard less frequently now, for commissioners are playing a more active part, and TANU people not only lobby for projects as they have done in the past, but also enter discussions

---

thorities in the form of grants towards development expenditure during the budget year 1964-65. (According to the *Five Year Plan*, this is to remain the average level of such grants during the *Five Year Plan* period.) This figure does not include grants to district councils for roads, drainage, or primary education. $1.7 million distributed over Tanganyika in unspecified funds is not a very large amount per district.

[28] Local Government Circular No. 20, 1963.

[29] This may account for what Nye, *loc.cit.*, called the "somewhat bureaucratic flavor" of minutes of development committee meetings. He cited statements to the effect "the locals agreed not to dig this road." Not all discussion finds its way into the final minutes, either because it may be perceived to be irrelevant or because people decide they do not want certain statements ascribed to them or on record at all. Inefficient minute-takers may leave gaps also.

about priorities, techniques, and control. Since TANU chairmen and district councilors may retain their posts for years, many people are becoming more experienced. Area commissioners also are acquiring experience, though they move from place to place.

It is, however, at the level of the RDC that the development committees really enter into formulation of the central plan. At the same time, the RDC is further removed from plan popularization and implementation, though it does have the crucial function of making district plans consistent and approving projects formulated lower down.

In an early stage of the *Five Year Plan*'s formulation, RDCs were asked to assess their contribution to the achievement of the 1970 goals for the nation. These assessments were expressed chiefly in terms of projected crop output and value added through the more elaborate processing of primary produce. There were some exceptions to this pattern—notably in Arusha and Kilimanjaro, Coast, Tanga, and Lake Regions (Mwanza and Bukoba), where local and municipal authorities are actively engaged in attracting new industries, and consequently are able to propose industrial possibilities to central government.

The Ministry of Development and Planning sent to the regions certain very broad targets, based on the data it already possessed.[30] The RDCs then compiled a regional development plan for the five year period, 1964-69. These plans were prepared very rapidly.[31] For example, the Mara Plan was prepared in six weeks with only minor assistance from outside, and followed the lines laid down by the Ministry of Development and Planning. Some of the plans pre-

[30] The Ministry of Development and Planning collated materials from other ministries in its own small statistical department before it absorbed the Central Statistical Bureau from the Treasury.

[31] I have been able to see the regional plans for West Lake Region, Mara Region, Arusha Region, and I have gone through the Kigoma Regional Plan with the regional agricultural officer.

327

sented a background of the region, some a detailed breakdown of the costs involved in their proposed projects. Some plans were projected in terms of per capita income figures as well as specific crop targets; others mentioned crop targets only. The plans that were sent back to Dar es Salaam also varied in the presentation of a detailed geographical breakdown.[32]

A thorough explanation of the way in which the RDC went about its business was given in the Mara Regional Plan. The regional commissioner gave the responsibility for preparing materials to a sub-committee of the RDC. Discussions were held and advice was sought from all heads of administration, from the agricultural and other departments, and from the DDCs. The RDC which usually met once a month, convened more frequently during the time of plan formulation. The bulk of the work was done by the regional agricultural officer who could draw on district agricultural personnel located at regional headquarters. The day-to-day work was done by a few heads of departments who kept the RDC informed of progress. The RDC approved materials as they became available.

More often than not, the RDCs found that the targets they had been sent initially were conservative.[33] They increased

[32] The West Lake Plan showed target figures for districts while the Mara Plan gave regional figures only. The West Lake Plan also had sub-district or divisional and sub-division breakdowns in an Appendix. Whether these were also sent to Dar es Salaam I do not know. The West Lake Plan notes that the questionnaire sent to the Ministry of Development and Planning include a district by district breakdown, although this had not been required. This was done at the request of the agricultural officer by district development teams for future reference.

[33] The minutes of the Arusha DDC show that three-fold increase in cotton production was called for. Eventually, Arusha District was slated for an increase of 200 per cent in the regional plan for cotton. The plan as put forward in the Arusha regional document called for a 90 per cent increase in value of crops by 1970 over the average value for 1961-63. The Ministry of Agriculture considered that a

the figures of the Dar es Salaam proposals, and so did the DDCs. At this point then, the center was not pushing the district and regional development committees to commit themselves to higher targets. Insofar as pressure came from local TANU people it was usually pressure for a new industrial project or for more social services in a particular locality.

The political representatives on the RDCs are in a much better position than those at lower levels to take an active part in setting targets. The TANU regional chairman is an *ex officio* member of the RDC and the regional commissioner is chairman of the committee. The civil service administrative secretary is RDC secretary, and the TANU deputy regional secretary has more status and plays a more important role in the RDC than the district deputy secretary of TANU plays at the DDC. This is in part a reflection of the gap in capabilities between deputy secretaries at the regional and district levels, which is probably greater in most cases than the gap between regional and area commissioners. MNE and MPs may also attend RDC meetings. But since there is no elected council at the regional level, there are no councilors to come to the RDC.

The position of area commissioners on the RDCs has not been standardized. In 1962 and the first part of 1963, all the area commissioners came to RDC meetings, but technical officials have said that they often talked so much and so irrelevantly that the agenda could not be completed and no work could be done.[34] Yet the area commissioners are the major

---

desirable target for increases in crop values would be 50 per cent for export crops. The projected value of livestock by 1970 represented an approximate increase of 167 per cent. Often the technical officers felt that they could have produced even more than the figures they sent off. There were some exceptions. The Mara planners felt that it was not possible to achieve the level of the national target of 80 per cent increase in livestock (which the guide paper from Dar es Salaam had set out). A 39 per cent increase in sales of livestock was planned.

[34] Personal interviews with regional and district civil servants.

liaison between regional and district development committees. And it would seem appropriate that they be present both to defend projects they want approved and to clarify orders sent to them. In small regions where communications are good, area commissioners can be brought in rapidly for consultation if necessary, but are not needed at each meeting. But it is in just those regions where communications are difficult and area commissioners lose a great deal of time traveling to and from RDC meetings that their presence on some regular basis (though not necessarily monthly) is most needed. At present, regions have no standard way of handling this problem: some area commissioners always attend the RDC meetings, others do not.

Despite the greater expertise of political officials at the regional level, technical officers sometimes complained that TANU people neither understood the political implications of the policies they wanted, nor the capital and human resources required for the projects they put forward. But there were no complaints that TANU was trying to push target figures beyond reasonable levels or, for that matter, to reduce target figures so that they could easily achieve them.[35] TANU officials in the regions seemed relatively uninterested in statistical matters and gave the technicians a free hand. Civil servants objected to the fact that TANU officials, including commissioners, sometimes would not see a policy through if difficulties arose. More often than not, the agricultural officers felt that the commissioners kept local TANU organizations at bay, an opinion seconded by town clerks and executive officers. This situation exists because the TANU government is not pushing a forced draft development; regional and district officials have not, as yet, felt themselves under intense pressure from the center to implement the *Five Year Plan*.

In fact, it was the Ministry of Agriculture that lowered re-

[35] These judgments are based on interviews with district and regional agricultural and community development officers.

gional figures for crop increases, feeling the proposed increases were unrealistic. The Directorate of Planning did not always agree, and in fact, as late as June 1965, had not approved the regional five year plans for crop increases because it felt that the targets might be too low. The Directorate was conscious, however, that there must be markets, both internal and external, for increased crop outputs. Political leaders do not always take markets into consideration when they call for higher output. Thus, high-level political leaders accused them of being too deferential to the technical experts and not pushing hard enough for increases. They felt that the enthusiasm of TANU representatives on some RDCs had been vindicated by early reaching of crop targets.[36]

Since economic data is hard to come by, and since the central planning office is not well staffed, the planners themselves have expected some decentralization of economic decision-making to the regional level. Toward this end, the Directorate of planning presented the RDCs with guides which were intended to provide an internally consistent framework within which the RDC could elaborate its projects and open up communication with the central planning agency.[37] In order to make this process work within the planned framework, the guides describe what "product of a sector" is and how it can be measured. The guide enumerates in simplified language the basic elements of economic analysis with which regional personnel must become acquainted if they are to participate in the management and planning of economic development in a region. An attempt is being made to teach the

[36] Vice President Kawawa pointed out that the targets for cotton production for 1970 were going to be reached as early as 1966 in Mara Region. Interview, April 1965.

[37] The Directorate of Planning asked that no material be quoted from the sample guide. I am citing only from Mr. Simba's speech at Kivukoni, and not from the guide. Mr. A.Z.N. Swai gave a speech to a regional commissioners' Conference of October 2, 1964, where he covered much of the same material.

331

planners and the regional commissioners to speak the same language.[38]

The commissioners have been told to face up to their responsibilities even at the cost of making mistakes. "Mistakes will not be blamed."[39] The central planners are encouraging commissioners to take some economic initiative, rather than simply to wait for Dar es Salaam to send instructions. While regional offices were waiting for the *Five Year Plan*, technical officers, rather than commissioners, were initiating their own development projects. The nomination of civil servants to commissioner posts is likely to lead to better administration and a better understanding between commissioners and planners, but it does not guarantee economic initiative. Entrepreneurship is needed. The pervasive tendency to wait for orders from Dar es Salaam stems in part from a general feeling of insecurity. Commissioners are new to their jobs and aware of their lack of experience in high-level economic decision-making. Their movement from one place to another has not allowed them to become familiar with local conditions; and they operate in a situation where information is hard to come by.

At the regional level then, political officials in the RDCs have played a role in formulating regional five year plans, although it has so far been a limited one. They may play an expanded role as the *Five Year Plan*'s regional breakdowns are revised. But so far they have neither exercised pressure on technical personnel to increase targets nor forcefully put

[38] The need to be statistics-conscious had been recognized. The President told the regional commissioners that they must acquire a "veritable thirst for statistical data." At the same time, the President said the plan, national or regional, must not become a fetish with the people. The President also let it be known that it was the duty of every regional and district development committee to take stock of what is being produced and to calculate to what extent production can be expanded. President's speech to regional commissioners, published in the *Nationalist*, October 29, 1964, p. 4.

[39] Speech of Mr. Swai to regional commissioners.

forward political considerations at RDC meetings. No recognizable TANU regional policy is evident in the minutes of the development committees. And where civil servants have resisted the proposal of a commissioner or a TANU chairman for some social service or development project on the grounds that it is financially unfeasible, the political official has usually deferred.

CHAPTER X

TANU Tries to Reach the Villages

TANU and Rural Development

TANU sees itself as the propagator of social change. One of the ways it tries to effect social change is by supporting technical programs: mobilization of audiences to listen to technical officers; further support and explanation of the policies of the ministries; and follow-through on policies initiated by technical personnel. TANU personnel often accompany agricultural officers to rural areas to help put a project across. In an area which had resented attempts by the colonial administration to get cattle dipped or land terraced, there might be a residue of feeling against an African agricultural officer or the expatriate officer still on the job. In such cases, TANU was, and is, invaluable in organizing support for local programs: it has enough authority so that individual TANU members can bring civil servants to the people and support them as they explain a program. The very conditions which require civil servants to need TANU determine the nature of TANU's own contribution to developmental programs.

The fact that tasks are not easily separable into component parts is related to the nature of local societies. Development does not consist, for example, in deciding that a village needs a new well and then telling technical personnel to construct one. The decision to have a well, getting the villagers to accept the location of the well, and persuading individuals themselves to carry out much of the construction work in cooperation with technical specialists are all a matter of political concern. Thus it is crucial to the development effort that TANU make available numbers of men who can travel around making speeches and bringing people into contact with centrally or regionally established goals. Civil servants

334

in regional administration have office work to do; technical personnel from the ministries are in scarce supply, also have office work to do, and must spend a great deal of time on programs already underway. It would be a waste of scarce resources to have these men gather people together and then make speeches to get support for ministerial programs.

At independence, TANU's emphasis was on self-help and voluntary labor schemes, areas in which TANU officials could easily involve themselves. Later on, the new political heads in the regions and districts could also become involved in organizing self-help schemes, since little expertise was required. Commissioners in general were not inclined to interfere with the technical ministries, whose duties they saw at first as outside their field of knowledge. But in self-help projects, which required mobilization of manpower, the commissioners, who had been pre-independence TANU chairmen and organizing secretaries, could use their skills. Speech-making, arranging meetings, and employing persuasion—not unmixed with coercion—were jobs familiar to the commissioners. Here then was an area in which TANU could contribute. The commissioners became key men in TANU's process of organization around the local development projects; they toured the countryside organizing the people in self-help efforts.[1] The aim was to increase local political participation through the mechanism of the TANU local organizations and development committees, and at the same time to tighten TANU's control over localities by popularizing and implementing these programs.

By the spring of 1962, the interaction of many of these elements could be seen. A People's Plan for village develop-

[1] Nye, *op.cit.*, p. 36, says that the real elevation of self-help came after Nyerere had resigned and was faced with the task of reorganizing TANU. The decision to create the commissioners was announced in October 1961. Self-help was a logical way in which to reorganize TANU with the commissioners in key roles.

335

ment was launched by Prime Minister Kawawa in May 1962. This plan was based on autonomous development committees at the village level, whose task was to plan individual development schemes.[2] The idea was that economic development at the village level could take place only concomitantly with social change. The idea of community development came to the fore. The Ministry of Community Development in conjunction with TANU was to be the vehicle for bringing about social change conducive to economic development without creating the dislocations of many modernizing experiences. Community development workers were to bring new awareness to the leaders and the people at village, district, and regional levels. The small amount of money budgeted in the *Three Year Plan* for self-help schemes ($196,000) was in the community development budget.[3] And leaders told TANU regional, district, and local officials that they ought to be, in effect, community development officers.[4]

The responsibilities of the community development division itself were being increased by May of 1962, when the "People's Plan" was introduced because government was becoming more aware of the costs of unsupervised self-help

[2] J. Kasambala, "The People's Part," *Spearhead*, I, No. 2 (December 1962). Mr. Kasambala was Minister for Community Development and Cooperatives. The "plan" he referred to was much more an organizational framework to achieve aims than a plan.

[3] Nye, *loc.cit.*

[4] It appeared for a time that local community development officers hired by district councils would be recruited from TANU activists. Women branch TANU leaders were also being made community development assistants. However, after January 1965, community development assistants were to be hired centrally by the Ministry of Community Development and posted to localities. Just as the need for efficient staff made it necessary for government to take the hiring of divisional executive officers out of the hands of the district councils, similarly, local council hiring of community development assistants was curtailed.

schemes. Although labor was cheap, roads that washed out or went nowhere and schools that could not be staffed were a drain on scarce resources and were having a demoralizing rather than an uplifting effect. Thus, after the first year of independence, the emphasis shifted from self-help schemes per se to nation-building projects and a program which came to be known as "villagization."

The villagization program was designed to group a scattered population into villages in order to husband scarce resources—tractors, managerial personnel—and facilitate the provision of social services and the mechanization of agriculture.[5] Grouping people into compact villages would make central direction of agricultural development easier. At the same time, TANU leaders believed that stronger local political organizations could be built in such villages. The idea of villagization was originally tied up with voluntary-labor schemes to build the villages, and such self-help programs were to provide the focus for strengthening TANU at the local levels. This did not always happen as planned; and when local TANU organizations proved unable to lead self-help programs in certain localities, they were demonstrably weakened. By 1964, villagization had come to mean primarily large-scale, relatively capital intensive and technologically advanced projects. The focus was around pilot village projects controlled by the settlement division of the Ministry of Lands, Settlement, and Water Development which is responsible for the "transformation" approach to agriculture under the *Five Year Plan*.[6] (The Ministry of Agriculture is responsible for the "extension" approach.)

[5] Cf. "Rural Settlement Planning," issued by the survey division of the Ministry of Lands, Forests and Wildlife (now known as the Ministry of Lands, Settlement and Water Development) Dar es Salaam, 1964.

[6] Formerly, there was a Rural Settlement Commission which was in charge of the pilot projects. The commissioner for Village Settle-

Local TANU organizations did not organize themselves around the pilot projects, and thus could not strengthen themselves through building these projects. However, the pilot projects do provide a more conventional arena for bolstering local TANU organizations. These schemes dramatize for farmers and leaders alike that something is being done to change the rural patterns. Furthermore, if a project is going well, local TANU leaders are likely to concern themselves with it and make sure that it is brought to the attention of notables from Dar es Salaam. In determining the site of a pilot scheme, political as well as technical considerations come to the fore: regional commissioners must be consulted; and sometimes a national leader may want the village established in his home area. The "pork barrel" may be very small in Tanzania but it is not unknown. One of the most obvious ways for local politicians to become involved in the pilot projects is through the selection of farmers to work them.

It is important to distinguish between different types of agricultural projects. The village pilot programs which I have been discussing seem relatively free from political interference in both the selection of personnel and the running of the farms. It is laid down in the standards of selection established for the pilot projects by the Ministry of Lands that no unemployed or semi-unemployed persons should be chosen for the schemes, but rather people with farm experience. (In Tanzania, even city-dwellers usually have experience of farming; many have recently moved to the town, and some still grow crops in their own gardens or just outside the town.) When a new pilot village is established, the RDC delegates a sub-committee to handle the selection of farmers.

---

ment and his staff moved into the settlement division of the Ministry of Lands in 1964. The original document which outlines the functions of a Rural Settlement Commission with an executive Village Settlement Agency was a Confidential Ref. No. VSC/V.1/1/11 Memorandum No. 1 to the Rural Settlement Commission, Appendix A, B, and C.

(The regional commissioner may take an active part here if he wishes.) People living in the region have priority for selection. Technical managers of the farms, who often are still expatriates, have the right of veto over individual recruits. When pilot farms were started before the present villagization program came into effect, expatriate managers complained that politicians interfered in running the farms, and that costly schemes were kept going because of their location in a prominent national leader's home district. This kind of political interference seems less prevalent now. There are other types of rural development projects which are more overtly political.[7] A Circular Letter of May 21, 1963 told the regional commissioners to give the pilot villages priority over other village schemes. Despite this injunction, commissioners often respond to the great local pressures for getting funds channeled to locally initiated projects which are not budgeted under the *Five Year Plan.* Villagers may work out a scheme in conjunction with the district agricultural officer and/or the community development officer and proceed with it without getting approval from the development committees. Even if funds need not be committed initially by central government, government may feel that resources will soon be required that it cannot provide. Regional commissioners may try—sometimes with a heavy hand—to raise funds for such projects locally. The Treasury has channeled money to TANU projects, although complaints are still heard in the NEC that government has not supported TANU-sponsored agricultural programs with enough funds. At times, there have been mutual recriminations between participants in the pilot projects and the locally initiated schemes. Competition between

[7] I am indebted to Professor Raymond Apthorpe of Makerere College for making available to me his as yet unpublished material on rural projects in East Africa from a study he has undertaken for the International Labor Organization (ILO). He bears no responsibility for the use I have made of his materials.

339

pilot projects run by the Ministry of Lands and other types of rural development programs can become seriously disruptive for the development effort. At the present time, there are basically two other types of organized rural settlement programs aside from the pilot village schemes.[8]

Communal farms have been started and run by TANU or TANU Youth League district organizations.[9] The moving force behind the establishment of a TANU farm is usually one man and a small group of his followers. They clear the bush and organize families to move into the cleared land. The leader of the farm may be a district TANU leader; more likely he will be a branch leader. It has happened more than once that a successful farm leader, who had been a local leader, came to district and then to national prominence through his nation-building efforts.[10]

What were formerly small-scale and very local attempts to start TANU communal farms have now become more highly organized, or at least enveloped in a panoply of organizational forms. For example, the most prominent TANU communal farm is at Litowa in Songea, near the famous Perimiho Catholic Mission. A number of young men, some influenced by the Mission, established the Litowa farm entirely on their own. Now there is a Songea Development Association which does not itself operate agricultural projects but encourages their founding and assists them with finance and technical aid.[11] TANU has also started a communal farming and train-

[8] There are many different local resettlement "schemes" that are not organized by government or by TANU. Individuals simply regroup themselves on their own initiative.

[9] They may have no smallholding at all as distinct from pilot schemes.

[10] One man was offered an opportunity to become an area commissioner after he had started a farming scheme. But he chose to continue with the farm. One year later he was elected to Parliament.

[11] The committee which controls the Songea Development Association is composed of one councilor from each of the 5 divisions

ing center in Tarime District, Mara Region. Central government has played a much greater part in this scheme. At Litowa, government made tractors available on loans; at Tarime, it has provided specialists for training and has given equipment. This scheme is sponsored and supported by a prominent leader who comes from Tarime and is trying to mend his local fences.[12] Government intends to use the farmers trained at Tarime to form a nucleus for planned settlement schemes. "Loyalty" and "enthusiasm" have been explicitly stated as criteria for selection of these schemes.

The third category of rural settlement is that of tenant farmer schemes. These were run originally by the Tanganyika Agricultural Corporation (TAC),[13] but have since been inherited by the Ministry of Lands. Some of the farms run by TAC were projects for rural resettlement of urban unemployed. TANU is involved in them in three important ways: TANU National Headquarters recruit men, largely from Dar es Salaam; disciplinary matters that cannot be settled among farmers and manager are sometimes forwarded to TANU Headquarters in Dar es Salaam; and TANU raises money for the farms through regional assistance boards. Since these boards rely on voluntary contributions, Asian businessmen and traders are often asked for donations.

TANU district and regional organizations rarely come into the administration of rural projects, which is the work of government representatives. However, TANU regional/district leaders do solicit support for these projects; they may even

---

of Songea; the agricultural and cooperative officers; the district chairman of TANU and the TANU Youth League; the district secretary of TANU. There is also one representative of each project connected with the Association. The area commissioner is the chairman of the Association.

[12] I refer to Mr. I. Bhoke-Munanka, now Minister of State, and MP for North Mara East (Tarime).

[13] A public corporation run by the Ministry of Agriculture.

sponsor them and start them with local initiative. Many people in rural areas are eager to get new wells or dams or health services. It is TANU's job, together with the community development personnel, to make the people realize what they must do to have what they want. But there are great difficulties involved. Very often, government cannot supply goods and services and thus it tells people they must be self-reliant and by their own efforts achieve valued ends. Not everyone is willing to strike this bargain. And people's perceptions of the gains and effort involved are variable. This includes TANU people as well; not all TANU activists, let alone those who call themselves TANU supporters, opt for "modernity." It would be a mistake simply to conceive of a backward countryside seeded with TANU carriers of modern patterns of living. All the seminars, meetings, and exhortations that government civil servants and TANU people are involved in giving are aimed, after all, at other civil servants and TANU people and not at the population at large. It is not unusual to find recalcitrant individuals in a certain district being led by a man who calls himself a TANU leader. If those who object are not organized by such a leader, one will usually be forthcoming to capitalize on local discontent. It would be rare to find a monolithic TANU local organization ranged against the people; it might well be that a TANU organization at the district level is being opposed by a locality, including TANU people there, and even TANU divisional leaders.

Now the TANU government and TANU regional and district leaders are being confronted with the problems that beset the colonial government: how willing are we to oppose, or to use traditional leaders; to what extent should force be used in subduing opposition; and, more fundamentally, how can rural change be effected? Rural pilot projects can make an impact, but they cannot be established everywhere. Furthermore rural change involves persuading people to grow more and different crops, and perhaps to revolutionize their patterns of family life, hygiene, communications, and physical effort.

I have described TANU, and specifically the commissioners, as coordinators of a "team effort," as sponsors and sometimes organizers of change, though in the last category TANU efforts in self-help programs have given way to more technical and specialized work, such as managing pilot programs and TANU communal farms. Let us now turn attention to TANU as the enforcer of central edicts in the countryside.

TANU and Enforced Change

It is hard to come to grips with local issues because by their nature they are often submerged and not readily available to someone who does not reside in one place for a long period and who does not speak vernacular languages.[14] Yet many issues do recur from locality to locality. If we look at what has to be enforced in Tanganyika, this becomes clear.

The reasons for supporting a nationwide political party are usually local reasons. For example, in colonial territories demands for independence were translated into local grievances and vice versa. This was particularly true in Tanganyika, where local TANU organizations and small, dispersed groups of people had only intermittent contact with central leaders and with each other. TANU a useful instrument for manipulating local situations and achieving local ends; it was directed both against the colonial government and against one local group by another. Local leaders rose and consolidated their position in struggles against the colonial government and against other local leaders.[15] Early TANU

[14] I have relied on a growing body of anthropological literature which is of great use to political scientists studying Tanzania. I have also benefited from discussions with Raymond Apthorpe, Lionel Cliffe, Griffiths Cunningham, Violaine Junod, John Kesby, Norman Miller, John Morris, Daudi Mwakawaga, Bismark Mwansasu, and Paul Mushi, among others.

[15] See, e.g., John Kesby, " 'We and Them' Among the Warangi," Paper presented to a faculty seminar held at Makerere College, 1964.

leaders were spokesmen for local discontent which stemmed from land alienation or enforced agricultural change. Some have by now given way to new men; others—like the aforementioned Kirilo Japhet, first TANU chairman of Northern Province—are still regional or district leaders; a few have ascended to national prominence.

The struggle for local dominance through manipulation of the national political movement did not end with independence. Men still vie with each other to gain power or try to enter national politics from their localities. The context of the struggle, however, is changed. In the past, a man could oppose the central (colonial) government and, depending on the particular strengths and weaknesses of traditional rulers, he could take a stance against them, Anti-colonialism and anti-chieftainship were issues that could be grasped and moulded to local advantage. Now one cannot be staunchly anti-TANU and have a political future. The role of traditional rulers is still an issue because it is tied up with local clan politics and the place of the traditional ruler on the local scene. But there is no longer any question about the chiefs as national rulers or local government agents.

In general, sweeping issues cannot be found in local Tanganyikan politics, which are largely concerned with a struggle for jobs, status, and power. But there are examples of local politics revolving around national issues. In Tanganyika, the question of independence was broken down into a number of local issues—enforced agricultural change, the role of colonial civil servants and indirect rulers. These issues appeared everywhere and were perceived as national issues. Now, local communities do not pose their relationship to the center as a national problem.

The way development policies are carried out is an issue that recurs from place to place. Criticism tends to be localized because it is directed largely to specific people and things. This was true during the colonial period also, but then

344

the central government was open to attack, especially during the terminal colonial period. Now people are reluctant to criticize the TANU government in generalized terms. Central government leaders may be criticized for their actions locally, or their lack of attention to local issues, but they are rarely attacked over national policies.[16]

Both high- and middle-level leaders know that development is going to be hard to achieve. Yet they sometimes create the aura of repression without actually being effectively repressive. They may be overbearing because they are insecure and struggling to do a difficult job. In a situation where leaders are eager to achieve rapid development, there is a tendency to resort to coercion. The new village and district development committees have already passed rules which stipulate that minimum acreages of certain crops be grown. Government has ordered the farmers to plant sisal because of its export value, as well as cotton, coffee, and tea. In order to increase agricultural productivity, rules have been made by district councils which prohibit the drinking or selling of alcoholic beverages except on weekends. President Nyerere once suggested in Mwanza that if people did not cut their cotton stumps, TANU Youth League members might do it for them and charge them for the labor.[17] Nyerere also said, in a speech made in October 1964, while he was on tour in southern Tanganyika, that farmers who were lazy might go to prison where they could learn model farming techniques.[18] Regional authorities in West Lake threatened to close the *pombe* (beer or wine made from palm trees) shops unless the people started growing tea.

But while there have been threats and isolated cases of strong arming the local population, government has not en-

---

[16] See chap. xiii on the elections of September 1965.

[17] *Tanganyika Standard*, October 8, 1963.

[18] *Nationalist*, August 29, 1964. Whether or not the President was serious was not clear from the text.

forced many of these regulations so far. Cattle-dipping and other measures to prevent cattle disease from spreading have been taken when animal health was at stake. Local sanctions have also been invoked for failure to appear for self-help schemes; and stirring up sentiment against self-help is an offense punishable by imprisonment.[19] Individuals who are vulnerable within their local communities may be coerced. Asian shops have been closed when Asians refused to join a TANU-sponsored march of solidarity in protest against a purported American plot to overthrow the government. But there is little evidence that TANU has employed force as a policy to put across government's programs. For one thing, the instruments of coercion—an armed and operative army and police force—are not strong enough to put down large-scale discontent. And government has been very reluctant to push issues that are unpopular, such as increasing taxes or forcing cattle-culling. All the commissioners with whom I spoke insisted on the necessity for exhausting every possible means of persuasion before resorting to coercion.

During the terminal colonial period, district TANU leaders assured the people that government land regulations and other restrictions would be lifted once Tanganyika was independent; the pressure of government interest does seem to have eased in places.[20] This is not due to any insistence from local TANU leaders, nor to any feeling on the part of central government that it must honor pre-independence pledges

[19] The penalties are greater for dissuading people from taking part in self-help than for not taking part oneself. Act No. 3 of 1962 provides for six months in prison or $21 fine for obstructing self-help. One TANU leader who was traveling on a delegation sent by the National Executive insisted that people should be beaten if they did not work on self-help. And one regional commissioner illegally imprisoned a man and illegally had another man publicly whipped. But these are unusual cases; the regional commissioner was imprisoned for his offense.

[20] Kesby, *op.cit.*, p. 11, cites Irangi as a place where government pressure has eased.

made by local TANU people. Rather, central leaders have been occupied with building administrative structures, organizing TANU, and establishing goals. They are also conscious of the meager means they have of reaching down to the villagers to enforce change; they are aware that they have not yet forged an instrument for pushing unpopular policies.

As attention shifts more and more to implementation of the *Five Year Plan*, government may try to tighten its control despite the dangers and difficulties of doing so. This is likely to be true in cash-crop areas and potential cash-crop areas where the stakes are high. In early 1965, there were reports that an area commissioner had used his detention powers to arrest community leaders in a district where government met resistance in trying to increase sisal production.

What and how much the TANU government can enforce, operating under the new political conditions, remains to be seen. Reaction against enforced agricultural change was a major factor in the downfall of the colonial government.[21] Government, both at the center and in the regions, wants to be popular and responsive to local needs. And its stress on community development and local initiative emphasizes its essential commitment to voluntary change. The top-level TANU officials and many regional and area commissioners seem very aware of the costs attendant on the breakdown of communications between the villages, district, regional, and central headquarters. Yet they cannot abandon attempts to impose their will on the countryside, for without reaching the villages, government remains essentially confined to a few urban centers and towns. This was understood by Julius Nyerere when he said: "Others try to reach the moon. We try to reach the villages."

Time and again, leaders refer to TANU's organization as a "two-way street": information and orders from the center

[21] Cliffe, *loc.cit.*, has posed this very question in his study of the reaction to enforced agricultural change.

must flow down to the villages, and the needs and desires of the people must be conducted to the center. A number of organizational devices have been constructed toward this end. These "devices" are partially, but by no means wholly artificial. Traveling throughout Tanganyika, one may ask: what is the relevance of TANU cells and development committees in this place, so desperately in need of technical personnel? (Arguments like this are sometimes put forward by visitors to African countries.) But veterinarians and organizational committees are not mutually exclusive; in fact, as I have argued, they are mutually dependent. If the organizational forms appear as so many "instant contraptions," it is because they reflect conscious attempts to bring people into communication with each other and with levels outside their own communities.

At worst, the "instant contraptions" are the form of government without content; they can be the ritualization of government. In order for development committees and party cells to be instruments of central control they have to rest on a material base which Tanzania does not have, and be surrounded by the kind of party organization TANU does not have. At best, "instant contraptions" can play a constructive role. Political development in Tanzania involves bringing people together and making palaver possible; only in this way can government become relevant to people in their daily lives. And until government is able to provide villagers with implements or with technical personnel, "instant contraptions" may be the only way its presence can be brought to the basic village unit. Organize people, discuss needs and possible solutions with them, and collect taxes: this is not a poor formula for political development in Tanzania. Moreover, even though activity on a committee cannot always bring with it material benefits, it does provide men with the opportunity to exercise power by giving orders and receiving status. As I have suggested, these are important considerations in Tanzanian local politics.

Two major organizational devices have been constructed to further nation-building. One is the hierarchy of development committees, the other is a very recent innovation, the establishment of TANU cells in 1965.

Village Development Committees and Traditional Rulers

In discussing the role of the development committees in formulating the *Five Year Plan*, I paid relatively little attention to the VDCs because they did not effect the *Five Year Plan's* formulation in any significant way. Yet Vice President Rashidi Kawawa was not exaggerating when he said that the key to nation-building lay with the chain of VDCs:

> The Village Development Committees form a chain of command providing the essential two-way flow of ideas between government and the people. There has been a tendency to regard them as purely isolated committees for running self-help schemes—an illusion which must be dispelled once and for all. ALL development activities of government in their areas concern these committees; school attendance, health, education, game protection, to name but a few in addition to material schemes for the construction of roads, dams and buildings.[22]

What the Vice President was saying, somewhat elliptically, was that there was really no one else who could carry out development activities in the villages. Community development is short-staffed and could not have representatives on hand at all times. Government officers of the central ministries who are at regional and district headquarters do not reach down to the village as permanent staff. Thus, it is left to the village executive officers to maintain law and order, supervise collection of the taxes imposed by the district council, and in general, coordinate and stimulate the development

[22] From the speech of Vice President Kawawa to a seminar of regional commissioners, Mimeographed, January 12, 1963.

effort.²³ But because villages rarely have a geographic concentration, the village executive officer must operate over a wide area, even though he may be responsible for only three or four VDCs. Government in the villages means self-government—in deciding on and providing basic services. Thus the VDCs are now called on to do more than guide self-help programs or implement the *Five Year Plan*: they have become the organs of representative government at the village level.

From their inception, the VDCs were intended to replace directly elected village councils, which had existed more on paper than in fact. In 1963, when the old village headmen were removed, the village councils were amalgamated into the somewhat larger VDCs, which also remained a paper phenomenon until 1964. Today a purported 7,500 VDCs exist; although some of these may be formed only in theory, there are thousands which do have active members.

The community development staff was supposed to help local leaders set up these committees, but the lack of trained community development personnel hindered the rapid creation of a network of VDCs. And after committees were formed, it took time to explain the tasks expected of them. They were creations of central government and regional administration, not spontaneous expressions of local initiative; and there was little pretense about this. All the speeches made by national and regional/district leaders notwithstanding, little real attention or encouragement was paid by leaders after the VDCs had been established. Early members were sometimes even mocked by villagers for having been drawn into the arrangement.

Furthermore, the VDCs soon became the forum for local splits between lineage groups, between generational groups, and between those who were adopting what I have called a

²³ These village executive officers are patronage appointments of the district council. Many are ex-village headmen who existed before the colonial local government system was dismantled in 1962-63.

Swahili pattern of life and those who were more traditionally oriented. Splits were exacerbated as groups tried to command the new local government machinery. And new tensions were created, in sparsely settled areas, when people were all grouped together into one VDC; in densely settled areas, when the VDC did not include all the people that considered themselves part of a single unit. The community development officers who worked with the VDCs often could not, or would not, surmount the factions.[24]

The present VDC's functions are very diffuse. This is due in part to government's intention that the VDC should govern as a combination of village council, elders council, development committee, and TANU organization. One observer reported that in one month the VDC in his coastal village:

... held its regular meeting, decided a local adultery case, settled three other domestic quarrels, ran two self-help schemes, formed a committee to punish villagers who didn't participate in a self-help scheme, and met with four visiting officials. In short, by its nature the VDC deals with most of the vital issues that arise in the village.[25]

That the functions of the VDCs are so diffuse also must be related to the diffuseness of village authority where there is a situation of flux and where old authority patterns come in contact with new ones. TANU's presence means that traditional leaders will be challenged more frequently now than heretofore, though not necessarily more effectively.

In theory, a VDC consists of about 20 elected members; in fact, they still vary in size from place to place. The village executive officer sometimes serves as secretary to the VDC; sometimes there is an elected secretary. Although women are supposed to serve on every VDC, there are VDCs where women play no role.

[24] E. K. Mwalujume, "The Role of Village Development Committees in Tanganyika," *Mwenge*, IV (Dar es Salaam), 1964.
[25] Miller, *loc.cit.*

In the past, the village council and the TANU elected village committees were not necessarily composed of the same members. Where TANU was strong, its committee might even be making decisions without the formal approval of the village council or the early VDCs. Officially the VDC had the right to waive school fees and rebate local taxes with the approval of the district council, but the TANU village committee might do it instead. Then in 1964, government ordered that the TANU village committee be amalgamated with the VDC, and that the TANU village committee chairman be the unpaid VDC chairman. This edict guaranteed neither that village splits would cease, nor that TANU committeemen would dominate. The VDC chairman is supposed to be elected by the TANU committee, usually composed of 6 members. But apparently some villages have elected former VDC chairmen who were not TANU stalwarts to serve again as VDC chairmen and to become *ipso facto* TANU chairmen.

Government has been trying to breathe life into the VDCs by making them the official TANU organization at the village level. Another, no less important, aim is to activate local TANU organizations by making them part of the governmental structure (though members of the VDCs will not be paid). It remains to be seen whether combining two often moribund bodies will result in a vigorous new village organ.

Local leaders who have a high status in the village apart from any TANU connection play a crucial role. Some of these leaders may derive their authority from traditional sources. Not all traditional leaders are against social change. (There were traditional leaders who entered TANU early in the anticolonial period. Not all of these, however, were necessarily "progressive" about social change in their villages.) There are also those who lead by virtue of their personal characteristics alone, without reliance either on traditional sources or on TANU itself; some of them may not even be TANU supporters. Yet it is absolutely essential to economic development and social change that high-level TANU officials not undermine this latter type of leader when he stands for development and change. He can be undermined if he holds an official position—village executive officer or chairman of the VDC—and is commanded by leaders at the center to do things that his followers patently will not accept. TANU leaders have sometimes purposely harassed local leaders who refuse to shout TANU slogans and proclaim themselves dyed-in-the-wool TANU supporters. When this happens, TANU cannot be effective and Tanzania's development suffers.

Examples of this can be found in the history of independent Tanganyika. Though the chiefs were deposed qua chiefs as government officials after independence, government recognized that the deposition of chiefs, sub-chiefs, and headmen could break the link between a traditionally oriented people and the district administration. Thus, in many cases headmen not only became the new village executive officers, but they remained in their communities, contrary to the policy of transplanting traditional rulers when they became local government officials under the district councils. However, by 1963, the deposition of headmen and chiefs had created problems in getting support in some areas for self-help projects. Self-help had been the best-publicized socio-economic policy of Tanganyika's first year of independence and had been put forward as the "Tanganyika way," but it was not new to Tanganyika. Self-help had existed as voluntary, semi-voluntary, and forced labor, and had been an integral part of some traditional tribal systems. And it had been adapted, with varying degrees of success, by the colonial administration. When the independent Tanganyika government abolished the chiefs, sub-chiefs, and headmen, it altered fundamentally the authority system upon which the self-help schemes depended.

One observer, on the basis of his research in Ugogo—which is in central Tanganyika and is relatively undeveloped and traditionally oriented—suggests that self-help programs declined after the deposition of chiefs and headmen.[26] Chiefs in Ugogo were able to manipulate traditional values, including witchcraft attachments, despite the fact that they were partially outside of the traditional system themselves. Gogo chiefs were not always traditional rulers, but they had traditional legitimacy through blood ties with ritual leaders or through ritual links and associations. Wealth in cattle also gave status. Thus, the chiefs could reinforce their colonial-backed rule with traditional sanctions and rewards. Not all chiefs were able to retain their authority, and many lost favor in trying to put across enforced change. But they remained authoritative figures, and took over the running of the self-help programs in the first two years of independence because the village committees elected to do so were composed of younger men without the requisite authority.

There is another point to be made from Ugogo. Central Tanganyika suffered flood and then drought in 1961. The Gogo chiefs were put in charge of famine relief; if people refused to pay taxes or participate in self-help programs, the chiefs were authorized to withhold famine relief. They were constrained to take this stance and, in general, to be authoritarian because they were partially outside the Gogo traditional value system:[27] they were not always descendent from ritual rulers and yet they ruled. Furthermore, chiefs in Ugogo and elsewhere were often relatively educated men, and were not above making alliances with "modernized" young men who spoke Swahili rather than Kigogo. Chiefs could survive the downfall of the colonial administration because they could become local or central government officials.[28] But because

[26] Peter Rigby, "Politics and Modern Leadership Roles in Ugogo," Forthcoming in a volume to be published by Syracuse University Press.

[27] Rigby paints a picture of authoritarian Gogo chiefs. The conclusion is mine, however.

[28] This was even more usual where chiefs were better educated than they were in Ugogo.

they acted only partially inside the traditional system, they had to buttress their rule by acting dictatorially at times and by calling on regional government on occasion. If it is true that the more outside the traditional system a local ruler is, the more he must rely on regional or central power to back him up, some very great difficulties are posed for TANU.

I have described TANU officials as being "Swahiliized," and looking to the towns rather than to the villages of Tanganyika. Civil servants who come to the villages from district offices to help on village projects are also certainly more "foreign" to a traditional area than the chiefs or sub-chiefs who have become local government officers. Thus, they need to be backed up by district and regional authority. But in certain respects, the regional authorities are more ambivalent about exerting themselves at the village level than the colonial regime was. For one thing, regional and central leaders are more sensitive to what is happening in the villages than the colonial officers were, despite the image often put forward by ex-district commissioners.[29] Leaders may not understand every local situation; they may not respond sympathetically or intelligently in all cases. But they do visit the villages and try to keep informed of the various crosscurrents. And in the last analysis, they have less naked force at their disposal than their predecessors. Thus the attempt to invoke social change by speech-making, the commitment to voluntary change through community development action, the view of TANU as a community development organization at the local level. And thus the construction of "instant contraptions" to facilitate implementing social change and economic development. The latest such device, however, springs from different wells and reflects the beginning of a new style in Tanzanian politics, if not a new content. For whatever the organizational

[29] Ex-colonial officers are fond of saying that they never would have dared to be as coercive as TANU, and that TANU is less responsive to the people than was the colonial government. There is little evidence for this, however.

form devised, the basic facts of existence in Tanzania are very intractable. This must be kept in mind when considering the new TANU cells.

TANU Cells

TANU cells were first introduced in Dar es Salaam at the end of 1964. They were partially a response to the security problem (which is described in the next chapter), but more generally, they were a new attempt to make TANU's presence felt in the countryside.

TANU's Publicity Secretary, Dr. Wilburt Klerruu, said that TANU cells would be instituted in order to: (1) assess the strength of the party in Dar es Salaam and have an accurate and reliable record; (2) facilitate the easy and efficient collection of party dues and subscriptions; (3) make it cheaper and easier for party leaders to become acquainted with the morale, complaints, and feelings of the rank and file; and (4) help the Dar es Salaam city council, if need be, in its campaign against hooliganism, idleness, lawlessness, and delinquency.[30] Dr. Klerruu said that the growing population of Dar es Salaam posed hitherto unknown problems in transmitting information to members and executing TANU orders. Cells were necessary for unity, discipline, and efficiency.

TANU National Headquarters stated that each street in Dar es Salaam would be divided into cells of 10 houses: that is, on one street a group of 10 houses (5 on each side of the street) would become one cell which would elect its own leader. If the system proves workable, a cell will grow from 10 houses to 100 (again on both sides of a street) under one leader. This will later change to 1,000. Eventually, when the 10,000 mark is reached, a cell will be entitled to open a branch office; and when it reaches 50,000, a "full" branch office. In the initial period, the cell leader (of 10 houses) will be answerable to the current branch leader who will in turn

---

[30] *Nationalist*, November 6, 1964, p. 8.

be answerable to the TANU area secretary (Dar es Salaam area commissioner). It is not clear (and may not have been worked out at the time) whether the 10-house unit would retain any identity and keep a leader if further amalgamations came about. If the aim is tight control and the development of an internal security network through a system of block leaders/informers, the basic unit should be retained. A statement to the effect that "accurate records of membership must be kept if the party is going to know and efficiently plan its role in the Development Plan," implies a desire to develop a recording apparatus. Initially, the security aspects were not stressed as such. There was no implication that TANU was aiming at control over the population by hard-core cell leaders. Rather, a more general aim was put forward: to strengthen TANU in Dar es Salaam by organizing more political involvement through TANU cells.

When Dr. Klerruu announced the formation of TANU cells, he referred only to Dar es Salaam. But it soon became clear that cells were to be started throughout the Republic. As might be expected, there is little standardization in the form cells are taking in the countryside. For example, the Ujijii TANU branch in Kigoma Region adopted the same format as that announced for Dar es Salaam.[31] Groups of 10 houses were established, each headed by a chairman who had first-hand knowledge of the residents in his group.

When the Ujijii branch announced its procedures for establishing cells, National Headquarters gave another official version of the cell structure. A spokesman for TANU National Headquarters said that the formation of groups of 10 houses was *not* the one which had been agreed upon "during the last

[31] The Ujijii cells were directly linked to security problems. The towns of Kigoma and Ujijii are on Lake Tanganyika, opposite the Congo shores of the Lake where there was a great deal of fighting in 1964. Fleeing Congolese from various factions crossed into Tanganyika, and the cells were supposed to help keep order and spy out strangers. Notice in the *Nationalist*, December 24, 1964.

meeting of the National Executive." (Possibly, between the time that the cells were announced for Dar es Salaam—November 6, 1964—and the time the Ujijii branch stated its own intention to form cells—December 24, 1964—the NEC changed the form of cells. It is possible that the NEC never meant the Dar es Salaam formula to be followed throughout Tanganyika.[32]) Each TANU cell would be composed of 10 members. In the towns, a house might have up to 15 people living in it, in which case 10 would form one party cell and the remaining 5 would join another group which had only 5 members. This was indeed a cell-type organization which might be utilized for close supervision of the populace.

However, when the cells began forming outside the towns, they followed the original Dar es Salaam model after all! However, there were some deviations, since settlement patterns are so varied in the countryside. It is unrealistic to have 10 houses form one cell in many places: where one large family inhabits many houses, one cell may suffice; where 10 houses are widely separated, it is not feasible to have them make up one cell.

By the beginning of 1965, cells were being widely publicized. Just as TANU leaders had traveled throughout the country in order to make known the functions and structure of the development committees, they now travel to popularize the party cells. Second Vice President Kawawa has outlined the work of cells under three main headings: bringing peoples' problems and grievances to the party and government; coordinating the work of the cells with that of the development committees; and ensuring the security of the nation. Elaborating on the first point, Mr. Kawawa said that the purpose of establishing the cells was to ensure easy communication among party members so that common problems could be dealt with easily and quickly. With regard to the coordina-

---

[32] I am being very speculative because I was not able to trace the evolution of these developments.

tion of activities, the Second Vice President said that cell members would act as carriers of government programs to the people and vice versa.

You are the eyes of the nation. . . . For the purpose of development, you have to establish a harmonious connection between your cells and the party offices, Area and Regional Commissioners' Offices, as well as the development committees at all levels. . . . You are the pillars of our nation. You must expose dangerous characters like thieves and other infiltrators who may poison our nation and put its safety at stake.[33]

It is too early to evaluate the cells' functioning. About half of the TANU branches had formed cells as of April 1965.[34] Whatever final form they may take, the cells are an attempt to bring TANU to a very basic level and to introduce greater effectiveness in TANU control and communication. Yet nothing is being done at the center to create a TANU structure capable of controlling basic units. If cells do become meaningful units of political life, they will be controlled by districts, or more likely sub-district organizations, and not by TANU National Headquarters (with the exception of the Dar es Salaam cells), unless a central TANU structure is created. Thus, the cells cannot solve the major problem of central control over local units, without a building up of TANU at the center. By itself, the creation of a cell structure tells us little about political life in Tanzania, except that TANU is still groping for new forms to extend its reach.

Some TANU functionaries are concerned with building a strong TANU center. When queried about how this is to be done, the most common answers given were that educated people should come into TANU staff work, and that there

[33] *Nationalist*, January 6, 1965, pp. 1, 6; report of speech of Vice President Kawawa to Dar es Salaam cell members.

[34] Estimation of Vice President Kawawa in a personal interview, April 1965.

should be a continued amalgamation of party and state structures and personnel. There is the idea of taking university graduates into TANU National Headquarters in an effort to create a TANU research department. One high TANU official said that "the research department is a good place to put university graduates"—implying that there they would be out of harm's way.

In a one-party state where a party bureaucracy exists and has a large and well-coordinated central staff, a research department might be a formidable weapon. But such a department is useless as a level of political control without the necessary apparatus. At this point, a research department can only record the history of TANU and such basic things as its membership size, dues paid, and other essential, but as yet unknown data.

There have been important structural changes in TANU since its inception in 1954: the appointment of area and regional commissioners, the creation of development committees and TANU cells are all major innovations. However, it is necessary to see these structures as statements of intentions to change the face of the country and not as *fait accompli* of that change.

For all the innovations, TANU's rule has appeared not only loosely organized, but somewhat fragile at the center. TANU's district and regional oligarchies have revealed splits in many places. The army mutiny of January 1964 illuminated TANU's weaknesses and strengths. And the parliamentary elections of September 1965 gave new information about the TANU regional and district organizations and the popularity of many middle-level leaders. The concluding section takes up these events.

PART IV
Crises and Conclusions

CHAPTER XI

The Army Mutiny in Perspective

TANGANYIKA'S ARMY had never been a factor in politics prior to January 1964. It consisted of two battalions totaling 2,000 men: one was stationed in Dar es Salaam, the other in Tabora which was in the center of the country and astride the major rail links. Company elements were also located in Nachingwea in southern Tanganyika. The army took its origins from the colonial King's African Rifles, renamed the Tanganyika Rifles after independence. However, it remained British trained and British officered.[1] In mid-summer 1963, only 26 of the 63 commissioned officers above the rank of warrant officer were Tanganyikan.[2] By 1964, the army had still not been Africanized, and complaints began to arise within its ranks. Nor had it been politicized; promotions were not via political channels.[3] Some men had been sent to Israel for training and, upon returning, were promoted over long-time King's Rifles men. This was another cause for resentment. The policy of recruitment too remained the same.[4]

[1] Until the mutiny in January 1964, all officers above the rank of captain were British. Supplies and equipment were British. Until the end of fiscal year 1961-62, Britain directly contributed two-thirds of the maintenance cost of the army (1963-64 estimates for defense were $2 million). Harvey Glickman, *Some Observations on the Army and Political Unrest in Tanganyika* (Pittsburgh: Institute of African Affairs, Duquesne University, 1964), p. 4.

[2] All Tanganyikans were African with the exception of one Asian. If 28 warrant officers were included, Tanganyika made up 58 per cent of the army officer staff. Few officers were in the mill at Mons Officer Training School or Sandhurst. *Ibid.*

[3] There was a selection Board for Officers which included the chairman, Chief Adam Sapi Mkwawa of the Hehe tribe and speaker of the National Assembly; two African civil servants; the secretary of the Military Council, a British expatriate; the British Commander of the Tanganyika Rifles, Brigadier Sholto Douglas; and another British officer. Graduates of secondary school could apply. In 1963, there were 43 applications; only 3 were trained. *Ibid.*, p. 5.

[4] Recruiting safaris traveled about every six months holding meet-

Although there was talk about using the army as an instrument of social and economic development—talk which emanated largely from the Minister of External Affairs and Defense, Mr. Kambona—the army was not engaged in extensive nation-building activities. Thus, the army was not a political actor; but to all appearances it did not aspire to become one. There was no breakdown in civil control in January of 1964, nor any kind of economic crisis. What then accounted for the mutiny? And what did it reveal?

In order to understand the army mutiny, we must first examine the Zanzibar Revolution, which was one of its triggers. On January 12, 1964, the government of the Sultan of Zanzibar, which had only recently been installed as an independent government, was overthrown. The organization of the Zanzibar Revolution, the amount and kind of outside support, and the role played by Tanganyika remain largely murky.[5] TANU had ties with the ASP, and Nyerere had warned the British against turning power over to a minority government.[6] But the extent of Tanganyika's involvement and the part played by individual TANU leaders cannot be ascertained.[7] The impact of the Revolution on Tanganyika, however, can be stated with more certainty.

---

ings. The largest numbers of recruits came from the Hehe and Kuria tribes. In the last group of 280 new recruits before the mutiny, 28 tribes were represented; 25 per cent were Hehe and 25 per cent were Kuria. *Ibid.* There was no preference given for TANU or TANU Youth League people.

[5] The official history of the Zanzibar Revolution insofar as one exists is the anniversary edition of the *Nationalist*, January 12, 1965, pp. 5, 7, 8. This version says nothing about the place of John Okello, former Field Marshal of Zanzibar and apparent leader of the first military phase of the Revolution. It disagrees in many places with journalistic accounts of the Revolution.

[6] The ASP obtained a majority of votes over the combined total of the Zanzibar Nationalist Party and the Zanzibar and Pemba's People's Party but it had fewer seats in the Parliament after the June 1963 elections. Independence was declared on December 10, 1963.

[7] After the Revolution succeeded, it is reported that Sheikh Karume,

Never before in East Africa had a non-colonial government been confronted with force in the name of a revolutionary movement. Never, since the British overthrew indigenous rulers and drove the Germans out of East Africa, had force been successful in replacing one government by another. Thus the Zanzibar Revolution introduced violence as a means of changing a constituted independent government in East Africa.[8]

Tanganyika had been characterized, prior to 1964, as the one East African country where violence, as a means of obtaining change, had been virtually non-existent since the time of British rule. In the 1890's, the Hehe of the Southern Highlands under the leadership of Mkwawa had fought the Germans; and southern tribes had fought the Germans in the Maji-Maji Revolt of 1905-07. But these were the only widespread and intense struggles against colonial rule in East Africa until the outbreak of Mau Mau in Kenya in the 1950s. Since 1907, aside from the struggle between the British and Germans in World War I, Tanganyika has had neither revolts nor the large-scale tribal violence which has characterized separatist movements in Uganda. Thus, Zanzibar's violent overthrow of a constituted rule made an immediate and deep impact on Tanganyika. This impact was made even greater by the fact that the overthrow of the Sultan's rule was made not only in the name of African nationalism against a

---

President of the Zanzibar Revolutionary Council, "left secretly the following morning, by canoe, personally to inform President Julius Nyerere and the Secretary General of TANU, Oscar Kambona, of what had happened. For had not TANU helped and supported the Afro-Shirazi Party since its inceptions?" This is from a version of the first days of the Revolution published in the *Nationalist*. But there have been conflicting statements about when Karume saw Nyerere and about the relations between the two.

[8] It is true that this independent government was seen by many Africans as a colonially installed, racial minority government, a government of Arabs over Africans.

minority Arab rule supported by foreign imperialists, but also in the name of a class war of workers and peasants against exploiters. The shock waves from Zanzibar traveled rapidly across the narrow sea to Tanganyika.

The Army Mutiny

Late on a Sunday night, January 19, 1964, troops of the first army battalion left the Colito Barracks some 8 miles from the center of town and moved into Dar es Salaam. They quickly took control of key points: radio and police stations, airports and the State House, the home and office of President Nyerere. The President went into hiding. By Monday morning, January 20, the troops were still occupying the centers of communications and security in Dar es Salaam.[9] Nyerere was still in hiding. Rumors were rife, one of which was that the TANU government had fallen.

After deposing their British officers, the mutineers stated their demand, which was simply for higher wages. They met no resistance from the police force which had been weakened by the shipment of 300 of their members to Zanzibar to help stabilize the situation there. While the army demands were not overtly political, no revolt of a military force would be without major political implications. Furthermore, looting broke out in Dar es Salaam and it took on racial aspects as it spread to Asian areas. The infectious revolt spread in the course of the week January 20-27 to Tabora, Uganda, and Kenya. The President emerged on January 21 to hear leaders

[9] The army in Dar es Salaam appeared well organized as it moved to take over key points. This gave rise to rumors about the intervention of foreign powers. China was specifically mentioned. There appears to have been no truth to those rumors. On January 27, the government issued a press statement that the revolt was not connected with outside subversion and specifically that it was not in any way communist inspired. On January 30, government felt compelled to deny that the implication of the January statement was that the revolt was connected with any popular movement.

of the mutiny insisting they wanted no coup, but reiterating their demands for more than a double wage increase—for example, $15 a month to $37 a month for privates. Neither Mr. Kambona, at that time Minister for Defense and External Affairs, nor the President were able to get the troops out of battle dress and back to their barracks. On Saturday, January 25, British Commandos landed from HMS *Centaur* lying off the Coast and took over Colito Barracks. They chased the first battalion into the bush with some little loss of life, and brought to heel the battalion in Tabora and the company in Nachingwea, Southern Tanganyika.

Tanganyika had suffered a tremendous blow. It seemed that President Nyerere had lost prestige from the apparent loss of control of his government. Although shortly thereafter the top ranks of the army were indeed Africanized,[10] the army itself was in ruins, and its future was questionable. Extra money had to be allotted for the expenses incurred, particularly to pay the army higher wages. Many mutineers and civilians were put in detention. Yet President Nyerere was perhaps unduly pessimistic when he said: "It will take months and even years to erase from the mind of the world what they heard about the events this week." When he went before a meeting of the Organization of African Unity (OAU) —specially convened by him to explain his reason for calling in British troops and to ask for African troops to replace them.[11] (An action he considered necessary for the preservation of his and Tanganyika's position of leadership in the

[10] A former lieutenant who had trained in Britain, M.S.H. Sarakikya, was appointed Brigadier and Commander of the Defense Forces. Another British trained lieutenant, Elisha Kavona, was appointed second in command. He was put under preventive detention some months later. This action was not explained at the time nor has any explanation been given subsequently.

[11] Nyerere called in British troops only after the precedent had been set by Uganda. Nigerian troops were provided shortly thereafter and they stayed on for a number of months until new Tanzanian battalions were created.

national liberation movement in South Africa)—he was given a vote of confidence by the OAU. This endorsement was seconded at an NEC meeting on January 31, which approved his disarming of the mutinous troops and his recourse to British troops. Later in the year, as attention shifted to the Union with Zanzibar and the *Five Year Plan*, the events of January seemed to recede in importance. The short-term judgments about the disastrous effects of the mutiny appeared to have been overstated. But the import of the mutiny for the politics of Tanzania must be assessed.

If the Zanzibar Revolution provided one trigger, the old issue of Africanization and wage demands provided the other. Well before the mutiny, there had been discontent in the Tanganyika army (and the Kenya and Uganda armies, too) with the low pay and the continued rule of British officers after independence. The East African governments were reluctant to increase wages since this would mean inflation of their budgets for non-development items. The mutiny of the Force Publique in the Congo had made Tanganyika's leaders conscious of the dangers of a disgruntled military force; but they felt that they ruled with popular support and their armies would remain obedient. Moreover, the Congo warning cut two ways. Rapid Africanization of the army might pose difficulties for continued reliability of the military.

Nyerere made a major speech on January 7, 1964, asserting that preference in hiring would no longer be given to Africans over other citizens of Tanganyika. The former policy had been one of localization, but with an emphasis on redressing an imbalance in the number of Africans who held responsible posts. Now Nyerere linked a policy of no discrimination against Tanganyika citizens to the needs of the *Five Year Plan* which would require utilizing all the trained personnel available. This speech prompted the Assistant General Secretary of the Kenya Federation of Labour to be alarmed that Tanganyika had dropped its policy of Africanization. Both the army and the Tanganyika Federation of Labour took up this cry. Spokesmen for the railway, local government, and central government employees unions said that this was contrary to a policy of Africanization. One Teendwa Washington of the Local Government Workers Union said that Nyerere was taking Tanganyika back to the "colonial days."[12]

Nyerere's speech brought to the surface the attitudes on racial/economic issues which had caused him such difficulties in 1961-62. And he provoked many of the same middle-level leaders now that opposed him at that time. In all probability, he would have weathered this storm as he had done before. But the Zanzibar Revolution broke upon him and all East Africa. It is clear from the very fact of the mutiny that despite the popularity of Nyerere personally, he could neither preclude such a mutiny nor face it down once it occurred.

On the other hand, while the mutineers could have brought down the government in Dar es Salaam had they wished (if the British had not intervened), they could not have ruled Tanganyika themselves.[18] The mutineers would have faced all the problems that the present TANU leaders face: a sparsely settled country with its population in major clusters along the peripheries of the country; an economy which does not provide the material requisites for exerting central political control; regional and district and village organizations which operate with a great deal of autonomy; severe personnel shortages; the persistence of traditional patterns of political, social, and economic actions. Furthermore, the mutineers would be dislodging the figure with the greatest popularity and authority in Tanganyika: Julius Nyerere. They

[12] *Tanganyika Standard*, January 9, 1964, p. 3.
[18] For a discussion of military skills and political abilities, see Morris Janowitz, *The Military in the Political Development of New States* (Chicago: University of Chicago Press, 1964). See also, Henry Bienen (ed.), *The Limits on Military Intervention* (New York: Russell Sage, 1967).

would have had to rule without the center that did exist—those few national leaders who have the consent of their party and civil service hierarchies to rule even if they cannot exert close control over these hierarchies. And the army was itself without trained administrators.

It would be tempting to conclude that the government at the center must have indeed been fragile since a battalion of 1,000 men in Dar es Salaam could control the command points without opposition from either the inhabitants at large or TANU people. But this would be to miss the point. The mutineers were aided by the fact that Dar es Salaam is itself cut off from the rest of Tanganyika's population centers. People from outside Dar es Salaam could not easily be mobilized to move against the mutineers. Within Dar es Salaam, there was great confusion. Since the army did not claim to be ruling, a wait-and-see attitude prevailed even among TANU activists. Naturally, there was a disinclination for unarmed men to oppose armed men.

Outside of Tabora and Nachingwea, the regional centers and district headquarters continued to be run by the TANU offices and civil service. Although nervousness was evident in places, there was no looting in the towns or the rural areas. In some districts, the situation of instability at the center prompted an attempt to settle old scores, but only rarely did people try to get rid of local TANU leaders. When it was clear that order was reestablished in Dar es Salaam, local TANU leaders in at least one district tried to imprison those who had opposed them openly during the crisis and covertly in the past. But on the whole, the regions and districts stayed calm —probably due to their very lack of contact with the center —and high- and middle-level leadership in Dar es Salaam remained cohesive.

Since the TANU Annual Conference and the NEC were due to meet in Dar es Salaam just at the time the mutiny broke out, there was ample opportunity for TANU regional and district leaders to take part in the revolt along with middle-level leaders or dissident top-level leaders who lived in Dar es Salaam. Yet of all the TANU middle-level leaders gathered there—the commissioners, elected TANU regional and district representatives, and even parliamentary secretaries— only one was implicated in the mutiny. An area commissioner was arrested,[14] as well as a number of trade union leaders. It is not clear whether government believed that all the arrested trade unionists were implicated or whether it took the opportunity to imprison trade unionists who opposed reorganizing the trade unions as governmental bodies. It is unlikely that those trade unionists who did come out to Colito Barracks to put themselves forward as leaders of a real revolt were in on the mutiny from the beginning. What is striking is that so few people took advantage of a chaotic situation to try to further their own ambitions. Nor did the few African army officers try to channel the revolt into a wider political contest; they remained loyal and later became commanders of the newly constituted battalions.

At the top, the President and at least one of his ministers, Austin Shaba (Local Government), called attention to the loyalty of Oscar Kambona, the Minister for Defense. It was Kambona who negotiated with the mutineers the day after the mutiny, when Nyerere was in hiding and Vice President Kawawa had disappeared. It was he who announced on the radio that he had ordered the army to return to its barracks. When the President called attention to Kambona's courage and loyalty as having reduced the effects of the troops' mutiny, he was doing more than voicing his appreciation; he was asserting TANU's solidity during the crisis.[15] Shaba stated that the situation proved that members of the Cabinet, high officials of TANU, and the country generally were solidly be-

[14] Mr. Hongoli, area commissioner for Tabora District.
[15] See *Uganda Argus*, February 13, 1964, for President Nyerere's remarks.

371

hind the President.[16] True, the country was behind the President, but as one person said: "we were ashamed." When Nyerere apologized to the *Umoja Wa Wanawake Wa Tanganyika* (National Women's Organization) for having been forced to call in British troops, it was reported that several women shouted: "we forgive you."[17] Demonstrations were held in support of the President.[18]

There were very good reasons for the solid loyalty that Nyerere received, quite apart from his personal popularity. The dangers of trying to make common cause with the mutineers should have been apparent to any would-be leader of a coup. The mutineers did not distinguish between shades of political opinion within the Cabinet or within TANU: they roughed up middle-level leaders who had taken strong stands for rapid Africanization; they chased "radical" junior ministers down the streets. Any government official was an "in"; the mutineers saw themselves as "outs." They wanted a bigger slice of the pie right away. And if the mutineers perceived themselves and were perceived as "outs," what of the urban unemployed and those primary-school leavers who would have been glad for the salary of even a lowly private? These are truly the "outs." Once the dam burst, once the legitimacy of the government was pushed aside and Nyerere's person removed, there was no telling where the demands of the "outs" would end. And who could draw the line again between ins and outs? Thus, even if there were middle-level

[16] Shaba was in London when he called attention to Kambona's loyalty. His comments were reported in the *Tanganyika Standard*, January 30, 1964, p. 5.

[17] *Tanganyika Standard*, January 30, 1964, p. 1.

[18] One of the first groups to demonstrate in support of the President were the taxi drivers of Dar es Salaam. Months later, when allegations were made that the USA was going to try and overthrow the government, the taxi drivers were again first in the streets in support of the President.

leaders who had grievances, this was not the base of support they wished, and the demands of the mutineers were not the issues they wanted to exploit.

If there were revolutionaries in Dar es Salaam who were willing to use a mutinous army to call forth the urban unemployed and the rural underemployed, they did not take this opportunity. Of course, this was 1964, not 1966. The instigators of the Zanzibar Revolution were not yet high-ranking officials of the TANU government; the *Nationalist* had not yet begun to publish; the new ideological streams had not been vigorously propagated even among a small circle. But the middle- and high-level leaders who differed from Nyerere would have acted no differently in 1966 than TANU middle-level leaders acted in 1964. And the mutineers would be just as threatening to them (after all, they *are* leaders with vested interests) as they were to the constituted TANU government.

Although the mutiny received neither popular support nor support from TANU officials, government was very sensitive to its vulnerability on the issue of economic progress. Immediately after the mutiny, a government statement was issued insisting that "neither the people nor their government have ever failed to stress the need for economic and social advance as a corollary to independence, and the whole people are mobilized for this purpose."[19] Later on the Minister for Finance said that the legitimate grievances of soldiers were "part of the grievances of all our people, which is poverty."[20]

The reassertion of Nyerere's personal position as leader of TANU and Tanganyika does not end the story of the mutiny. The attempt that has been made since to build a new security force also adds significantly to the picture of rule in Tanzania.

[19] *East African Standard* (Nairobi), January 31, 1964, p. 1.
[20] *Sunday News* (Dar es Salaam), February 7, 1964, p. 7.

Reconstruction of the Security Forces

The bulk of the two battalions in Tabora and Dar es Salaam were dismissed after the mutiny, and the mutineers were sent home;[21] individuals had to report periodically to the area commissioners in their home districts. Internal security was provided by British and then Nigerian troops, but a new army had to be constructed. Tanganyika's leaders now became particularly security-conscious, not only as a result of the mutiny. Tanganyika's borders had become very unstable in the course of 1963-64: the crisis in the Congo brought Congolese troops into Tanganyika; large-scale violence in Rwanda brought in Tutsi refugees by the thousands. After Malawi became independent, Dr. Hastings Banda accused Tanganyika of harboring his enemies, and relations became strained. Internal strife in Malawi took place in the area bordering Tanganyika. Tanganyika sponsored nationalist groups from Mozambique who infiltrated back into their country.[22] And even the Zambia border became disturbed during the Lumpa uprising in 1964.

Last but not least, the Zanzibar Revolution and the subsequent Union of Tanganyika and Zanzibar brought East-West and Sino-Soviet struggles to mainland Tanzania, as the great powers sought to influence the Revolution and gain position in East and Central Africa. The attempt to build a new security force became entangled in different foreign aid programs and various foreign military missions in Zanzibar and Tanganyika. These missions retained independent identities in Zanzibar and Tanganyika even after the Union.

It is in this context that we must view the TANU government's determination to create a national service which

[21] The leaders of the mutiny were tried by a special court and given jail sentences.

[22] The government requested British marines to disarm an "army" of 400 in training for the liberation of Mozambique after the mutiny. Glickman, *op.cit.*, p. 7.

would provide army recruits and also engage in nation-building activities.

Immediately after the landing of British troops on January 25, Nyerere called for a new army to be built around the TANU Youth League (TYL). However, by February 12, Vice President Kawawa said that although the Youth League was "another nation-building group," it lacked leadership. A new group—National Servicemen—would be instituted to provide the necessary leadership. TYL members would be recruited into special village schemes with National Servicemen at the head of each.[23] Youth League members flocked in to be recruited into the National Service. Local TANU secretaries used the promise of an army job to get people to take out TANU cards or pay back dues. (Some of the people promised army positions by local secretaries were patently physically unfit.) Recruitment was carried out by traveling teams, which moved from place to place reviewing men assembled by the regional police officers and the regional commissioners. Parliamentary secretaries—among them John Mwakangale, Richard Wambura, and John Nzunda (who was also Deputy Secretary General of TANU)—along with those non-commissioned officers who had been loyal also helped recruit.

Although many TYL members were eventually recruited into the army, the idea of using them to form a new army was not sustained, and soon gave way to the more encompassing concept of the National Servicemen. The new recruits had to have exhibited political loyalty; they had to be citizens aged 18 to 25, able to read and write Swahili. Infantry officers had to have completed Standard XII.

In a change of portfolios in May 1964, defense became the responsibility of the Second Vice President, Mr. Kawawa; both the National Service and Youth sections and the head-

[23] *Tanganyika Standard*, February 12, 1964, p. 5.

quarters of the Tanzanian People's Defense Forces are now part of his portfolio. A regular army of two battalions and an air wing are being formed. After three months of National Service training, which includes taking part in nation-building activities—for example, bush-clearing or road-construction, recruits may join the army, the police, or a specialist unit for paramilitary training in the last six months of their training. Those who do not enter the armed forces are to establish new village settlements; they may settle there if they want, but are recallable for military duty. Initially, it was stated that all young men would be liable for national service duty, but limited funds restrict the number of national servicemen to about 3,300 during the *Five Year Plan* period.

Government has adopted a number of measures aimed at ensuring political loyalty and integration of the armed forces with TANU. All members of the military and the police can now join TANU. On June 24, 1964, Second Vice President Kawawa told recruits that they were citizens of the country and could participate fully in the politics of the United Republic. The former practice of refusing soldiers the right to political participation had been instituted by the colonialists, said Mr. Kawawa.[24] (The independent Tanganyika government took three years to change this rule.)

Police and soldiers have responded en masse to TANU's invitation. In fact, they enroll as whole units; company commanders are heads of the TANU committee established in the company. Officers are expected to do party liaison work and to explain to the troops their role in Tanzania's development. President Nyerere granted an honorary commission in the People's Defense Forces with a rank of colonel to S. J. Kitundu, the Coast Regional Commissioner and a resident of Dar es Salaam. Mr. Kitundu was also appointed by the President as Political Commissar of the Tanzania Defense Forces with effect from November 6, 1964. This post is not a listed

[24] *Nationalist*, June 25, 1964, p. 2.

position of the Ministry of Defense; it is designed to give a TANU official a high army position. However, Mr. Kitundu has had no operational direction of the armed forces so far.

Before the mutiny, TYL members were often given policing duties at meetings or formal roadblocks; they were instructed to prevent smuggling and sometimes even to collect taxes. In certain places, TANU people did constabulary work. But these informal and irregular procedures have now been formalized.[25] To prepare them to defend Tanzania in the event of an attack, members of the nation's Police Force, Prisons Service, National Service, and TANU Youth League are to undergo full military training with modern weapons. The defense force is to be expanded beyond the limited number of National Servicemen and army by creating a national reserve. A Field Force of militarized police will exist in each region, and special village police, consisting of volunteers working under two regular policemen, will be posted to villages—particularly border areas and other places where there has been occasional trouble.[26] The people have been told that they are obliged to help these policemen.

It remains to be seen whether such a national reserve will become an effective force. Villages that are in fact sparsely settled areas spread out for miles and are hard to police. And Tanganyika has had one of the smallest salaried police forces in the world in relation to the population and the size of the country. In response to this situation, a Special Constabulary of volunteers has been established who train for police work; special constables have been recruited from the TYL. Most regions have such a force, but it is best organized in Dar es Salaam where there are almost 250 uniformed special constables and over 60 women constables.

[25] The Reserve Forces Bill legalizes paramilitary training and functions of the TYL.

[26] *Reporter* (Nairobi), February 12, 1965; *Nationalist*, February 2, 1965, p. 1.

None of these measures guarantees a loyal and pliable security force. For one thing, an army with a large element of politically aware TYL youth may be difficult for the leadership to digest. The TYL has been troublesome in the past, but despite sporadic attempts to governmentalize it by incorporating it into a Ministry of Culture and Youth, the TYL has managed to retain its identity. Difficulties not related to the new recruits have also sprung up in the army since the mutiny. When the Congo border became very unstable, the government decided to allow some of the disgraced mutineers back into the army as a stop-gap measure; shortly thereafter, trouble broke out in the army for which there has been no explanation.[27] There have also been rumors to the effect that a Zanzibari unit which was posted near Mozambique was very undisciplined and had to be shipped back.

Aside from the difficulties in building a loyal and stable force, the Tanzanian government—which now has an integrated Zanzibar and Tanganyika Peoples Defense Force—has problems in financing and training its security forces. The latter problem has created international incidents. President Nyerere's decision to accept a Chinese training team for his army provoked warnings from an outraged West. The President replied that the maximum risk was that the army would revolt, and this had already occurred with an army that was not Chinese trained. Nyerere's reply was just. His present military helpers could hardly be more varied. Israel helps with the National Service and West Germany was training

[27] The September 12, 1964 headline of the *Nationalist* read: U. R. [United Republic] ARMY ARRESTS. The text of a government announcement was printed. "In active pursuance of its duty to maintain the integrity and safety of the United Republic the government yesterday found it necessary to arrest and detain a small number of servants of the Republic. This number included Officers and other ranks of the United Republic Army, who were of doubtful loyalty and guilty of insubordination by default." It was on this occasion that Elisha Kavona was arrested.

an air wing before the crisis in West German-Tanzanian relations, after which Canada took over this training. The Zanzibar units receive Chinese, East German, and Soviet training and equipment. Not only do these arrangements pose technical difficulties for training, but Tanzanian security is a function of international politics in a very marked way.

Nonetheless, it is clear that Tanzania means to have a security establishment closely tied to TANU. The different militarized forces are designed to guard against any one branch repeating the January mutiny. But the government is not primarily concerned with insurrection; it is worried about its own inability to exert force internally.

Thus, here again the central problem of the TANU government is shown: How can it assert itself in the countryside? The National Service, the TYL, the Field Force of Military Police, the special village police are all attempts to make the central will be felt through creating new organizational forms. Another characteristic response has been the merging of TANU organizations and the defense forces. We can think of this as politicizing the security forces; but perhaps it is just as useful to see the enrollment of army and police in TANU and the creation of defense TANU units as an attempt to strengthen TANU. The parallel with the entrance of civil service into TANU is clear. By incorporating these functional units, TANU does not so much extend its control—for we have seen that the TANU center is limited in its ability to do this with its own territorial organizations—as give itself more concrete meanings and manifestations. TANU's diffuse functions become specific by incorporating functionally specific organizations. TANU is short on executive and administrative personnel, so it recruits civil servants and policemen.

All groups and individuals must be within TANU so that no group or individual can threaten it from outside. TANU leaders feel that separatisms can be contained within the party's embrace, and that the major reason why the army mutinied

379

was because it did not have contact with TANU leaders and was not informed with TANU goals.[28]

Conclusion

The stark facts of life in Tanganyika were driven home by the mutiny: the center was basically cut off from the rest of the country, both geographically and politically; fewer than 1,000 armed men could bring the government down, but the TANU organizations outside Dar es Salaam could keep "ruling." The army mutiny illustrated the discontinuities between the center and the districts. It also illuminated an interesting paradox: the very absence of central political control has permitted a relatively stable situation in the countryside, which was not deeply affected by the turmoil in Dar es Salaam during the mutiny, nor subsequently by all the concerns of East African Federation, planning, international politics, and ideological struggle.

President Nyerere has "fitted" as a leader in this situation. He has not tried to enforce close control within his own Cabinet much less over TANU, nor has he encouraged TANU to rule with a short rein. He has been realistic about the possibilities of doing these things. But more than this, his "style" has been to propose, convince, but not to impose or coerce.

President Nyerere retained the loyalty of his national and middle-level leaders in the face of the army mutiny. Although Nyerere now shares political space with new national leaders who hold their own beliefs and programs and are closer in thought and spirit to the middle-level leaders, no other national leader could hope to assert the degree of control Nyerere does—over non-central TANU organizations, over the population at large, and at the center itself. For he does this more by the force of his own personality than by any grasp of central control mechanisms. We have seen that such mechanisms do not exist in Tanzania.

[28] This judgment is based on personal interviews.

After the mutiny, entrance into TANU became, more than ever, the *sine qua non* for being part of the nation. The security forces had to be linked closely to TANU before TANU leaders could feel confident in them. TANU became more embracing, but at the same time it was called on to be more disciplined in order to effectively implement the *Five Year Plan*. Would there be a tension between these two aims?

TANU tried to provide answers, in advance, via the *Presidential Commission Report on the Establishment of a One-Party State*. The Presidential Commission was not brought about by the mutiny; it was the result of a decision made before the mutiny to have a one-party system *de jure* in Tanganyika. However, the timing of the announcement of the Commission's convention was significant: the President announced his Commission on January 28, 1964, only a few days after British troops had reestablished order in Dar es Salaam. The Presidential Commission was called not only to shift attention away from the mutiny, but more importantly, to carry on the search for TANU's and Tanganyika's identity. The mutiny had called into question the most fundamental assumption of leaders: that TANU was unassailable. They were aware of their problems in enforcing central rule in the regions, districts, and villages, but they had not anticipated that the established rule would be shaken at the center itself.

The TANU government was going through a process of reassuring itself about its place in the nation throughout 1964-65. The elections for President and for Parliament in 1965 were meant to ratify the popularity of TANU and its leaders and to establish a new framework for political competition in Tanzania.

CHAPTER XII

The Elections of September 1965

Electoral Framework

TANZANIA elected a new National Assembly and reelected Julius Nyerere as President of the Republic at the end of September 1965.[1] This was the first national election held after the Union of Tanganyika and Zanzibar, and it was the first election for the National Assembly since October 1960, when the pre-independence Legislative Council had been elected. For the first time parliamentary elections were held without seats being kept in reserve for minority races. The presidential election of 1962 had taken place under universal adult suffrage, but less than one-quarter of the adult population had voted. Could TANU now get out the vote? Would the election manifest parochialism or racialism? Would TANU leaders be rejected? And, if so, how would they react? On what issues would the elections turn? Leaders in Dar es Salaam could estimate the popularity of their colleagues and themselves. But no one could even guess what would be the precise outcome.

The system was not "informationless": people in general were aware of the local issues involved and had an idea of the eventual victors. But this information did not travel upward to the leaders. There are different ways for leaders to handle their own ignorance when it comes to elections. If they are completely in the dark, they may not risk holding any elections at all; they may rig elections so that huge majorities are guaranteed; or they may even start out to hold free elections and then change their minds in mid-stream.[2]

---

[1] Polling took place on two separate days, September 21 and September 26 in order to facilitate running the election.

[2] The suggestion has been made that a 1960 election in Ghana was rigged after the first results came in. The Convention People's Party (CPP) candidates did not do as well as expected in the first phase

In Tanzania, the NEC decided to hold elections which would be free within a stipulated framework. But because of the severe lack of communication which prevented any possibility of predicting the total effect of the election, the election itself was a kind of crisis for the constituted leaders.[3] The election, in ways different from the mutiny, showed Tanzania under stress; it was illuminating not only for the final results but because we can see the responses by leaders and the populace to the electoral process.

The elections held in September 1965 might have led to the replacement of many TANU leaders, but not the major ones. There was little possibility that Julius Nyerere would be voted out of office and 6 important figures in the old government ran unopposed. Thus, it could not be said that even a change in governments, much less in regime, would come about. TANU would remain the ruling party, *de jure*. Nonetheless, the TANU government was putting the election forward as the first real test of the possibility of a one-party democracy in Tanzania; outside observers went so far as to call it the first real test in the possibility of a one-party democracy in all of Africa.[4]

We have seen that TANU leaders had faced the question as to how open elections should be. It was determined that TANU would be *de jure* the single party in Tanzania.[5] And

of the election; then the second phase showed overwhelming majorities. Cf. Dennis Austin, *Politics in Ghana, 1946-1960* (London: Oxford University Press, 1964), pp. 390-92.

[3] I do not mean to say that a crisis atmosphere existed in Dar es Salaam in August-September 1965, as it did in January 1964, when the army revolted. Perhaps the only time anything approaching a crisis atmosphere came about in the 1965 election was when the first phase returns came in and showed 2 ministers and 4 junior ministers beaten. There was some apprehension in Dar es Salaam that more ministers would go but there was no panic among leaders.

[4] Colin Legum, "One-Party State Passes Its Test," *Observer* (London), September 26, 1965, p. 4.

[5] In practice, Tanganyika is a one-party system and so is Zanzibar with its Afro-Shirazi Party.

for the first time a choice among TANU candidates existed because two candidates ran under TANU sponsorship.[6] It also was decided that TANU candidates would be processed through a preselection primary-type poll in TANU district conferences.

The Presidential Commission recommended that any person who could obtain 25 signatures of registered voters on his petition should be allowed to put himself before the TANU district executive committee in the constituency concerned. Each member of the district executive committee would select from among those nominated 3 candidates of his choice. The full list of those nominated would then go to the NEC along with a tally of the votes each candidate had received in the district executive committee. The NEC would not be bound by the district executive committee votes for a candidate.[7] The NEC would select 3 candidates to stand in each

---

[6] Julius Nyerere has said, with much truth, that for the first time people were offered a real choice. In the 1958 elections, the choice was between TANU and a colonial government-sponsored party (the UTP); and then in the 1960 elections, most TANU candidates ran unopposed. See Nyerere's Speech to the National Assembly, October 12, 1965, reported in the *Nationalist*, October 13, 1965, pp. 1, 2, 6, 8.

[7] *Presidential Report*, p. 20. The Presidential Commission considered, but rejected, limiting the number of candidates by requiring a deposit which would be forfeited if less than a certain number of votes were obtained. The stated grounds for rejection were that a great many potential candidates of high quality would be excluded for lack of financial sources unless TANU itself provided funds. And if TANU did that, the whole purpose (limitation) would be defeated. Nor did the Presidential Commission favor the idea of permitting only nominees who were nominated by a specific number of voters. The commission objected that if the number was sufficiently large to be an effective limitation, the practical task of checking nomination papers would "be very likely to overwhelm the Returning Officers. Moreover there is a very real danger that a good candidate with popular support could be disqualified by inadvertent failure to meet the nomination requirements." However, the Commission was committed to a positive role for TANU district and national organs and it rejected the other procedures in order to channel the preselection process through TANU.

constituency, taking note of the 3 most popular choices in the district executive committee vote.

The joint session of the TANU and ASP NECs amended the report so that 2 candidates would stand in each constituency and the first preselection would be made not in the district executive committee but in a special district conference of TANU where each voting delegate of the TANU district conference cast one vote (by secret ballot), but the delegate chose 2 candidates on the single vote.[8] President Nyerere explained that reducing the candidates from 3 to 2 would guarantee that a person who did not enjoy the popular support of the people in his constituency did not get elected. "If you have three candidates there is the risk that a candidate of the minority might get elected. A candidate rejected by 60 per cent of the voters would represent the constituency."[9] Whatever the merits of this argument,[10] it appears that the NEC was concerned about minority candidates being elected. It would have been a mistake to reduce the number of candidates from 3 to 2 if the elections were between one TANU candidate who was more "official" than another: if this was to be the pattern, the 2 "less official" candidates could split the vote against a district-organization-sponsored candidate. However, there was no one official candidate of the TANU district conference.

The TANU conferences themselves were often split between candidates, and they were unable to influence the voting pattern in the district. Thus, reducing the candidates from 3 to 2 worked to reduce the number of real alternatives offered to the voters. Since so many "ins"—former MPs, TANU chairmen, area commissioners, junior ministers—went out, and

---

[8] The two candidates with the most first choices were selected.

[9] *Daily Nation* (Nairobi), May 7, 1965, p. 1.

[10] A transferable vote system could have avoided this. Voters could indicate a first and second choice and the second choices of the candidate who came bottom could be distributed between the other two candidates if three ran. Sanger, *op.cit.*, p. 21.

since so many candidates who polled low votes in the district conference vote won seats in the election, it became clear after the fact that reducing the number of candidates worked to reduce real competition. It is very likely that 3 candidates would have split the districts more than 2 did, and that the electorate would have divided so that many minority candidates would have been elected.

The NEC was probably aware that this would happen. Thus, the decision to reduce the number of candidates reflected more than a fear of minority candidates being elected; it was also an attempt to reduce the number of splits in the TANU district organizations and in the electorate induced by the election. However, the decision to have the selection poll take place in a district conference rather than in the district executive committee worked just the other way. The TANU district executive committee, as a smaller body, would have produced fewer splits within the TANU district leadership simply because there would be less bodies to disagree. The TANU district conference which acted as a preselection primary included all the TANU district officers, regional officers resident in a district, constituency MPs, branch chairmen, 2 branch delegates and delegates from affiliated agencies. The sizes varied from under 20 to over 100 delegates.

One important study of the election reports that the major determinant for choice in the district poll was that the candidate be well known.[11] Delegates and some area and regional commissioners tried to influence the choices by lobbying.[12] There were rumors of some intimidation. The failure of 2 junior ministers, 6 MPs, an ambassador, and the chairman of the Agricultural Marketing Board to secure either first or second place in the district poll foreshadowed that other emi-

[11] Belle Harris, "Tanzania Elections 1965," *Mbioni*, II, No. 5 (Dar es Salaam, 1965), n.p.
[12] *Ibid*. In some district conferences only the area and regional commissioners questioned prospective candidates; in others, more delegates interviewed them.

nent people would also lose in the final election. And the cause of defeat was often the same: failure to keep in contact with one's locality.

The decision to hold preselection in a district conference is testimony to the strong urge of many TANU members in the NEC to widen and thus democratize the procedures at least within a TANU framework.[13] It is also a vivid illustration of the lack of consistency, which has applied elsewhere in decisions of the NEC. The TANU NEC, like many party organizations in Africa, simply refuses to be either Leninist or democratic, elitist or representative, self-serving or altruistic. It is all these things at once. To label the NEC one thing or another is to miss the complexity of the body; and this is true of TANU as a whole.

Election Results

The new Tanzanian National Assembly has 199 members. When the voters in Tanganyika went to the polls in September 1965, they elected 101 MPs. There were 107 constituencies to be filled, but Second Vice President Kawawa, 4 ministers (Oscar Kambona, Job Lusinde, Michael Kamaliza, and Austin Shaba), and 1 junior minister (F. V. Mponji) ran unopposed. Zanzibaris could vote for or against Julius Nyerere's presidential candidacy, like their mainland compatriots; but they could not vote for Zanzibari representatives to Parliament.[14] Zanzibar is represented in the Tanzanian National Assembly by 23 members of the Zanzibar Revo-

[13] In fact, members of the TANU district executive committee and branch secretaries who attended the meeting had no voting rights in the district conference poll.

[14] The *Presidential Report* had expressed the view that the NECs of TANU and the ASP should be jointly charged with the duty of nominating a single candidate for President of the Republic. In the event of the nominee's failure to get a majority, it would be the duty of TANU and the ASP to put forward an alternate name. The NEC decided that an electoral conference should be constituted from the National Conference to nominate the presidential candidate.

lutionary Council, 3 regional commissioners from Zanzibar and Pemba, and 14 Zanzibari MPs who are not members of the Revolutionary Council.[15] Other MPs include 17 mainland Tanzanian regional commissioners and 10 nominated MPs from Tanganyika.[16] There are 15 national members who are elected by the National Assembly after approval by the TANU NEC. The NEC rejected all the nominees submitted by 7 National Institutions as their prospective representatives in Parliament for these seats because nearly all the institutions submitted names of people directly connected with them.[17] The new provisions stipulate that National Institutions should submit names from both within and without their organizations.[18]

There can be no doubt that the constituency seats were truly contested. The TANU district conferences held their

[15] First Vice President Karume enters the Parliament through the Revolutionary Council, as does Aboud Jumbe, minister of state in the First Vice President's office. Ministers Babu, Hanga, Makame, and Wakil, and Junior Ministers Rashid and Mwalim enter as appointed Zanzibari MPs.

[16] The President used his prerogative for appointing members to restore Paul Bomani, former Minister of Finance, to the National Assembly. Bomani was the only defeated minister or junior minister to be appointed to the National Assembly. He reentered the Cabinet as Minister for Economic Affairs and Development Planning. The President also appointed Lady Chesham, a former MP who had been elected to a seat reserved for Europeans in 1960; Chief Fundikira who had resigned his seat in 1963; Joseph Namata, principal secretary in the President's office; Mark Bomani (brother to Paul Bomani) the Solicitor General; Ali Migeyo, an early TANU founder and resident of Bukoba. He also appointed 4 Zanzibaris who did not come in as Council members or appointed Zanzibari MPs: Bibi Jokha Sulemani, Sheikh Umbaya Vuai, Ahmed Seleman Ali Riami, and Himid Mbaye.

[17] National institutions include: NUTA, the Cooperative Movement, the University College, the Association of Chambers of Commerce, the Tanganyika African Parents Association, and other institutions that may be designated by the President. They may each nominate up to 5 persons.

[18] Bibi Titi Mohamed and Mr. Timothy Samjela withdrew their names from the list because they had been defeated in constituency races.

preference polls toward the end of July.[19] The results of the polls were published in full so that the public could know how many votes each individual received in the district conference. No campaign activity could begin openly until the second week in August, when the NEC announced the candidates. The election was held during the last week of September. Thus the candidates had about six weeks for electioneering. The election rules forbade individual campaigning. All election activities were controlled by the district executive committee, which arranged the meetings between candidates and provided the forum for debates. Both candidates had to be present; if one was ill, electioneering activities were halted until he regained his health. Candidates had to address crowds in Swahili or through an interpreter if they did not speak Swahili.[20] They took turns addressing each meeting first. Three-men committees were formed from people outside a constituency to ensure that fair play prevailed and that no campaigning took place on the basis of tribal or religious ties. High officials in TANU, NUTA, and government were warned not to try and intimidate candidates. And it was explicitly stated that all individuals chosen had TANU support. Nonetheless, "private" campaigning did take place, and individuals did use their family connections or ties with TANU and local government bodies. And local TANU officials did sometimes unofficially try to influence voters.

Each candidate was given a symbol—either a house (*nyumba*) or a hoe (*jembe*)—chosen by the Central Com-

[19] On the day that the district conference met, candidates were expected to be near the meeting room so that they could be asked a few questions. No candidate was allowed to make a speech to the delegation.

[20] Some campaigns by the TANU organizations for getting a pro-Nyerere presidential vote were organized separately from the parliamentary campaign and the local language was used. Harris has noted that many voters were unfamiliar with the Swahili word *rais* for president.

mittee and distributed to candidates by the NEC.[21] President Nyerere announced that the symbols were issued simply because many voters were illiterate, and had no significance in themselves; voters were to choose a man, not a symbol.[22] Nonetheless, candidates did try to exploit their symbols. For example, one would say: "The hoe has never failed you; choose the hoe." Another (the mayor of Dar es Salaam): "Choose the house so that I can serve you. Do not choose the hoe whose owner does not even own a farm."[23] In this instance, and in many others, the hoe proved more popular: 59 winning candidates had the hoe; only 41 had the house.[24] This is a large enough discrepancy to make one wonder whether or not the NEC had some pattern in their distribution of symbols. But incumbents and TANU district or national leaders ran under both hoe and house equally. Distribution was done in order of constituencies, the first candidate being given alternatively a house or hoe; in the case of ministers and junior ministers an exact distribution was made. During the campaigns, those candidates who had the hoe symbols exploited them, while those who had the house were defensive about it. Reports of the campaign speeches show that many statements were made to the effect that "the hoe is traditional" or "all wealth comes from the hoe." Apparently, in very few constituencies was the house symbol actively exploited. In Mbeya, the local-born candidate emphasized his local ties by saying: "Our homes are here." He won.[25]

[21] It is reported that it took the Central Committee over five hours to choose symbols it felt to be of equal value.

[22] Radio broadcast of September 10, 1965, reported in the *Nationalist*, September 11, 1965, pp. 1, 4, 7.

[23] My report of campaign activities is based on campaign stories from the *Nationalist* and from reports by on-the-spot observers. I had left Tanganyika by the time the election was held.

[24] I have no record for the remaining candidate.

[25] Reported by Harris, *loc.cit.* Harris reports that in 8 cases at least the symbol obviously influenced the result. Of the 13 TANU chairmen who were defeated, 10 had the house as a symbol.

A number of themes emerged from the campaign speeches. Candidates stressed local ties, if they had them (for example, Otini Kambona's[26] opponent: "I am a farmer, and like most of you have firsthand knowledge of the pains endured by farmers"). "Locals" stressed their work in local development projects or adult literacy programs when they were running against incumbents or against TANU leaders who had been in Dar es Salaam for most of the last five years. They also accused those in the capital of not having done anything for their home districts. Thus I. Bhoke-Munanka faced the charge that he had promised villagers in North Mara cooperation, but had done nothing for them. His opponent said that of the 76 new schools in the country, none were in Mara Region. Mr. Munanka's answer was characteristic of that of most central leaders: many improvements had been made since independence; TANU's promises had been fulfilled. Munanka refuted allegations that jobs were given only when bribes were offered, but, like other leaders, was clearly on the defensive. And it was only after charging that he, unlike his opponent, was a founder of TANU and had suffered during the fight for independence that Munanka was able to gain the offensive.

However, being a leader or a founder was often more of a liability than an advantage. People were not interested in hearkening back to the anti-colonial struggle; they wished to know why their district had not received more benefits and why leaders in Dar es Salaam were living so much better than they were.[27] And President Nyerere himself made it clear

[26] Otini Kambona is Oscar Kambona's brother.

[27] And when leaders tried to take credit for accomplishments, their opponents turned the tables on them. E.g., the Mayor of Dar es Salaam pointed out that he was Acting Chairman of the National Housing Corporation and that the Corporation had built many new homes. His opponent (who beat the Mayor, 44,602 to 7,282) argued that "A housing program is included in the *Five Year Plan*. This means that whether Mr. Kirundu is Acting Chairman or not, the houses will be built." *Nationalist*, August 26, 1965, p. 2.

before the election that individuals could no longer take refuge from the people's anger behind TANU or their past work. After the election was over, he said:

> Nothing can take away from the honour which was earned by the founder members of TANU, and those other Members who suffered in the independence struggle. . . . But elections are not a vote of thanks. It would be quite wrong to elect a person to Parliament because in the past they have done good work. The elections choose people for the future. . . . Politics is, and must be looked upon as a field of service, not as a means of earning a living.[28]

This speech was a response to the heavy toll taken by the election on incumbents and TANU regional, district, and national leaders. Mr. Bhoke-Munanka survived, but many others did not. TANU leaders were indeed in a difficult position; they were a focus for whatever anti-TANU sentiment existed in the district. It is logical to suppose that leaders would attract an anti-TANU vote. There is evidence that this happened. When the voters cast their ballot for an MP, they also voted for or against Nyerere for President. Nyerere received a massive majority—2,519,866 votes out of the 2,612,225 votes cast on the mainland and on Zanzibar and Pemba.[29] Zanzibar and Pemba gave Nyerere the same kind of majorities as he received on the mainland.[30] It is thus very striking that in those constituencies where there was a greater than average "no" vote, sometimes a TANU leader was running unopposed or very often a well-known TANU official was

[28] President's Address to the National Assembly, *Nationalist*, October 13, 1965, p. 2.

[29] See *The People's Choice* (Dar es Salaam: The Ministry of Information and Tourism, 1965), p. 3. Election statistics have been gathered from this document, from the *Nationalist*, and *Tanganyika Standard* of September 22—October 1, 1965.

[30] Nyerere received 133,227 "yes" and 326 "no" votes in Zanzibar. He got 82,961 "yeses" in Pemba and 1,148 "nos."

running. In the former case, the only outlet for any anti-TANU sentiments would be a vote against the President. The most striking example of this occurred in Dodoma South where Job Lusinde ran unopposed. There Nyerere received 24,540 votes for and 7,309 against him—almost 8 per cent of total "no" votes.[31] In those constituencies where junior ministers lost, the vote was heavier than usual against Nyerere. I am not arguing that Nyerere hurt TANU leaders. Rather, unpopular leaders probably led to a higher than average vote against Nyerere. However, whatever anti-TANU vote existed was focused against them.

It was not, however, a generalized anti-TANU sentiment which brought down 2 ministers; 6 junior ministers; 3 present or former TANU regional chairmen; 13 district chairmen; 5 former or present MNE; a regional commissioner who gave up his post to run; the mayor of Dar es Salaam; a former minister and ambassador to China; the former Vice President of TANU and member of the Central Committee; 5 present or former area commissioners (only 3 area commissioners won); the chairman of the Mwananchi Development Corporation; the Deputy Commissioner of the Civil Service Commission and former editor of *Mwafrica*; and 9 back-benchers in the former Parliament (one of whom we have accounted for as an area commissioner and another as the Mwananchi man). This long list does not even do justice to the fall of past "ins" because 3 present or former junior ministers and 6 present MPs did not make it through their district polls, and 27 backbenchers from the outgoing Parliament did not stand—many because they had no chance of nomination. And some of the most devastating defeats were

31 In another Gogo constituency, there were about 14 per cent "no" votes. In Oscar Kambona's constituency, "no" votes for the President were more than 5 per cent compared to the less than 2 per cent national figure. In the other four constituencies where candidates ran unopposed, the "nos" were about the same per cent as the national figure.

incurred by the mayor of Dar es Salaam; by former junior ministers;[32] one minister,[33] and TANU MNE and regional chairmen.[34] All told, 22 out of 31 TANU officeholders were unsuccessful;[35] and 16 out of 31 MPs lost.

These men were all defeated because they faced a "throw-the-varmints-out" sentiment, which fed on seeing leaders living in high style. Exhortations by leaders to the effect that people should make sacrifices and work harder were difficult for the people to swallow: on the few occasions when they did see their leaders, it was not in the fields planting cotton or sisal but going by in high-powered Mercedes. These sentiments hit the junior ministers hardest of all because they had all the liabilities of being out of touch and antagonizing people by their relative wealth.[36] Even though the ministers could count on much closer association with Nyerere than could the junior ministers,[37] 2 ministers lost and 2 barely squeaked in. The TANU regional chairmen and MNE who had been able to perpetuate themselves within the TANU regional oligarchies had much less success before the body politic. They too were "ins"; and though they were in their regions much more than ministers and junior ministers could be, they

[32] Bibi Titi Mohamed, Junior Minister and TANU Women's leader, polled less than half the votes of her opponent. The Junior Minister for Education, Frank Mfundo, received a quarter of his opponent's votes. The former Minister for Home Affairs managed one-eighth of his opponent's totals.

[33] Paul Bomani, Minister for Finance, was undoubtedly hurt by his association with the development levy which falls on cotton farmers in Sukumaland. He had also been out of his home area for years as he had been a minister from the beginning. He was defeated by a farmer, 14,146 to 9,639.

[34] D. Misano, T. Ambrose (Mwapanduji), R. S. Tambwe, F. Hosea Irungu, H. Hamisi, O. Lema, T. Songoro, and H. Swedi all lost badly.

[35] Including TANU deputy secretaries and branch officials.

[36] Of the 14 junior ministers, 6 lost at the polls, 3 failed to gain nomination; 3 were elected; 1 did not stand; 1 ran unopposed.

[37] Of 15 ministers, 2 were defeated at the polls, 8 were elected, 5 returned unopposed.

had to be at the regional capital much of the time. Thus they were often out of the constituency where they had to run. All the defeated officials had one thing in common: they had ceased to be "locals." But the people fixed on local issues: they wanted MPs who were personally connected with them and could channel their desires to the center. Many of these defeated candidates had done a good job in Dar es Salaam, but simply could not spend the time needed in their home areas. This lack of contact might have been compensated for by a rising standard of living; but the TANU government had not been able to provide vast programs for social welfare and economic development in the countryside. Incumbents promised new programs, but the people remained skeptical.

To call this a politics of parochialism would be somewhat of a misnomer. The people were not always looking narrowly inward to tribal or religious considerations.[38] Granted, they were concerned with local issues; and they preferred candidates whom they knew and who had been active in their localities. But this kind of parochialism is perhaps better called "grass rootsism"; it is one so pervasive that it surmounted racial considerations. An Asian defeated the African chairman of the Mwananchi Development Corporation on Mafia Island, who was running there because the Dar es Salaam constituencies were filled. He was open to the carpet-bagger charge.[39]

One of the most interesting things to emerge from the elec-

---

[38] Harris, *loc.cit.*, reports the absence of a religious vote and says that only in about three constituencies was it seen as a determinant of voting behavior. In more cases tribal considerations played an important part and people divided on language or some other cultural trait associated with "tribe."

[39] When President Nyerere in his post-election speech said that the people had rejected racialism he was referring to the fact that an Asian minister won reelection (Amir Jamal) as did a European minister (Derek Bryceson). The terms Asian and European simply denote large racial categories in terms of old pre-independence reserved seat schemes.

tion was the relationship between the vote in the TANU district conference preference poll and the final election returns. I have produced below a scattergram (Fig. 3) which shows the percentage of votes received out of total votes in the district conferences on one axis and the percentage of votes each candidate got in the election on another. The failure of the dots to form a line is a significant result. Because sometimes as many as 16 candidates ran in some district conference polls and 8 or 10 often ran, the percentage of the total that each of the 2 winning candidates received was between 0 and 30 per cent in more than half of the polls.[40] I correlated 90 constituencies where more than 2 men ran in the district poll. Of the 180 candidates, the breakdown shown in Table 13 holds for various shares of the district preference polls.

TABLE 13

Share of the District Preference Polls	
Percentage	Number of Candidates
0 - 10	14
10 - 20	32
20 - 30	49
30 - 40	23
40 - 50	29
50 - 60	10
60 - 70	6
70 - 80	10
80 - 90	5
90 - 100	2

Forty-nine out of 90 constituencies showed the front-runner in the district poll-winning.[41] If we look at winners and losers in terms of preference poll percentiles, we get the breakdown shown in Table 14.

[40] 713 candidates were in the district polls; 222 were chosen.
[41] In two cases there was a tie; in one the man on top of the poll was not chosen by the NEC, but the second-place man ran and won.

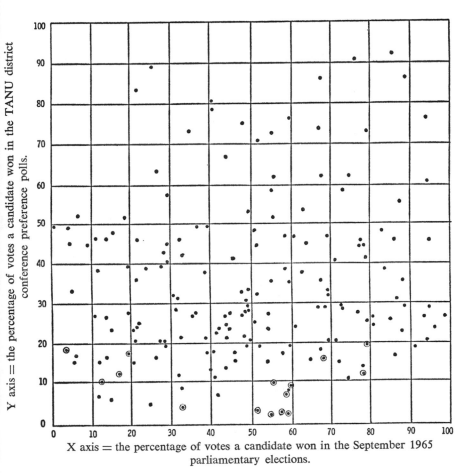

Y axis = the percentage of votes a candidate won in the TANU district conference preference polls.

X axis = the percentage of votes a candidate won in the September 1965 parliamentary elections.

Fig. 3.—Scattergram of Election Returns, 1965

⊚ = Candidates chosen by NEC.

TABLE 14

Preference Percentiles of Winners and Losers

Preference Percentiles	Winners	Losers
90 - 100	2	0
80 - 90	2	3
70 - 80	7	3
60 - 70	4	2
50 - 60	6	4
40 - 50	14	15
30 - 40	11	12
20 - 30	22	27
10 - 20	14	18
0 - 10	8	6

Thus there is almost a symmetry between losers and winners in terms of percentiles. People neither consistently voted against high-preference winners nor for them. I conclude two things from the results of the scattergram. First, the people at large did not care how a candidate fared in the district poll. The results were made known to them not only by the press in Dar es Salaam (which would not necessarily guarantee knowledge of it in the constituencies), but also by the district conference members themselves. But people viewed the poll as the work of the district conference and in no way binding on an individual's vote. This was also President Nyerere's attitude, and he insisted that the two candidates chosen were equal in the eyes of TANU.

When President Nyerere first held out the possibility that candidates might run under a TANU rubric, he awakened the desire for office in many men. But only those who were either in the TANU district oligarchy or on the periphery of it had a chance because it was the district conference after all which chose the candidates. This leads to my second conclusion from the results of the scattergram: that the TANU district organization is the loosest of oligarchies. Individuals who were

398

members of the present or past TANU district conferences—
even former members of the TANU executive committee in
the district—might be removed from the inner core of TANU
leaders. It was these men who had a chance in the district
conference poll, but would have had much less chance if the
district executive committee had chosen the candidates.

In the past, when the TANU executive committee was nominating candidates for town and district councils, TANU district leaders—the district secretary, district chairmen, and
working committee members—had a difficult time enforcing
their will on the executive committee.[42] The inner-core lead-

[42] One district secretary is on record as saying: "When the time
came for an election (to a town council in this case) what I had to
do was the following.

(1) To consult responsible officers of local and central government regarding the extension of franchise.
(2) Encourage the public to register themselves.
(3) I wrote to communities and clubs for their support.
(4) When the nomination day was nearer I sent out circulars in-
viting applications of those who required TANU support (all
who wanted to stand).
(5) The district committee was called to recommend to headquarters probable candidates.
(6) On behalf of the National Executive, the Central Committee
approved all names recommended by the District Committee
except one.
   So far it was all right, but there are problems and difficulties
in the system:
(a) The district committee consists of people from branches
and many of them outside the town. They don't know any
of the candidates who applied, therefore it is very difficult for the Secretary and Members of the Working
Committee to convince the executive committee in recom-
mending candidates.
(b) If it is even more difficult for the district committee to
know worthy candidates a question arises: why should the
National Executive or Central Committee be given the
final authority? How would they know worthy candidates?
I am citing a written report of one district TANU secretary written in
1962. It is a nice irony that the secretary, an appointed official from
the center, questioned the center's right to be the final arbiter of the
nominees.

ers lost control of the determination of nominees under the new procedures. A wider chorus of TANU district voices made themselves heard, and the NEC stepped into the process more than it had in the past. The outcome was an infusion of new blood into the Parliament.

Looking at the biographies of the winners,[43] it is striking how many new MPs have been active in the cooperative movement or have been teachers, or both. Many have been members of district councils. Those who trained at Kivukoni College or at civil service training centers (at fairly low-levels) and then came back to work in their localities as co-operative secretaries or established local farming organizations were very successful. (See Table 15.)

Successful candidates were potentially more effective in obtaining local benefits and voicing local grievances. And here relatively higher education was an important factor. In all but 8 of the 40 constituencies where there was a marked difference between the educational qualifications of 2 candidates, the candidate with the most education was successful. Of the 8 exceptions, 6 were former MPs, including 1 minister and 2 junior ministers.[44] The relatively poor showing of long-time TANU officials is related to this preference for electing people with higher education.

These men and women were able to get in because the Parliament had been enlarged, providing new seats in districts where TANU founders had been ensconced. Their chances were made even better when the reservation of seats for minority races was done away with. But above all, they had a chance in the district conference because they had often been members of it in the past, had friends there, and could use their popularity in the constituencies. Many individuals who were second in the district poll proved to have more popularity in the final election where constituency pop-

[43] Short biographies were published in the *Tanganyika Standard*, October 2, 1965.
[44] *Ibid.*

TABLE 15

Occupation of Candidates

	Successful	Unsuccessful
MPS	15 (+6 unop- posed)	16
TANU officials	9	22
Coop and NUTA officials	12	6
Local government[a] (political)	14	14
Local government[a] (civil service)	4	2
Area commissioners	3	2
Civil servants	13	4
Teachers (including education assistants)	11	4
Farmers	8	13
Traders and trans- porters	4	—
Business (managerial and sales clerks)	3	3
Lawyers/magistrates	2	—
Miscellaneous	2	7 (including one unemployed)

SOURCE: Harris, *loc.cit.*

[a] I have broken Harris' local government category into political and civil service.

ularity counted. TANU district and regional leaders were not operating at the constituency level because constituencies were smaller than districts. Thus, there was not even a formal TANU constituency party organization which might have influenced voters directly.

The TANU organizations were often split. This could be seen when two very well-known TANU district leaders ran against each other. For example, Kirilo Japhet, leader of the old Meru Citizens' Union and a TANU district chairman, ran against Obed Ole Mejooli, a TANU district council chairman

401

and former TANU secretary. The vote was close in the poll and very close in the final election. Elsewhere, however, two well-known figures might run neck and neck in the poll, but one would defeat the other badly in the election. The breakdown of the preference polls has shown how split the district organizations were. It remains to be seen whether the new MPs will also take hold as district leaders. Most likely, they will play a role in district politics and further fragment TANU's district and regional organizations.

It is very significant that the election was fought almost exclusively within the framework of the district poll. This might not have occurred if either of two things had happened. First, the NEC had the prerogative to disregard the first two candidates in the district poll and choose some other name from the list; as the scattergram shows, the NEC did this in 15 out of 180 possible cases. Of the candidates it chose, 10 were successful and only 5 lost. It is not entirely correct to say that there was no resentment against candidates chosen by the NEC simply because they were successful twice as often as not. The victories of these candidates were narrower than average victories, and the losers had greater than average losses. In two cases at least, the NEC apparently tried to pick weak candidates to run against individuals it hoped would be reelected. In Mwanza East, it went to the bottom of the list to choose a candidate who had received less than 2 per cent of the district conference vote to run against the Minister for Finance, Paul Bomani. Similarly, in the Mafia Island race, the NEC picked a man who had received 1 vote out of 52 in the district poll. In both cases, the strategy, if such it was, backfired. The NEC did not consistently favor regional leaders who lost in the polls. In some cases, it did choose regional chairmen or MNE who did not run first or second, but in another it struck down a regional leader.[45] Nor did the NEC see fit to reinstate national leaders

[45] Twaibu Songoro, Dominic Misano, and R. Nyembo were in-

who had run poorly in the polls.[46] Most of the candidates the NEC refused to endorse had tarnished TANU records rather than no TANU records at all.[47]

While the NEC cannot change the face of Tanzania by fiat, while it cannot control the operations of the district organization, it does have free hand in personnel matters. Just as commissioners can be transferred around without being vetoed by local organizations, so the NEC can determine candidates for Parliament. It did not choose more candidates because this would have been against the stated aim of the election if the NEC had intervened widely. But this should not obscure the fact that one real power of the center is to determine the people it wants to be officials and to veto pos-

---

stalled. Bibi A. Maufi was disallowed. S. W. Majaliwa was not boosted from a third in his poll. All these names appear in Tables 2 or 3, chap. iii.

[46] Thus neither George Kahama, a former minister and Ambassador to West Germany, nor Roland Mwanjisi, former Junior Minister to Home Affairs and editor of *Uhuru*, got a second life from the NEC. There were others in the same position. After the election, the President brought Bomani back into the Cabinet. This apparently led to resentment in the country. See *Reporter*, IV, No. 13 (October 8, 1965), 11. Also see "We Had Our Say," letter to the editors of the *Nationalist*, September 29, 1965, p. 4, by Alfred Juma. The President also gave Waziri Juma, a former regional commissioner and defeated candidate, an ambassador post. J. Kasambala, the other defeated minister, was made chairman of a number of government boards. Edward Barongo was made a regional commissioner. The President was on solid ground when he argued that good men with scarce skills were needed. See *Nationalist*, October 13, 1965, p. 6. Most of the defeated former "ins" were not brought back. Their possible dissidence was a worry to Nyerere even in advance of the election. In every major pre- and post-election speech he urged defeated candidates to return to the country's service in some other capacity; to accept the verdict of the people even if the people were mistaken; not to feel shame for no shame attaches to defeat. *Ibid.*, p. 2, and *Nationalist*, September 11, 1965, p. 7.

[47] Six names refused were connected with misappropriation of funds. Two withdrew; in one case the use of religious influence was rumored. Harris, *loc.cit.* Harris says that 5 candidates the NEC refused had "a poor TANU record," but does not explain what this meant.

sible representatives; district organizations have the same prerogatives in the preselection process vis-à-vis lower levels. This is possible because the TANU framework—the rules established at the center—are accepted by the people at large and by the TANU organizations at various levels. In this case, authority can be translated into power.

A second way in which the framework could have been rejected would have been through low registration. In 1962, when Nyerere was first chosen President of Tanganyika, there was a registration of 1,800,000 people. But only 64 per cent of these (less than 1,200,000) voted. In the 1965 election, some 2,266,000 people recorded their choice for MP and 2,612,000 voted for or against the President.[48] (The mainland vote represents more than half the possible voters.) It is true that there was more interest than ever before because these were real parliamentary contests. But this should not detract from TANU's accomplishment in involving so many people in the election. The 50 per cent of the adult population which voted represents a real achievement in a free, honest election and registration. Thus, although the actual registration of 3,175,617 was short of the 4 million hoped for (which would have been 80 per cent of estimated eligible citizens), it is a more impressive figure than the bogus 95 per cent plus registrations and majorities in many African countries.[49] And although the number of abstentions was past 55 per cent in some constituencies and averaged

[48] The discrepancy is accounted for by Zanzibar and Pemba voters having a ballot for President but not for MPs. There were also the 6 uncontested Tanganyika constituencies. There were 125,000 more votes cast in the presidential than parliamentary elections on the mainland.

[49] The TANU government did run into difficulties when it tried to register voters. Second Vice President Kawawa said that people should not be deceived by false rumors and that the "registration [for the 1965 election] was not connected with tax at all." See also the editorial in the *Nationalist*, July 6, 1965, p. 4.

around 24 per cent per constituency, the total vote also represented a major achievement.

Conclusion

The election in Tanzania has been heralded as "the first real test in Africa of the possibility of a one-party democracy in Africa."[50] We should not forget as we consider the democratic aspects of the system that the NEC could and did step in to void the district poll, and that TANU district conferences did determine the only legal candidates. Still, a competitive election has been held in a *de jure* one-party state. A balance between freedom and a strong, effective single party is being attempted. The balance is all the more precarious because that strong and effective party has not yet been created. But it is the very openness of TANU, which was demonstrated in the election, that makes the experiment possible. However, some of the features of the election which were heralded as indicating the democratic nature of the system (for example, the dramatic turnover in the National Assembly as a whole, the pronounced uncertainties of the outcome, and particularly the lack of information among TANU leaders)[51] reflect the information gaps in Tanzania and the absence of a strong party organization to process information and affect outcomes.

[50] Legum, *loc.cit.*

[51] See Ruth Schachter Morganthau, "African Elections: Tanzania's Contribution," *Africa Report* (December 1965), pp. 12-16.

CHAPTER XIII

Conclusions

IN STUDYING the new states which have emerged since World War II, we search for similarities and differences. The African countries are particularly susceptible to this kind of treatment because there are so many of them, and they are new nations. And, while many of them are similar in size, population, and resources, and have a legacy of colonialism and a ruling single party, the style of rule often seems very different. We want to know if the differences are only variations in rhetoric of leaders and their penchants for organizational forms, rather than important variations in the way people are ruled.

Obviously, only empirical studies can tell us, for example, how specific parties perform. And a case study such as this cannot itself provide answers to general questions about political development. These questions can be approached only through the accumulation and analysis of data about many societies—data informed by and related to theoretical frameworks. And in fact the comparative treatment of new states has often meant analyzing individual political systems so that a detailed knowledge of one country's politics is presented in a way that makes comparison and generalization feasible and allows us to qualify our past statements in the light of new data. Rarely will one scholar undertake concrete comparisons between systems in a single work. A number of works have also appeared which are devoted to building toward a theory of political development by presenting data from different systems within more or less explicit theoretical frameworks.

My own focus on party and economic development in Tanzania allows me to examine the nature of the connection between economic development and national integration, in order that the Tanzanian materials may be relevant for comparison and generalization. By analyzing intra-TANU relationships—in terms of recruitment, ideology, and political functioning—within the context of party interaction with its economic environment, I have tried to stress the importance of seeing political institutions as the concrete links between politics and economics in studies of development.

One possible interaction of a ruling party with its environment is for the party to become increasingly centralized and bureaucratized as it undertakes economic tasks. The party becomes the agent for economic growth as it undergoes changes in organization and personnel. The system as a whole moves in one direction because the party affects economy. This is not the pattern in Tanzania. The party does not provide an institution which can transform the economy and make itself more effective in the process; it is too weak and too loose and has too few material and human resources to tackle developmental problems. As we have seen, the state administrative agencies are so weak that resources cannot easily be borrowed or appropriated to strengthen TANU.

Thus, generalizations from this study arise out of the relationship between levels and structure of economic development and (1) the possibilities for exerting political control at different territorial levels and (2) the nature of the internal arrangements within a political party or between a party and other groups. Thus I question whether countries with economic structures similar to Tanzania's can have Leninist parties—that is, parties ruled from an authoritative and monolithic center. Other variables aside from economic ones operate, of course. *Lingua francas*, cultural traditions, individual leaders, the nature of indigenous traditional small-scale political communities and the presence or absence of statewide structures in the past are obviously relevant. I have tried to take account of them in my study. One does not have to be committed to a determinist's understanding of change

407

to argue that economic development conditions the possibilities and sets the limits for many kinds of central intervention in society. However, after examining Tanzania, I am immediately suspicious of any categorizations which lump together Ghana, Guinea, Mali, and perhaps Tanzania as "mobilization systems," "revolutionary states," "mass-party" or "one-party" states, and set them against Uganda, Senegal, or Ivory Coast which have been called, by social scientists and "one-party" leaders alike, "conservative," "partyless," "pluralistic." There are differences and similarities between these systems, but they cannot be comprehended by typologies which have been constructed around party ideology or even party structure. Despite the obviousness of this statement, it apparently requires saying.

How then can we come to grips with the seeming variety of African political systems? There is no short cut: we must see what various structures actually do before we can compare them meaningfully. We have to understand the political functioning of various institutions in their own contexts. This entails understanding how they relate to both the modern and traditional sectors of society. And it involves spelling out the environment in which political institutions operate in some detail so that we may gauge how they affect that environment and how they change internally over time. We have to try and specify when a political institution acts as an independent variable not only in the social system as a whole but in the economy in particular; we have to see in what ways the economy is an independent variable and the party a dependent one. I have argued that it is hard for TANU to become an independent variable in the sense that the levels of development are so low that an initial critical stage cannot be easily reached after which the party will become a force for economic growth.

The internal structure of TANU can be changed; new organizational devices can, and in fact have been adopted. But

CONCLUSIONS

TANU cannot become a tightly disciplined, hierarchically organized party which rules from the center without first effecting fundamental changes in the relationship of the party to economic tasks and without structural changes in the economy taking place. There will have to be a shift away from the present ratio of subsistence to monetary sectors, a change in the proportion of subsistence farmers to total working force, a rise in the level of productivity and per capita income. And, TANU itself will have to organize development projects and be constantly engaged in administering them before it can become a centralized party.

President Nyerere has said, and the slogan for the *Five Year Plan* has become: It Can Be Done, Play Your Part. But what can be done, and what are the roles for individuals, groups, and TANU itself? These are still open questions; TANU still searches for its place within Tanzania. Entrance into TANU is the *sine qua non* for being part of the nation; however, TANU itself is without specific function or definition. TANU's search for purpose and identity is inextricably linked with the identity of Tanzania as a nation. Thus, the *Five Year Plan* and the *Presidential Report* are not merely statements of intention and stipulations for action in the economy and polity; they are themselves responses to the problem of identity, and they reflect the struggle to come to terms with the tasks of rule. Before independence, Tanganyika had an administrative and international identity by virtue of the German and then British colonial control. The formation of TANU as a *national* union was a crucial step in the formation of the idea of a Tanganyika nation. TANU's founders intended it to be a national movement. TANU gathered momentum in the 1950's and was able to dominate the anti-colonial struggle without a powerful center able to force its will upon regional, district, and village organizations. It was able to monopolize African national politics because other African political organizations were either sub-regional groups, who had neither the ambition nor the capabilities of becoming national, or splinter parties from TANU's own body. TANU had great advantages over these parties. It was the first national political party, and tried to reach into the villages and the towns. As the first nationally oriented party, it inherited the existing local organizations of its predecessors: the Tanganyika African Association and the tribal unions. TANU also had Julius Nyerere. And it was neither continuously nor strenuously opposed by the colonial government.

Thus TANU was able to form the first independent government for Tanganyika. It was national in size and scope—it had 1 million members, loosely defined, out of a total population of 10 million; and it was represented in all districts and sub-divisions. But in fact, TANU coexisted with a host of traditional authorities and local leaders. TANU regional and district organizations did not dominate the countryside, and often TANU's presence had little impact upon the daily lives of the people outside of minor towns and settlements. The dominant single party was a grouping of organizations that functioned under a few well-known national leaders. It was politicizing new groups and including within itself a heterogeneous body of individuals and associational and social groups. As it was becoming the ruling party, TANU was becoming looser, not more disciplined and monolithic. However, TANU could ensure that all organized politics took place within the frameworks it set up. Thus political competition takes place within TANU institutions.

When TANU formed the government for Tanganyika, it had to rule the civil service apparatus inherited from the colonial government, and it was forced to form a center capable of directing the TANU regional, district, and sub-district organizations. Even before independence, in 1958-59, appointed officials were instituted as the first step in trying to control these organizations. In 1962 area and regional commissioners were instituted as agents of the center in the regions and districts. They were also meant to make the NEC more responsive to central leadership.

All along, one of the major problems within TANU has been the lack of an institutionalized center to direct internal party affairs. TANU has not been able to use the government machinery and patronage powers to build a center. It is the ruling party in a one-party system; but its National Headquarters staff has well under 25 full-time administrative and executive employees. Its national officers are also government ministers who, when not outside the country, are often busy with their ministries. National Headquarters has not progressed beyond its position at independence. If anything, it has atrophied, since it is no longer responsible for the appointment of area and regional TANU secretaries. The Central Committee has also been unable to consolidate power within TANU and determine the way regional and district organizations will operate. It remains a small group of Cabinet ministers, junior ministers, and co-opted Dar es Salaam TANU elders, with neither a staff that works to it, nor any mechanisms with which to exert internal control.

The most important of the central TANU organs is the most difficult to assess: the National Executive Committee. Clearly, the NEC is not a pliable instrument of the central leaders. It is essentially a non-central, national organ, whose members like to think of it as analogous to the Central Committee of the Communist Party of the Soviet Union. The analogy begins and ends in imaginations. Many of the members are from the regions and come to the NEC as regional TANU chairmen, regional secretaries, or MNEs. Thus, it has an important elected-representative nature. The NEC is supposed to make policy which is then carried out by the government. However, it has not "made" policy outside of TANU's internal affairs. It did not inform the *Five Year Plan* with its own sentiments, nor can it control the implementation of day-to-day policy. The district and regional TANU organiza-

411

tions do not function as agents of the NEC, or as agents of any other TANU central body.

TANU's non-central bodies are oligarchical, but they are internally competitive and house different elected and appointed hierarchies. Regional and area commissioners are able to prevail only through a process of compromise and consensus; they do not rule by fiat, and are not political bosses who tightly control either TANU elected officials or ministerial representatives. Functions are still very diffuse, a reflection of the diffusion of authority among many people, both in and out of TANU, in the countryside. TANU organizations have had such a difficult time making an impact on the dispersed population, let alone ruling the countryside, that every time a district headquarters wants something accomplished, TANU personnel swarm into the surrounding area.

How do regional and district leaders dominate their organizations in a system where elections count? The answer is that they can prevail only where there is a party machine which local political leaders can manipulate, or where they can consolidate support by other institutional arrangements —for example, through the distribution of goods and services. And here lies the crux of the problems of central/local control in Tanzania.

District, regional, and national leaders have a say in determining candidates for elections. This is important because to become an MP is to get a high salary; to become a member of a district council is to become available for giving and receiving favors. But the material and human resources do not exist for building a party machine. Marginal increments to income may be highly valued, but there is a very small pie to distribute. Government cannot give its local TANU leaders the goods and services which would enable them to reward or punish on a wide scale. One vicious circle of underdevelopment is: limited resources→weak organizations→limited resources. After individuals are elected to office, there is

412

no organization which can closely control their activities. The recent elections to Parliament revealed the decentralized and loose regime in this one-party state once TANU decided to operate without a restrictive and explicit ideology to which members had to conform, and once electoral competition was allowed within the specified limits. There was no attempt to impose the façade of a monolithic party. But TANU is even less centralized than the election shows because only two candidates were permitted.

TANU does not have the instruments of coercion or the internal cohesion to enforce its views. How then does the system keep operating? TANU's theme song is *TANU Nchi Yajenga*—TANU Builds the Nation. TANU can "build the nation" without central institutions which closely control other TANU institutions and associational groups. TANU itself is a congeries of regional, district, and sub-district organizations which communicate with each other and with Dar es Salaam only intermittently. Furthermore, these organizations do not attempt to regulate the lives of the people in the countryside continuously or closely. Thus, some political competition and the very looseness and non-directiveness enable TANU as a whole to continue to "rule" mainland Tanzania.

The regional and district organizations are not independent of the central leaders because regional and area commissioners do transmit orders and because the leaders try to give the non-central organizations definition and purpose. The regional and district organizations are "TANU" because there is, after all is said and done, a TANU center. It is a center because it purports to be one. No regional or district organization makes this claim. Central definitions may not become operative, but people are aware that central leaders have ideas about what TANU should be, and they look to the center for proposals. However, the center does not propose and the regional, district, and village organizations obey. Neither does it propose and they deliberately disobey. More accu-

413

rately, the center has ideas and programs which reach the territorial organizations in different forms from the original plans. Then, much on their own, development committees, commissioners, TANU chairmen and their executive committees, representatives from the ministries all do their job as they conceive it. What results is not the final, predictable output of orders sent along a chain of command, but rather the widely varying, often bewildering actions of men thrown back on their own resources, trying to prove that It Can Be Done if each man plays his own highly individualized part.

Is this situation likely to alter soon? How would TANU and Tanzanians respond to any attempts to tighten the system? The economy of Tanzania cannot change quickly. If all the goals of the *Five Year Plan* are fulfilled by 1980, Tanzania will still be only just emerging from its underdeveloped state (by present standards) even in the eyes of the planners themselves. More people will be in the agricultural sector than are there today, though the planners hope that agriculture will be less subsistence agriculture than modern farming for markets.[1] Wage-earning workers will still be less than 6 per cent of total population. Even if all the proposed new settlements are open, people will remain widely separated. Major communications routes will undoubtedly be improved, but this will not make people appreciably more accessible to district headquarters. The countryside will still be physically cut off from a few main centers. We can, however, state the general conditions for more far-reaching and pervasive social and political change.

Even if a new ideology—call it Marxism-Leninism or

[1] The number of people in the traditional agricultural section is expected to increase absolutely by 1980. The planners calculate that the number of people deriving their incomes largely from wages will increase by approximately 100 per cent. The number of those in the traditional sector will increase by 25 per cent. It is also expected that the traditional agricultural sector will move more into the market economy.

Maoism—were raised on high and even if a new *Five Year Plan* were instituted calling for breakneck development and steeply rising rates of taxation, the facts of Tanzanian economic development could not be denied. The situation is not static. The kinds of political leadership, the values and programs espoused are important; but the possibilities are defined and limited. Only if economic development takes place will the conditions begin to exist for a centralized TANU capable of directing economic change in the future.

At the present time, it is hard to see a full interaction between economic and political variables. We can stipulate what the present economic conditions mean for present political problems. We can see what the existing political organizations do, and can do, to affect economic development. We can even say how future economic development will affect political development in terms of possible directions of change. We can say, for example, that there is no possibility of TANU becoming a bureaucratized party in the near future. The experience of the Communist Party of the Soviet Union where party membership changed as the party took on technical and administrative tasks and where control of the party became increasingly vested in centralized organs, is not going to happen in Tanzania in the foreseeable future. Tanzania does not have and cannot quickly produce thousands of technically trained people able to administer over the rest of the population. Without the people to enforce central orders within the cells, the VDCs, and the TANU district and regional organizations, these institutions retain both their autonomy, to varying degrees, and their representative nature. This does not mean that political leaders sit back and wait for enough economic development to take place to change the social structure and to enable them to control their outlying organizations. They are active agents in the process of making change.

Many political leaders in new states have equated mo-

415

APPENDIX I

Tanganyika: Economic Abstract

Size: Tanganyika is the tenth largest country in Africa south
of the Sahara, with a land area of 341,150 square miles
and a water area of 20,650 square miles of which the
Tanganyika part of Lake Victoria comprises 13,450
square miles.

Population: The 1957 census estimated population at 8.7
million. It is now estimated at over 10 million. Population density is around 34 per square mile. There is a
great deal of regional variation. The center of Tanganyika is arid and tsetse infested; some districts have as
few as 2.8 people per square mile (e.g., Mpanda),
others as many as 150 people or more per square mile
(e.g., Moshi).

Birth and death rates also vary regionally: death rates
are higher in central Tanganyika at 27 per 1,000 than
in Tanga Region on the Coast with 18 deaths per 1,000.
Life expectancy is 38 years.

Indices of Development: Tanganyika compares unfavorably
in per capita physical output figures to many African
countries. It has comparatively low yields for cotton
and for major staple food crops.[1] Tanganyika has one

[1] Figures for per capita production of electricity can be found in
Economic Survey of Africa Since 1950 (New York: United Nations
Department of Economic and Social Affairs, 1959), p. 133. Source:
United Nations, *Statistical Yearbook*, 1955 and 1958 calculations
done by the Bureau of Economic Affairs. Figures for cement can be
found in *Economic Survey*, p. 37: Sources: United Nations, *Year-
book of International Trade Statistics*, 1957, Vol. I; *Statistical Year-
book*, 1958; Monthly Bulletin of Statistics, January and May 1959.
Tanganyika's yields *per hectare* for groundnuts was the lowest of the
African countries listed, including Madagascar, Uganda, Ruanda-
Urundi, French West Africa. It was less than half of the average
yield for all of Africa. The same was true of cotton and cassava.
Economic Survey, p. 26. Source: *Yearbook of Food and Agricul-*

419

mile of road per 61 square miles of land area compared to 119 for Uganda and 118 for Kenya. For each vehicle in Tanganyika there are 223 persons; in Uganda and Kenya, the figures are 167 and 99 respectively.

The 10 per cent of Tanganyika's population which is literate compares unfavorably to Kenya's 25 per cent and Uganda's 30 per cent. Tanganyika also has fewer radios and telephones per person as compared to Uganda and Kenya, although it does not compare so unfavorably in these respects to other sub-Saharan African states.[2]

In general, the different indices which describe the Tanganyikan economy between 1954 and 1963 show positive gains. (See Table 17.)

---

tural Statistics, 1958, Vol. xii, Part i. Cotton yields have been improving in Tanganyika since this survey was made.

[2] See Almond and Coleman, *op.cit.*, Table on Economic Development in Underdeveloped Countries, pp. 580-82.

TABLE 16

Tanganyika Gross Domestic Product at Factor Cost, 1960

Sector	1960
Monetary Economy £'000	
Agriculture	40,765
Livestock	4,096
Forestry	2,775
Hunting and Fishing	502
Mining	6,970
Manufacturing	7,541
Craft Industries	—
Building and Construction	6,369
Public Utilities	1,140
Transport, Storage, and Communications	13,334
Distribution	8,600
Ownership of Dwellings	3,699
Public Administration	13,266
Miscellaneous Services	5,390
Total	114,447
Subsistence Economy £'000	
Agriculture	41,747
Livestock	14,297
Forestry	2,261
Hunting and Fishing	3,061
Craft Industries	5,910
Building and Construction	4,500
Total	71,776

SOURCE: *Three Year Plan*, p. 3.

TABLE 17

Indicators of Economic Trends in Tanganyika
(£ million, unless otherwise indicated)

	1954	1958	1962	1963	Rate of Growth 54-58 %	Rate of Growth 58-62 %
GDP, Monetary	79.1	97.9	123.3	140.3[f]	+5.5	+5.9
GDP, Volume[a]	74.8	101.8	124.7	131.3	+8.0	+5.2
Agricultural Product	35.1	39.2	48.5	60.4[f]	+2.8	+5.5
Non-Agricultural Product	44.0	58.7	74.8	79.9[f]	+7.5	+6.2
Gross Investment	21.8	22.7	24.4	25.1	+1.0	+4.2
Investment/GDP Volume	29%	22%	20%	19%		
Non-Agricultural Employment	221.0	217.5	195.8[d]	[g]	+0.4	−3.2
Exports, Foreign	36.2	41.7	51.2	63.6	+3.5	+5.3
Imports, Foreign	32.0	33.6	39.8	40.4	+1.2	+4.3
Trade Balance[e]	5.8	10.3	13.6	24.5		
Government Current Expenditure[b]	14.3	17.3	19.6	—	+4.9	+3.2
Tax Revenue[b]	18.5	20.5	23.4	—	+2.6	+3.3
Current Budget Surplus[b]	4.2	3.2	3.8			
Import Prices (Index)	100	95	89		−1.2	−1.5
Retail Prices (Index)[c]	100	103	100	100	+0.7	−0.7

SOURCE: Paul Clark, "Foreign Aid, Domestic Finance, and the Development Plan," in *Problems of Foreign Aid* (Dar es Salaam: Tanganyika Standard Ltd., 1965), Table I, p. 100.

[a] Agricultural exports at 1960-62 prices.
[b] For fiscal year beginning in calendar year, excluding financial transfers.
[c] June.
[d] 1961.
[e] Including re-exports.
[f] Increase in new series added to old series for 1962.
[g] Decrease.

APPENDIX II

The *Five Year Plan*

TABLE 18

Five Year Plan Projection

	Recent Past[a]	Future Plan[b]
GDP Volume, Growth Rate (%)	+5.2	+8.5[c]
Agricultural Product, Growth Rate (%)	+5.5	+7.3
Non-agricultural Product, Growth Rate (%)	+6.2	+9.2
Non-agricultural Employment, Growth Rate (%)	—3.2	n.s.
Gross Investment Share (% of GDP)	20	26[d]
Government Investment (£ million)	6.6	14.2
Other Public Investment (£ million)	2.9	14.9[d]
Private Investment (£ million)	14.9	18.6[d]
Government Development Budget, Annual Average (£ million)	8.0	20.4
Actual Development Expenditure, Annual Average (£ million)	6.7	
Foreign Finance, Development Budget, Annual Average (£ million)	4.5	15.9
Domestic Finance, Development Budget, Annual Average (£ million)	2.2	4.5

SOURCE: Paul Clark, "Foreign Aid, Domestic Finance, and the Development Plan," in *Problems of Foreign Aid* (Dar es Salaam: Tanganyika Standard Ltd., 1965), Table I, p. 100.

a The recent past in Tanganyika is 1958-62 with respect to growth rates; for investment, 1962; for Tanganyika's development budget, 1961-64 (the *Three Year Plan* period); and for Tanganyika's actual expenditure and finance, 1961-63. The recent past is at current prices with adjustments for agricultural export prices. GDP volume is adjusted for agricultural export prices 1960-62. These are the largest price changes in the economy.

b Future plan is 1961-62 average to 1970 for Tanganyika's growth rates, approximately 1967 for investment and 1964-65 to 1968-69 for budget and finance. Prices are constant prices but Clark has made some revision with future expectations.

c In chap. ix, I have cited an annual growth rate of 6.7 per cent. The above Table, using Clark's figures, cites a growth rate of 8.5

423

per cent. The earlier figures include both subsistence and monetary sectors while the 8.5 per cent is for the monetary sector only. The subsistence sectors pull down the total rates of planned growth. After subtracting population growth, individual incomes would grow at an average rate of 4.5 per cent per year. GDP estimates since 1954 show an annual growth rate of 4.5 per cent at current prices and an annual rise in per capita income of 2.7 per cent. Population has been growing at 1.8 per cent per annum. The basis of the growth as already noted has been increase in export receipts from the main agricultural products. Nineteen sixty/62-70 growth in the subsistence sector is planned at 2.1 per cent (cf. *Five Year Plan*, p. 10). The *Budget Survey, 1963/64* estimated that GDP in 1963 would be on the order of 5.7 per cent real growth (if the sisal price element was not held constant, it would be in the order of 9 per cent growth). With this 5.7 per cent figure, by the end of 1963 income was estimated to have risen 10 per cent above the 1960 pre-famine level. Allowing for a population growth of 6 per cent in the intervening years, this would represent an increase in real income of 4 per cent. But this figure is for real income over a three-year period or about 1.3 per cent a year. This is considerably less than the proposed growth of 4.5 per cent (after population increase is subtracted) of the *Plan*.

d Estimated from government and government-financed public investment in 1966-67, investment plans 1964-69, projected 1967 GDP.

TABLE 19

*Comparative Structures of Gross Domestic Product
in Tanganyika*

	Average % 1960-62	Target 1970	Target 1980
Primary Production (all rural and mining activity)	60.0	50.0	39.0
All Industrial Activity	13.0	19.4	26.7
(of which manufacturing and processing)	(4.0)	(7.5)	(13.3)
Basic Facilities	(5.6)	(6.3)	(7.1)
Construction	(3.4)	(5.6)	(6.3)
Tertiary Activities (services, distribution, rent, and administration)	27.0	30.6	34.3
Total GDP	100	100	100
Subsistence sector	32.5	21.7	13.7

SOURCE: Ghai, *op.cit.*, p. 1, and *Five Year Plan*, p. 11.

The evolution of the GDP can also be expressed in terms of £ s for sectors of the economy (see Table 20).

TABLE 20

Evolution of the Gross Domestic Product
(£ million)

	ACTUAL Average 1960-62			1970			AVERAGE 1980		
	M[a]	S[b]	Total	M	S	Total	S	M	Total
Crop Husbandry[c]	37.7	45.7	83.4	72.2	54.6	126.8	126.8	65.4	188.8
Livestock[c]	5.9	12.3	18.2	10.6	15.1	25.7	20.9	18.8	39.7
Fishing and Forest Products[c]	2.4	1.9	4.3	3.7	2.4	6.1	5.9	3.1	9.0
Mining and Quarrying	5.2	—	5.2	7.5	—	7.5	10.3	—	10.3
Processing and Manufacturing	7.4	—	7.4	25.0	—	25.0	84.9	—	84.9
Public Utilities	1.3	—	1.3	3.7	—	3.7	9.0	—	9.0
Construction	6.3	—	6.3	18.5	—	18.5	40.0	—	40.0
Transport and Communications	8.7	—	8.7	17.2	—	17.2	35.8	—	35.8
Distribution	22.1	—	22.1	44.2	—	44.2	93.5	—	93.5
Rents and Royalties	8.0	—	8.0	17.0	—	17.0	33.5	—	33.5
Public Administration and Defense	12.6	—	12.6	25.2	—	25.2	54.4	—	54.4
Other Services	6.9	—	6.9	15.0	—	15.0	37.2	—	37.2
Total GDP	124.5	59.9	184.4	259.8	72.1	331.9	548.9	83.3	636.1
Population (million)			9.4			11.3			14.1
Per capita GDP			£19.6			£29.3			£45.1

SOURCE: *Five Year Plan*, p. 9.

[a] M = Monetary.　　[b] S = Subsistence.

[c] Primary rural product for the year 1960-62 valued at 1960 prices. Other sectors' product in current price.

425

APPENDIX III

Village Plans

NOT ALL REGIONS produced village plans within their regional five year plans. The West Lake plan did contain a breakdown for villages in Buhaya, which was composed of Bukoba and Karagwe Districts. There was a section on divisional targets for a few crops, and an outline for self-help construction programs. Under the division headings, the *gombololas*[1] or subdivisions listed (a) nation-building work (*Kazi za kujenga Taifa*) and (b) crops. The nation-building work was for the *gombolola* as a whole; usually three or four projects were listed. Of the 31 *gombololas* listed, 21 of them planned to build TANU offices. It is interesting that in 1963, 21 out of 31 sub-divisions did not have a TANU office building. (One enterprising sub-division determined to build by self-help a TANU office in each of its villages.)

Of the 10 that did not plan a TANU office, 6 were in Karagwe District. Either Karagwe already had TANU office buildings, or it was satisfied to make do with makeshift quarters in *dukas* (stores). Possibly Karagwe citizens were giving priority to the other nation-building projects that appeared on most sub-division lists: schools, dispensaries, clinics, community centers, roads, wells. Schools had pride of place and were usually first on the list; the building of TANU offices was usually put last. This was consistent with the tenor of the remarks of President Nyerere, who when laying the foundation stone for one TANU edifice or another, has often rather wistfully remarked how a dispensary might be more directly useful and desired.

Crops targets were broken down for each village development committee. These crop figures were prepared by the

---

[1] *Gombolola* would not be used everywhere in Tanganyika for sub-division. But West Lake Region borders Uganda, and the term has come into use from Buganda.

village development committee for the first year of the *Five Year Plan* period. The draft proposals of the *Five Year Plan* which were sent out to regions and districts during the *Plan* formation period did not go down to the village. The villagers produced what they called *Mipango Ya Uchumi Na Kazi Za Kujenga Taifa* 1962-63, or literally, Arrangement of the Affair of Nation-Building. But the *Plan* overtook their works which were outside its framework for target increases. The regional agricultural officer of West Lake thought that the VDCs had been too ambitious with their crop targets; he doubted whether the targets, if they could be produced, could be marketed. Targets were expressed in this Appendix in terms of acreage to be planted. The number of people in the village was given and the number of acres per person was set. Though Buhaya is a cash-crop area, primarily for coffee, the crops targeted were maize, peanuts, and beans. In other words, the VDC ignored the major cash crop, and did not consider a wide range of economic activities. The regional and district agricultural officers felt that they would have to visit the villages and set more realistic targets. (The village development plans for Karagwe District called for an increased production of groundnuts from an estimated total production, including internal consumption, of 148 tons to 1,374 tons within a year.) The West Lake regional plan took little notice of the target figures set by the VDCs.

427

Selected Bibliography

BOOKS

Almond, Gabriel, and James Coleman. *Politics of the Developing Areas.* Princeton: Princeton University Press, 1960.

Apter, David. *The Political Kingdom in Uganda.* Princeton: Princeton University Press, 1961.

―――. *Ghana in Transition.* New York: Atheneum, 1963.

―――― (ed.). *Ideology and Discontent.* Glencoe: The Free Press, 1964.

Ashford, Douglas E. *The Elusiveness of Power: The African Single Party State.* Ithaca: Cornell University, Center for International Studies, 1965.

Austin, Dennis. *Politics in Ghana, 1946-1960.* London: Oxford University Press, 1964.

Bantu, Kasela. *What Is TANU and What Does It Do?* Dar es Salaam: n.d.

Barongo, Edward. *Tanganyikan African National Union.* Dar es Salaam: Thakers Ltd., 1962. (Swahili)

Burke, Fred G. *Tanganyika: Preplanning.* Syracuse: Syracuse University Press, 1965.

Cameron, Sir Donald. *My Tanganyika Service and Some Nigeria.* London: Allen and Unwin, 1939.

Carter, Gwendolen (ed.). *African One-Party States.* Ithaca: Cornell University Press, 1962.

Chidzero, B.T.G. *Tanganyika and International Trusteeship.* London: Oxford University Press, 1961.

Cole, J.S.R., and W. N. Denison. *Tanganyika.* London: Stevens and Sons, 1964.

Coleman, James S., and Carl Rosberg, Jr. (eds.). *Political Parties and National Integration in Tropical Africa.* Berkeley and Los Angeles: University of California Press, 1964.

429

Cory, Hans. *The Ntemi: The Traditional Rule of a Sukuma Chief in Tanganyika.* London: Macmillan, 1951.

———. *The Political Indigenous System of the Sukuma.* London: Oxford University Press, 1953.

Cory, Hans, and M. M. Hartnall. *Customary Law of the Haya.* London: Laird Humphries, 1945.

Cory, Hans, and W. Malcolm. *Sukumaland.* London: Oxford University Press, 1953.

Duverger, Maurice. *Political Parties.* London: Methuen and Co., 1955.

Easton, David. *The Political System.* New York: Alfred Knopf, 1960.

———. *A Framework for Political Analysis.* Englewood Cliffs, N.J.: Prentice-Hall, 1965.

The Economic Development of Tanganyika. Report of the International Bank for Reconstruction and Development. Dar es Salaam: Government Printer, 1961.

Fainsod, Merle. *How Russia Is Ruled.* Cambridge: Harvard University Press, 1957.

Farer, Tom J. (ed.). *Financing African Development.* Cambridge: M.I.T. Press, 1965.

Fortes, M., and E. E. Evans Pritchard, *African Political Systems.* London: Oxford University Press, 1940.

Friedland, William. *Unions and Industrial Relations in Underdeveloped Countries.* Bulletin No. 47. Ithaca: New York State School of Industrial and Labor Relations at Cornell University, 1963.

Friedland, William, and Carl Rosberg, Jr. (eds.). *African Socialism.* Stanford: Stanford University Press, 1964.

Geertz, Clifford (ed.). *Old Societies and New States.* Glencoe: The Free Press, 1964.

Gerschenkron, Alexander. *Economic Backwardness in Historical Perspective.* Cambridge: Harvard University Press, 1962.

Glickman, Harvey. *Some Observations on the Army and*

BIBLIOGRAPHY

Political Unrest in Tanganyika. Pittsburgh: Institute for African Affairs, Duquesne University, 1964.

Goldthorpe, J. E., and F. B. Wilson. *Tribal Maps of East Africa and Zanzibar.* Kampala: EAISR, 1960.

Hailey, Lord. *An African Survey.* London: Oxford University Press, 1957.

————. *Native Administration and Political Development in British Tropical Africa.* London: H. M. Stationery Office, 1940.

————. *Native Administration in British African Territories,* Part I. London: H. M. Stationery Office, 1950.

Hatch, John. *Africa Today and Tomorrow.* London: Dennis Dobson, 1962.

Hirschman, Albert. *Latin American Issues.* New York: Twentieth Century Fund, 1961.

Hodgkin, Thomas. *African Political Parties.* Baltimore: Penguin Books, 1961.

————. *Nationalism in Colonial Africa.* New York: New York University Press, 1957.

Hughes, A. J. *East Africa: The Search for Unity.* Baltimore: Penguin Books, 1963.

Hunter, Guy. *New Societies of Tropical Africa.* London: Oxford University Press, 1962.

Ingham, Kenneth. *A History of East Africa.* London: Longmans, 1962.

Janowitz, Morris. *The Military in the Political Development of New States.* Chicago: University of Chicago Press, 1964, pp. 107-25.

Key, V. O. *Politics, Parties, and Pressure Groups.* New York: Thomas Cromwell and Co., 1958.

Klerruu, Wilbert. *One-Party System of Government.* Dar es Salaam: Mwananchi Publishing Company, Ltd., 1964.

LaPalombara, Joseph (ed.). *Bureaucracy and Political Development.* Princeton: Princeton University Press, 1963.

Lasswell, Harold, Daniel Lerner and C. Easton Rothwell. *The*

431

Comparative Study of Elites. Hoover Institute, Series B, No. 1. Stanford: Stanford University Press, 1952.

Lerner, Daniel. *The Passing of Traditional Society: Modernizing in the Middle East.* Glencoe: The Free Press, 1958.

Marsh, Zoe, and G. W. Kingsnorth. *An Introduction to the History of East Africa.* Cambridge: Cambridge University Press, 1965.

Moffett, J. P. (ed.). *Handbook of Tanganyika.* Dar es Salaam: Government Printer, 1958.

Nye, Joseph, Jr. *Pan-Africanism and East African Integration.* Cambridge: Harvard University Press, 1965.

Nyerere, Julius. *Democracy and the Party System.* Dar es Salaam: Tanganyika Standard Ltd., 1963.

―――. *The Courage of Reconciliation.* Dar es Salaam: Government Printer, 1964.

―――. *The Second Scramble.* Dar es Salaam: Tanganyika Standard Ltd., 1962.

―――. *TANU Na Raia.* Dar es Salaam: TANU Press, 1962.

―――. *This Is the Way Forward.* Dar es Salaam, 1963.

―――. *"Ujamaa": The Basis of African Socialism.* Dar es Salaam: Tanganyika Standard Ltd., 1962.

Peacock, Alan, and Douglas Dosser. *The National Income of Tanganyika, 1952-54.* London: H. M. Stationery Office, 1958.

Pye, Lucian. *Politics, Personality and Nation-Building in Burma.* New Haven: Yale University Press, 1962.

―――. *Aspects of Political Development.* Boston: Little, Brown and Co., 1966.

Richards, Audrey (ed.). *East African Chiefs.* New York: Frederick Praeger, 1959.

Segal, Ronald. *African Profiles.* Baltimore: Penguin Books, 1962.

Stahl, Catherine. *History of the Chagga People of Kilimanjaro.* The Hague: Mouton and Company, 1964.

―――. *Tanganyika: Sail in the Wilderness.* The Hague: Mouton and Company, 1961.

Swerdlow, Irving (ed.). *Development Administration*. Syracuse: Syracuse University Press, 1963.

Taylor, J. Clagett. *The Political Development of Tanganyika*. Stanford: Stanford University Press, 1963.

Tucker, Robert. *The Soviet Political Mind*. New York: Frederick Praeger, 1963.

Who's Who in East Africa. Nairobi: Marco Surveys Ltd., 1964.

Wood, Alan. *The Groundnut Affair*. London: The Bodley Head, 1950.

Young, Roland, and Henry Fosbrooke. *Land and Politics Among the Luguru of Tanganyika*. London: Routledge and Kegan Paul, 1960.

Zolberg, Aristide. *Creating Political Order: The Party-States of West Africa*. Chicago: Rand McNally, 1966.

──────. *One-Party Government in the Ivory Coast*. Princeton: Princeton University Press, 1964.

ARTICLES AND PERIODICALS

Austen, Ralph S. "Notes on the Pre-History of TANU," *Makerere Journal*, No. 9 (March 1964), pp. 1-6.

Bennett, George. "An Outline History of TANU," *Makerere Journal*, No. 7 (1963), pp. 15-32.

Bienen, Henry. "Foreign Aid versus National Independence," *East Africa Journal* (February 1965), pp. 19-26.

──────. "National Security in Tanganyika After the Mutiny," *Transition*, v (April 1965), 39-46.

──────. "The Party and the No-Party State: Tanganyika and the Soviet Union," *Transition*, III (March-April 1964), 25-32.

Bretton, Henry. "Current Political Thought and Practice in Ghana," *American Political Science Review*, LII (March 1958), 46-63.

Cameron, Sir Donald. "Native Administration in Nigeria and Tanganyika," Supplement to the *Journal of the Royal Africa Society*, XXXVI (November 30, 1937), 1-20.

Clark, Paul. "Foreign Aid, Domestic Finance, and the Development Plan," in *Problems of Foreign Aid* (Dar es Salaam: Tanganyika Standard Ltd., 1965).

Cory, Hans. "Reform of Tribal Political Institutions in Tanganyika," *Journal of African Administration*, XII (April 1960), 77-84.

Deutsch, Karl. "Social Mobilization and Political Development," *American Political Science Review*, LV (September 1961), 492-514.

Eberlies, R. F. "The German Achievement in East Africa," *Tanganyika Notes and Records*, No. 55 (September 1960).

Ehrlich, Cyril. "Some Aspects of Economic Policy in Tanganyika, 1945-1960," *Journal of Modern African Studies*, II (July 1964), 265-77.

Friedland, William. "Tanganyika's Rashidi Kawawa," *Africa Report*, VII (February 1962), 7-8.

George, John B. "How Stable Is Tanganyika?" *Africa Report*, VIII (March 1963), 3-9.

Ginwala, Frene. "No-Party State," *Spearhead*, III (February 1963).

Harris, Belle. "Tanzania's Elections 1965," *Mbioni*, II, No. 5 (1965).

Johnson, Harry. "A Theoretical Model of Economic Nationalism in New and Developing States," *Political Science Quarterly*, LXX (June 1965), pp. 169-85.

Keith, Robert. "Self-Rule in Tanganyika," *Africa Special Report*, IV (December 1959), 8.

Kilson, Martin. "Authoritarian and Single-Party Tendencies in African Politics," *World Politics*, XV (January 1963), 262-94.

Kitchen, Helen. "Why Did Julius Nyerere Resign?" *Africa Report*, VII (February 1962), 7.

Leys, Colin. "The Need for an Ideology," *Kivukoni Journal* (1961), p. 4.

————. "Tanganyika: The Realities of Independence," *International Journal*, XVII (Toronto: Summer 1962), 251-68.

Liebenow, J. Gus. "The Chief in Sukuma Local Government," *Journal of African Administration*, XI (April 1959), 84-92.

————. "Responses to Planned Political Change in a Tanganyika Tribal Group," *American Political Science Review*, L (June 1962), 442-61.

————. "Tribalism, Traditionalism and Modernism in Chagga Local Government," *Journal of African Administration*, X (April 1958), 71-82.

Lowenkopf, Martin. "Outlook for Tanganyika," *Africa Report*, VI (December 1961), 6.

————. "Tanganyika Achieves Responsible Government," *Parliamentary Affairs*, XIV (Spring 1960), 244-57.

McAuslan, J.P.W.B. "The Republican Constitution of Tanganyika," *International and Comparative Law Quarterly*, (April 1964), pp. 502-73.

Mazrui, Ali. "Tanzania versus East Africa," *Journal of Commonwealth Political Studies*, III (November 1965), 209-25.

Mwalujume, E. K. "The Role of Village Development Committees in Tanganyika," *Mwenge*, IV (1964).

Mwanjisi, W.B.K. "Tanganyika African National Union," *Africa Today*, VIII (December 1961), 10-11.

Nyerere, Julius. "Tanganyika Today: The Nationalist View," *International Affairs*, XXXVI (Toronto: January 1960).

————. "Will Democracy Survive in Africa?" *Africa Special Report*, V (February 1960), 3-4.

Pratt, Cranford. "Multiracialism and Local Government in Tanganyika," *Race*, II, No. 1 (November 1960), pp. 33-49.

Rothchild, Donald. "Progress and the One-Party State," *Transition*, III, No. 10 (September 1963), 31-34.

BIBLIOGRAPHY

Sanger, Clyde. "The Changing Face of Tanganyika," *Africa Report*, VII (July 1962), 3.

————. "Tanzania's Presidential Commission Report," *East Africa Journal* (June 1965), pp. 19-23.

Schachter, Ruth. "Single-Party Systems in West Africa," *American Political Science Review*, LV (June 1961), 294-307.

Shadbolt, K. E. "Local Government Elections in a Tanganyika District," *Journal of African Administration*, XIII (April 1961), 78-84.

Shils, Edward. "Primordial, Personal, Sacred and Civil Ties," *British Journal of Sociology*, VIII (June 1957), 130-45.

Smythe, John. "Political Projects," *Spearhead* (November 1961), p. 6.

Tordoff, William. "Parliament in Tanzania," *Journal of Commonwealth Political Studies*, III (July 1965), 85-103.

————. "Regional Administration in Tanganyika," *Journal of Modern African Studies*, III (1965), 63-89.

Van Arcadie, Brian. "Gross Domestic Product Estimates for East Africa," *Economic and Statistical Review*, IV (December 1963), ix-xii.

Whitely, Wilfred. "Political Concepts and Connotations," in St. Clair Anthony's Papers, No. 10. *African Affairs*, No. 1, ed. Kenneth Kirkwood (London: Chatto and Windus, 1961), pp. 7-21.

OFFICIAL PUBLICATIONS

Constitutional Development Commission. Dar es Salaam: Government Printer, 1953.

Development Plan for Tanganyika, 1961/62-1963/64. Dar es Salaam: Government Printer, 1962.

Oldaker, A. A. *Interim Report on Tribal Customary Land Tenure in Tanganyika.* Dar es Salaam: Government Printer, 1957.

BIBLIOGRAPHY

The People's Choice. Dar es Salaam: Ministry of Information and Tourism, 1965.

President Nyerere Opens Dar es Salaam University Campus. Dar es Salaam: Ministry of Information and Tourism, 1964.

Report of the Africanization Commission of 1962. Dar es Salaam: Government Printer, 1962.

Report of the Presidential Commission on the Establishment of a Democratic One-Party State. Dar es Salaam: Government Printer, 1965.

Sikukuu Ya Saba Saba (Seventh Day of the Seventh Month Festival). Dar es Salaam: Ministry of Information and Tourism, 1964.

Sikukuu Ya Taifa Ya Tanganyika (National Festival of Tanganyika). Dar es Salaam, 1964.

Statistical Abstract, 1962. Dar es Salaam: Government Printer, 1963.

Tanganyika (Constitution) Order in Council S.I. 1961 No. 2274, Schedule II.

Tanganyika Data Book: Commerce and Industry. Dar es Salaam: Government Printer, 1961.

Tanganyika Five Year Plan for Economic and Social Development, Vols. I and II. Dar es Salaam: Government Printer, 1964.

Tanganyika Press Directory. Dar es Salaam, 1962.

The Union of Tanganyika and Zanzibar. Dar es Salaam: Tanganyika Information Services, 1964.

TANU PUBLICATIONS

TANU Sheria na Madhumuni ya Chama. (TANU Constitution). Dar es Salaam: Mwananchi Publishing Co., Ltd., n.d.

TANU Souvenir. Dar es Salaam: Tanganyika Standard, Ltd., n.d.

437

BIBLIOGRAPHY

KENYA GOVERNMENT PUBLICATION

African Socialism and Its Application to Planning in Kenya. Nairobi: Government Printer, 1965.

UGANDA GOVERNMENT PUBLICATION

Uganda Government 1963 Statistical Abstract. Entebbe: Government Printer, 1964.

UNITED NATIONS PUBLICATION

Economic Survey of Africa Since 1950. New York: United Nations Department of Economic and Social Affairs, 1959.

UNPUBLISHED PAPERS

Cliffe, Lionel. "Nationalism and the Reaction to Enforced Agricultural Change in Tanganyika During the Colonial Period." Paper presented at the EAISR Conference, December 1964.

Ehrlich, Cyril. "The Economy of Tanganyika, 1945-60."

Ghai, Dharam. "Reflections on Tanganyika's *Five Year Plan.*" EDRP Paper No. 34 (June 1964).

————. "Some Aspects of Income Distribution in East Africa." EDRP Paper No. 51 (November 1964).

Glickman, Harvey. "Traditionalism, Pluralism, and Democratic Processes in Tanganyika." Paper presented at the annual meeting of the American Political Science Association, Chicago, Illinois, September 9-12, 1964.

Glynn, F. J., and John B. Seal, Jr. "Job Analysis Report on the Regional Administration." Dar es Salaam: Government Printer, 1963. (Processed)

Jellicoe, M. R. "Political Parties in Tanganyika Since Independence." Makerere College, University of East Africa, 1963.

Karmiloff, G. "Planning Machinery and Its Operation in Tanganyika." Paper presented to the University of East

Africa Public Policy Conference, Kampala, October 1963.

————. "Problems of Regional Development and Industrial Location in East Africa." Paper presented to the Seminar on Problems of Economic Development in East Africa, Nairobi, September 1964.

Kesby, John. " 'We and Them' among the Warangi." Makerere College, University of East Africa, 1964.

Lee, Eugene. "Local Taxation in Tanganyika." Institute of Public Administration, Dar es Salaam, May 1964.

Lowenkopf, Martin. "Political Parties in Uganda and Tanganyika." Master's thesis, London School of Economics, 1961.

Lury, Dennis. "Brief Statistical Background for East African Federation." Paper presented to the Second Conference on Public Policy on East African Federation, Nairobi, November 26-30, 1964.

Maguire, Gene Andrew, "Toward *Uhuru* in Sukumaland: A Study of Micropolitics in Tanzania, 1945-1954." Ph.D. dissertation, Harvard University, 1966.

Miller, Norman. "Village Leadership in Tanzania." EAISR paper, December 1964.

Redmayne, Alison. "Preliminary Report on a Hehe Community." EAISR paper, 1962.

Reining, P. "Village Organization in Buhaya." EAISR paper, 1952.

Rigby, Peter. "Modern Leadership Roles in Ugogo." Forthcoming in a volume to be published by Syracuse University Press.

Southall, Aidan. "Traditional Role Structure and the Formation of Elites in East Africa." Paper presented to the African Studies Association, Philadelphia, October 1965.

Van Arcadie, Brian, and Philip Nedgwa. "Future Trade, Balance of Payments and Aid Requirements of East Africa." EDRP Paper No. 31, May 1964.

BIBLIOGRAPHY

NEWSPAPERS AND PERIODICALS

East African Standard (Nairobi).

Kenya Weekly News (Nakuru).

The *Nationalist* (Dar es Salaam).

Pan-Africa (Nairobi).

Reporter (Nairobi).

Sunday News (Dar es Salaam).

Tanganyika Standard (Dar es Salaam).

Uganda Argus (Kampala).

Vigilance Africa (Dar es Salaam).

Index

26, 303-04. *See also* economy of Tanganyika

economy of Tanganyika, structure of, 6*n*, 264-72, 297-98, 301, 419-22; development of, 274-77, 422. *See also* economic development and political change; economic nationalism; *Five Year Plan*

elections, *1958-1959*, 50-54, 65; *1960*, 55-56; *1962*, 56-58, 404; *1965*, 382-405

Five Year Plan, and civil servants, 152; and TANU goals, 220-21; slogans for, 226, 409; formulation of, 266, 280-81, 291-95, 327, 411; system of planning, 284-91, 426-27; targets of, 295-96, 304, 415, 423-25; financing of, 297-301, 305; and commissioners, 321; mentioned, 264

Fundikira, Chief A., 59, 60, 68*n*, 302

German rule, 22, 36-37, 65, 365, 409

Hanga, Kassim, 79, 221-23, 388*n*
Hussein, Sheikh Yahya, 59

Ideology, and typologies, 5-6; and economic factors, 203, 212, 250-51; and social change, 205, 255-56; and opposition to Nyerere, 207. *See also* African Socialism; economic nationalism; Nyerere, on democracy and the one-party system

Jamal, Amir, 285*n*, 295*n*
Japhet Kirilo, 26, 344, 401

Kamaliza, Michael, 79, 185*n*, 255, 387

Kambona, Oscar, background of, 47; importance in TANU, 77, 79, 255, 282; ministerial portfolios, 79*n*; on TANU elections, 110; gives up teaching, 126; and appointment of commissioners, 132; and civil servants, 150; and expulsion of Europeans, 165*n*; Secretary General, 194*n*, 197; in the *Nationalist*, 210; member of Presidential Commission, 239*n*; and army mutiny, 364, 367, 371; and Zanzibar Revolution, 365*n*; and 1965 elections, 387, 391*n*, 393*n*

Kandoro, S., 143, 187*n*
Karume, Sheikh Abeid, 79*n*, 186*n*, 210, 388*n*
Kasambala, Jeremiah, 304, 403*n*
Kawawa, Rashidi, Minister for Local Government and Housing, 67; importance in TANU, 77, 79, 255, 282; on TANU elections, 210; and appointment of commissioners, 132; and civil servants, 148-49; on TANU appointed and elected officials, 156; Vice President of TANU, 158*n*; on life-presidency for Nyerere, 159*n*; succeeds Nyerere as Prime Minister, 164-65; member of Central Committee, 185*n*; and Islam, 188; Chairman of Presidential Commission, 239*n*, 248; on one-party democracy, 241; on dissemination of government policy, 321-22; on *Five Year Plan* goals, 331*n*; on village development, 336, 349; on TANU cells, 358-59; and army mutiny, 371; and TANU Youth League, 375; and National Service, 376; and 1965 elections, 387; mentioned, 210

INDEX

445

Other books published for
The Center of International Studies
Woodrow Wilson School of Public and
International Affairs

Gabriel A. Almond, *The Appeals of Communism*
Gabriel A. Almond and James S. Coleman, editors, *The Politics of the Developing Areas*
Gabriel A. Almond and Sidney Verba, *The Civic Culture: Political Attitudes and Democracy in Five Nations*
Richard J. Barnet and Richard A. Falk, *Security in Disarmament*
Henry Bienen, *Tanzania: Party Transformation and Economic Development*
Cyril E. Black and Thomas P. Thornton, editors, *Communism and Revolution: The Strategic Uses of Political Violence*
Robert J. C. Butow, *Tojo and the Coming of the War*
Miriam Camps, *Britain and the European Community, 1955-1963*
Bernard C. Cohen, *The Political Process and Foreign Policy: The Making of the Japanese Peace Settlement*
Bernard C. Cohen, *The Press and Foreign Policy*
Charles De Visscher, *Theory and Reality in Public International Law*. Translated by P. E. Corbett
Frederick S. Dunn, *Peace-making and the Settlement with Japan*
Herman Kahn, *On Thermonuclear War*
W. W. Kaufmann, editor, *Military Policy and National Security*
Klaus Knorr, *On the Uses of Military Power in the Nuclear Age*
Klaus Knorr, *The War Potential of Nations*
Klaus Knorr, editor, *NATO and American Security*
Klaus Knorr and Sidney Verba, editors, *The International System: Theoretical Essays*
Sidney J. Ploss, *Conflict and Decision-making in Soviet Russia*
Lucian W. Pye, *Guerrilla Communism in Malaya*
James N. Rosenau, editor, *International Aspects of Civil Strife*
James N. Rosenau, *National Leadership and Foreign Policy: A Case Study in the Mobilization of Public Support*
Rolf Sannwald and Jacques Stohler, *Economic Integration: Theoretical Assumptions and Consequences of European Unification*. Translated by Herman F. Karreman
Richard L. Sklar, *Nigerian Political Parties: Power in an Emergent African Nation*
Glenn H. Snyder, *Deterrence and Defense*
Harold and Margaret Sprout, *The Ecological Perspective on Human Affairs, With Special Reference to International Politics*
Thomas P. Thornton, *The Third World in Soviet Perspective: Studies by Soviet Writers on the Developing Areas*
Sidney Verba, *Small Groups and Political Behavior: A Study of Leadership*
Karl von Vorys, *Political Development in Pakistan*
Myron Weiner, *Party Politics in India*